HAVE WE DELIVERED?

YOU BE THE JUDGE . . .

Subscribe now to Issue #4 of *Gauntlet.* We guarantee controversy, irreverence, unique perspectives . . . and we'll never compromise our principles to pander to chain bookstores to sell copies.

We'll step on toes, provide censored material you won't find elsewhere, outrage and cause discomfort. We'll provoke plenty of thought and will never be dull, If you agree . . .

CUPEC '91

The ball's in your court!

Send me (check):
___Issue #4 for $12.95 + $2.00 p&h   ___Issues #4 & #5 for $24.00 + $4.00 p&h

Back Issues available:
___Premiere Issue for $10.95 + $2.00 p&h   ___# 2 for $10.95 + $2.00 p&h

Check or M.O. to: *GAUNTLET*, 309 Powell Rd Dept GS92, Springfield PA 19064 **U.S. Funds Only**
Canadian Orders add $4.00 p&h   Foreign Order add $7.00 p&h

Name _____

Address _____

City/State/Zip _____

GAUNTLET T-Shirts for issues 1-3 of *GAUNTLET* are available. Shirt for the premiere issue (right, pictured @ left) is gold with black imprint. Shirt for #2 (left, pictured @ left)—the *Stephen King Special*—is blue with a black imprint. A black and white rendition of both the front and back covers of this issue will be available within 8-10 weeks of publication (color of shirt to be determined).

Cost: $12 plus $2 p&h
Allow 6-8 weeks for delivery

Make check payable to **GAUNTLET**,
Mail to: **GAUNTLET**, Dept. SH92,
            309 Powell Rd., Springfield, PA 19064.
            U.S. Funds Only.

Send me _____ PREMIERE ISSUE T-Shirt(s)

Send me _____ STEPHEN KING ISSUE
                     T-Shirt(s)

Send me _____ POLITICALLY (IN)CORRECT
                     ISSUE T-Shirt(s)
                     (Indicate front or back cover)

Size: **Large** or **X-Large** (circle preference)

I enclose a total of _____

Name _____

Address _____

City/State/Zip _____

☐ **Check here if interested in color poster of back cover #3 and send SASE.**

GAUNTLET
Exploring The Limits Of Free Expression

Published by **GAUNTLET**, Inc.
Barry Hoffman, President

FOUNDER/EDITOR-IN-CHIEF
Barry Hoffman

ASSISTANTS TO THE EDITOR
David Reed & Cheryl Meyer

RESEARCH ASSISTANT
Dara Lise

COLUMNISTS
John Sutherland, Tom McDonald, Matthew Costello, Linda Marotta, Rex Miller, John Rosenman, Richard Chizmar

CORRESPONDENTS
Donna Bocian, Mike Baker, Duane Swierczynski

LAYOUT AND DESIGN
Thomas F. Monteleone

TYPESETTING
Borderlands Press

COVER PHOTO
Walter Cessna © 1991

COVER LAYOUT
Lisa Steinmeyer

COVER MODEL
Rhonda

COVER CONCEPT
Adam Alexander

ORIGINAL ARTWORK/CARTOONS
John Callahan, Russ Miller, Trina Robbins, Harry Fassl, Harry O. Morris, Charles Dougherty, Ron Leming, David Chlystek, Roger Gerberding, Kenny Ray Linkous, Michael Vickery, Harold Cupek, Michael Taylor, John Longhi, Alfred Klosterman

GAUNTLET BOB CONCEPT
Russ Miller

LETTERS/QUERIES/ORDERS TO:
GAUNTLET, Dept. A92, 309 Powell Rd., Springfield, Pa. 19064

ADVERTISING RATES: Full page—$400; Half Page—$250; Quarter Page—$175; Inside Cover—$500

SUBSCRIPTIONS: *GAUNTLET* is an annual, published each March. One year subscription is $12.95 plus $2 p&h; 2 Years $24 plus $4 p&h. Canadian Orders add $4 postage per issue; Foreign Orders add $7 postage per issue. Checks made payable to *GAUNTLET*, Inc. sent to the above address. **U.S. Funds Only.**

BACK ISSUES: Issues #1 & #2 are available in limited quantities. Send $10.95, plus $2 p&h for *each* issue, payable to *GAUNTLET*, Inc. to the above address. A **limited** quantity of the hardcover Stephen King limited, **signed by Stephen King** and over 30 other contributors is available. Query with SASE.

GAUNTLET CORRESPONDENTS: *GAUNTLET* seeks journalists/investigative reporters from around the country willing to track down and investigate stories dealing with censorship and free expression issues. Query with SASE.

ARTISTS/CARTOONISTS: *GAUNTLET* seeks artists and cartoonists. Send samples of your work to be kept on file to Cheryl Meyer, at above address. Enclose SASE.

ADVERTISING EXECUTIVE: *GAUNTLET* seeks an advertising executive, to be paid with a generous commission. Work from your home. Query with resume and SASE.

GAUNTLET seeks original commentary and satire (up to 1500 words), fiction (up to 2500 words unless commissioned), original comics and editorial cartoons. Use this issue as a guide to the appropriate content and style. Send submissions or query for guidelines, along with SASE to the above address.

EDITORIAL MEANDERINGS

There was no single example of overt censorship in 1991 comparable to the 2 Live Crew flap, the Robert Mapplethorpe brouhaha, the NEA battle, or directors bucking the MPAA's "Dreaded X," that captured the nation's attention in 1990 and galvanized the forces of free expression against would-be censors.

The Persian Gulf War *could* have been that issue, if the war itself was anything like the hype of the buildup. But BB-guns versus "smart bombs" don't make for much of a war and Sadaam Hussein's forces were quickly vanquished before governmental censors had to really flex their muscles. Moreover, to a great extent, the media abdicated its role in favor of cheerleading and allowed itself to be unmercifully manipulated. This isn't to say there wasn't censorship during the Persian Gulf War (see "Desert Storm Confidential" beginning on page 56), but it dwarfed that of Vietnam and what could have been in an extended conflict.

No, 1991 was more comparable to George Orwell's *1984*—thought control, taking center stage, in the guise of "political correctness." Liberals ran around like chickens with their heads cut off (apologies to PETA), afraid of alienating minorities whose causes they espoused (i.e. the Clarence Thomas hearings put them in a real quandary - blacks versus feminists) whereas the right laughed itself silly viewing the carnage from the sidelines, while remaining unscathed.

This issue of *Gauntlet*, therefore, focuses on the theme of political correctness. Readers may find portions of the "PC" section contradictory—one article,

for example, labeling animal rights activists "PC"; another taking an opposing point of view. This is intentional. *Gauntlet* is meant to initiate dialogue and provoke thought. Our contributors view similar events from differing perspectives, hence the apparent contradictions. *You* are the final arbiter as to what is political correctness and where you stand. Hell, straddle the fence, if you wish, as there are no easy answers. And, as Bill Paige so aptly states, when discussing political correctness, beware of wolves in sheep's clothing. Those who feel disdain for the politically correct may feel a wee bit queasy finding themselves in bed with the likes of David Duke. Sorry, it comes with the territory. Navigating the minefield of political correctness is no simple matter, as you shall see.

Gauntlet's distribution continues to grow, though once again, you won't find it in your local Waldenbooks. As before, the problem is one of controversial graphics. One of *Gauntlet*'s cornerstones is not merely discussing censored material, but wherever possible letting the reader *see* what's been attacked, and then read the commentary to make an *informed* decision. Censored material is by its very nature controversial; hence Waldenbooks and some other chains, with the AFA peering over their shoulder, may be leery of letting us enter its doors. Why not ask your local Waldenbooks or chain if they carry *Gauntlet* or special order it for you. If they won't tell them you'll take your business to your local independent. Most of those will be glad to order you a copy through our nationwide chain of distributors. And while you're at it, bug your local or college library to stock a copy. After all, there is no other publication that deals with First Amendment issues. *Gauntlet* a natural for libraries.

On a brighter note, issue #2 was welcomed in Canada without controversy and English customs okayed distribution in that country. This issue has an international flavor, with contributors from England, Canada and Germany.

An Apology is in order: In 336-page publication, edited by a staff of one, there are bound to be errors. Issue #2, thankfully, had precious few. However, inadvertently, the pull-quote in Andrew Vachss' short story, "Cripple", gave away the ending, denying the reader of the element of surprise (this error was corrected in the 2nd printing). Such an oversight, however unintentional, is unpardonable. I apologize to Mr. Vachss and those readers denied full enjoyment of his exceptional story.

I could go on—there's so much to say after a year—, but it's best to let *Gauntlet* speak for itself. A final note of thanks to all contributors who made this issue possible and a special thanks to Allen Sonnenschein and Leslie Sternbergh for their invaluable assistance.

Enough already . . . read on.

—*Barry Hoffman*
February 3, 1992

Gauntlet's survival, beyond this issue, remains in doubt. There will be a #4, *but* without some cash infusion (printing costs alone run near $25,000) *Gauntlet* will have to be drastically altered—in all probability to a 100-page trade paperback. We will obviously have to be far more selective in what we print—books reviews, the quantity of fiction and the like may have to be cut. Quality, as well as quantity, will suffer as it will be difficult to offer debates (one of *Gauntlet*'s staples) in a downsized publication.

The reality of the situation is *Gauntlet* is *solely* financed on a teacher's salary and money is *lost* with each copy sold to distributors. We would hope there are one or two individuals interested in discussions of uncensored First Amendment issues who would financially back us so these cuts will be unnecessary. For now, the ball is in your court.

OPENERS

Tattooed Fetus and the Art Critic

An anonymous critic, with a can of spray paint, defaced this photo by Charles Gatewood at an exhibit entitled "Art and the Forbidden" at San Francisco State University in April 1991. Gatewood's camera had documented the art of tattooist Spider Webb—a human fetus that Webb tattooed with a heart on its chest.

Gatewood's reaction to the deface-ment: "Oh well, the last time I showed 'Tattooed Fetus' at the Foto Gallery in New York there were bomb threats and calls from the Attorney General."

Gatewood's artistic philosophy is, "the role of the artist is to deliver a wake-up call. That call will, by definition, come as quite a shock, but the right artistic shock can change your being forever."

Gatewood's new book, *Primitives* of his still photography is expected to be published in late-1992. For additional in-formation contact: A. Mutt Press, P.O. Box 410052, San Francisco, CA 94141.

—Submitted by Michael Perkins

Talk About Having No Balls

The cover for the second album from David Bowie's new group, Tin Machine, was too much for 60% of the record stores and chains shown a copy in advance. The uncensored cover, of classical Greek statues known as Kouroi (naked forms from 6th Century B.C. representing a boy or young man) on display in museums throughout the world (including the Metropolitan Museum of Art in New York and the J. Paul Getty Museum in Los Angeles) was released worldwide *except* in the U.S.

Victory Music, a fledgling record company, sensing a possible problem, showed the proposed cover to top retail chains, 60% of which found it offensive. Fearing a retail shutout, the company of-fered a compromise—a black band around the shrink wrap over the offend-ing genitals—but this, too, was rejected. The outlets feared complaints from parents once the shrink-wrapped jock straps were removed at home. Victory gave in, castrating the offending mem-

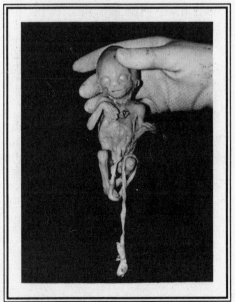

Photography by Charles Gatewood

bers. The retailers, with selective memories, have no problems with similar nudes (of both nude men and women) which adorn a number of classical works they carry.

Bowie notes, "The accepted cover says more about today's confused morality than a thousand words."

The original artwork was also rejected for a billboard rental on Sunset Strip. The group's response: "There are so many pricks in Hollywood, we didn't think they would notice 4 more."

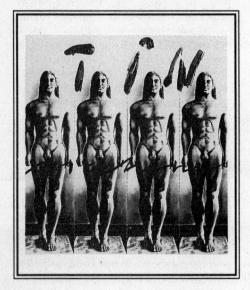

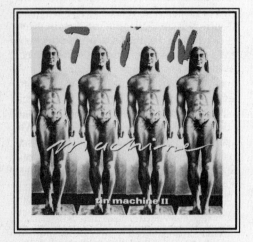

Cube Iced

Korean American merchants went on the offensive to protest rapper Ice Cube's song "Black Korea" which warns Asian merchants to stop harassing black customers. Some of the offending lyrics:

So don't follow me up and down your market

Or your little chop-suey ass will be a target

Of the worldwide boycott . . .

So pay respect to the black fist

Or we'll burn your store right down to a crisp

And then we'll see ya

Cause you can't turn the ghetto into Black Korea

Korean merchants rather than ranting and raving for the singer's head, or censorship of his album *Death Certificate* quietly made their point with a boycott of St. Ides, a high-strength malt beer popular in black neighborhoods, which Ice Cube promotes with TV and radio spots. Korean owners of inner-city convenience stores pulled the beer off the shelves and even drove caseloads back to the distributor, according to the *Philadelphia Inquirer*.

Within a month, the brewer of St. Ides capitulated. Cube was dissed (taken off the air) and the brewer promised to donate up to $90,000 to Korean American groups.

Of note, the Korean American Grocer's Association conducted the boycott primarily in Korean-language newspapers. They wanted action and respect, not publicity. And, they pledged the money the McKenzie River Corp. donated would be used for a program to train *black* youths for jobs and go into a multi-racial scholarship fund.

'Outing' Of Those Seeking Abortions

Taking a cue from some segments of the gay community which "Outs"—names—prominent celebrities and politicians who are allegedly gay, but don't want to go public, anti-abortionists outside a Livonia, Michigan clinic in June waved placards displaying the names of 2 women—one a minor—who had obtained abortions there.

Organizer of the demonstrations Lynn Mills, refused to divulge how she obtained the names which were to remain confidential under Michigan law.

The tactic was criticized by some leaders of the anti-abortion movement. John Harrington told the *New York Post* "It's not an appropriate tactic at all. Women should not be punished for having an abortion."

Curious. If women did *not* seek abortions, would there be abortions? Why don't pro-life advocates advocate punishing women seeking abortions instead of solely attacking those who perform them? Could it be because it would be political suicide?

An unrepentant Mills refused to apologize for using the tactic and said, "I may do it again."

Not likely. Not only didn't the tactic catch on, as some feared, but in late-December the 2 women publicly named sued Mills for violating a state privacy law that protects the confidentiality of medical information.

That's called payback.

Florida . . . Could It Be The Water?

Is it our imagination or was Florida in the headlines an inordinate number of times this year; headlines that heaped ridicule on the State. Here's just a sampling:

✧ Pee Wee Herman was exposed in an adult movie theater (Sarasota)

✧ a 52-year old grandmother was arrested, strip-searched, and jailed overnight for selling a copy of *Playboy* to 2 sixteen year olds. (Miramar) See below for more details.

✧ William Kennedy Smith was charged, tried and acquitted, in 77-minutes, of date rape. (Palm Beach)

✧ A federal judge ruled pictures of nude women posted at a Jacksonville shipyard was a form of sexual harassment. The judge ordered the pictures removed, the workers educated about sexual harassment and provided penalties including suspensions and firing of workers who violated his orders.

✧ As part of an alternative sentencing program, 12 people convicted of misdemeanors, ranging from shoplifting to soliciting for immoral purposes, were ordered to purchase classified ads that would include their photo and the charges. David Davis who pleaded no contest for soliciting for immoral purposes said, "I felt like I was innocent, but I didn't have the money to fight the charges. Now this is just more humiliation." (Escambia County)

✧ Ft. Lauderdale's Vice-Mayor, Doug Danziger, who successfully fought topless bars and adult bookstores in that city, resigned when his name surfaced in a sex scandal. His name was on a list of alleged clients of Kathy Willets, arrested for prostitution. Her husband, a police deputy, was suspended *with* pay after being charged with living off of the earnings of a prostitute. Their defense: Kathy Willets suffered from nymphomania and having sex with different men was a form of treatment for the disorder.

✧ Obscenity charges were dropped against a man arrested for displaying an obscene bumper sticker because of an error in the deputy's paperwork. The offending sticker: "The New Kids (as in the New Kids on the Block—the singing group) Suck" (Daytona)

✧ Two consenting adults were arrested and charged with having sex in their own bathroom; the act videotaped by a neighbor. (Tampa) See details below.

Is all of this a coincidence? A conspiracy? Or maybe it's something in the water . . .

Where Were The Police When You Needed Them?

As reported above, in Miramar, Florida last February, a 52-year old grandmother was arrested for selling *Playboy* to 2 sixteen year old boys. Elaine Ott, 52, who'd never been arrested before, was strip-searched and jailed overnight; placed in a cell with drug addicts and drunks. Arrested for a 3rd degree felony, she faced a penalty of up to 5-years in prison and a $5000 fine. The police who caught her in the act were at the store working an undercover robbery detail.

In an ironic twist, the night after his wife's arrest, Richard Ott, who also worked at the store, was robbed at gunpoint of $40.

A lawyer for *Playboy* agreed to defend Mrs. Ott at no cost. "I will not leave her dangling in the wind."

Charges were later dropped and Mrs. Ott has since filed a civil suit against the City of Miramar, the police chief and the two police officers.

By the way, the gunman who robbed the store escaped—presumably without a copy of *Playboy*.

Don't Like The Speaker?
Cancel The Event

A Catholic hospital, the New York Foundling Hospital, specializing in prenatal and infant care, crossed New York's John Cardinal O'Connor in November by extending an invitation to Representative Susan Molinari to speak at a fund-raising luncheon.

While it could not be confirmed whether O'Connor knew of the invitation, the *New York Post* reported the Cardinal "hit the roof" when he learned of it.

In 1986 the New York Archdiocese issued an edict barring anyone who disagrees with Church teachings from speaking at parish-sponsored events. Molinari's crime: she is pro-choice on abortion. Molinari, then, would have become the first pro-choice politician to speak at a Church-sponsored event since the edict.

Molinari believed she was invited because, "I spend a lot of my time in Congress focusing on children, child abuse, day care and a lot of family-friendly legislation."

Rather than dis-invite Molinari, the hospital, a week later, cancelled the luncheon, that was to raise money for poor children.

No one disputes the Archdiocese's Constitutional right to control free speech. That doesn't make it right, however. And what of the children who would have benefitted from the luncheon? A good question for the good Cardinal in these recessionary times.

Molinari is also in hot water with 8 anti-abortion groups, who two weeks earlier, petitioned Pope John Paul II to excommunicate her and 26 other U.S. politicians who don't follow the party line on abortion.

No decision from the Pope, as we went to press, who might have better things to do with his time.

Want To Be A Cop? Value Your Privacy? Forget It

With police departments being exempt, under state and federal law, from restricting the kinds of questions employers may ask of applicants, if you want to uphold the law you may be forced to submit to a lie detector test and answer these questions pertaining to your sex life, according to the *Philadelphia Inquirer*:

Have you had sex with animals? Are you homosexual? Have you had sex with more than one person at the same time? Other than masturbation and intercourse, have you engaged in any other kinds of sex acts?

Proponents of this invasion of privacy argue those who aspire to be police have to be screened more closely than other job applicants. According to Henry L. Canty, of the American Association of Police Polygraphists, "Say it's bestiality. Well, that's illegal in some states and, I dare say, a bit kinky, myself. If a guy has a fetish for a chicken, do you really want that guy out there guarding your neighborhood? Especially if you're a chicken farmer."

David Rudovsky, a civil rights lawyer in Philadelphia, is uncomfortable with the practice. "The danger is: Having asked the questions, how do you know it won't be used against you?"

Jury Duty:
Gays Need Not Apply

New York State Supreme Court Justice Ralph Sherman ruled, in late October, that lawyers could question jurors about their own sexual orientation in a gay-bashing case. "We intend to ask prospective jurors if they're gay or if they have any gay family members," the defense said.

Countered Brooklyn District Attorney Charles J. Hynes to *New York Post* columnist Mike McAlary, "The belief that a gay person can't fairly decide a case like this is a stretch. It's insensitive. It's like Outing someone."

McAlary suggests such questions are illegal. "Something called the Batson ruling precludes the systematic exclusion of jurors." He contends the defense is "intent on getting a straight jury to hear the case. He [the defense attorney] is of the belief . . . gay people would be unable to deliver a fair verdict in a case involving a gay victim." Most troublesome, the judge apparently concurs.

McAlary equates this to a judge excluding black jurors judging the guilt or innocence of a white defendant, or Italians from a case of a Mafia kingpin, concluding, "Can questions about religious preference be far behind?"

Conform Or Else . . .
By High Noon

The Clarence Thomas hearings certainly inflamed passions. When the Compton branch of the NAACP unanimously voted to approve the Thomas nomination, they were threatened with expulsion if they did not get in line with the national groups opposition to Thomas.

William Penn, the NAACP's director of branches, told the *Washington Post*, "Positions contrary to [those] articulated by the national NAACP cannot be issued in the name of a NAACP branch. The president of the Compton branch has been informed this matter must be resolved by 12 noon . . . "

In an abrupt about face the next day, after the incident received nationwide exposure, the national NAACP decided not to punish the Compton branch. "The national NAACP has no reservations about individual members of the Compton branch, or any branch, expressing opinions as individuals. Membership does not require conformity."

Odd . . . it did a day earlier.

More Dukes
On The Horizon

On the day the *Philadelphia Inquirer* reported on David Dukes defeat in his run for the Governorship of Louisiana, another article was buried deep within that could have far-ranging ramifications.

The grand wizard of Duke's old Klan group said he is building a training camp for white supremacists who share Duke's beliefs and aspirations, but don't carry his excess baggage (direct ties to the Klan and Nazi sympathies).

"Louisiana has one David Duke," said Thom Robb. "We plan to give America a thousand of them." Robb shares Dukes political strategy: replacing racist rhetoric and violence with carefully crafted and articulated campaigns against affirmative action, welfare, AIDS victims and drugs.

At a summer camp, Robb said, students would learn traditional Klan beliefs, but political leaders, "will be taught to avoid statements that sound hateful and turn people off." Their dress and speech would be honed, he continued. "If you're a person who wants to take some kind of leadership position and you've got bad teeth, get your teeth fixed."

Duke Clones . . . a truly frightening thought; more so in that is not that far-fetched.

Privacy Takes Another Beating

The saga of Alfred Stephens and Janet Paddock, arrested in Tampa, Florida, for having sex in their own house took many unexpected and sobering turns.

In July, police were summoned, according to the *New York Post*, after an 8-year old saw the two making love in a hot tub in Stephen's bathroom and told his mother, "Mommy, Mommy, they're having pony rides." A neighbor, Lew Adler, filmed the event for . . . who knows what?

The two were taken in, charged with a lewd and lascivious act in the presence of a child under 12 and later released on $15,000 bail each. Charges were later changed to disorderly conduct.

End of story? Hardly. In August, Adler was busy on the talk show circuit. *A Current Affair* interview was already complete and approaches had been made by *Oprah* and *Donahue* among others. "Everybody wants the tape," Adler told the *Post*'s George Rush. "They all want it exclusively. But they won't come up with a figure."

In late-August, Stephens proposed marriage to Paddock, who accepted during a taping of *The Maury Povich Show*. Tom Owens, a friend of Paddock's, composed a song, "Sex Behind the Mini Blinds" which was getting airplay on Florida radio stations. The chorus:

One minute you're making magic
Then you're making license plates
Because priorities are twisted
In these United States

Finally, it was reported, in the *USA Today*, in late-September, that Janet Paddock attempted suicide by taking a drug overdose.

Unmasking The Klan

Shade Miller, a member of the Georgia Ku Klux Klan, who purposely orchestrated his arrest to challenge a 1951 anti-mask law, was acquitted by a jury in September. Michael Hauptman, Miller's lawyer, said that at a mall in February 1990, "He [Miller] got out of [a] truck, said 'God Bless America' and put his hands out to be arrested." Police had been tipped anonymously in advance.

Miller's guilt or innocence hinged on whether the mask-wearer "knows or reasonably should know that the conduct provokes a reasonable apprehension of intimidation, threat or violence." The prosecution could not produce such a witness, other than the arresting officer.

Earlier, the Georgia Supreme Court, ruling on the same case, forbade mask-wearing based on threat of intimidation. Chief Justice Harold G. Clarke, writing for the majority, said a hooded Klansman was a "nameless, faceless figure [who] strikes terror in the human heart.

"But remove the mask, and the nightmarish form is reduced to its true dimensions. The face betrays not only identity, but also human frailty."

Atlanta Journal columnist Elliott Brack applauded the Supreme Court ruling against mask-wearing."People of this nation don't need the misguided techniques of the Ku Klux Klan. They don't need their ranting and raving, their ignorance and hatred, their deepseated misunderstanding of the modern world."

Upon hearing Miller had been acquitted in a jury trial on the same charges, Brack quipped, "The Bill of Rights works for *him*."

It turned out to be a hollow victory for the Klan. Without a conviction the Constitutionality of the anti-mask law itself cannot be challenged. Whether the Klan has the right to wear a mask, even if it causes intimidation, has yet to be decided.

Cleansing Libraries

Each summer librarians, often aided by parents and teachers, clear public school libraries of outdated books (i.e. "Someday man will land on the Moon"). Some schools have decided *outdated* means a book that contains words or phrases that might offend someone, sometime, reported the *Philadelphia Inquirer*. Thus, in Edgewater Parks Mildred Magowan School in New Jersey, *Read About Policeman, First Book of Nurses* and *The Negro in America* were yanked. "These [were] pulled due to racial, ethnic and sex bias in content, pictures, etc.," said a library spokeswoman. Apparently a book that refers to a nurse only as a *she* and a police officer only as a *he* has no place in a growing number of school libraries.

Doris Ebler, Pennsylvania Director of the School Library Media Services Division would go further—a book with the theme of males as bosses and females as secretaries would be banished if she had her druthers.

Judith Krug, Director of the Office of Intellectual Freedom of the American Library Association disagrees with the practice. "What's politically correct today may not be politically correct tomorrow."

Writer Imprisoned

Reminiscent of Salman Rushdie, Egyptian writer Alaa Hamed, according to the *Philadelphia Inquirer* was sentenced, December 26, to 8 years in prison for questioning the value of religion in his 1988 novel *A Distance in the Man's Mind*. His publisher and a book distributor also received prison terms. The book was accused of being blasphemous to Islam.

UPDATES

One of the results of "sound bite" journalism are stories splashed on page one which are then ignored, as editors scurry to capture the reader with even more attention-grabbing pieces. Reporters, themselves, often don't show the initiative of following a story to its conclusion. We're not talking Pulitzer-winning investigative journalism here, just slice-of-life pieces that often unfold at a snails pace.

Call it editorial prerogative. Actually, it's shoddy journalism. Even though *Gauntlet* is an annual, it is our goal to update readers on stories that appeared in previous issues. An update on 2 Live Crew appears on page 72 and the case of Father Pfleger (p. 28 of #2) can be found on page 78. Here are some additional updates:

Brooklyn Korean Boycott

(p. 15 of #2)

Black activists picketed a Korean deli in Brooklyn, New York after a Haitian woman alleged she was roughed up by one of the stores co-owners, Pong Ok Jang, in January 1990. The good news for Pong is a jury cleared him of assault charges a year after the boycott began. The bad news . . . demonstrators didn't go away, and with his business crippled Pong decided to sell his Family Red Apple grocery, the *New York Post* reported in May. Pong's health, the paper reported, had deteriorated as a result of the boycott. "Before he had black hair and now, in a year, it's all white," employee Kyongha Joo told the *Post*.

An ironic sidebar: while the *USA Today* reported business was off 30-40% at the neighboring M&R Meat Market, during the boycott, owner Mike Popilevsky saw a silver lining—"all the police around here have sent drugs dealers elsewhere."

Son of Sam Laws

(p. 274 of #2)

Last issue, convicted serial killer Gerard Schaefer debated the merits of Son of Sam laws, which seize money criminals earn from telling their stories and awards the cash to crime victims, with regular *Gauntlet* columnist John Sutherland.

In December, the U.S. Supreme Court unanimously ruled New York's Son of Sam laws a violation of free speech. Justice Sandra Day O'Connor, writing for the Court, said under the wording of the New York statutes authors ranging form Malcolm X to St. Augustine (who confessed he stole pears from a neighbor's vineyard) would have been subject to the law if it had been in effect when they wrote.

NC-17

There were few waves as a result of the MPAA's new NC-17 rating, despite threats from the likes of Donald Wildmon. Blockbuster Video, America's largest video retailer (1600 outlets), however, announced in January 1991 it would not stock *any* videos carrying a NC-17 designation. Ron Castell, a Blockbuster spokesman, said, "We don't carry any movie that the [MPAA] rates X. So we are saying that since NC-17 is the same criteria as the X we're not going to carry it."

Many theater chains, video stores and newspapers have indicated they would judge films rated NC-17 on a case-by-case basis, and that seems to have been what occurred in 1991.

✦

If readers come across clippings updating stories covered in any issue of *Gauntlet*, please send it to the editor for inclusion in the next issue—indicate Updates on the envelope.

Needs for Issue #4

We are looking for first hand accounts—from any point of viewfrom those in special interest of pressure groups (i.e. PETA, ACT-UP, Operation Rescue, the AFA) on just what makes these groups tick, the commitment of its members as well as anecdotes that might be of interest to readers.

It's best to query the editor with ideas first, but unsolicited manuscripts up to 2500 words are welcomed

---

Gauntlet welcomes local or regional items of this nature which too often don't draw the national attention they merit. Send news or magazine clips (with the name of the paper and date of the article) to **Gauntlet Openers** *for inclusion in future issues. Many thanks to all those who provided material for this year's* **Openers**. .

TRIAL BY MEDIA?

Melinda McAdams

S hould men accused of rape be named in the news media?

Journalists routinely name people accused of murder, robbery, child abuse, and other crimes. The announcement of an arrest or a search for a known suspect gives the reporter license to publish or broadcast that person's name and other relevant facts, such as the individual's address and place of employment.

The media's right to do this has long been established, partly because once the police identify a suspect, that person's name becomes public record. The public record becomes public in the media.

But the rape victim's name is also a matter of public record. The police do not withhold it from the press; the press has traditionally withheld it from the public. Students in journalism schools all over the United States learn the rule early in their first basic reporting

and terrorists—that is, *alleged* killers and terrorists—apprehended on Page One or at the top of the 11 o'clock news; we expect to see their faces, hear their names. But for those crimes, and others, we have also learned the names of their victims and their accusers.

Only the person who alleges rape is anonymous. Only she, among adult victims, levels a charge from a protected position.

She can avoid the stigma of rape at least so far as the harsh light of publicity is concerned. But the accused cannot escape stigmatization. And the accused, whose name, face, and personal life might be slathered across front pages nationwide (you can think of at least one), could be an innocent man.

Could be. Maybe not, but the cornerstone of our justice system is that he *could* be. The decision is supposed to be made in a court of law and not in the minds of the public, and certainly not on the front page of the local newspaper. The special situation of rape, however, invites us to jump to judgment. *She knows who did that to her,* we think. *And she* wouldn't put herself through this if it hadn't really happened.

If we believe that to be true in every single case, then it is time to reread *To Kill a Mockingbird*. Any number of women might have any number of reasons to fabricate a rape. Given the undeniable trauma of going to the police with an accusation of sexual assault, not many women would do it without real cause. But some have.

It is distasteful to me, a woman, to admit that the charge of rape is sometimes a lie, because saying so makes some people less likely to believe the real victims. A woman who has been raped should be believed. She should be treated with respect and kindness, gently handled, listened to with the greatest seriousness. No one should say they doubt her word. No one should ask what she was doing in a pool hall after midnight, or where her husband was, or why she wears short skirts.

That does not mean that a woman's word alone should be allowed to send a man to jail. There are courts, juries,

> Only the person who alleges rape is anonymous. Only she, among adult victims, levels a charge from a protected position.

class: Do not publish the name of a rape victim.

"Unless the victim died, or she's a very public figure, most newspapers and broadcast media decline to name the victim unless she requests to be identified. That's the prevailing way that journalists have decided the question," said H. Eugene Goodwin, Professor Emeritus at Penn State's School of Communication and author of the book *Groping for Ethics in Journalism.*

"In other kinds of crimes, we try to give the victims and the accused equal treatment," Goodwin said. "The argument against that in rape cases is that rape is a special kind of violent crime that carries a special stigma that in some ways makes the victim a double victim."

Not all media outlets follow the rule at all times. In some highly publicized cases recently, the name of the accuser in a rape case has been revealed. In response, debate about using a rape victim's name has flourished among journalists, media watchdogs, feminists, and others.

Few people question the publication of the name of the accused. Why should they? We are accustomed to seeing killers judges; there will be a trial.

But should the woman's word carry enough weight to put an innocent man's reputation in question?

Should her word alone—her anonymous word—put his picture on the front page with the weighted label ACCUSED RAPIST beside his name?

At the end of July in Sanford, Florida, near Orlando, a 33-year-old woman told police she had been abducted and raped by more than a dozen men. Three men and a juvenile, 16, were quickly arrested and held without bail. About 50 deputy sheriffs had accompanied the accuser to Midway, the neighborhood where the alleged rape occurred, to identify and pick up the suspects, according to a report in the *Orlando Sentinel*, which named the four men but not their accuser.

The accuser's charges were called into question almost immediately. People who had been in or near the boarding house where the alleged crime occurred said that the accuser had agreed to trade sex for drugs and was not forced to do anything. Eventually the accuser admitted she had made up parts of the story she told police.

A grand jury considered the evidence and issued a "no true bill," meaning that there was no indictment; the criminal investigation was closed and the accused men were let go,according to Assistant State Attorney Jack Scalera in Sanford.

In the Midway case, the ability of the accuser to identify her alleged attackers set a train of events into motion: the police had seemingly solid grounds for arrest; they were able to find the accused men in the community where they lived; the press had a straightforward story about four men arrested on sexual-assault charges. But after the men's names were published on page 6 of the *Sentinel* (in the continuation of a Page One story), the case unraveled and ultimately came to nothing.

"These are judgment calls," journalism professor Goodwin said. "There might be cases where everything a journalist knows about it suggests that it may not be a legitimate charge of rape. In that case, you might not want to identify the accused man. I think we have to be more careful about naming the accused rapist in those cases where there are real doubts. But we also have to be careful about creating more policies about not telling what we know."

It's a journalistic cliche that when you get arrested in a topless bar your picture will be on Page One, and when you win the town's good citizen award you'll be on page 65. There begins the argument for caution in publishing names of men accused of rape: Will any story about dropped charges be noticed as much as a story about an arrest?

"Our sense of fairness is that if you run the charges on the front page, you should run it on the front page when they're cleared," said Greg Miller, an assistant metro editor at the *Orlando Sentinel*. When the grand jury declined to hand up an indictment in the Midway case, the *Sentinel* put the story on Page One, Miller said. The next day, the paper also ran a Page One story on reactions from people in the Midway community.

WFTV, the ABC-affiliate station in Orlando, covered the Midway case as a major story, using the four men's names and repeatedly running video of their arrest. The station also ran reactions from the accused men after the charges were dropped. "We did many stories on the grand jury meeting and making the decision, and two or three stories after the men were cleared,"said Tom Cook, 6 o'clock news producer at WFTV. "That was probably as big a story as the original story."

While the station did not change its policy on rape stories as a result of the Midway case, "it brought home to us that when people are cleared, we need to make some public announcement of that," Cook said. "In the past we may have been less likely to do that. This holds true for any crime, not just rape cases."

Steve Olson, a reporter for WFTV in Seminole County who covered the Midway case, concurred. "If you're going to give it a big splash when the men are arrested, you have to give it just as much coverage when the men get a no true bill."

Until some legal evidence is pieced together, a rape case rests on a woman's word against a man's. There are seldom

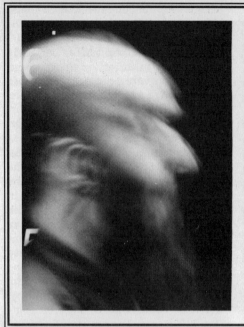
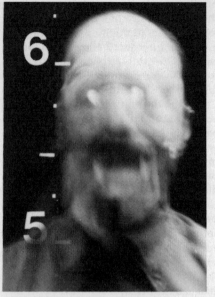

any witnesses to corroborate her accusations. If the man did not do it, the facts
that prove it will not emerge right away.

The accusation stands, however, in
the man's community. Long after the
charges are dropped and the newspapers
have been buried in landfills, the accused
man's neighbors will remember.

In Rhode Island last May, a young
man was accused of rape by his former
girlfriend. Soon it became obvious that he
could not have raped her; he had not left
Chicago, where he lived. Within two
days, the accuser's story had disin-
tegrated and the man was cleared. Police
charged the woman with filing a false
report, to which she eventually pleaded
no contest and received a suspended six-
month jail sentence. But the man's name
and picture had already been broadcast in
local TV and radio news reports and
printed in the newspaper.

"Your name is really all you have.
Without your name, you're nothing. Customers have to be able to trust a person
before they'll buy something," the man
told the *Providence Sunday Journal*. At the
time of the charge, he was planning to go
back to Rhode Island to work at his
stepfather's marketing firm. "Once I say

my name, they're going to think, 'K——
E——. That's that kid who raped that girl
not long ago."

The accuser's story convinced state
police, who were brought in because the
fabricated crime involved taking the
woman from one town to another. The
health service at the University of Rhode
Island, where she was a student, confirmed that the woman had had sexual
intercourse. Because she said she had
been abducted at gunpoint, the state
police wanted to move quickly, a police
captain told the *Journal*.

Police issued an arrest warrant on a
Friday afternoon, several hours after the
woman made her accusation. The TV
evening news carried the story, along
with a picture of the accused man. The
Saturday *Journal-Bulletin* ran the story,
with a picture of the man, at the top of
page 3. On Sunday, the *Journal* carried a
story on Page One declaring that the
police felt no rape had occurred.

In the Rhode Island case, it is difficult
to say that anyone acted irresponsibly—
except the woman who lied. The man,
who was clearly innocent, spent a sleep-
less night chain-smoking and wondering
why his ex-girlfriend would want to do

such a thing. He was never arrested. But his plans to return to his home state were thrown into question. "Now I don't want to [go]," he told the Journal several days after the incident. "I'm afraid to see people."

E—— did move to Rhode Island this fall, but in December he went back to Chicago. "People come up and say things about it," he told *Gauntlet* the day before he left Rhode Island. "I would go play basketball, and I'd hear people on the tennis courts beside the basketball court saying it. There were several instances like that."

It happened at his job too, he said. "I started working with my [stepfather]. It's selling; he represents jewelry lines, so you're dealing with the public. You know, Rhode Island is a small state. People are always saying something. In Chicago, they won't know me."

The man went back to his job as a computer operator in Chicago, but the pay, he said, "is a third, or even a fifth, of the money I could get here." If not for the rape accusation, he said, "Probably I would stay in Rhode Island."

He never found out why the woman accused him. The frightening part of the experience, he said, was that "if I'd been in Rhode Island [at the time of the alleged crime], I could have been convicted and got 20 years in jail." Even so, it's not over. "I'm still suffering now, and it's seven months later," he said. He is now suing the woman for slander.

In his case, the man said, the newspapers were not at fault. He blamed the state police for not investigating his whereabouts more thoroughly before issuing a warrant.

Ken Mingis, a reporter for the *Providence Journal-Bulletin* who covered the false rape story, said that afterward there was "some feeling that the state police should have checked things out more before they released [the accused man's] name." But he did not think the newspaper had done anything wrong. "The paper did its best to try to track this kid down before we ran our story," Mingis said.

The paper's policy on rape stories has not changed as a result of the incident,

Mingis said, "but there's a very clear sensitivity now, and maybe we would not be so quick to use the name of the accused." In the future, reporters will be more likely to discuss with editors whether to print the accused's name, but the decision will be left to the editors and will be decided on a case-by-case basis, he said.

The Providence papers, like the *Orlando Sentinel* and WFTV, maintain a policy of not naming rape victims (although the Sunday *Journal* named the woman who accused E—— in the same story that reported his having been in Chicago). Many journalists disagree with the policy, Mingis said. "You can't say use the victim's name in all cases, but many reporters, including me, believe that by shielding the victim we set rape aside as a different kind of crime," he said.

"Rape crisis centers emphasize that rape is not about sex; it's violence. If that's the case, the rules that apply to other kinds of violent crimes apply to rape," Mingis said. "By withholding the name, you make it seem different, and maybe that implies that the victim somehow invited this crime."

Some people argue that printing the accuser's name would eliminate false rape charges, but victims' advocates say it would only reduce the number of reported rapes. A better guarantee might be to hold back the name of the accused until a prosecutor gets an indictment.

"The threshold for us is clear when the proper agencies involved make a determination that they have enough evidence to arrest someone," said Miller of the *Orlando Sentinel*. "If they had gone straight to the grand jury without arresting anyone, we probably would not have printed any names. We can't determine whether someone is guilty or innocent. We can only report what is known and what is being done by the supposedly responsible agencies. There's news value in that. The public wants to know."

Let's assume, for the sake of the women who have suffered the awful reality of rape, that most women who say they were raped are telling the truth. And certainly it is less traumatic for those women to remain unnamed in the news media than for them to cope with public prying into their experience, although that question is not the issue here.

Now let's also put a little faith in the U.S. criminal justice system; let's assume that a rape case doesn't go to trial unless there is some solid evidence (which of course still does not mean the man is guilty). Once the man is indicted or enters a guilty plea, there is ample reason to identify him in the media.

But before that—before there is any more evidence than an accusation from an alleged victim who speaks from behind a veil of anonymity—the press could tread with more caution. All the journalists interviewed for this article agreed that the question of naming the accused in a rape case is a legitimate one precisely because of the custom of protecting the accuser's identity. In the two cases described here, though, the reporters felt that the media had acted responsibly, even admirably, and no one regretted having used the name of the accused.

But journalists could afford to let the dust settle before printing names and pictures; the story can be told just as well with anonymity on both sides. There will be time enough later to fill in the details if the charge turns out to be supportable.

Melinda McAdams is a free-lance writer who lives in New York City.

Accused Rapists Do **Not** Have the Right to Anonymity

Natalie LaTorre

When Raymond Donovan, Labor Secretary under Ronald Reagan, stepped from a New York courtroom after being found Not Guilty on corruption charges, reporters thought they were about to face a man giddy with redemption. Instead, they were surprised when he seemed to rain on his own parade. "What I want to know," he demanded angrily, "is where do I go to regain my reputation?" It was an excellent question which remains rhetorical for all accused persons who suddenly find themselves exonerated in the eyes of the law, but not the public. The question has been made tougher recently when applied to those accused of one of the more notorious crimes, rape. The debate over whether or not to release an alleged rapist's name has sprung out of the issue of whether the victim's identity should be revealed. If the victim has the right to remain anonymous, should the accused?

Recently, several high-profile cases have occurred in which rape accusations were either recanted by the victim or the prime suspect was proven innocent as the result of a police investigation. In one

case, a group of Sanford, Florida men were charged by a woman of committing a gang rape against her. The number of men she cited in the attack—as many as 15—and the length of the attack—34 hours—made it a sensational case in the eyes of the media and public.

But then the case became muddied. The woman admitted going to the building in which the attack occurred in order to purchase drugs. The men involved in the alleged attack said the woman agreed to take drugs in exchange for sex. Residents of the building corroborated this. Then the woman changed other key points to her story. She had not been at the building for 34 hours; she'd been there half a day. As their case seemed to dissipate, police released the accused men until a grand jury could review the evidence.

In another Florida case, a man singled out by a rape victim as her attacker was arrested and charged with rape and other offenses. He spent 9 days in prison before police determined that he had worked the day of the attack and couldn't possibly have committed the crime. He was released, his name already imprinted upon the collective mind of the community.

The right of anonymity afforded rape victims is almost universally honored by the media, making it unique, and that is what has sparked the recent debate about publicizing an alleged attacker's name. As the previous examples show, it can be enormously humiliating for a man to be incorrectly charged and then released for committing rape. (Although in the first instance, in which the accused maintain they traded drugs for sex, they have hardly ennobled themselves in the community either way you look at it. Nonetheless, rape is more severe than employing a prostitute.)   However, withholding the name of an accused rapist would be tantamount to preferential treatment, and would set a precedent that would have to be honored by the police and media - that all accused criminals remain anonymous until conviction.

The public's right to know—which is sometimes a vague notion—can probably be invoked here as reason enough to publicize the names of all accused criminals, rapists or otherwise. An alleged offender is assured of certain rights in this country: the right to trial by a jury of his/her peers; the right to a speedy trial and the right to legal representation. For better or worse, confidentiality is not protected under the Constitution and is not a jurisprudential right. During the interim between being charged and being convicted (or acquitted), the accused's name is part of the public domain and as long as the media has access to police reports, that's the way it is going to remain.

It is the rule of the system that a defendant is innocent until proven guilty, and the release of an accused person's name is not a declaration of guilt. Raymond Donovan was irate because he felt that the system had failed him, since he was held up for judgment. No doubt the scrutiny he endured was unpleasant, but when it was over he was ostentatiously declared free of verifiable sin. Just as the

> If you grant anonymity to rape suspects, then you must also grant it to accused burglars, killers, extortionists, etc.

charges had been headline news, so was his acquittal. It may not be much consolation to a man with the experience of a jury trial fresh in his memory, but someone should have told Donovan that reputations, like babies, are more resilient than they appear.

If you grant anonymity to rape suspects, then you must also grant it to accused burglars, killers, extortionists, etc. This is unacceptable, because it lessens the social stigma placed on criminals by offering them a sort of cozy hovel of secrecy, where they may crouch incognito while conferring with their lawyers. Every time a suspect's name somehow leaked out, defense attorneys would be shrieking for acquittal on grounds of prejudgment. This would mean the deification of public opinion, giving it more weight than written law. From that point on, society could look forward to a diverse festival of crimes of unknown authorship.

Natalie LaTorre writes for **WOAR** (Women Against Rape).

In God's Name

Barbara L. Delhotal

A civil war was waged in Wichita, Kansas, in the summer of '91.

The invading army of men, women, and children called itself Operation Rescue and drew its soldiers from all across the United States. It had been invited by local clergy to protest against three abortion clinics and Dr. George Tiller, a nationally-known physician, one of the few who will perform second-, and sometimes third-trimester abortions.

Its' leader, Randall Terry, and his followers gathered to spend a week to "stop the killing of unborn babies." Its' ranks were swelled by an unlikely combination of Catholics, fundamentalists, and members of pro-lifer groups who live in Wichita and have been carrying on a low-key protest of the clinics for years.

Wichita was a city vulnerable to at-tack in the summer of '91. It had been a bad year for Wichita's citizens. Property reappraisal had increased most people's taxes, sometimes doubling them; and yet the Chamber of Commerce was beating its drums for a revitalization of the downtown (which had lost at least three major businesses in the year) by raising more taxes.

Both City and County Commissions were voting themselves salary raises. The School Board, which had elected three new members, hired a new law firm to investigate the possibility of firing the School Superintendent; after spending $150,000 of non-allocated school funds, the Board was told that the law firm could find no grounds for the firing.

The City enforced mandatory water rationing because of the drought. And in

> "I live two blocks South of the clinic and was greeted with cries of 'babykiller!' as I walked to and from work."

a record-setting meeting, City Councilman Frank Ojile spent more than 10 hours trying to pass a City Ordinance restricting abortion in the city, finally standing and, with tears in his eyes, asking the others to join him in voting for the ban. (It was defeated.) With all the problems on the minds of Wichitans, news of Operation Rescue was first shoved to the back pages of the local newspaper, *The Wichita Eagle*. But there were signs that news of the protest would not be content to stay there for long.

Roger Christman, owner of Hair Masters, a hair salon across the street from the Wichita Family Planning Clinic, remembered:

"At first, it appeared that the protest would really hurt my business. The Police used my parking lot, and the protestors tried to take over the rest of it so that my customers had no parking. The Police just stood by, watching.

"I also live just two blocks South of the clinic and was greeted with cries of 'Babykiller!' as I walked to and from work. The protestors assumed I was pro-choice when I actually don't believe in abortion."

The second or third day of the protest, he put the following message on his portable sign, "Freedom of Choice. God Bless America."

"By Thursday, I was trying to think what I could do to protect myself and my business."

Christman called Peggy Jarman, spokesperson for Dr. George Tiller, who owned one of the targeted clinics, for ideas. He told her, "We need some help as to what to do in the neighborhood." He had never been active in anything like this before, he explained.

That Saturday, Jarman came in the salon and became his first pro-choice customer. At the rally the following day, she thanked him publicly for his sign; and Christman began actively protesting the protestors. "At this point," he added, "I just wanted those people out of my neighborhood."

Christman's 72-year-old mother lives with him and is on dialysis. The first week, the handicapped bus that picks her up for her treatments couldn't get to the house because of the protest, and she had to walk to the end of the block, a hardship for her in her condition.

Clinic patients began coming to the salon to wait safely for their turn in the clinic, and the protestors followed with their signs. Customers would find nails carefully placed under their tires, forward and back, so that they could not be avoided unless noticed and removed. Christman's walk-in trade suffered, and in the first 3-4 weeks of the protest, he lost $1,000 in business.

Christman didn't change his attitude about abortion because of the protest; he's still against it. But he believes everyone should have the freedom of choice. The protest caused him to look closely at the issue. "As a citizen, I do not understand how or why anyone would allow one individual to persecute and torture another individual under the guise of freedom of speech."

An unexpected side effect of his anti-protest protest was an increase of 80 customers, all pro-choice. "I've met so many wonderful people who care."

During the first week of Operation Rescue's "Summer of Mercy", the three targeted clinics (Tiller's Women's Health Care Service, Wichita Family Planning Clinic, and Planned Parenthood) remained closed to patients. The admittedly pro-life mayor, Bob Knight, advised Police Chief Rick Stone to avoid confrontation with protestors; and Governor Joan Finney, also admittedly pro-life, spoke at an OR rally. Pro-choice groups were advised to avoid waging battle with the protestors, part of the theory that OR would then "just go away;" and for the first six days, there were no arrests.

At the end of the week, Operation Rescue claimed a victory in stopping abortion in the city, but behind the lines, the citizens of Wichita were mobilizing.

Signs worn by "rescuers" are tiny fetus feet.

✧

Dr. Tiller was the major target of Operation Rescue, and Alan Phares is one of his patients.

"George Tiller is my primary physician and has been for the last five years. He coordinates treatment for my heart condition with my cardiologist," Phares began. "I had been scheduled to go in for routine blood work on the Monday that the protest started, and George called me and said 'Let's put it off a week. We don't need any further confrontation.' Then he called me to cancel again the following week. I was unable to get normal medical health care for three weeks because of the protestors."

When Phares finally could get an appointment, he had to park three blocks away because the protestors had taken all the available parking spaces. He told the policeman at the gate of the clinic that he was there for an appointment. "I guess because I was in a suit, he decided I wasn't a protestor,"

Phares added. He was escorted inside by clinic personnel without harassment. "Because I was a man, I guess the protestors were surprised. They moved, I went in and did my blood work, went out, the police asked them to move again, they did, and I was gone."

The protest didn't affect how Phares feels about abortion.

"I live in a house divided, and I'm in the middle. But I can tell you that I'm an advocate for women's rights. I've worked with handicapped families and saw the agony that they go through.

"I'm just glad that I wasn't really sick in the middle of the protest. Despite the inconvenience and the parking, I got ongoing medical care, unlike the women patients."

The three clinics opened the second week, and the battle lines were drawn. Fueled by rallies for both the pro-life and pro-choice sides, protestors dug in and clinic supporters defended the gates to the clinics. Residents began to take sides, and the editorial section of the local newspaper was flooded with letters:

"The pro-choice people, by their very arguments in favor of it, have convinced

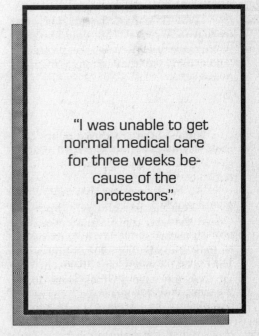

"I was unable to get normal medical care for three weeks because of the protestors".

me that abortion on demand is not only morally wrong, but the worst legal move the Supreme Court has given our country . . . Legalized abortion is numbing America to violence."

" . . . Let me finish by saying I am neither for thoughtless abortions or against all abortions. The individual case is the answer with careful thought."

"But I am very much against these intruders in our streets."

" . . . I am proud of the people who are willing to take a stand and be clear about this issue (anti-abortion) . . . I will continue to pray for a renewed respect for life."

"Wow, Wichita as the center of social change in America! This would be great if only Operation Rescue were protesting and gaining public attention for the right reasons."

✧

Button at the pro-choice rally: "God says She doesn't know Randall Terry."

✧

When the pro-choice supporters joined the war, confrontation escalated. OR protestors sat or lay in front of the entrances to abortion clinics; and when carried off by police they either went limp or took tiny steps, which came to be known as "the Wichita walk." The police released protestors after payment of a $25.00 fine, and buses from a local Pen-

tecostal Church returned them to the blockades. Finally, the clinics, fed up with what they felt was a lack of police protection, petitioned the Federal Court to restore order; and Judge Patrick Kelly invoked a 120-year-old civil rights law (Originally used against the Ku Klux Klan) to limit unlawful blockades and harassment of patients and staff by OR.

Judge Kelly ordered federal marshals to ensure that the Order of the Court was enforced and that the clinics stayed open. OR filed an appeal with the Tenth Circuit Court to stay Kelly's injunction, and despite the intervention of the Attorney General of the United States, the injunction was upheld. Kelly's life was later threatened, and one OR official claimed he would go to the Vatican to ask the Pope to excommunicate Kelly. Speaking at a pro-life rally, Pat Robertson asked for Kelly's impeachment.

As the number of arrests exceeded 1,000, the protestors became more aggressive, kicking at police, climbing fences, locking arms and hurling themselves at lines of supports and Police at clinic entrances. Such tactics brought national publicity to the protest, adding reporters and the Donahue Show to the battle and increasing donations of time and money to both sides.

✧

Sign: "Put feet on our prayers."

✧

Mary Triana, a Wichita resident and grandmother, was one of the protestors who went to jail for 28 days.

August 2nd, the 18th day of the protest, Triana was arrested for the third time. She was loaded in a bus with other protestors and taken to the Police Academy building. But instead of pleading "Not guilty" and being released, Triana and the others were handcuffed in threes and taken to the Sedgwick County Jail.

"I believe the reason we were put in jail was as an example to the others," she explained. Once processed and searched, all personal items such as jewelry and purses were taken from the prisoners and they were fed, showered, and all clothing except underwear was taken from them. They were given two-piece orange outfits to wear and placed in 12-person unitsconsisting of a day room and 12 individual cells.

"The majority of the time we were kept separated from the other prisoners," Triana added. The 12 women in her unit were all protestors. "Some had been arrested in other places before, and some were with Operation National.

"We were really surprised (to be arrested). We really truly didn't expect to be jailed. We felt we had done nothing to be jailed for and refused bail. We wanted the City to suffer the consequences: crowded dockets, crowded jails. Most of us knew this was going to happen eventually. We were concerned about our families, but no one was really unhappy. We felt that God had done this to give other people the incentive to come and 'rescue.' There was a lot of prayer and hymn singing. There were I don't know how many denominations in there, but the Christian unity was unbelievable."

Triana used her one phone call to contact a friend and ask her to call an attorney. She did not call her daughter, Theresa Rogers, because "I knew she wasn't in sympathy with what I was doing."

During the day, the protestors prayed and read the Bibles provided them in jail. Triana had requested a rosary, but the matron ran out. "Lots of things are made in jail from toilet paper. I wet some and stuck it on the desk in my cell in the shape of a rosary." They asked the guards how they felt (about abortion), but they would point to their uniforms and say that they couldn't answer that question.

Triana told of a priest's visit. "He said that it (being in jail) was kinda like a retreat. I said it was better than a retreat, because in a retreat you have one retreat

"We are trying to change the world. Liberalism is way out of hand."

master and one set of things to study. In jail, there were many people who said things that were spiritual food for thought to me.

"We are trying to change the world. Liberalism is way out of hand."

Triana still refuses to pay her fine and is scared only that she will be jailed again because of her refusal. She has nothing but praise for Operation Rescue and its' leader. "I think that every group that wants to accomplish something needs someone like Randall Terry. A focus. He has the ability to gather people and arouse in them the desire to do God's Will. I don't want anybody to feel we were doing Randall Terry's will.

"No way. Operation Rescue came in to lead the fight, recruit, and rouse the troops. Pat Mahoney is called 'God's Cheerleader,' but they all make you excited to do what God wants you to do."

✧

One of the most controversial issues of Operation Rescue's tactics involved the use of children as protestors. Children could be seen walking the line in front of clinics, carrying signs they could hardly see over. One mother was warned by a policeman that she was endangering her infant by carrying it outside in over-100 degree weather and said he would charge her with child abuse if the baby became ill.

Ellen Donnelly, 16, of Ypsilanti, Michigan, lay in the street to block traffic with her seven brothers and sisters, ages 9 to 17. When asked about her actions, she said her parents did not object. "They said it's between us and God."

One protestor argued, "If a woman at the age of 15 is old enough to make a conscientious decision to murder a child in her own womb, without instruction or parental consent, then a 15-year-old is old enough to make a decision to rescue a child from murder."

Cartoon from the *Houston Post*: Man wearing an OR button and holding a sign proclaiming that "Abortion is murder" is telling a trio of children, "Remember, Children . . . Life is sacred. Now lie down in front of that car."

Co-workers, friends, and relatives found themselves on opposite sides of the issue, even on opposite sides of the street. The newspaper ran a photo of two sisters embracing in the midst of a protest: one carried a pro-life sign, the other carried a pro-choice one.

Theresa Rogers, Mary Triana's daughter, hasn't talked to her mother about her views on abortion. "I'm against abortion morally and in my heart, but I'm a foster parent. I've seen children who are physically, emotionally, and sexually abused, and I've seen children that nobody wanted."

She added, "I wouldn't let her views come between us. That was her thing, and she can do whatever she wants. I try to understand. But it (Triana's decision to go to jail) lets you know where you stand. That (the protest) comes first. It would be nice if she were there for her own family rather than for unborn children. Family ought to come first."

Rogers especially disagreed with the use of children as protestors. She explained, "Children shouldn't fight adult battles. They are just doing what their parents want them to do to get the parents' approval. People who take kids down there, let them lie down in front of cars, leave them of curbs when they're arrested, make them carry signs, are hypocritical. They say they are fighting for the lives of children and they are putting their own children's lives in jeopardy."

Triana's arrest widened the rift between mother and daughter. "I could hardly talk to her anymore because that's all she could talk about. I had arguments with my husband over my helping out at Mom's house while she was in jail. I felt pulled apart. If I helped her, I was making him angry. And if I didn't go see her (in jail) and water her plants, I was letting her down."

Roger's friends say her mother is a saint, that she's the bravest woman they know. "I let everyone know I wasn't going to fight about this. I said a jillion times, 'Let's change the subject.'"

After 46 days of "rescue," Operation Rescue left Wichita, turning over control of the movement to local anti-abortion organizations. It claimed a "stunning victory." But, what in God's name did they actually accomplish?

OR left behind a legacy of debts, lingering resentment, increased levels of crime, and a proliferation of newly-formed pro-life groups:

Over 2,600 arrests were made during OR's war, at a cost to Wichita taxpayers of more than $650,000 in court costs, police overtime, unpaid fines, and property damage.

Two groups of Wichita clergy with opposing views on abortion have discontinued meetings designed to ease tensions and find ways to cooperate. One of the members of the Wichita Rescue movement wrote in a letter from jail:

"I want to propose a plan that will end child-killing in Wichita. We will have to be prepared to polarize the community. We could lose all that we own. We should expect even our relatives to turn on us. We will be hated by many because of the vicious lies in the press.

"We will have to resign ourselves to losing our very lives."

Persistent and increasing hostility has marked protests at abortion clinics, and both sides complain of pushing, shoving, and harassment by the other. An aura of paranoia surrounds both camps. The Pro Choice Action League had its headquarters swept for a bugging device because it felt the opposition knew too much about when patients' appointments were scheduled and what kinds of cars they drove. The Reverend Joe Slovenec, a national Operation Rescue leader, was arrested upon returning to Wichita for failure to post a peace bond of $100,000. He claimed, "I woke up yesterday morning, and I thought I was in America. Then when I got off the plane, I realized I was in Wichita, where Judge Kelly rules and the Constitution means nothing."

Criminals committed a record number of robberies, burglaries, and auto thefts in July, according to police records; and Operation Rescue's protest is partially to blame. Response time to calls also increased, due to the tremendous demands on police resources. The impact on the police department's budget may be as much as $500,000.

Pro-choice and pro-life advocates reported an increase in supporters as a result of the "Summer of Mercy." Colleen Kelly Johnston, Wichita NOW President, said, "NOW has had a 13 percent increase in membership since Operation Rescue, and we thank them for it." The Reverend James Conley of the St. Paul Parish-Newman Center said, "Operation Rescue definitely strengthened those who were already committed. It put new life into the existing pro-life movement."

The image of Wichita as a peaceful midwestern city of more than 300,000 people has been changed as well. Wichita now must face an image as a city with weak leadership that was intimidated and blackmailed with the threat of national humiliation by an out-of-state organization. It was an expensive lesson. During a subsequent attempt by Operation Rescue to blockade an abortion clinic in Iowa City, pro-choice supporters pushed protestors back, chanting, "This is not Wichita."

An editorial in the nearby *Hutchinson News* summed it up when it stated:

Time may heal all the summer's wounds, but the perceptions will linger. The view is of a city divided, racked by crime and sorely lacking a unified vision.

That is bad for Wichita, but it is equally harmful to the state as a whole.

Barbara Delhotal is a freelance magazine writer for Midwest **Living** *and* **Kansas** *and is at work on her first novel.*

Burning Issue · A TRUE STORY

ONE SUMMER AFTERNOON, IN A SMALL TOWN IN THE COUNTRY, A YOUNG WOMAN NAMED *ALFI* TRIES TO TAKE HER MIND OFF THE OPPRESSIVE HEAT BY THINKING OF ANOTHER TIME...

WHEN I WAS YOUNG, THINGS WERE SO *DIFFERENT!*

I CAN REMEMBER VISITING MY COUSIN...

...IN THE CITY. MY PARENTS AND THE OTHER GROWN-UPS WERE ALWAYS TALKING *POLITICS*, BUT *I* WAS ONLY INTERESTED IN THE LATEST FASHIONS!

ISN'T THAT *COOL*, ALFI?

I CAN'T WAIT 'TIL I'M OLD ENOUGH TO WEAR STUFF LIKE *THAT!*

BUT BY THE TIME I WAS OLD ENOUGH TO WEAR STYLISH CLOTHES, THINGS HAD... *CHANGED.*

CONSERVATIVES HAD TAKEN OVER, AND MY HUSBAND INSISTED I DRESS AS PLAINLY AS ALL THE OTHER WOMEN.

WHERE HAVE YOU BEEN?

AT THE *DOCTOR'S.*

JUST A ROUTINE CHECKUP.

I JUST *CAN'T BELIEVE* IT... THE DOCTOR TOLD ME THAT MY STOMACH HAS BEEN HURTING LATELY BECAUSE I'M *PREGNANT!*

BUT I'M NOT *READY* FOR A CHILD YET!

THERE WAS *NO* ONE TO TURN TO.

I DID WHAT I *HAD* TO DO, *MYSELF.*

SCRIPT
LAMAR WALDRON ·

ART
TED BOONTHANAKIT ·

LETTERS/EDITS
SUSAN BARROWS ·

RESEARCH/CONCEPT
TERI

Reprinted from **Choices**. See page 267 for review.

PROFILE IN COURAGE:
BILL BAIRD

Harvey Wood

Talking to Bill Baird these days is both an inspiration and an ordeal. To hear him tell his story is reminiscent of watching the performances of Lenny Bruce in that comedian's later years, after his many arrests, trials and persecutions had left him almost unable to talk about anything else. Baird is not as funny as Bruce; but like Bruce, he is consumed with anger at the injustices he has suffered; like Bruce, he surrounds himself with clippings, letters and other documentation, which he refers to almost compulsively, circling back again and again to quote passages which particularly anger or please him; like Bruce, he sees himself as a fighter for freedom, who has been repeatedly betrayed by the very people he fought for, as well as by his natural enemies; like Bruce, he is driven, obsessive and sometimes irritating. And, like Bruce, he is right.

For almost thirty years Bill Baird has fought, unceasingly and usually alone, for the right of women to make their own reproductive choices, particularly as regards birth control and abortion. From the days when even advocating the use of contraception was illegal in most states— and abortion was illegal everywhere— Baird has been in the front lines, defying the opposition and waving his more timid followers on to battle. In the process he has lost his family, risked his safety, and sacrificed such luxuries as a private life or a reasonable income. He has been arrested eight times in five states, has been firebombed, spit on and shot at, and has received numerous death threats. He has also been responsible for a considerable portion of the progress that has been made since those early days. His name is on three landmark women's rights decisions by the United States Supreme Court, one of which was a direct precursor of Roe v. Wade, the ruling that legalized abortion. He was instrumental in liberalizing the birth control laws of several states, including New York and New Jersey. And through his day-to-day work in his non-profit reproduction counselling clinics, he has personally helped thousands of women, many of whom were too poor or afraid to go anywhere else.

It all started—very dramatically—in

1963, when Bill Baird, a thirty-year-old ex-Sunday School teacher who had grown up poor in the slums of Brooklyn, gone to college with the goal of becoming a doctor, and dropped out of medical school for lack of money, was working as clinical director of a large drug company, marketing and distributing contraceptive foam. While on a business visit to Harlem Hospital in New York, he heard a scream in the hallway. Rushing out, he found a profusely bleeding woman with part of a coat hanger lodged in her uterus. The woman died in his arms. That moment changed his life.

Abortion, of course, was illegal, and whereas there were illicit abortionists—ranging from licensed physicians to backroom operators who were neither particularly skilled nor sanitary, and who often demanded sex from their clients as part of their payment—self-induced abortion, especially among poor women, was very common. The coat hanger was only one method. Women would douche themselves with such substances as bleach, Lysol or turpentine—all of them highly dangerous. "They would stand up against the wall," Baird says, "and let their husband or boyfriend punch them—out of love—to try to abort them, or throw them down a flight of stairs."

Fired by the idea that women should at least be able to obtain the knowledge which would allow them to avoid such danger and suffering, Baird bought an old United Parcel van which he converted to a mobile counselling center, and began distributing birth control information in the poor sections of New York in his off-hours. To avoid prosecution, he formed a non-profit organization, the Parents' Aid Society, "with the hope that the Attorney General would be overworked and wouldn't see what I had in my charter. In my charter it said, 'to help with reproductive health care, abortion and birth control'—clearly against the law." It worked; the state chartered him to give this illegal information.

In 1965 Baird opened his first clinic in Hempstead, Long Island—the first clinic in the United States to openly offer abortion counselling. In the same year he was arrested for disseminating birth control information in violation of state law. His arrest got him fired from his job; the only employment he could find was as a security guard at a mental hospital, where for two dollars per hour he helped carry away dead bodies at night.

The publicity from Baird's trial was instrumental in the liberalization of New York's birth control laws, two months after his arrest. The charges were dropped, and a year later, ironically, Baird was asked to become family planning adviser to New York State. The same thing happened after his arrest in New Jersey in 1966, where he served his first jail sentence. Baird accepted both positions. "I would always say the same thing: there should be no law on birth control. They asked me what my law was, and I would give them a blank piece of paper, and I said, that's my law."

In 1967 began the events that led to what is perhaps Baird's most important victory, the 1972 Supreme Court decision in Baird v. Eisenstadt. During a lecture on birth control at Boston University, Baird was arrested for handing two contraceptive devices to a female student. This was a deliberate effort to test the constitutionality of a 125-year-old Massachusetts statute dealing with "crimes against chastity, morality, decency and good order," which, among other things, prohibited dissemination of birth control materials or information to unmarried people. (The Supreme Court, in Griswold v. Connecticut [1965] had given contraceptive freedom to married couples, but not to singles.)

Baird was found guilty on two counts, and sentenced as a felon to three months in prison, the judge accusing him of being "a menace to the nation." In prison he was repeatedly strip-searched and had to cope with such pleasantries as rats in his cell and bugs in his food. Though the governor of Massachusetts suggested parole, the District Attorney refused. One prosecutor was quoted as saying, "Baird is such a menace I would not allow him in the same room with my daughter." He served thirty-six days before a Federal court ordered his release pending appeal.

The Massachusetts Supreme Court upheld the conviction, and the case was then appealed to the U.S. Supreme Court, which had been Baird's ultimate objective. The Court at first refused to hear the case; but that ruling was reversed due to the persistence of Justice William O. Douglas, who later said in his book *The Douglas Papers*: "The teachings of Baird and Galileo may be of a different order, but the suppression of either is equally repugnant."

Finally, in 1972, the court ruled 6-1 that the Massachusetts law was unconstitutional, thus extending the right of contraception to everyone, regardless of marital status. In a significant and often quoted opinion, Justice William J. Brennan wrote: "If the right of privacy means anything, it is the right of the individual, married or single, to be free from unwarranted government intrusion into matters so fundamentally affecting a person as the decision whether to bear or beget a child."

This statement, with the important phrase "bear or beget," clearly looked forward to future cases dealing with abortion. And indeed, in the 1973 case of Roe v. Wade, which finally made abortion legal, the precedent of Baird v. Eisenstadt was referred to five separate times in the majority decision.

Baird put his name on legal history again in the two Supreme Court cases entitled Baird V. Bellotti, as a result of his filing a claim on behalf of the right of teenagers to obtain abortions without parental permission. In Baird v. Bellotti I (1976) the Court ruled that parents could not have an absolute veto, but directed the states to investigate the feasibility of "judicial bypass." In B v. B II (1979) the Court ruled more specifically, saying that an abortion could be obtained provided a

judge, considering the plaintiff's maturity and best interests, decides that she may have one.

(These rulings, as well as others concerning abortion, have since been weakened by the Webster ruling of 1979, which effectively turned abortion decisions back to the states.)

In 1989 Baird's help was requested by the family of Nancy Klein, a comatose pregnant woman whose husband sought an abortion to safeguard her health. In a

widely publicized case, the abortion was opposed by right-to-life people, two of whom applied to become guardians of Klein and of the fetus she was carrying. After lower court rulings in the Kleins' favor, the anti-abortionists went to the Supreme Court, where two justices declined appeals to review the case, this allowing the abortion to proceed. Klein later came out of her coma, and is currently recovering.

Baird's accomplishments in the realm of reproductive freedom, of which these are only some of the highlights, were not won easily. He has been the constant target of right-wing groups, right-to-lifers and the Catholic Church, as well as hostile police and public officials. Judie Brown, of the anti-abortion American Life League, called him "a religious fanatic who believes in the freedom to kill babies." (Hardly religious in any conventional sense, Baird is an ex- Lutheran who became a Unitarian because, he says,"Unitarians accept anybody.") He has been called a "corrupter of morals," a "peddler of death," "the Devil himself," and a man who makes "whores and prostitutes out of women." In 1971 he was arrested while lecturing in Huntington, N.Y., on charges of impairing the morals of a minor—the minor being one fourteen-month-old infant (with a vocabulary of three words) carried by her mother, who had been unable to find a baby-sitter. (The mother was arrested also.) Despite the fact that the police lied at the trial in an attempt to strengthen their case, Baird was acquitted. He sued the police, won $8,000, which he split with the mother, and with his half set up the Bill Baird Suffolk County Police Abortion Fund. Nonetheless, the morals charge haunts him to this day.

After the Huntington arrest, threats against him and his family grew so severe that Baird decided to move his wife and four children to another state. He has lived apart from them ever since. Though he still sees them when he can, and though they remain on good terms, they have grown apart from him politically, and now largely embrace, he says, all the stultifying values he has always fought against.

In 1971 two firebombs were thrown at a building in New Bedford, Massachusetts where Baird was speaking. In Wisconsin someone shot at him with a rifle; the shooter was not found. In 1973 he clashed with the Catholic Church when he was arrested for disturbing the

peace while he stood in a Virginia motel corridor waiting to deliver a request to speak at a meeting of Roman Catholic bishops. When the case was thrown out of court, Baird announced plans to file a false-arrest suit against the National Conference of Bishops, and to build the Bill Baird Catholic Abortion-Birth Control Clinic with the proceeds. The next day the charge was reinstated, and again dismissed, but lack of promised funds prevented the suit. The Church struck again in 1974, when priests in Marlboro, Mass. refused to baptize an infant because the mother was a Baird supporter.

In 1979 Baird's Hempstead clinic was destroyed when one Peter Burkin, an unemployed drifter with ties to anti-abortion groups, walked in with a jug full of gasoline and a flaming torch and set fire to the place, which at the time was occupied by thirty-five patients and fifteen staff members. Fortunately all escaped unharmed, due largely to Baird's having prepared and rigorously trained his staff for just such an event. One counselor saved two terrified patients by running back into the building and pulling them out by their hair. Burkin was charged with arson. According to Baird, the Nassau County District Attorney—who had previously said that he would not prosecute anyone who blockaded a clinic because they were doing God's work—barely went through the motions in prosecuting the case. Burkin was sentenced to less than one year in a mental hospital. The Hempstead clinic was relocated a few blocks away.

Last year a scheduled abortion debate at Catholic University of America in Washington, D.C. was canceled due to religious protests. Baird, claiming that six cardinals had brought pressure on the school, fought to receive full payment of his promised fee, vowing to use it to open an abortion fund for poor Catholic women. After some resistance, the fee was paid.

With the exception of the separation from his family—which obviously grieves him deeply—and in spite of his indignant denunciations and insistent self-justification, one feels that Baird takes the consequences of these attacks from his right-wing enemies with relative equanimity. In fact, he seems almost to relish his battles with the Church and the anti-abortion fanatics, and to take pride in the strength and cleverness with which he opposes them. (Though his manner is low-key, he is not exactly self-deprecating; he is given to such grandiose statements as "I see myself as the candle that lights the darkness of ignorance and sexism.") But when he speaks of his relations with the feminist movement, and how he has been repeatedly attacked and excluded, mainly because of his sex, by the people he feels should be his natural allies—from the relatively conservative Planned Parenthood organization to the National Organization for Women (NOW) to the ultra-militant feminists of the left—his tone changes.

"I'm not black, but I fought for black rights. I'm not gay—I long fought for gay rights, before there were any gay groups . . . I thought people would help people. That's my philosophy, loving people, caring about people . . . But I'll be damned, it's suddenly now the very people who are oppressed who oppress others, by saying, you're not our color, you're not our sexual preference . . . I've been shot at, firebombed, punched, kicked, separated from my family, paid my dues—and I'm still told, you can't be with us because you're a man."

Baird's conflicts with the people whose rights he fights for go back at least to the beginning of Baird v. Eisenstadt in 1967. Planned Parenthood, which believed in gradual change through legislation rather that court battles, refused to become involved in the case, saying there was "nothing to be gained," a quote which Baird comes back to again and again, his blue eyes shining with indignation—which turns to pain as he quotes a NOW official as saying, re the same case, "If William Baird's name was Wilhelmina Baird, we would have acted."

"I called NOW later," he says. "And they were very angered by that. And I said they were later in understanding what the issues of women's rights were . . . Three U.S. Supreme Court cases I had, that dealt with millions of women. Would you like to take a guess as to how many amicus

> . . . he quotes a NOW official as saying: "If William Baird's name was Wilhemina Baird, we would have acted."

briefs were filed [by NOW] that basically say, we support the arguments before the Supreme Court? . . . A hundred? Fifty? One from each state? One from every other state? Zippo. Not one. Now what does that say?"

Although his work has been commended from time to time by NOW and other women's groups, Baird has also been prevented on a number of occasions from speaking at abortion rallies or debating abortion issues because he is male. In 1975, invited to debate a right-to-lifer at a Connecticut college but denied access by militant women, he filed a sexual harassment suit with the Human Rights Commission. The Commission claimed the suit was filed too late; Baird claims the HRC was simply not interested in handling a reverse sexism charge.

After that, Baird says, the feminist attacks on him intensified. Betty Freidan accused him of being a CIA agent. ("I wouldn't know a CIA agent if I fell over one," he says.) Robin Morgan, long-time militant feminist and currently editor of *Ms.*, implied in her book *Going Too Far* that Baird was in the women's movement in order to enhance his sex life, which he says is an insult to women as well as to him.

"To this day," Baird says, "I cannot get . . . any one of those so-called feminists to remember that they came to me in the sixties, when there was no one else in the United States who would publicly say they would help . . . So when I see the abuse that women endured, way before there was a NOW, and that Planned Parenthood never came out in support of abortion until . . . years after I did . . . and now to tell me, as a true pioneer of this movement, go away, we don't want to know you—has filled me with rage and anger."

Baird says that though he is angry, he is not bitter; but the line often seems finely drawn. Though he never raises his voice, the emotions come across loud and clear. In past interviews he has said that the constant threats and attacks have led him to believe that he would not survive to fight to the end. That's still true, he says, but he wonders now about a different kind of vulnerability. "If you have somebody beat you up for thirty years, you're telling me that after the thirty-first year, or the thirty-fifth, or whatever it may be, that you can't be broken? . . . If somebody says, Bill Baird, you've lost a family, you're deep in debt . . . you're being barred from campus after campus—not because of your message but because of your sex—people pray for your death, people write editorials, I am the devil; then you've got the women's movement who says, we'll castrate you if you show up—I'm surprised I haven't been broken . . . I'd like to say to you honestly that . . . I can't be broken even now. I couldn't do that . . . Any one of us can be broken. And I know that can happen to me."

But this mood doesn't last; he is off to fetch more clippings, more documentation; his energy seems inexhaustible. He's fit and trim, looking far younger than his nearly fifty-nine years. Sometimes one wishes for less energy as the barrage of facts, assertions, quotations and denunciations streams on. Bill Baird is relentlessly anxious to get his story told—every bit of it. But there can be no doubt that it is a story worth telling. And there can be no doubt either that through all the obsessiveness, anger and pain shine the qualities that are the true essence of the man—his unlimited compassion, his undeniable courage, and his undiminished and apparently bottomless dedication.

"People have said, he's a great social reformer, and the letter I've got here compares me to Dr. King, to Ghandi, to Thoreau—direct quote. Others compare me to Hitler. And I'm neither. All I am is probably the most stubborn man you'll ever meet, who won't surrender one inch for the principle that you and I have a right to differ, you and I have a right to make our own judgements. That's what my whole life's battle has been—the word called freedom . . .

"So . . . I say in spite of all of you—in spite of all of you—I will chart the course that I know is right, and that is not that abortion is right or wrong, but every American has the freedom and the right of privacy to make his choice. And I live for those words of Justice Douglas: 'The teachings of Baird and Galileo may be of a different order, but the suppression of either is equally repugnant.' And better than that is Justice Brennan: 'If the right of privacy means anything, it is the right of the individual . . . to be free.'

"That's my tombstone," Bill Baird says.

Reprinted from October 1991 issue of **Penthouse Forum.** *Harvey Wood a writer for Penthouse Publications also writes fiction and non-fiction on a free-lance basis*

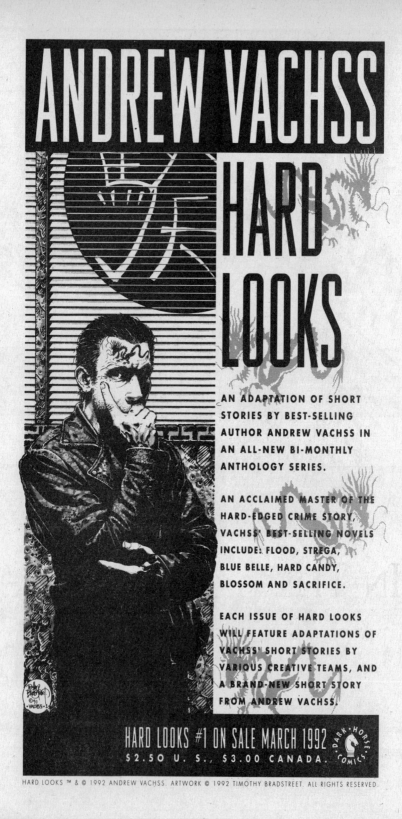

ANDREW VACHSS

HARD LOOKS

AN ADAPTATION OF SHORT
STORIES BY BEST-SELLING
AUTHOR ANDREW VACHSS IN
AN ALL-NEW BI-MONTHLY
ANTHOLOGY SERIES.

AN ACCLAIMED MASTER OF THE
HARD-EDGED CRIME STORY,
VACHSS' BEST-SELLING NOVELS
INCLUDE: FLOOD, STREGA,
BLUE BELLE, HARD CANDY,
BLOSSOM AND SACRIFICE.

EACH ISSUE OF HARD LOOKS
WILL FEATURE ADAPTATIONS OF
VACHSS' SHORT STORIES BY
VARIOUS CREATIVE TEAMS, AND
A BRAND-NEW SHORT STORY
FROM ANDREW VACHSS.

HARD LOOKS #1 ON SALE MARCH 1992
$2.50 U. S., $3.00 CANADA.

DARK HORSE COMICS

POLITICAL
AND
CORPORATE

IN THE LAND OF THE FREE

John Shirley

Just before the 1984 presidential election, ABC World News Tonight stopped three stories—"spiked" them, in the vernacular—that could have hurt the Republican campaign. One of the stories involved a documentation of serious health and safety violations at nursing homes owned by U.S. Information Agency director Charles Wick—a close friend of Ronald Reagan's; there was the story of the FBI's cover-up of Labor Secretary Ray Donovan's association with organized crime; there was a report on Reagan crony Paul Laxalt's attempt to stop a Justice department probe of his campaign contributors. All three stories were stopped. The spiking was "political pressure," according to senior ABC Producer Marion Goldin.

When Jon Alpert, a stringer for NBC news for 12 years, returned from Iraq with some striking videotape of civilian areas of Iraq devastated by U.S. bombing, NBC president Michael Gartner not only ordered that the footage not be aired, but forbade Alpert from working for the network in the future.

William Randolph Hearst III put columnist Warren Hinkle of the *San Francisco Examiner* on a three-month "vacation" as soon as the war began, after *forbidding publication* of a Hinkle column entitled "If Saddam is Hitler, Then Bush is Tojo".

New York Times correspondent Raymond Bonner dared to report on the mass graves near the capital of El Salvador where government-sponsored death squads left their mutilated victims in the early 1980s. As a result Bonner was yanked from Central America and was pressured to resign from the *Times* shortly thereafter. *Washington Post* correspondent Alma Guillermoprieto was also pulled from El Salvador after she reported on massacres by U.S.-backed forces—it was made clear to her that she had overstepped the bounds of allowable reporting.

✧

Isolated incidents? Not according to "Project Censored," initiated by Professor Carl Jensen at Sonoma State Univer-

> When Jon Alpert, a stringer for NBC news for 12 years, returned from Iraq with some striking videotape of civilian areas devastated by U. S. bombing, NBC president Michael Gartner not only ordered that the footage not be aired, but forbade Alpert from working for the network in the future.

sity. Suppressed stories cited by Project Censored in recent years include drug trafficking by CIA directed Nicaraguan Contras, sloppy biological warfare research in university laboratories, and the abuse of children incarcerated in U.S. prisons.

When truths are uncovered, you find them like rough gems in a strata of ironies. Here's an irony we'll have to dig through: the claim that the political left is perpetrating a "PC" censorship—a censorship of those who are not "politically correct", who are not playing along with the counter-culture agenda. People who've done substantial research on political censorship in the United States shake their heads and laugh sadly when that canard is foisted on the public.

"PC" censorship? If there is any, it's a handful of grains beside the mountain of censorship and "spiking" routinely carried out by Big Business, Big Government, and powerbrokers in the areas where those categories of power overlap.

Most political and corporate censorship isn't perpetrated as blatantly as it would be in a place like Communist China. Carl Jensen explains, "Censorship is the suppression of information by any means. It doesn't have to be direct, official government censorship. It could mean overlooking a story, or under-covering a story, or rejecting a story because it would mean alienating a sponsor." A sponsor who may have a relationship with the government—as for example General Electric, who has dozens of contracts for weaponry and related technology used in the Gulf War.

According to Chris Welles, a former journalist who teaches at Columbia School of Journalism, "I daresay anyone who has been in the business for more than a few months can cite plenty of examples of editorial compromises due to pressure, real or imagined, from publishers, owners and advertisers."

The best single documentation of political and corporate-interest censorship in America is currently found in the book *Unreliable Sources: A Guide to Detecting Bias in News Media,* by Martin A. Lee and Norman Solomon. From the book: "A more insidious and widespread form of censorship occurs when reporters give up trying to write about subjects they know will not be acceptable. Alert to the preferences of their higher-ups, journalists learn they must adjust to the constraints of the corporate workplace." Lee and Solomon quote former FCC-Chief Nicholas Johnson: "The story is told of a reporter who first comes up with an investigative story idea, writes it up and submits it to the editor and is told the story is not going to run. He wonders why, but the next time he is cautious enough to check with the editor first. He is told by the editor that he'd better not write that story. The third time he thinks of an investigative story idea but doesn't bother the editor with it . . . The fourth time he doesn't even think of the idea anymore."

The authors of *Unreliable Sources* quote a news producer who worked at CBS and NBC for nine years on the pressures that encourage self censorship: "People are even more careful now, because this whole notion of freedom of the press becomes a contradiction when the people who own the media are the same people who need to be reported on. There are political limits I perceive, and you

have to work within those limits, because ultimately it's unacceptable to stray beyond them."

Self Censorship was widespread during the Gulf War. Los Angeles' KABC-TV actually *banned* coverage of peace demonstrations soon after the war began, according to *L.A. Times* TV critic Howard Rosenberg. A KABC staffer told Rosenberg, "Nothing is on paper but it's understood and it's been reaffirmed repeatedly . . . . We may occasionally drop in a line [about anti-war demonstrations] at the end of coverage of pro-war demonstrations, but we do not put those protest stories on the air."

Only fools and paranoids claim that the American media is 100% controlled. Stories opposed to the interests of the Bush administration crop up fairly often in the media, and some of them are persistently troubling to the status quo. For a while there was a flap about the strong possibility that friends of the Reagan campaign arranged with the Iranians to delay the release of the American embassy hostages till after the election. True, this story has fallen by the wayside recently—but that could be simply because it was obliterated by other, more pressing stories, or because there have been no new developments.

Still, in this context it's worthwhile to note that one form of political censorship is the cold-shouldering of a major story once it has been raised in the media. They "just don't follow up on it", even though it's often a very big and trenchant story. In some cases this may actually be the result of phone calls made at high levels.

20/20 ran a story about the embarrassing ignorance and incompetence of many American ambassadors to foreign lands. Normally *20/20* offers transcripts and cassettes of its' stories—but after this one aired, no copies were available, and none of the usual follow up was done. No one else reported on the issue. "Pressure from above" was cited by some *20/20* personnel.

60 Minutes did a rather courageous story about the Pentagon's cover-up of *thousands* of needless civilian deaths in Panama at the hands of invading U.S. troops—and the military's dumping of

> "When the entire environment is controlled, a journalist ceases to be a reporter . . . He works a lot like the PK [the Nazi propaganda corps] . . . "

the bodies into mass graves. It was a *big* story, well documented, *reeking* of scandal, but it was never heard from again.

Maybe that's just coincidence.

Voice or no voice, the people can always be brought to the bidding of the leaders. That is easy. All you have to do is tell them they are being attacked, and denounce the pacifists for lack of patriotism and exposing the country to danger. It works the same in every country . .
—Hermann Goering

The Gulf War pointed up the apparent willingness in the media to accept informational spoon-feeding from the White House and especially the Pentagon. The following comes from *Extra!* the journal of FAIR, Fairness and Accuracy In Reporting, Volume 4, #3: "A recent study conducted by the University of Massachusetts' Center for Studies in Communication, found that the more people watched TV during the Gulf crisis, the less they knew about the underlying issues, and the more likely they were to support the war. When the research team tested public knowledge of basic facts about the region, U.S. policy and events leading up to the war, they discovered

that 'the most striking gaps in people's knowledge involved information that might reflect badly upon the Administration's policy'."

In a related piece, *Extra!* maintains, "The extent to which war reporting was controlled by the Bush administration was seldom detailed by the press and hence widely misunderstood by the public, which largely bought the argument that restrictions were necessary for some vaguely defined 'security' reasons. Such arguments were belied by the Pentagon's arbitrary ban on coverage of coffins returning to Dover Air Force Base, and by the '48 hour news blackout' at the beginning of the ground war, a blackout that was abandoned as soon as the news turned out to be good for the Pentagon . .

Extra! continues:
" . . . *I've never seen anything that can compare to it, in the degree of surveillance and control the military has over the correspondents,"* stated *New York Times* correspondent Malcolm Brown (*Newsday* 1/23/91). *"When the entire environment is controlled, a journalist ceases to be a reporter. . . He works a lot like the PK* [Propagandakompanien, the Nazi propaganda corps] . . .

"The key principle used by both Reagan and Bush is that if you can control where and when journalists (particularly TV journalists) can report, you can control the imagery and its emotional impact on the public. Michael Deaver, Ronald Reagan's minister of photo opportunities, marveled at the Pentagon's media mastery: *If you were going to hire a public relations firm to do the media relations for an international event, it couldn't be done any better than this is being done."*

Ironic that he should put it that way—a few years back the Pentagon *did* send key information officers to an information-managing school put on by a P.R. outfit.

Extra! notes that "the prime function of the pool reporting concept was to limit the imagery available to TV cameras. Thus we saw much heroic imagery of missiles rocketing off into the wild blue yonder; images of soldiers killed or wounded by friendly fire or 'non-combat related accidents' were not considered suitable photo opportunities. As Howard Stringer, president of the CBS Broadcast Group reported, *There are more people routinely killed across the spectrum of American television in a given night than you saw in any coverage of this war*

" . . . When Robert Fisk of the *Independent* tried to report without official permission on the battle of Khafji, NBC correspondent Brad Willis reported him to the Marines. *You asshole*, the NBC reporter told Fisk, *You'll prevent us from working. You're not allowed here. Get out. Go back to Dhahran . . . .*

"Reporters who tried to cover the war outside the Pentagon's press pools were sometimes detained and threatened by U.S. soldiers. Marines held a wire service photographer for six hours, threatening to shoot him if he left his car—*We have orders from above to make this pool system work*, they told him. A French TV crew was forced at gunpoint to turn over to Marines footage of soldiers wounded at the battle of Khafji.

" . . . Military officials had right of approval over final copy and footage . . . The censors were known to delete details that struck them as embarrassing—the fact that stealth pilots were watching X-rated movies before bombing missions, for example . . .

"The Center for Constitutional Rights, on behalf of a number of journalists, filed a lawsuit seeking the abolition of the restrictions on the grounds that there is no wartime exception to the First Amendment. But not only did mainstream media not join the law-suit...they hardly even reported on the suit."

One correspondent in Saudi Arabia told *Newsday*: "We have sort of become adjuncts of the government. The line between me and a government contractor is pretty thin."

According to *Extra!* writer Robert Krinsky, "In the weeks before President Bush dispatched orders to bomb Baghdad, CNN and network affiliates in Washington, DC, rejected efforts by the Military Family Support Network, a group of relatives of service-people who opposed the Gulf War, to purchase time for an anti-war TV ad. *It is a very sad day*

when in these troubled times the media thinks the feelings of military families are too controversial to be broadcast, observed Alex Molnar, MFSN co-chair."

Clearly, when complaints about media management and censorship are aired in *Newsday* and in other publications, there is no consistent censorship of media—but media critics would argue that the government, the Pentagon and Big Business simply censor where they can get away with it. And they get away with it with chilling frequency. The suppression we hear about is only the tip of an iceberg that is decidedly submerged.

As worrisome to me as Pentagon management of news sources, is the chummy understanding that exists between news media and the bigger corporations.

Indeed, sometimes the media *is* just a branch of some other kind of big business. General Electric is the owner of NBC. GE is also one of the biggest investors in nuclear energy. In March 1987, NBC News broadcast a special "documentary" entitled, "Nuclear Power: In France It Works." According to *Unreliable Sources*: "In an upbeat introduction to the so-called documentary, NBC anchor Tom Brokaw neglected to state that his corporate patron is America's second-largest nuclear energy vendor, with 39 nuclear reactors in the U.S. and the third-leading nuclear weapons producer—facts which gave rise to the moniker 'Nuclear Broadcasting Company' among disgruntled NBC staff."

NBC's report on nuclear energy was, well, glowing. With respect to the thorny problem of nuclear waste disposal, it concluded, "The French will probably succeed in their disposal plan for the same reasons the rest of the nuclear program works . . . The French have more faith than we do in the government's competence to manage the nuclear program, and the French government has had less tolerance for endless dissent."

"Unfortunately," Solomon and Lee tell us, "faith and lack of tolerance for dissent will not solve critical nuclear problems, even in France. One month after NBC aired its pro-nuclear broadcast, there were accidents at two French nuclear power installations, injuring seven workers . . . . polls show a third of the French public opposing nuclear power. While the accidents were widely discussed in the French media and some U.S. newspapers, NBC did not report the story . . ."

NBC News' blatant conflict of interest, its willingness to act as a shill for nuclear power while pretending to do an objective documentary, is to me something chillingly close to Orwellian brainwashing. There was a kind of *a priori* censorship, in the case of NBC's hour-long commercial for nuclear power, of any information that would reflect badly on the industry. Particularly shocking is the hint in the actual script of the broadcast—"less tolerance for endless dissent"—that significant degrees of dissent should no longer be tolerated.

Extra! reports that a *Today* show report on defective bolts in airplanes, bridges and nuclear plants was originally sharply critical of GE. Every reference to GE was removed before the segment aired. And, "when NBC *Nightly News* runs 14 minutes of coverage on a new type of machine to detect breast cancer, it seems relevant to mention that GE produces the device. Although the network devoted the equivalent of half a newscast to the subject over three consecutive days, it never found time to mention that its corporate parent makes the expensive devices. Neither ABC nor CBS found the subject newsworthy . . ."

FAIR's Todd Putnam got a call from NBC's *Today* show saying they were interested in airing a story on consumer boycotts. She asked for information on "the biggest boycott going on right now". It turned out to be the boycott of GE products prompted by GE's leading role in the production and promotion of nuclear weapons".

When told that the owners of NBC were the object of the biggest boycott in the country, Amy Rosenberg of the *Today* show responded, "We can't do that one. Well, we *could* do that one, but we won't."

And they didn't.

> For example, a gas company sponsoring a TV version of *Judgement at Nuremburg* demanded that producers delete references to "gas chambers" from accounts of Nazi concentration camps.

More from *Unreliable Sources*: "Dependent on corporate sponsors for financial sustenance, TV Networks are under tremendous pressure to shape their product in a way that best accommodates the needs of their advertisers. *I would say they are always taken into account,* Herman Keld of CBS acknowledged . . . For the most part, however, advertisers wield influence by restricting and watering down show biz content . . . One way they do this is by yanking—or threatening to yank—financial support from certain programs . . . Corporate sponsors figure they are entitled to call the shots since they foot the bill—an assumption shared by network executives, who quickly learn to internalize the desires of their patrons. For starters they are likely to frown upon programming that puts a damper on the 'buying mood' that advertisers require . . .

"These are the principal guidelines, explicitly spelled out by big-league sponsors, that TV censors follow:

"Make sure nothing in a script undermines the sales pitch for the advertised product. For example, a gas company

sponsoring a TV version of *Judgement at Nuremberg* demanded that producers delete references to "gas chambers" from accounts of Nazi concentration camps. Pharmaceutical firms won't tolerate scenes in which someone commits suicide by overdosing on pills ...

"*Portray Big Business in a flattering light.* Procter & Gamble, which spends over a billion dollars a year on advertising, once decreed in a memo on broadcast policy: 'There will be no material that will give offense, either directly or indirectly, to any commercial organization of any sort.' Ditto for Prudential Insurance: 'A positive image of business and finance is important to sustain on the air.' If a businessman is cast as the bad guy, it must be clear that he is an exception...

"*Cater to the upper crust.* To impress potential sponsors, ABC once prepared a booklet with a section called, "Some people are more valuable than others." If the elderly and low-income counted for more in the advertising department, their particular concerns would figure more prominently in ... TV programming.

"*Steer clear of overly serious or complex subjects and bleach out controversy whenever possible.* Dupont, a major advertiser, told the FCC that commercials are more effective on "lighter, happier" programs ... 'You can't take up real problems seriously,' complained Charles Knopf, a TV scriptwriter and former president of the Writer's Guild ...

"The 1988 season-opening episode of the dramatic series *MacGyver* was censored by ABC in response to complaints by the National Rifle Association (NRA). The episode in question included flashbacks of a shooting incident that took the life of MacGyver's boyhood friend. The show was to have closed with statistics as to how many children are killed each day in handgun accidents."

"Things have opened up as far as four-letter words are concerned, but as far as political content goes, I don't see anything changing," said Tommy Smothers. The Smothers Brothers were recently back on the air—twenty years after CBS cancelled them for expressing their views on the Vietnam War. In 1989, Smothers said, "four or five years ago, Lou Grant [Ed-ward Asner] was put off the air because of his opinions on Nicaragua. I'm sure not going to start getting on their case now about getting out of Central America. I'll be out of work for another 20 years."

I recently taped an interview with one of the authors of *Unreliable Sources*, Norman Solomon. Here are some excerpts from our conversation:

Norman Solomon: The web of corporate control extends so widely now that keeping an independent media is really a battle. ... General Electric, for example, not only owns NBC, they're spread all over the national airwaves . . . They're buying major time on all the networks so the net result is there's one corporation with a huge amount of power over what's said and not said.

John Shirley: A lot of the censorship you were talking about often takes the form of something called Spiking, right? Which is basically, it seems to me, cowardice. It's people afraid to risk their jobs.

NS: Yeah. We've been conditioned to believe that censorship only happens when it's imposed by a dictator . . . and yet in the United States we have censorship all the time that comes through the corporate mechanisms. And a lot of journalists are consciously or unconsciously naive about that form of censorship . . . If you work for a daily newspaper, your top boss is the interface between owners and the beat reporter. The executive editor functions at the behest of the owners . . . A lot of the time I'll talk to a reporter who says, "Well nobody ever told me what to write." There are a couple of problems with that response. One is that journalists are told what to write all the time, it's just couched in professional terms . . . it's euphemistically put. The other problem with that claim is that journalists have been pretty much conditioned to stay within narrow bounds. If you don't have to be told to stay within boundaries, then you've internalized the censorship process. You stay inside the mental cage without having the door locked. If you do bolt, you find out what happens. And our book talks about people like Raymond Bonner, who covered El Salvador, and Francis Cera (who covered problems at the Shoreham nuclear power plant)...when they stepped out of line they were dumped off their assignment and given a demotion. That kind of object lesson is not lost on working journalists who are after all functioning in an industry that is contracting, and many newspapers have hiring freezes. We say in the book that, although there are many hardworking, intelligent journalists they are increasingly working in an industry that has as much to do with independent journalism as *Safeway* has to do with family farming. There's this whole corporate ambiance where it's not only Tom Brokaw deferring to the people who cut his paycheck at General Electric, but also there's a corporate sensibility in the workplace, in the newsroom, in the editing process, so that owners and managers in glass suites can't throw stones . . . Nobody at CBS is going to raise questions about the impact of corporate ownership on the news reporting of NBC [an issue that's been raised to reporters at other networks, with no luck] when CBS is owned by a real estate and tobacco tycoon.

We quote in the book an assistant managing editor at *TV Guide* whom I interviewed, who acknowledged that *TV Guide* doesn't go after the networks for their patty-cake treatment of the cigarette industry, because every issue of *TV Guide* has full-color cigarette ads. And here you have this conflict of interest that is not being acknowledged . . .

JS: And in the current atmosphere where people are being laid off in the corporations, right and left, they might be more willing than ever to play ball . . . You know the major book publishers have been bought by huge conglomerates, in some cases oil companies, and I used to think it was just these multinationals doing a kind of knee-jerk investment thing, but now I wonder if they didn't do it in order to protect themselves—to get control to some extent over books that might be threatening to them. I suppose that's just paranoia . . .

> One of our challenges is to call things by the right name, to call this corporate dominance *censorship* . . .

NS: No, I think you're being very realistic. The fact is, look at a corporation like Time-Warner which was a new entity after the merger in 1989. Time-Warner publishes many magazines, and an average rack in the store is nearly *filled* with Time-Warner magazines. Warner of course has Warner books, films, videos. They can broadly, then, exclude media and creative efforts that don't "fit in". I think you're right that the publishing industry is increasingly dominated also by people like Gulf & Western . . . One of the problems is that not only do you have these corporations with their fingers in so many corporate pies, but also they're interlocking directorates so for instance the New York Times company has on its board of directors people who are also on the board of directors of major nuclear-invested utilities and the virtual *hysteria* of *New York Times* coverage in favor of nuclear power has something to do with the corporate interlock on their own board . . .

JS: Certain stories that made Bush nervous were spiked before his election, at ABC [the reports on Laxalt's attempt to squash an investigation of his financing;

the FBI's cover-up Raymond Donovan's organized crime connections; Reagan crony Charles Wick's involvement in nightmarish conditions at nursing homes he owned] . . .

NS: As we put it in the book, higher-ups at ABC got cold feet. We quoted Senior Producer Marion Goldin at ABC, "It was political pressure, classic spiking . . ."

. . . Sometimes it happens on a particular broadcast where you would think censorship wouldn't occur. One example is the "The Nelsen Mandela 70th Birthday Tribute" concert in Britain in 1988, carried by the Fox Network and we quote Little Steven in the book [a performer in the anti-apartheid concert] as saying that when he got back to the USA and saw what was actually broadcast it was "a totally Orwellian experience" . . . What they cut out was political statements, and political songs...

JS: Right, it was censored by arch-conservative Fox-owner Rupert Murdoch who makes no bones about censoring anything that politically offends him. An atrocious outright censorship in this case.

NS: . . . One of our challenges is to call things by the right name, to call this corporate dominance *censorship*, a censorship which has a different style than stereotyped censorship but much the same function. In the book we quote Ben Bagdikian, author of *The Media Monopoly*, who says that the corporate executives are ready, willing and able to restrict the flow of information for their own purposes as much as any dictator anywhere on the planet.

JS: Some of the mechanism is probably a kind of cronyism sometimes, since they're cronies, the heads of big business and the people in government, and sometimes the business people literally are the government people—they wear both hats. A lot of people in big business and government go to the same retreat, this place in Northern California . . .

NS: Bohemian Grove? Right.

JS: And they mingle there, Kissinger and the CEOs of major corporations and Reagan and the people from the New York Times and Time-Warner . . . it's really worrisome how much social life there is in common, between media, big business and government. And since someone's access to a government figure, to someone they need to get access to for photo ops and sound-bites and footage— since that access relies on good relations with those people, they don't want to rock the boat by running risky stories.

NS : Right. . . . I think another key point is repetition and pursuit of a story. There can be a probing investigative piece put out but if there isn't a follow up the story tends to just die. And whether there's a follow up or not often depends on whether officials in high places are pushing the story. Actually this was the case in Watergate where you had some people in the CIA and elsewhere who wanted to bring Nixon down so there was a constant flow of information, and another irony is that investigative reporters such as Bob Woodward are often the most compromised—because they have to have a constant quid pro quo, they have to be enmeshed in the web of sources that will continue to give them information . . .

JS : What about this PC Censorship business—maybe it's paranoia but I noticed that articles about "Politically Correct pressure" appeared almost simultaneously in various major publications—but only in the really big publications. It wasn't as if it was a grass roots thing, there was very little of that.

NS: The Political Correctness matter is one of the great frauds of recent years in the media. The *real* PC police are in the executive suits of the major news media of this country . . . They are the ones who decide whose opinions can be disseminated and reach the American people . . .It's a very typical inversion of reality. I would compare it to, in the Gulf War when the United States was dropping this horrendous quantity of bombs on human beings in Iraq—yet the single pilot who's shot down, early on, is shown on the cover of *Newsweek* and portrayed as the Victim. That's an inversion. You go and incinerate thousands of civilians and the person who's dropping the bombs on them is the victim!

This PC thing—the very forces who are trying to enforce *their* political correctness agenda on media are turning around and accusing the minority of trying to do the same thing. You're quite right: all of a sudden it was these major news magazines launching this ferocious assault on "political correctness" which was really an assault on affirmative action, on multicultural diversity, and it was an attempt to fight back against people expressing their own cultural realities— people with very little power in the media, African Americans, Latinos, gay men, poor people . . . . This ferocious attack on them under the banner of fighting for free expression. It's an absurdity! Here you have George Bush with very little criticism from the mass media making this huge speech from the University of Michigan where he attacks this supposed intolerance in campuses— here's someone who wants to gag doctors from explaining abortion options to pregnant women, who is appointing Supreme Court judges who are cutting back on First Amendment rights, in practice, and

yet somehow the real enemies of free expression are the supposed PC fanatics running around the campuses . . . I think the real "PC Police" are the mass media editors and powerful executives. We quote in our book for instance studies of the MacNeil-Lehrer NewsHour and Nightline on ABC—they are basically 90% white, 90% male, the guests on those programs are overwhelmingly of a conservative bent, and the programmers are the real PC Enforcers . . .

Unreliable Sources is a stunning, startling book, well documented and altogether a reliable source in itself. Another great source is *Extra!*, the journal of FAIR, available from the *Extra!* subscription service, 175 Fifth Avenue, Suite 2245, New York NY 10010.

The truth will make you free. How free do want to be?

John Shirley is the author of numerous novels, including **Eclipse** *and* **In Darkness Waiting**. *His new novel* **Wetbones** *from Ziesing Books was published in late-1991.*

Louisiana Governor Buddy Roemer was excommunicated by the Orthodox Catholic Church, in July, for vetoing 3 bills in 2 years banning abortions. Roemer, a Methodist, does not belong to the Orthodox Catholic Church. The Rev. Lee McColloster, however, said his church can excommunicate non-members.

The Boy Scouts and Freedom From Religion

Donna Bocian

A young boy and his father walk down a long, empty, echoing hallway together. Behind them are the shouts and laughter of a group of boys. They are the only two leaving the building. The rest of the boys have been accepted into the club; only this one child is excluded . . . because of his father . . . because his father is—

What do you think? Black, before integration?

As a matter of fact, that was the father's thought, "This must be just a small taste of what it was like, being black in the south before desegregation." But this time the discrimination was not based on skin color. This time it was based on religion. The boy was initially excluded from the Boy Scouts because his father is agnostic. The lowest level of scouting, the Tiger Cubs, requires that an adult guardian join as a "leader" of sorts. As part of the application, the adult must subscribe to the Declaration of Religious Principle which says, in part:

"The Boy Scouts of America maintains that no member can grow into the best kind of citizen without recognizing an obligation to God and, therefore, recognizes the religious element in the training of the member, but it is absolutely non-sectarian in its attitude toward that religious training."

The father is Elliott Welsh; the boy is Mark Welsh. When presented with the Declaration of Religious Principle, Elliott Welsh asked if there would be a problem with his agnosticism. He expected the BSA to have a different form with alternate wording he could agree to sign. Elliott was told there would indeed be a problem, and that his boy would not be allowed to join unless Elliott signed the form as-is. Being a man of conscience, he couldn't and wouldn't sign, so he and his son left.

Mark was disappointed. His friends were joining the scouts, but he wasn't allowed to because of his family's religious beliefs. "I felt pretty sad," he said, but Elliott added that Mark didn't cry.

And so the battle began. Elliott Welsh is not a man of incredible wealth who could hire a lawyer to sue. So he began making phone calls and writing letters. The BSA stood firm. No agnostics or atheists allowed. The fact that Mark was not even seven years old at the time, and might change his mind about religion before adulthood didn't seem to matter.

Elliott Welsh was a Boy Scout when he was young, and talked to his son about the fun he had, when Mark first expressed an interest. No one had ever asked young Elliott about his religious views, and if they had, he would have replied that he and his family were Christian Scientists. It was only later that Elliott changed his mind; later, despite his years in scouting, that Elliott became agnostic.

The ACLU looked into the case. One woman there suggested that Elliott "think of 'God' as a metaphor." But to Elliott, the language was pretty clear: the Boy Scouts meant "god" or they would have used another term. He wrote more letters and made more telephone calls.

Finally, Elliott found a lawyer who was willing to take the case on a pro bono basis. In March of 1990, a suit was filed. In May, the BSA filed a motion to dismiss. In

infringed upon, or whether the BSA is, in fact, a public accommodation, and thus not allowed to discriminate on the basis of religion.

No matter what the outcome of the trial, it's expected that the losing side will appeal, and that the appeal process will continue until, perhaps, the Supreme Court. The judge, at one point, commented that she hoped the case would be over sometime before Mark was married. It might not.

While there is the legal question of whether the scouts can discriminate based on religion which involves a lot of legalese and obfuscation, logic asks whether discrimination against non-religious boys makes sense in an or-

Elliott (left) and Mark Welsh

August Judge Ilana Rovner filed a 52-page opinion denying the motion to dismiss. The two sides were brought together to negotiate before the case came to trial. Information was presented by the Welsh's lawyer showing the various ways the Girl Scouts accommodated non-religious members, and suggested alternatives the BSA might consider.

The answer for the BSA: The Girl Scouts are totally different. The case now hinges on whether the BSA can be considered a private club, and that by being required to admit agnostics and atheists their right of free association would be

ganization that allows boys of any and every religion to join. The BSA maintains that having non-religious youths within the group would be disruptive. How? The BSA, in their non-sectarian stance, surely would admit, along with boys from Christian denominations, boys who profess to be Hindu, Buddhist, or Jewish. Moonies, Jehovah's Witnesses, Pagans, and Christian Scientists are equally welcome. This despite the fact that some established religions have multiple Gods while others have none.

The BSA goes to great lengths to be sensitive to the different religions involved in scouting. During Desert Storm, the BSA wanted to compose a prayer that would be acceptable to all denominations. After much consideration, it was decided that a silent prayer would be best. How could an agnostic boy who was not praying at all disrupt a silent prayer?

It might even be said the divisiveness between some religions might be greater than that between a religious boy and one who simply doesn't care about the religious views of the other. After all, wars have been fought between religious factions, but it is difficult to argue with a person who says, "Believe what you want. It doesn't affect me."

The scouts do not discriminate against the handicapped, although a boy in a wheelchair might have problems on a nature hike. The Boy Scouts do not discriminate against vegetarians, although it might be inconvenient at the campfire weenie-roast. The Boy Scouts do not discriminate against boys with allergies, speech impediments, or nervous tics. Accommodations are made for these boys so they can participate in scouting.

Elliott Welsh learned that many Buddhist scouts don't say "God" when they recite the Boy Scout oath. Their religion doesn't include a belief in a God, and they simply omit the word, assuming it to be the accepted thing to do. This practice hasn't been questioned.

The BSA won't admit Mark Welsh because without religion he is unable to grow into "the best kind of citizen." You'd think the BSA would welcome the chance to turn Mark into that model citizen, rather than excluding him. Mark's father, without religion, is apparently "not the best kind of citizen" either. Nope, not a moral man at all. He refused to lie on the application for admission to the Boy Scout program, even though some outwardly religious people urged him to sign it anyway, and no on would know. Homosexuals and girls are also being kept out of the Boy Scouts, and are fighting to get in. As a compromise, the BSA has decided to develop a new program called "Learning for Life," separate from the scouts, but administered by the local councils who choose to have it.

Richard Grossman, lawyer for Mark

> The BSA [Boy Scouts of America] won't admit Mark Welsh because without religion he is unable to grow into "the best kind of citizen."

Welsh, doesn't find this new program acceptable for Mark. "All his friends are in the Boy Scouts, and that's why he wants to join—so he can be with them."

The irony of this affair is that if the BSA does win the battle, they may actually lose more than they gain. The BSA gives the appearance of a civic organization, not a religious one. Thus, they receive funding from groups like the United Way, which will not donate to groups who discriminate. The BSA also works through the public school system, distributing information in the classrooms, and using public schools facilities as meeting places. The schools may forced to treat the scouting groups as religious entities; not allowing the distribution of information through classrooms, and charging them for meeting space. Forest Preserve facilities and military bases are often used by scouting groups at no charge, which could not be done if the scouts were seen as a religious organization.

Mark, now 8 years old, admitted he was a bit tired of all the media attention, but he still would like to join the scouts. He has friends in the group, and he'd like a chance to be with them and do the fun things scouts do—swimming, camping, bonfires. As far as the Scout oath, Mark doesn't want the BSA to abandon it, "just let me not say the part about God."

DESERT STORM

Ed Cafasso

Every war leaves a legacy.

The horrors of World War I, through the eyes of Ernest Hemingway, produced a generation of living dead—lost souls wandering amid civilization's moral ruins.

"The War to End All Wars" introduced the modern dilemma of mass destruction as an instrument for both war and peace in the form of Nazi death camps and American nuclear fusion.

The frustrating conflicts in Korea and Vietnam taught us never to lose sight of the politics of war.

But the legacy of the Gulf War defies the convenient broad brush strokes of both hindsight and history.

One year later, it remains the ultimate moving target—a public relations tour de force micro-managed by computers on the battlefield and packaged on edited videotape for homefront distribution.

"As far as everyone knows, we won the Super Bowl. No one stops to think that we never really saw the game," said Karen Hardwick, of Massachusetts, whose 22-year-old son, Blaine, was among the war's 540,000 American players.

Like many Desert Storm veterans, Blaine Hardwick is just now beginning to discuss the battlefield carnage he witnessed with the 82nd Airborne as part of the famed "Hail Mary" pincer that slammed the door of retreat on the shellshocked Iraqis.

Hardwick still has to stop himself from attacking anyone who playfully sneaks up on him. And he still awakens from occasional sweat-soaked nightmares shouting, "I'm green!"—apparently fearing he wore the wrong color camouflage for a desert war.

Some of his war memories are horrific. During his unit's lightning advance, part of Hardwick's job was to inspect disabled or destroyed enemy vehicles for intelligence information, kills and booby-traps.

The grim task often involved removing charred enemy bodies, sometimes limb by limb. In one case, the shriveled, blackened head of an Iraqi soldier simply tumbled to his feet when he nudged the dead man's body.

Such battlefield experiences haunt Hardwick far more than the fact that he, his best friend, Brian Markham, and several other members of the 82nd were used by their superiors as human guinea pigs to test for the presence of biological and chemical agents.

Markham, a 22-year-old New York City native, learned he was expendable on a moonless night at the crest of ridge near the Iraqi border.

Surrounded by a half-dozen Army buddies wearing gas masks and protective suits, the stunned soldier was ordered to hand over all his weapons and breath deep—at gunpoint.

"I felt alone the whole time," he says of his 45-minute ordeal. "I knew it was totally standard procedure, but I didn't know it was going to be me."

> The grim task often involved removing charred enemy bodies, sometimes limb by limb. In one case, the shriveled, blackened head of an Iraqi soldier tumbled to his feet when he nudged the dead man's body.

It was 1 a.m. on the war's third day. Markham was on guard duty at an edgy camp astride French tank forces whose chemical detection equipment had already triggered a number of false alarms. He heard a U.S. chemical alarm siren sound, put on his protective gear and began waking up his compatriots.

Ten minutes worth of tests showed the air to be clean, but, in a war that showcased billions of dollars in high-tech weaponry and gadgets, that wasn't assurance enough.

"I don't know who elected me or how the decision was made, but I noticed all of a sudden that everyone was watching me. I didn't have a rifle in my hands, but they did," Markham says.

"They asked for my knife, my bayonet, my Swiss Army knife. They told me to sit down—not under the tent, under the stars. I sat down on a rock. They said, 'Take off your mask. Unmask.'"

A bizarre interrogation commenced. What does the air smell like? Does it smell like lemons. Does it smell like almonds. Are your eyes watering? Is you nose running? Are your muscles twitching. Are they cramping? Are you having problems breathing? What's your name? What's the password?

"I knew what was happening. I'm a professional soldier. I may not have liked it, but I knew what had to be done. I just answered the questions," Markham recalls.

When his superiors were satisfied and the all-clear sounded, the soldiers who had surrounded him straggled away without a word and went back to sleep. The incident was never mentioned again.

That night, Markham spent the last 10 minutes of guard duty realizing why the soldier picked as the guinea pig is never forewarned.

"The message is that someone is expendable. Telling a guy before he goes into war that he's so completely expendable—that he's marked—is just not good for morale," he says matter-of-factly.

"You just can't put 100 percent faith in machinery. If all that (testing) equipment is wrong, at least only one person gets killed. If everyone had just unmasked and it had turned out to be a real chem attack, I would have felt worse."

Hardwick's wife, Sarah Hennessey, explains the mindset from a civilian's perspective.

"That's what their job is. You are prepared to die for your country and if your country tells you to do something, you do it because it's your job," she says.

What Markham remembers most about the conflict was the "intense adrenalin rush" of the ground war.

"It was the weirdest thing of the whole experience. For four days, I felt invincible—like I couldn't be touched or hurt in any way," says Markham, who blasted heavy metal tunes on his Walkman as his unit stampeded across the border into Iraq.

His stunning account of his stint as a chemical weapons guinea pig was first published in the *Boston Herald* on March 25, 1991. He immediately received calls from a number of major media outlets, including Larry King Live and the Associated Press, but decided not to speak with anyone else.

"He didn't want to look like a weenie in front of his company," a friend says.

Markham's story was lost in postwar euphoria, but there are other tales from the all-too-human underbelly of Desert Storm that occasionally bob to the surface.

A congressional inquiry, initiated in part by Democratic presidential candidate, Sen. Thomas Harkin of Iowa, is underway to determine whether anti-chemical warfare drugs given to Gulf War veterans are responsible for miscarriages and infections of the uterus and placenta in some female soldiers and the wives of male soldiers.

"Very disturbing" was how Adelita Medina, executive director of the Military Families Support Network in Washington, D.C., described the women's tragic experiences.

"We're getting a dozen calls here, a dozen calls there and we thinks it's a problem that merits attention and investigation," she told the Chicago Tribune. "We're not necessarily attributing these miscarriages to the drugs; we just want to find out if they're connected."

In the weeks before the war began, hundreds of thousands of American soldiers were inoculated against potential biological attack with anthrax vaccine, botulinum toxoid and pyridostigmine—the latter two being so-called "investigational drugs" that required a Food & Drug Administration waiver for use.

The drug's histories appear to contain little evidence of medical side effects that could complicate pregnancy, but the Pentagon has begun tracking those involving Gulf War veterans—all the while reminding the concerned parents-to-be that such factors as stress, age, health and hormonal fluctuations also play a role in miscarriages.

The 33,000 female soldiers of Desert Storm have their own stories of combat to tell. Unfortunately, many of them fought the battle of the sexes with men who had grown bored and lonely in a faraway land whose religion placed women off-limits.

"I wish the men out here would stop and think real hard about the vows they made to their wives back home," Army Spec. Tina Johnson, 22, of Michigan, said as she stood in the aisle of the Dhahran PX in the waning days of 1990.

"The desert is not the end of the world, so I hope they'll repent if they have a conscience or they'll regret it when they get back home."

When they weren't arming attack planes, prepping MASH units, manning Patriot missile batteries or staffing critical supply lines, female soldiers like Johnson were filing sexual harassment complaints detailing their colleague's and superior's derogatory sexist remarks and incessant sexual advances.

"They make constant jokes about how we could learn something about subservience from the Saudi women," one Air Force lieutenant told the Washington Post. "We don't think it's very funny."

There were even reports of rape that led to courtmartials, but the Pentagon prefers not to discuss such accounts and the victims aren't talking.

"Some guys hadn't seen a woman for five months and they acted like animals," one female Gulf veteran said.

When the war ended, the Pentagon flew counselors onto returning ships and to European air bases to advise soldiers how to relate to the opposite sex.

Said counselor Catherine Stokoe: "Some guys fantasize about their girlfriends while they're away. They think it was better than it was. Our job is to give them a dose of reality."

Desert Storm, and kid brother Desert Shield, saw their share of consenting adults too.

By the time the war had finished its first month, more than 1,200 pregnant soldiers had been evacuated from the region—despite the fact that the military had issued more than one million condoms.

The Navy found itself crunching numbers to help minimize the fact that 36 of the 450 female crew members who had served aboard the destroyer-tender, Acadia, became pregnant while the ship was on duty in the Gulf.

During its 7 1/2-month deployment, the Acadia—known in Desert Storm lore as "The Love Boat"—stopped for liberty in Honolulu, the Philippines, Singapore and seven other Far East ports, the Navy explained.

And, spokesmen added, 14 of the women were pregnant before they even came aboard.

Although one expert described the Gulf deployment as "one giant Alcoholics Anonymous meeting," American ingenuity—not to mention U.S. dollars—helped bring some Western-style recreation to the Mideast.

Army Capt. Roger Mansfield, 30, of Kansas, called for a congressional investigation into "widespread" drug use by U.S. soldiers in the Gulf—just before he pleaded guilty and was sentenced to three years in prison as part of the plea bargain that concluded the war's only drug-related court martial.

Before and during the war, Mansfield, the chief pharmacist for an Air Force medical group, admitted writing false prescriptions for amphetamines, specifically the diet pill dextroamphetamine, and illegally distributing triazolam, a sleeping pill known as Halcion, and the potent inhalable anesthetic isoflurance, marketed under the name Forane.

Before admitting that "a man of stronger will and character would not have done the things I've done," Mansfield wrote a letter to Rep. C.W. "Bill" Young, a Florida Republican, noting that he had filled "numerous prescriptions for senior officers for large amounts of tranquilizers."

He also hinted that the heart attack that claimed the life of a 21-year-old airman a few days after the war began was triggered by a very deep whiff of Forane.

For its part, the Pentagon says there were only 10 drug-related investigations during the Gulf deployment—a far cry from the marijuana and heroin-laced homestretch of Vietnam.

In the dry land of Saudi Arabia, without access to opiates and hashish from Iraq, disciplinary problems were cut in half and there was a significant decline in motor vehicle accidents.

Alcohol, drugs and prostitutes were all available on the Saudi black market, but the penalties were so severe and the hassles so forbidding that few soldiers apparently bothered.

Eight desperate soldiers built stills in

the desert and ended up in the hospital with alcohol poisoning.

In the end, the U.S. government paid $31 million for two luxury cruise ships to provide the soldiers who had been "in country" the longest with some good old-fashioned "R&R" for the three weeks before the war began.

"It was a drunken bash," Markham recalls of his three-day, post-New Year's visit to the Cunard Princess. "The biggest complaint we had was that the bars didn't open until 11 in the morning."

Ed Cafasso is a reporter for the **Boston Herald.**

DISGRACE BEHIND THE GLORY

Leigh Roche

I remember the day I left for Saudi Arabia. I thought I'd be afraid. I was going to war, and there was the very real possibility that I might not come back. But I was calm. I knew I had a job to do and that my chain of command would protect me.

Or so I thought. I learned that I don't count in today's Army because I'm not an NCO. And I also learned what it means to be a female in our unit.

There were ten of us to approximately 150 males. Though we had a separate tent, we still were around males most of the time. We'd been given classes on sexual harassment to help deal with any situations that might arise, but nothing could have prepared us for what did happen.

Most of the males were pretty good. Some were even protective of us. Then there were the others . . . . We had a lot of trouble with the young Black males, who believed that females existed for their pleasure and entertainment. But it was the NCO's we had the most problems with. Harassment came from as high as the First Sergeant and became as violent as rape.

It started with a Staff Sergeant (SSG).

At first, he was everywhere she was, showing up even at the latrine when she had to go. He's also nose around, asking her female friends if she was a virgin, and about her sexual preference. Next he made sexual remarks about her, explicit enough to offend several other males.

This occurred during a respite from work. Everyone was lying on their bunks, talking about a very familiar topic: home. Specifically, what kind of food they missed the most. "A cold Budweiser!" one male volunteered. "Pizza!" said another.

But food wasn't what the SSG missed, and he said it aloud, accompanied by a leer at the female, and a grin. The other males reacted angrily when they saw him rub his crotch slowly, making no effort to conceal his erection.

She had to work with him later that night . . . alone, in the dark. It wasn't until they were out there that she fully began to comprehend what could happen to her. They were far enough away that he could do *anything* he wanted to her, and no one would be able to hear her cries.

She tried to tell herself she was imagining things, but that didn't quiet the alarm bells going off in her head. She knew she was right. She had reason to be afraid.

She couldn't even look him in the eyes as they worked; she didn't want him to see the fear she was trying to hide. It took an extra effort for her to just concentrate on her work. But she remained aware of his every move.

Nothing happened. But the other males recognized that there was a danger and moved in to protect her. It wasn't

> All she wanted to do was escape from him, even if it was only for a few minutes. Out there, in the desert, she found only one way to escape.

enough. One night, that NCO saw that she was too close to another male and he locked and loaded an M16 on him.

It was the SSG's word against two witnesses and the female. All he received was a counseling statement. The female was told she was "being childish" by her platoon sergeant. Then everyone in her chain of command slammed the door shut on her and pretended like nothing had happened. The only people who asked her if she was okay were the ones who'd tried to protect her.

She sought comfort in a diary, just a simple lined notebook that was a friend who always listened, even when she ranted and raved; the words distorted into meaningless scribble by rage. She loathed him, and hated the sound of his voice. But hate was a dangerous thing out there, and she kept it confined to her personal journal.

A few males asked what had happened; they showed concern. But then the incident was forgotten, quietly tucked away where no one would have to deal with it. *Except her*. She still had to see him from time to time, and knew she couldn't stay angry. That anger would destroy her. She accepted what happened, and that she was powerless to do anything to change the situation. Her only choice was to try to avoid him as much as possible.

She hoped she would not have to rely on him if war broke out.

Two weeks later, a female private was raped. She was returning from the port with her Platoon Sergeant, an Sergeant First Class (SFC).

He pulled off to the side of the road, in the darkness, claiming he had to use the side of the truck. The next thing she knew, he was inside the truck, his hands reaching in her uniform, groping and grabbing at her breasts.

Then it was all over, and they continued on their way as if nothing had happened. But it had, and the next day she wrote out a statement and filed charges.

Since it was a serious accusation, Criminal Investigation Division (CID) was summoned to investigate the situation. They were bland, colorless men who had already made up their minds about what had really happened. They called her in and then all her friends.

Questions were asked, many having nothing to do with the actual incident. It was her word against his, and they wanted to know if she was a liar. She was, after all, a rather unattractive woman, and there was no reason why the SFC should be interested in her.

The SFC drew a reprimand, not for what had happened in the desert that night, but because he had perjured himself. Otherwise, CID said, the unit did not seem interested in pursuing the issue. They just quietly disappeared one day, and the female was left to deal with the rage over a man she still saw every day.

But she had no place to go with her anger. There was so much of it inside her that she couldn't even talk about what had happened. It came out anyway, directed at anyone, any rank. And, it wasn't good anger that releases what's inside. It was an anger intermingled with self-pity.

It was everyone's fault, she decided. "You don't care about me!" she'd scream at people who desperately were trying to reach for the terribly hurt person inside. But the anger had formed an impervious wall around her. None of her friends could get past it.

One day she picked up her M16 and 180 rounds and thought about what she could do to her assailant, and the thought pleased her. "He'd better watch his back," she said aloud.

Her weapon was taken away, and she was sent to a unit nearly a day's travel away. There, in the safety of people who did not know what had occurred, she carefully tucked the anger away, hiding it deep within so she wouldn't have to face it. But she changed that day, from an adult back into a child.

The SFC was sent just down the road apiece, only after rumors began circulating that he might not live through the war.

The third female nearly didn't.

The NCO would barge into her tent on a daily basis, hoping to catch a glimpse of something more than a uniform. There were ten females to pick from, but he had something on her. He used it to blackmail her.

She was trapped. She couldn't do anything at all without getting herself into trouble. And he was in the perfect position to claim that she was only making things up to escape charges of alleged adultery. It had never happened; people just had seen what they wanted to see. But it didn't matter.

He started with sexual remarks. Soon it became gestures, and he got alarmingly close to her. Every day, he was around, waiting for her. He was very careful, of course. There were never any witnesses.

All she wanted to do was escape from him, even if it was only for a few minutes. Some kind of safe haven where she could hide. Out there, in the desert, she found only one way to escape.

She tried to commit suicide.

An overdose of the Army's magic pill, Motrin, bought her a ticket home for mental observation. She expected to escape from his influence, but it reached her, even 10,000 miles away. Fortunately, she had her boyfriend to confide in.

It was rough in the beginning. He didn't want to listen. There were many fights. She could see the doubt within him; he thought *she* had done something to provoke the NCO. But gradually, as he really did begin to listen to her, their relationship began to blossom. He wanted justice for what had happened, and he encouraged her to press charges.

She had fantasies of seeing the Military Police arrest the NCO when he returned from Saudi. Reality was that the Army couldn't touch him because he had over twenty years in the service.

He was her First Sergeant. The Army is thinking of promoting him.

What of the others? They're all back from Saudi Arabia now. The SFC requested a transfer to another post. He works in recruitment now. The SSG is preparing to get out of the service.

The three females are still in the same unit. One is writing, using her art to struggle through her own anger. She still sees the NCO who harassed her. They greet each other, but their voices are stilted. Because of what happened, she still cannot quite bring herself to trust any men.

Another has accepted things as they are and has gone on with her life. The third still has her anger, buried deep within. Its presence has seriously damaged her self-esteem, she's become anorexic, and she needs men to make her feel better about herself. She chooses ones who verbally abuse her.

Recently the hurt inside her emerged, if only briefly, during a sexual harassment class. All three females attended, this time with a different perspective. Two listened to the stories of the other females they'd served with and were shocked to find they weren't alone. The third cried for a few minutes, then carefully hid the anger and hurt away once again.

Then the emphasis of the class was on when a female says, "No," that's exactly what she means.

Most of the males just listened quietly, though the younger Black males thought the whole thing was a joke. And one male in particular, a Sergeant, was appalled. 'No' always meant 'yes' in his book.

The Equal Opportunity representative tried to explain that this attitude was wrong, but all the NCO wanted to know when he was finished was, "Well, what about a man's pride?"

This is today's army.

Leigh Roche, is the pen name of a Private, who served in the Persian Gulf War. She is currently attending college as a communications major.

FEMALE WAR RESISTOR STANDS HER GROUND

Aaron Nauth

In the midst of the Persian Gulf War-tooting, yellow-ribbon entrenched Americana, a woman from Southern Illinois acted upon her personal convictions and resisted the call of brainwashed duty.

"I wanted to be out of the military for a long time, so it was a combination of events," said Stephanie Atkinson, the first female war resistor to the Persian Gulf conflict. "I thought I was already out, but I wasn't"

Atkinson had signed up on an eight year enlistment agreement when she was at the impressionable age of 17, coming from a small town and what she calls, "politically backward" parents.

"I feel especially empowered now, because a woman can stand up in the face of authority. That took a lot for me. This is really the first time I stood up for myself and really had a voice about something. It was frightening but at the same time [it gave me] self-confidence and self-respect."

She had just finished her six years of active reserve participation when her unit was activated. President Bush signed a stop-loss order on August 22, 1990, giving the Secretary of Defense power to retain anyone who had served in the military. Thus, Atkinson was involuntarily extended.

At first she reluctantly accepted the extension, but upon a closer look, decided to stay honest to her true feelings.

"I made a will and other plans as if I was going to kick the bucket, and that was very spooky. Then [I thought] 'This is ridiculous. I know I can't do this.' I read an article about a couple of guys who had been resisting, and it really impressed me and made me realize I was in the same situation and I wasn't going to go, even if it meant going to jail. I don't regret making the decision."

With the decision made, she became a public figure, was arrested, jailed, and even received death threats. Atkinson had applied for Conscientious Objector status. She was eventually given an other-than-honorable discharge, in lieu of a court martial. Basically, they let her off because she was too much trouble.

> "Adjusting to the military lifestyle was really difficult.It's really sexist, racist, homophobic and has nothing as far as an alternative lifestyle."

"One [reason they let me go] was that I was a woman. I was white, college educated, semi-articulate, and well-publicized, and the military thought it was an isolated incident. There were only two or three guys before me who had done that and they didn't have a scope of what was going to happen.

"I was lucky. But when I came home, I was like, well it's still not over because there's still going to be a war, and there are these other people who are doing this. And it turned out there were 2,500 people who resisted, or more."

Atkinson went to Philadelphia and got a job with American Friends Service, working with people who wanted out of the military; ones like herself. Having struggled through six years of service before realizing what war was really all about, she put her knowledge to use in this program, as well as through public speaking.

Atkinson was vehemently opposed to the Persian Gulf crisis, and the underlying classist, economic motivations of our government, but she also had been at odds for a while with the way the United States military operated.

"Adjusting to the military lifestyle was really difficult. It's really sexist, racist, homophobic and has nothing as far as alternative lifestyles. It's just an oppressive atmosphere. People get killed in training accidents and I was discontented with that. Then I started going to school here [Southern Illinois University-Carbondale] and got into the whole punk-rock thing. That was difficult for me; to be in school, punk-rock and being in the Army at the same time."

As Atkinson challenged herself in civilian life, she said she opened her mind away from the brainwashing influence of the military. A major criticism of her action was that she should have never signed up to begin with, but Atkinson said she was extremely naive at the time, coupled with the fact that recruiters prey upon young, impressionable people.

"I had no political sensibilities when I was growing up. I didn't have anybody as a role model as to what war was. I didn't have any dad or uncles from that generation who were in Vietnam. I really had no idea what the military was about."

Due to their naivete, high school students are easy targets for recruiters because they are not sure enough of themselves to make an informed decision. On top of this, Atkinson said, the military spends $2.3 billion a year on advertising alone to manipulate as many distraught, young minds as possible. The bait for people to get hooked into the military mind mill is a way to pay for college.

"They totally sell you. They want people they can manipulate. If you're not sure of yourself at that age, it's too easy to buy what they're selling you—and I bought it."

Atkinson was caught in the military trap and realized she wanted to swim away. She decided to finish up her degree in English, however, hoping to complete her enlistment agreement without ever having to actually engage in combat. Once immersed in Army reserve lifestyle, she began to see the manifestations of mind control.

"They just treat people like shit—you're an indentured servant. In the enlistment agreement—which most people call a contract, but it's not—there's a paragraph that says the military and the government can change anything about your pay status, your rank, where you live, and what sort of job you perform. They can change anything about you, anytime they want, with no [reciprocation] of anything to you. That's how I was involuntarily extended.

"People don't realize it, but when you join up, your body becomes government property. If you get a sunburn, you can get an Article 15, which is a non-judicial punishment, like a fine. People that try to kill themselves, in the military, not only get charges surrounding suicide, but things like attempted destruction of government property."

Atkinson also became knowledgeable of the military clampdown during wartime and its effects on unruly soldiers.

"There were people who tried to be conscientious objectors and submit their applications. Their commanding officers would rip them up, or people would threaten to beat them up. Some guys were put in straight jackets and waist shackles and flown into the Gulf. Some people weren't issued chemical protective gear.

"All the service people were inoculated before they left for the war. Only one guy refused. It was an experimental drug for a nerve agent and everybody had to take it. The FDA regulations were waived because they were military members. Now they're coming back, and the wives of a lot of guys are having miscarriages. So they were pretty much used as guinea pigs for a drug."

After the main conflict was over, she heard even more stories from talking to people who came back.

"I think there was an attempted mutiny by a company that was primarily black, but I don't know if that was just a rumor. A lot of people who resisted, especially Marines, got sent to Camp Lejeune,

in North Carolina. They really got a lot of shit there. They were beat and locked up in closets."

The Marine brig was also a topic of military horror stories for people who did not conform. "Most of them are in medium security, which is like a general prison population, and they have tasks like jobs. If you mess up there, they send you to segregation. They make you sit in a chair all day and you can't fall asleep. You have to sit at attention. If you still won't shape up, then they put you in what they call the dog cage, which is basically a big cage you would keep a St. Bernard in. You get bread and water and have to sit there in your underwear. Most of those people have been adopted by Amnesty International. There's like 25 fugitives that are political prisoners in the United States that our country doesn't recognize."

Now that Atkinson's life has taken on an active cause, she wants to get a doctorate and develop an educational program which informs people about the hazards and history of the United States military, using a multi-media presentation to make her point. Whether or not she does this in a classroom setting, Atkinson will keep up the struggle for peace.

"People need to be encouraged to be pro-active in their government, rather than just waiting for things to happen. Otherwise, they're just going to be used and defeated."

Aaron Nauth is a freelance, underground culture journalist from Illinois, now living in Minneapolis, covering everything from music to politics. The full interview transcription of this article can be found in an upcoming issue of Profane Existence [P.O. Box 8722, Minneapolis, MN 55408].

I met a young woman the other night. It seems, at one point, I had spoken to her class at Kutztown University about the circumstances that led to my firing.

In February, 1991, I was dismissed from my job as editor of a local weekly newspaper, *The Patriot*, for writing an anti-war editorial. Because of my stand, and the subsequent national attention my dismissal received, I was asked to speak at several colleges.

The young woman just wanted to tell me how badly she felt about my plight. In fact, she was almost in a panic about it, as if she couldn't get over the shock that this could happen in America.

For a few moments I felt that perhaps it wasn't a good thing that my firing got so much attention. When people find out it happened once, that knowledge serves to scare them into line, make them think they'll pay a high price if they, too, buck the system.

My own tale of editorial woe first appeared in the *Philadelphia Inquirer*. It quickly zipped through the wire and across the country.

I had dared to challenge the reasons behind the slaughter in Iraq, and my boss decided I was no longer good for business.

For a time, I was a minor media celebrity. My home phone rang constantly, from 8AM to 10PM for three straight weeks.

One of those calls was from a Washington D.C.-based radio station. It was one of those 'point-counterpoint' type of shows. One caller, while I was on the line, finished his statement by proclaiming, "Well, your boss was an idiot." That started the ball rolling. Soon, both hosts were proclaiming, "Yeah, you worked for idiots." Idiot became the buzzword.

After a few moments, strangely enough, I found myself defending my boss, saying he wasn't that bad. Suffice it to say, I wouldn't do that any-more. I'd have to be an idiot.

Like anyone else who faces some sort of crisis, I learned just who I could count on. Although the media painted my plight as one man standing up against an overwhelming majority favoring the war, I never felt as if that was the case. I never saw the widespread support for George Bush's atrocity.

Yes, there were a lot of yellow ribbons hanging from poles in Kutztown, but one man can hang 100 yellow ribbons in a short time. My boss first indicated he got a lot of angry letters and subscription cancellations as a result of my "How about a little PEACE" editorial. It turned out he got no cancellations at all. There were, however, cancellations *because* he fired me.

For about a three-week stretch, I received phone calls from around the globe; one as far as Sydney, Australia. My phone literally rang as soon as I put down the receiver. People were supportive. There was a lot of disgust over what the Bush Administration had undertaken.

Here in Kutztown, people called to say they thought I got a raw deal. To this day, some members of the community come up to say they feel sorry about what happened.

In my 5-1/2 years as editor of the *Patriot*, I was known for writing what I felt and believed. The community had learned to accept that. I was open to their right to disagree. My impressions were

FIRED FOR PEACE

Joe Reedy

they were grateful I took a stand. I respected the readers. All I ever aspired to do was a complete job. I was a one-man show, doing the writing, editing, layout and photography, with the help of an assistant. I was an active editor; I did a lot more than just write editorials, and I injected positive themes into the paper. That was my style.

It was easy to tell those who thought, in some way, I deserved to be fired. Those whose eyes never met mine. Those who sold the Dessert Storm T-shirts and bumper stickers. Those to whom profit represents morality. Local businessmen didn't rush to offer me employment. I wasn't a member of the regional men's-type business buddy clubs, as was my boss. Some folks prefer to let the clique make their decisions for them. It's easier that way.

Kutztown is no different from any town in the United States. You have your commonfolk, your working people, and your elitists; the rich society-types and the society wannabes. Businessmen, more than anything else, strive to be "politically correct." Today's rules are easy to follow: Check the polls before offering an opinion. If they read 50-50, say nothing at all. Patriotism, to certain folks, isn't speak-

Joe Reedy

ing your mind, it's backing the right horse; going with the flow. Nonetheless, you no more get points for patriotism because you display a flag and wear a yellow ribbon than you get a Super Bowl share for wearing a 49ers jersey.

The yellow ribbon proponents were the real traitors during the war in the Gulf. They betrayed the spirit of America. They blotted out the meaning of the U.S. Constitution, ignoring the horrible realities of warfare and painting military action as glorious.

As did the major media. Don't get me wrong, I got a few moments to tell my story, but I was an exceptions. The pro-war folks got the press. Bush, Dan Quayle, Dick Cheyney and any military man who wanted to don a uniform and talk about bombs and guns were like TV camera magnets; modern Dr. Strangeloves. There was little objectivity as the theory of "Manifest Destiny" once again surfaced in American hearts.

At one point, I was contacted by an ABC News crew. The producer wanted to come and interview me about my firing. While I was talking, the network correspondent got on the speaker phone. We set up an appointment for a Friday afternoon. I told them, it would have to be late because I had to sign up for my un-

> The yellow ribbon proponents were the real traitors during the war in the Gulf. They betrayed the spirit of America.

employment that day.

Suddenly, the correspondent, doing his best "Broadcast News" routine, jumped. "That's it," he said. "Where do you have to sign up? We'll met you there." I said, no, that I wouldn't feel comfortable with that. He pushed forward. "No, see, you're unemployed, and you're going to the unemployment line. See that? It fits." I told him I didn't want to go into that office with the rest of those poor souls while being trailed by an ABC News camera crew. He still persisted, but his producer, a kinder, gentler newsperson, nixed the idea.

ABC never showed. First, they cancelled when the ground war appeared imminent because they had to go to a military base and do one of those "worried wives" stories. The second appointment was cancelled for the same reason when the ground war began. War got the priority. Peace could wait. Why is it you are never perceived as fighting for your country while you are on domestic shores?

I was frustrated with the continual polls, which lied about U.S. opinion, and the arrogance of those supporting this "just" massacre. I was comforted, however, by dozens of letters and hundreds of phone calls from ordinary people, who read about my plight and reached out to me.

Their letters and words were compassionate, kind and intelligent. Their own anti-war logic was flawless. World War II veterans called me and related their own tales of combat's horror. "No one who has ever seen combat would willingly send another man into battle," they said. Schoolchildren told me they were shocked I was fired, that the action went against the spirit of our Constitution they were studying.

Men and women from Oklahoma, Texas, Maine, Florida and Massachusetts phoned me after I appeared on National Public Radio. Some said they had sons and daughters in the Persian Gulf, and although they didn't tell their siblings, they were active in the anti-war movement back home.

Not one called to disagree with my stand. Actually, no one could give any

Copyright © 1992 by Jon Longhi

reason why we were bombing Iraq. Too many political zombies just argued that "we" had to, that there will always be wars and we may as well just accept it. When you think about it, it is kind of sick that a nation at war actually has the luxury of taking polls on whether or not the war is popular.

I say 'popular,' not 'fair' or 'just." Popular is all that matters to the mass murderer in the White House. Those who took Bush's word that this massacre was necessary agreed to skip Chapter 1 in the book. We opened with Chapter 2, where Sadaam Hussein was Hitler and out to conquer the world.

In Chapter 1, you could read about Kuwait's refusal to pay war reparations to Iraq for the latter's protection during the Iran-Iraq War. You could have discovered Kuwait was drilling into disputed oil fields and pumping enough oil to lower OPEC's prices, thus hurting the entire Arab economic fabric. Finally, you could have discovered the arrogance of Kuwait which defied Iraq, bragging its 'white slaves' would defend it.

That proved too true. Don't get me wrong, I didn't support the invasion of Kuwait, it's just that two wrongs don't make a right. Violence begets violence.

The war may be over now, but there will be resentment and repercussions for generations to come. Although we had all sorts of wasteful, boring parades, I fail to see what we won. Tremendous environmental sins were wreaked upon Mother Earth. Close to a half million human beings are dead. You couldn't possibly believe in Christian values and support such a mass inhumanity.

In America, it's back to business as usual—well—that is, unless you count the recession.

I sit, unemployed, trying to overcome morning anxiety attacks, feeling rejected. It is odd meeting strangers who have heard about you, odder still hearing them tell you their friend's opinion of you. It's funny how the story gets twisted.

It is tough to look into the faces of potential employers, who hear the reasons for your dismissal and aren't sure they believe you. It's painful to get the polite rejection notices a few days later. "Sorry, Joe, but I think you're a little too hot to handle right now."

For the most part, the news media has gone on to other topics. I continue to get invitations to speak. I talked at several local colleges and to a citizens groups in Maine. Unfortunately, I don't get Ollie North-type speaker's fees. Then again, I'm proud of what I wrote, and I don't own a shredder. I'd write it again, only bigger, better and with fewer spelling errors.

Now and then, a friend or acquaintance stops me on the street in Kutztown, asks about me, and tells me he or she is proud I stuck to my beliefs. I don't know what to say but, "Thanks." It means a lot, and makes me feel a little better. Somewhat better.

During the Gulf War, I wasn't very proud of a lot of my countrymen. I felt they were like lemmings. They let mob hysteria overcome logic. They adopted simple-minded slogans (Support the Troops—what does that mean?) to override morality. They supported a slaughter in the name of the red, white and blue. I always felt proud to hear the National Anthem. Now, I feel its spirit has been perverted by mindless, ribbon wearing zombie zealots.

However, when I look at my stack of letters I saved, and feel the support of my family, all of whom backed me 100-percent, and friends; when I think back to the moments where I let my conscience by my guide and wrote what I believed to be true, I know one thing for sure:

I am still proud to be an American. I fought for my country, too, and furthermore, I look forward to doing it again. We're all raised to believe that what happened to me shouldn't happen in America. All I can do is work to stop it from happening again.

That's my right—employed or not.

Joe Reedy, former editor of the **Kutztown Patriot** *remains unemployed—over a year, as this issue goes to print.*

Update From Broward County, Florida:

2 Live Crew,

The Sheriff,

&

The Store-Owner

Deborah Wilker

There is a long tradition in show business of insincere people aligning with popular causes when it suits them, and then hastily abandoning such allegiances when the allure dims.

Such is the case with the hot topic of 1990: music censorship. Lots of entertainers spoke out on the issue but few took decisive action, particularly when it came time to support such vilely graphic rappers as 2 Live Crew and others of that genre.

The Crew's Luther Campbell has never received the mainstream support of Hollywood, the entertainment business or the music industry. No one has thrown him a fund raiser to support rally. He makes scant TV appearances and has been having trouble getting his tours off the ground.

He is, however, still selling records.

One major company that had initially stood by 2 Live Crew was Atlantic Records, now part of the massive Time-Warner. Throughout the 1990's firestorm, Atlantic piously acted as if its affiliation with the Miami rap group was an altruistic gesture, when it was strictly a typical money-making venture.

ts the time, the 2 Live Crew founder, Luther Campbell, was a sizzling hot commodity. He was a ghetto kid who had built a multi-million dollar independent record company from scratch. When Atlantic signed him to a distribution deal, Campbell's Luke Records took advantage of the mammoth Warner retail network, while Warner got a big chunk of Campbell's profits.

But now that Campbell has become a mere footnote to an issue that has worn thin and numerous rappers have proven they can also sell with—and without—violently rough language, Atlantic appears edgy, as if it would prefer to quietly ease itself out of the picture.

Atlantic's discontent with the Crew began in the summer of 1990 as Campbell was creating the Crew's latest recording, "Sports Weekend (As Nasty as They Wanna Be II"). The disc—released in two versions (one clean; one dirty)—hit stores during October 1991, but according to Campbell, Atlantic seemed to want no part of it at first.

During production of the new release, Atlantic had received word that the product to come was reportedly so vulgar, so explicit and so infantile, that record company executives requested that the album not carry the Atlantic logo or name.

Though Atlantic eventually rescinded that decision, the sting has lingered. While the battle brewed, Campbell issued a terse statement claiming that Atlantic did not have faith in them. He also feared a bigger problem: that Atlantic is not genuinely committed to providing retail support implicit in such distribution deals. Campbell has said repeatedly that he'd be just as happy to go back to distributing on his own and keep all profits to himself.

Atlantic confirms that scenario but remains tight-lipped. A spokeswoman said: "Our logo will appear. That's all we can say."

Bottom line: Atlantic was there when it suited them; there when money was to be made and willing to be gone in a flash once it was no longer fashionable to defend such juvenile rap ramblings. As show biz hit-and-runs go, this one was a classic.

When it came time for the album to finally hit store shelves, the logo and the Atlantic name did indeed appear, but 2 Live Crew spokeswoman Debbie Bennett says she is suspect of the motive.

"I guess they didn't want to look bad after saying they were for freedom of speech and making a whole big deal about it when they signed us."

Atlantic also knew there was still money to be made. The dirty version of the new recording made its debut at No. 25 on Billboard's Top 200 Albums chart. The clean version had not charted by mid-fall '91.

Meanwhile the hypocrisy of all this has only muddled an already confusing situation. Though "Sports Weekend" is equally, if not more, graphic than the original "As Nasty As They Wanna Be," it is readily available in Broward County as well as nationwide, as are the Crew's three other explicit albums.

Broward County Sheriff Nick Navarro has not pursued a ban on the new record as he did last time out. Former Governor Bob Martinez, another zealous anti-Crew crusader, is now the nation's new Drug Czar. Miami lawyer Jack Thompson, who initiated the Florida censorship craze, had briefly turned his attention toward the rap group N.W.A., but after receiving little response, has apparently given up.

With myriad product on record store shelves of an adult, graphic nature, politicians apparently have realized that taking on the massive music business is a daunting and useless fight.

Campbell's Miami-based Luke Records still has about 25 artists on its roster; 20 full-time employees and a seem-

> Though "Sports Weekend" is equally, if not more, graphic than "As Nasty As They Wanna Be," it is readily available in Broward County

ingly healthy, if not spectacular, future in the rap and dance music industry.

And even though the first "Nasty" album was deemed by court ruling to be illegal to sell in Broward (appeals are pending) it still can be found in a variety of independent and smaller chain record stores.

Said store owner Pete Azzopardi in an interview with the (Fort Lauderdale) *Sun Sentinel*: "We never actually stopped selling it."

Like many independent retailers, Azzopardi believes he won't get in trouble. "I think it's pretty much blown over," he told the *Sentinel*.

But for one record store owner, the nightmare continues.

Courtesy Atlantic Records

Charles Freeman, the retailer who took a stand against Navarro's censorship crusade in June 1990 by loudly proclaiming he would sell the "Nasty" disc, has had nothing but legal troubles ever since.

First Navarro made an example of him by having his deputies storm Freeman's tiny EC Records in northwest Fort Lauderdale before noisily arresting him in front of several TV cameras.

During the same time-frame 2 Live Crew members and the band Too Much Joy were also arrested for singing material from the album. Hollywood, Florida nightclub owner Kenny Gheringer also was arrested for presenting the performers.

But when all was said and done, only Freeman was convicted (his appeal is still pending).

The performers were exonerated, and by the time Gheringer's trial was to take place in January '91, the Persian Gulf War had begun and the nation was distracted. Seeing that he had wrung all the mileage that he could from the issue, Navarro quietly dropped the charges against Gheringer and the issue disappeared.

But not for

Chas. Freeman—the only one convicted in the 2 Live Crew case

Freeman. Legal bills piled up. His store went bankrupt and reported promised help from Campbell never materialized. The two had known each other years before this controversy when both worked as street party DJ's and that's why Freeman thought he could depend on Campbell, he said.

But Campbell turned a cold shoulder, as did Atlantic Records, the rest of music and entertainment industry, and the nation's various, powerful record retailing associations.

"We sent out flyers asking retailers not to sell the album once the ruling came down," Bennett said. "I'm not sure what he expected Luke to do for him in the way of help. If we had bailed out Freeman, we may have been asked to bail out a couple thousand record stores."

Languishing in debt, Freeman closed his shop in December 1990 and six months later was arrested again on a far more serious charge: cocaine conspiracy.

The charges, which allege that Freeman was part of a 20-person gang that sought to distribute more than 100 kilograms of crack cocaine, were still pending in late-'91.

From his jail cell at the Wakulla prison in upstate Florida, Freeman said he wasn't holding out much hope.

"My lawyers are being paid very little," Freeman said. "I don't think they have the money to defend me right." Trial, which was tentatively set for November '91, could again be delayed, Freeman said. "They don't have many judges up here."

He is facing 30 years to life.

Freeman, a father of four small children, said he has all but lost his house, his marriage and family. "The mortgage is five months overdue. My wife's trying to work something out, but when she cries to me on the phone there's little I can do but hang up. I just can't help her from here."

Freeman, who adamantly proclaims his innocence, is convinced he is the victim of political posturing. He admits knowing three of the other people involved in the crack conspiracy, who have since been convicted.

"But that's just guilt by association," he says. "I don't think it's just a coincidence that Martinez is the Drug Czar now."

Freeman's plight has attracted little attention from the media or ACLU.

Says Bennett: "All this is behind us now. People don't care any more. They just wanna go out and buy what they wanna buy."

Deborah Wilker is a reporter for the **Fort Lauderdale Sun Sentinel.**

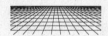

In December, a California appeals court struck down a "Gang Mom" law that held parents responsible for the criminal activity of their children, because it didn't define "responsible parenting."

2 LIVE CREW:

The Double Standard Is Alive And Well In The Nineties

Trina Robbins with Carol Leigh

"No man is an island . . . never seek to know for whom the bell tolls; it tolls for thee." —John Donne

The second issue of *Gauntlet* features interviews with Luther Campbell of 2 Live Crew, and Penelope Ann Spheeris, who filmed a documentary on the controversial rap group. Both Campbell and Spheeris are asked a similar question: how do you feel about women objecting to sexism in the group's lyrics? Campbell's answer: "We talk about a certain type of woman who exists, let's face it . . . I wouldn't put a lady of the night in the same boat as Bush's wife . . . We . . . talk about the ones who sleep around with all the guys in the building. I'm not talking about a nice, decent woman . . . I'm talking about the other woman who slept around."

Spheeris almost paraphrases Campbell: "I didn't really have a problem with the sexism because, from what I can tell, the kind of people they're talking about I can't even begin to relate to. I don't feel they're talking about me. I feel a lot of their lyrics refer to prostitutes, and loose women, and I'm neither one." Later, in answer to the repeated question, "What about women's complaints that the lyrics are degrading to them?" she reiterates, "As I said, they're not talking about me."

It's hard to decide whose answers are more horrifying, the rappers' or the film makers'. Certainly, Campbell reflects a classic 1950s-style double standard. Is it okay for *him* to "sleep around" with all the *girls* in the building? How many women has he had sex with, or *would* he have sex with, given the chance? Does he, or has he, patronized prostitutes? Or is he a priest?

Spheeris, obviously, is a nun. Yet even nuns, I have been led to believe, have compassion for their fellow man and woman. Spheeris exhibits none for her sisters in the sex industry—an industry which depends for its existence solely on male support. It's okay to insult prostitutes, reasons Spheeris, because I'm a "nice girl." If 2 Live Crew were a neo-Nazi rap group, would she say she doesn't mind them attacking Jews because she's not a Jew? Has Spheeris ever read John Donne? Does she care?

I wonder if Campbell or Spheeris is aware of the figures: Studies indicate that up to 85% of juvenile prostitutes are survivors of incest. One study on street prostitutes found that 70% had been raped on the job, although only 7% had sought help and only 4% reported these attacks to the police. In fact, the prostitute is considered fair game for abuse by police, customers and vigilante groups (i.e. the recent harassment of street prostitutes in the East Village). Murders of prostitutes are rarely investigated by the police until 10 or more women have been killed, or until the killer begins to attack "good women." The Hillside Strangler, the South Side Slayer and the Green River Killer are just a few examples. In addition, laws against prostitutes are enforced in a highly discriminatory manner. Spheeris, who seems so concerned with racism, should know that although a majority (70-80%) of prostitutes in this country are caucasian, 85% of those sentenced to jail are women of color.

Campbell says, "I wouldn't put a lady of the night in the same boat as Bush's wife." How ironic that he uses Barbara Bush as his definition of a "nice girl"! It is common knowledge that Mrs. Bush is pro-choice, yet she suppressed her own beliefs in favor of her husband's anti-choice stand, and now refuses to publicly give any opinion on the subject. In other words, she had traded her ideals for the luxury and power of being the President's wife. As far as I'm concerned, that makes Barbara Bush the First Whore of the United States.

The forces that George Bush represents with his anti-choice stance are also against all forms of birth control and sex education in public schools. If these people had their way, our country will see an unprecedented increase, not only in unwanted babies, but in women dead and permanently maimed from back-alley abortions, and newborn babies left to die in dumpsters and garbage cans.

Campbell finds no fault in this—Barbara Bush is a "nice girl"—but he feels that prostitutes and "loose women" deserve to be insulted and degraded because they have been forced for economic reasons to provide sexual services to men.

If he really feels this way, why doesn't Campbell donate part of his profits to organizations that help get women off the streets? Possibly because, then, he won't have anything to write or sing about anymore. Campbell knows that his misogyny is making him rich. At the end of his interview he is asked if his future lyrics might include something about "the joys of fatherhood," to which he replies, "No. Nobody's gonna buy it. It won't sell."

Carol Leigh, aka Scarlot Harlot is responsible for all the facts and figures on prostitution. She is a prostitute, and award-winning filmmaker and one of the founders of ACT-UP.

FATHER PFLEGER: ROUND TWO

Donna Bocian

(Editor's Note: In issue #2, Donna Bocian reported on the arrest of Father Pfleger who allegedly advocated the defacement of billboards in minority neighborhoods that advertised cigarettes and liquor. Pfleger felt that minority neighborhoods had been specifically targeted for these advertisements, and he was determined to force them out. What follows is the result of Father Pfleger's trial)

I t sounded like a David and Goliath story: Father Michael Pfleger against R.J. Reynolds and the rest of the alcohol and tobacco industry. And like that

story, the little guy seems to be winning.

In round one, the case against Father Pfleger for encouraging the defacement of billboards, the jury found the painting priest not guilty. The billboard company countered by filing a $100,000 suit against Father Pfleger, and also getting a court order to keep him away from their billboards, which according to Father Pfleger, "would mean I'd have to move out of Chicago," a reference to how prolific the billboards are in many areas.

R.J. Reynolds pulled all of its billboard advertising from black and hispanic neighborhoods in Chicago, citing "business reasons" and not because of Father Pfleger's influence. Pfleger says it was, of course, a business decision, and that had the billboards remained, R.J. Reynolds would surely have lost some business. They just don't want other cities to follow Chicago's lead, according to Pfleger. But he intends on encouraging other cities to put the pressure on, as well.

Father Pfleger has sent letters to various presidents of companies that advertise in heavily black and Hispanic neighborhoods, and as we spoke he had letters from Phillip Morris and Seagrams on his desk that had just come in the mail.

He is also working with members of Chicago City Council where he hopes to develop legislation to curb the use of billboards targeted at poor and minority neighborhoods.

Father Pfleger was also instrumental in halting the production of Powermaster Malt Liquor (a product with a higher alcohol content of malt liquor which was to be marketed towards blacks). He and Father Clemens, also from Chicago, went to LaCrosse, Wisconsin, after failing to meet with anyone at the Chicago office of G. Heileman, maker of Powermaster. No one in LaCrosse would meet with them, so the two refused to leave the premises, and were arrested. Father Pfleger went to the mayor of LaCrosse, and suggested that if a meeting did not take place, he would bring in busloads of people, and for the good of the city, perhaps the mayor would be able to arrange a meeting.

On July 3, 1991, a two hour meeting was held in Chicago, where officials said that they recognized the problem, and agreed there would be no billboards. This wasn't enough. Father Pfleger wanted the product pulled. He had groups in ten cities lined up, ready to announce boycotts, and said that a new city would be added to that list every day for twenty days. Shortly after the meeting, several groups across the country announced their boycott.

By 3:30 that afternoon, production of the malt liquor was ceased, but G. Heileman asked for a 90-day extension to sell what was already produced. Father Pfleger agreed, so long as none was shipped to Chicago. And now those few cans produced are on their way to being collectors items.

Donna Bocian, a free-lance writer, is **Gauntlet's** *Chicago correspondent; a hotbed of censorship and anti-censorship activity in the past three years.*

Salman Rushdie: Year 3 In Captivity

When Salman Rushdie resurfaced for his first trip abroad—to speak at the Columbia University Graduate School of Journalism's Salute to the First Amendment—since publication of his *Satanic Verses* led to a bounty being placed on his head three years ago, he eloquently explained the cause of seemingly contradictory decisions that had troubled some of his supporters: embracing the Muslim religion, his statement he regretted writing the novel, opposition to further translations and publication of a paperback edition of his novel.

In his speech, excerpted in the *New York Times* he said, "At the end of 1990, dispirited and demoralized . . . I determined to make peace with Islam, even at the cost of my pride.

". . . I spoke the Muslim creed before witnesses. But my fantasy of joining the fight for the modernization of Muslim thought . . . was stillborn. I have never disowned the *Satanic Verses*, nor regretted writing it. I said I was sorry to have offended people because I had not set out to do so."

Rushdie met with 6 Islamic scholars on Christmas Eve 1990, at which time they agreed the novel had no insulting motives. Rushdie tells what happened next. "Now we will launch a worldwide campaign on your behalf to explain that there has been a great mistake," he quotes them.

"It is in this context," he went on, "that I agreed to suspend—not cancel—a paperback edition to create what I called a space for reconciliation.

"Alas, I overestimated these men. Within days all but one had broken their promises and recommended to vilify me and my work as if we had not shaken hands. I felt . . . a great fool. The suspension of the paperback began at once to look like a surrender. I accept that I was wrong to have given way on this point. *Satanic Verses* must be freely available and easily affordable, if only because if it is not read and studied, then these years will have no meaning. Those who forget the past are condemned to repeat it."

Rushdie determined to risk the trip abroad after the book's Italian translator was severely wounded and its Japanese translator stabbed to death.

LENNY BRUCE Is Dead

Harlan Ellison

Lenny died in 1966. Gee, how time flies when they're busy bumping off the good guys.

It came over the 11:00 news, and they ran some film clips. The usual sort of flaming-stick-in-the-eye sensationalism: Lenny in a wheelchair after his 1965 window-falling accident; clips from some forgotten college gig, with Lenny satirizing a cop at one of his nightclub performances trying to take notes about his act for an upcoming obscenity trial, while roaring with laughter; some random photos of mother Sally and daughter Kitty.

And then they ran a seventeen-second interview with one of the cops who was on the scene of his death. A swell human being named Vausbinder. He could as easily have been talking about a garbage bucket or a side of beef as one of the sharpest social critics this country ever produced. "Lenny Bruce, whose real name was Leonard Schneider, died at 6:10 tonight. There was evidence of narcotics on the premises and—"

—and they couldn't even let him die with a little dignity.

We learned later, years later, that they had gone in, found him dead, and propped him up on the toilet with the spike sticking out of his arm. They hounded him and stole his days and they crippled his humor, turning him into a pudgy bore worrying court transcripts like a withered old man with prayer beads, and they broke him financially supporting lawyers, and they wasted his life in courts for "offenses" that were as substantial as fog, and then the creeps rearranged his limbs and wouldn't even let him die without calling him filthy names.

He was surely the most moral man I

ever knew.

He saw clearly enough to know it was a terrible world, filled with hypocrisy and casual, random viciousness; and he talked about it. Because he was a comedian, a nightclub comic, a *shtickmeister*, and not Eric Hoffer or William Buckley, his mercilessly accurate social criticism was labeled "sick," and his lampooning of the powerful and pious was impermissible of entry as "philosophy." He talked about what was wrong with us in the Fifties and Sixties in the language of the hipsters and the poor Jews and the showoffs. The language that made you sit and laugh till you thought you'd drop from an infarct. He talked about the most serious concerns of decent men and women the way the guys on the corner talk—honestly, slyly, phonographically reproducing the way people *really* talk about such concerns, rather than in the simpering, mealy-mouthed "at this point in time" corruption of language employed by frauds and thugs and those shining the seats of power with their pants.

His was the humor of painful truth; and he was driven by the sheer absurdity of it all—or fearless beyond a sense of his own survival—so that he kept talking; never able or willing to back off, even when they told him they would drive him, chivvy and harass him, harry him to a nuthouse or to the grave. He persisted, nonetheless. He was in the American grain of great humorists: Chaplin, Twain, Benchley, Thurber, W. C. Fields. He told them more than they wanted to hear. And they killed him for it, as they had promised. Then they propped him up on the can, and stuck the spike in his arm.

What was his crime? As the creator of *archy & mehitabel*, the journalist Don Marquis put it: "If you make people think they're thinking, they'll love you; but if you *really* make them think, they'll hate you."

And rearrange your limbs in death.

I never knew him as awfully well as many others did. But we had a special liaison in that I was the guy who got him to write some of his material for magazines, and I edited and arranged

those higgledy-piggledy columns of prose, and published them in a magazine called *Rogue* from 1959 through 1961.

I met him in Chicago soon after I started editing for *Rogue*. I was fresh out of the Army, and Lenny was the hottest new comedian in the country. He was the darling of Rush Street, and having heard a couple of his albums for Fantasy Records, I was determined to get him to do a regular humor column for the magazine. It was a time when men's magazines were emerging as more than publications displaying the naked female form, a time when *Playboy* was publishing better and more daring material than any other periodical in America, and *Rogue*'s publisher wanted a similar claim to legitimacy. So, though he'd never even heard of Lenny Bruce, the publisher gave me the go-ahead to try and snare him for the book.

He was working Mr. Kelly's on Rush when I connived an introduction, and we hit it off. I'd been doing standup comedy on one coast while Lenny was working similar material on the other coast, and we spent many nights prowling and dunking doughnuts in coffee. He was friendly (and always funny) and outgoing; and even then near the beginning, a little wary of

> He told them more than they wanted to hear. And they killed him for it, as they had promised.

how people wanted to use him, then revile him in print.

He had cause to be wary: already they had started in on him, the Catholic Church, the politicos, the big, Irish cops of Chicago who were coming to scope his act so they could go back to their superiors and report that that motherf- - - - - - Bruce was using awful words like motherf- - - - - right from a public stage and wasn't it a motherf- - - - - - shame that a filthy blue comedian like him was littering up motherf- - - - - - Rush Street with his foul mouth!

His columns for me were always brilliant. Sometimes they were disjointed and rambling, the way his rap on stage was; sometimes he mailed them in to me from somewhere on the road, scribbled on menus and cocktail napkins; sometimes he'd call me and dictate the copy, and I'd sit there at three in the morning writing furiously, trying to capture the cadence and inflection that made the material work. But they were always pertinent. They were funny and sharp and insightful . . . and they hurt. Which is what good satire is supposed to do. He knew how to write, even if it was verbal writing off the stage; he wrote a swell book, even if it was ghosted; he produced great American humor. Human and universal . . . and dangerous.

His records are for always. They capture only a small corner of the arena he ruled, but even they, incomplete as they are, will last. Because he talked of his times, and the dishonestly of his times, and the absurdity that he saw in the most loathsome lies his times could tell.

It is now twenty-five years since Lenny went down. They don't have him to harass any longer; they've gone on to other poor bastards who believe in crazy stuff like the First Amendment. They got their heart's desire: the junkie, the pervert, the foul-mouthed Lenny Bruce is dead.

And they made a movie about him, because even in rearranged, disreputable death, legends do not die if they're played by Dustin Hoffman. That's called irony. Gee, how time flies when Hollywood's having a bout of conscience, particularly if there's a kopek to be made from it.

Sticks and stones did not break his bones, names never really hurt him. But they broke his heart and they silenced his voice, a voice we needed so urgently, then *and* now, and the malicious, stupid motherf- - - - - s still don't realize that they killed one of our few heroes.

Harlan Ellison's latest books are the upcoming **Slippage** *and* **The City on the Edge of Forever.**

LENNY & ANDREW

Allan Sonnenschein

Andrew Dice Clay, in perfect form, once told me that most comics are "motherfucking, backstabbing scum bags;" offering a litany of in how many ways they have wronged him. Included in the Dice man's complaints was how comic notables, like Jay Leno, Richard Belzer and Sam Kinnison have enlisted with the critics to deplore his lack of sensitivity when the subject turns to women, gays and assorted other politically correct favorite minority groups.

As one who has met some of Clay's comic critics, I would say they were for free speech; well, almost. It's not like, in criticizing Dice, they were endorsing Donald Wildmon and his polyester horde of storm trooping censors; only, they were liberals and liberals aren't censors, but politically correct thinking citizens.

Dice's complaint left me thinking about Lenny Bruce. The pioneer of comic free speech. The Jesus Christ of standups who was forced to suffer on the cross of censorship so today's comics could utter a fuck or two on Showtime. One must search far and wide to find a young comic who does not acknowledge the sufferings of Lenny Bruce and his debt to that Patriarch of Comedy. Unfortunately, it's all bullshit.

There is barely a comic around today, and I'm not talking about the Burns, Berle or Youngman crowd, who ever saw or heard Lenny Bruce perform. Most of today's Improv and Comedy Store phenoms weren't even toilet trained when Lenny was ODing on his toilet seat. But it has become *de rigueur* for them to kiss Lenny's ashes. If they had witnessed a performance of their patron saint of comedy, they would not be calling Andrew Dice Clay insensitive. Hell, if Lenny was alive today, he wouldn't be allowed to work the bathroom at a NOW convention.

Would Andrew be insensitive if he talked about a five year old, stupid kid who fell in a deep well, and while war, famine and plague was going on all around us, the only thing the world cared about was getting the brat out of the hole? Say the Dice man created an imaginary convention of world religious leaders.

How can you explain all the reverence for Bruce and the hatred for Clay? The answer has little to do with comedy . . .

about the over the hill, unfunny comic bombing at London's Palladium, is a classic. It's what Bruce did best; taking you to places you don't want to be, but like the automobile accident on the road you can't help but look. You want to die with the dying comic at the Palladium, but Bruce makes you laugh. You want to cringe at his growing frustration and hostility towards the staid London audience, but, somehow, Lenny has you laughing uproariously.

Yet, there are times I find Andrew Dice Clay and a dozen other comics funnier than Lenny Bruce. How can you explain all the reverence for Bruce and hatred for Clay? The answer has little to do with comedy. There is little doubt that Lenny Bruce tested and crossed the borders of censorship, and, after it was too late for him to profit by it, opened the borders to where comics can travel anywhere with their material. That is their debt to Lenny Bruce.

On the other hand, it is fantasy to believe that he woke up one morning and decided to embark upon a free speech mission. Hey, we're talking about a heroin user who snitched on his wife to keep out of prison. Such men, folks, are not moralists and martyrs. Lenny Bruce happened to be around when certain prosecutors in the United States, especially, Richard Kuhn, a New York City Assistant District Attorney, were tired of the ambiguity and confusion of obscenity laws. They wanted the courts to define obscenity once and for all. Can you say "fuck" in New York City and not in Florida? That was the question Kuhn and others were asking, and Lenny Bruce was the perfect test case. Oh, Bruce fought them, but what was his option? The man had to make a living.

Lenny had one thing going for him that Andrew has not: Support from communities of entertainers and artists. From the man who invented show business, Steve Allen, to the man who turned Jewish guilt into a literary form, Phillip Roth; Bruce had a support system of artists. In fact, as Albert Goldman recounted in his biography of Lenny Bruce, Phillip Roth would take the subway each day to cheer on the comic in court, but on the

Would he be insensitive to include at the gathering a greedy rabbi, an illiterate black preacher and a grease ball pope? And, this you don't have to imagine, how great would be the cries of insensitivity if Dice had a routine where he kept repeating to his girlfriend to "shutup bitch?" Pretty insensitive, Andrew Dice Clay's comic critics would all agree, but that was the typical stuffing in Lenny Bruce's material. So, why the big fuss over Andrew Dice Clay? Why the holy reverence for Lenny Bruce?

I have interviewed many comics for *Penthouse* Magazine, and they all had the same word when the discussion turned to Lenny Bruce. Genius. Yet, I have listened to hours and hours of Lenny Bruce albums made during the final five years of his life and found myself using a different word. Boring. His routines were endless hours of reading court transcripts detailing his prosecutions and persecutions by various state and federal prosecutors. Rarely, is any of it funny. Always, it is pathetic.

There was, however, an earlier Lenny Bruce; one who knew how to turn things upside down for an audience. While I wouldn't use the word genius, his routine

CALLAHAN

end. Future comics gained the spoils of Lenny's war; but rather than appreciate that he was there to fight for another generation of entertainers, they choose to gush sentimental over a comedic genius they never saw or heard. Also, in the case of Andrew Dice Clay, they've got it all wrong. They've seen and heard the Diceman's comedy and choose to deplore it, not because it's funny or not, but it goes beyond the very borders Lenny Bruce opened. Now, they would like to reestablish the borders of censorship. They wish to join the unholy alliance of the reactionary Donald Wildmons and liberal politically correct thinking Jay Lenos and Richard Belzers. One can only say: Forgive them Lenny for they know not what they are doing.

way home would complain, not about injustice, but that he was funnier than the defendant. Andrew Dice Clay cannot lay claim to supporters among the rich and famous. And that brings us back full circle to what it's all about—politically correct thinking.

Lenny won the battle but lost the war. The trials, drugs burned him out in the

Allen Sonnenschein is special features editor at **Penthouse**

AN INTERVIEW WITH WILLIAM M. GAINES

Steve Ringgenberg

Mad Magazine publisher William M. Gaines is no stranger to censorship battles. In 1954, at the height of the anti-comics hysteria largely generated by a book entitled *Seduction of the Innocent*, which blamed comics for everything from juvenile delinquency to the younger generation's bad grammar, Gaines voluntarily testified before the Senate subcommittee on Juvenile Delinquency. Gaines was there because he was the publisher of the legendary (or infamous, depending

on your point of view) E.C. Comics line. In addition to publishing Mad in its original incarnation as a four-color comic, E.C. also put out some of the best-written and illustrated shockers ever to grace the pages of a comic book. Titles such as *The Vault of Horror, Tales From the Crypt, The Haunt of Fear, Crime Suspenstories, Shock Suspenstories, Weird Science* and *Weird Fantasy* carried in their pages stories about werewolves, vampires, axe-murderers, zombies, cannibals, and man-devouring alien plants. Crime and Shock, while they ran some science fiction and terror stories, mainly concentrated on searing tales of rape, murder, racial prejudice, drug addiction and other modern horrors.

E.C. comics were strong stuff for the conservative 1950's. Gaines's trio of horror comics were his most popular titles and were the best-selling horror comics of the '50's. Because E.C. was so successful and because E.C. comics were so graphic, William Gaines wound up taking a lot of heat for what he was publishing. Parents' groups, headline-seeking politicians, and of course, the retailers and wholesalers who controlled the comics business, singled E.C. out as among the most flagrant offenders of the public taste.

Gaines freely admits that the comics E.C. published were gruesome and often explicit in their gleeful depictions of torture, dismemberment, cannibalism and murder. But, unlike most of its competitors, E.C.'s horror comics were done with tongue firmly in cheek. Gaines and his writer/editor Al Feldstein dished up their horror with large helpings of black humor, which is one of reasons why E.C. comics are still being reprinted and read today.

But, because E.C., and some other comics companies were seen as a threat to the morals of America's youth, the Comics Code Authority was inaugurated in October of 1954. The Comics Code Authority was an organization designed to assure America's parents that the comics bearing its seal were clean, wholesome entertainment. Every comics publisher that subscribed to the Code was expected to submit its comics to a review board for approval before publication. The Code specifically forbade the use of the words "Horror" and "Terror" in comic titles, and the word "Crime" could only be used if it was used with "restraint". The code also forbade "All scenes of horror, excessive bloodshed, gory or gruesome crimes, depravity, lust, sadism, masochism..." as well as the "walking dead, torture, vampires . . . ghouls, cannibalism and werewolfism."

Gaines knew his days as a horror publisher were numbered when he couldn't get distribution for his non-Code approved comics, so he killed them off and created a new line of titles, his "New Direction Line". These comics, with titles like *MD*, *Psychoanalysis*, *Valor*, *Impact* and *Piracy*, while more restrained than the original E.C. line, were still intelligently-written, beautifully drawn comic books. Unfortunately, they weren't as successful as the more shocking stuff, so after a year of trying, Gaines killed off the "New Direction Line" and turned *Mad* the comic book into *Mad* Magazine. Gaines maintained the anarchic E.C. spirit in *Mad*, which has gone on to become one of the two most successful humor publications of the 20th Century.

Despite being out of reach of the Comics Code Authority, *Mad* has not escaped controversy. In the nearly forty years since its inception as a magazine, *Mad* has been accused of everything from being a bad influence on the minds of America's children to being unpatriotic to simply being in bad taste. *Mad* also has the distinction of being sued by one of America's most eminent composers, Irving Berlin. Back in the '60's, Mr. Berlin took exception to several parodies of his songs in *Mad*, feeling that if his work was being parodied, he was owed royalties. He was wrong and the ensuing court case set a precedent about how much parodists can take from the source material they are lampooning.

The 1990s find William Gaines still at the *Mad* helm as publisher, even though he sold Mad back in the 1970s for what was reputed to be a tidy sum. Because of his previous battles with censors and bluenoses, Gauntlet asked me to look up Bill Gaines in his cluttered Madison Avenue office and get his opinions on the current censorship climate in the Land of the Free and the Home of the Brave.

RINGGENBERG: Having lived through the repressive censorship climate of the 1950s, how would you compare the current climate in this country?

GAINES: Well, they don't seem to be bothering publications today. Today it's music they're after. And the only censorship problems I've heard about are what the musicians and the record companies are having.

R: So, do you think the climate's changed since the fifties?

G: Oh, yeah.

R: Do you think that there are any limits about what should be published in a comics format?

G: Well, if you're excluding . . . I guess there's nothing left, no. . . . I was going to say excluding pornography, but of course you have the underground comics and they've been pretty pornographic for years, so I guess there's nothing left.

R: Is there anything that you personally would find objectionable?

G: I can't think of anything.

R: Would you censor anything if you had the power?

G: Oh, I've never believed in any kind of censorship against anything in any way for anybody nohow.

R: What do you think of the current crop of comics?

G: I'll be perfectly honest with you. I don't know. Once I got out of comics I stopped reading them, and I don't have any idea of what's going on. I understand that some of the companies are putting out a very good product today. More expensive stuff, printed on better paper, with supposedly very fine art. But I really don't know . . .

R: As far as censorship goes, what battles do you think have already been won out there in the trench?

G: Well, to the best of my knowledge, the Comic Magazine Association does not have the power that it once had. As you may know, Russ Cochran is reissuing all my old horror comics and he is doing this through the distributor who was most unhappy with me back in the fifties. And this same distributor is now distributing the very same material that he was condemning back in the fifties, and without the Comics Code seal. One of the conditions I made was that Russ Cochran cannot put the (Comics Code) seal of approval on any of the stuff that he's publishing. And as a matter of fact, he's putting all of the material back in its original condition before it was censored, to the best of his ability.

R: Could you tell us the story behind the Jack Davis cover that was censored in the fifties? It was *Tales From the Crypt #38*— the Davis cover where the man was chopping an axe into a casket. There was a body in the casket, and there were pieces of hair and flesh flying up.

G: Well, it was obviously censored by one of the associations. There were two of them that I was involved in.

R: Did they force the E.C. art staff to censor it themselves?

G: No. Well, yes. Well, I mean they forced them to make the changes. I wouldn't say to censor it themselves . . . Now I know there's a cover kicking around where we took a meat cleaver out of a head. Do you know that?

R: That's the Johnny Craig cover. (see panel at right)

G: Okay, so that meat cleaver has been put back into the head. But that was probably a simple matter of peeling off something which had been . . .

R: A paste-over or something?

G: A paste-over, yeah.

R: So, it was the objections of the Comics Code people, or the wholesalers to the Davis and the Craig covers that caused the changes?

G: Oh, well, the Comics Code was formed because of the objections of parents and wholesalers. So, you might say in a sense that the wholesalers started it, but the wholesalers were upset because the parents and newsdealers were upset, probably. So, one thing led to another.

R: During the time that your work was being censored like that, how was it affecting your sales?

G: Back then?

R: Yeah, back then.

G: It wasn't affecting them at all until we had to drop all those titles and put out new titles. And those new titles never sold, for a variety of reasons. So, in that sense we were affected, but I don't think the average reader knew what had been censored. So, what he didn't miss, he didn't worry about.

R: Well, given that the Comics Code expressly forbid the use of the words Weird, Horror and Terror, did you feel that your company was being particularly targeted?

G: I would say so, yes. (chuckles)

R: Did you change *Mad* from a comics format to a magazine format to escape the censors?

G: No. No, I did not. I changed it because Harvey Kurtzman, my then editor, got a very lucrative offer from, I believe, *Pagent* magazine, and he had, prior to that time, evinced an interest in changing *Mad* into a magazine. At the time I didn't think I wanted to because I

Copyright © 1981 by William M. Gaines (*Vault of Horror #32*)

didn't know anything about publishing magazines. I was a comics publisher. But, remembering this interest, when he got this offer I countered his offer by saying I would allow him to change *Mad* into a magazine, which proved to be a very lucky step for me. But that's why it was changed. It was not changed to avoid the Code. Now, as a result of this, it *did* avoid the Code, but that's not why I did it. If Harvey had not gotten that offer from *Pagent*, *Mad* probably never would have changed format.

R: Before you changed *Mad* over to a magazine, you did a whole new line of magazines, or comics, rather; the New Direction line. Were titles like *MD* and *Psychoanalysis* an attempt to mollify the criticism from some of your detractors?

G: No. They were . . . What do you mean to mollify them?

R: Well, I mean . . .

G: I was putting out comics that I thought would not be criticized. But I didn't do them to mollify anybody. We put out a whole new line of comics. *Extra!*

was about newspaper reporters, *Piracy* was about pirates. *Aces High* was about World War I aircraft. *MD* was about doctors, and *Psychoanalysis* was because I was undergoing it at that time.

R: So you were interested in that process? That's what prompted the title?

G: Yeah, So was my editor.

R: During the time when E.C. Comics was being criticized most harshly in the fifties, during the juvenile delinquency hearings, Senator Estes Kefauver singled out one of your covers. It was *Crime Suspense #22*, the Johnny Craig cover with the severed head. At the time, Kefauver accused you of indulging in, at the very least, bad taste, and you countered with the argument that you thought the cover was not in bad taste.

G: Yes. And what Kefauver didn't know, and I did know was that when Craig originally brought that cover in there was blood dripping from the neck. The head had been held higher so that you could see the blood dripping from the neck and I, myself, had suggested that he raise the bottom of the cover up to cover the neck, so the neck was cut off before it was shredded, and I made one or two other minor changes which would soften the cover. And that's why when they said do I think it's in bad taste, knowing what it had been originally, I said, 'No, this is in good taste.'

R: One thing I'm curious about is the Jack Davis baseball story in *Haunt of Fear #19*. That was the one where the evil baseball player was dismembered.

G: One of our worst.

R: I was wondering, was this a deliberate attempt to bait the people who were criticizing you, or just a miscalculation?

G: No, no. No, it's just that Al and I were turning out a story a day and

it's not easy to turn out a story a day. And that day we were probably very late coming up with a plot and so we took this thing, and did it out of desperation because we absolutely had to have a story written that day. It was a bad story, it was a stupid story. It was certainly in bad taste. And I'm sorry we did it, but we did it.

R: Well, is there anything else that E.C. put out that in retrospect you wish you hadn't done?

G: No. Not that I can think of.

R: Let's jump ahead a little bit ... to the New Direction comics. In *Impact #4* you had a story called "The Lonely One," which was about prejudice against Jews. The Jewish soldier in the story had a very bland name. It was "Miller".

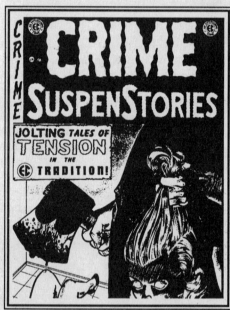

Copyright © 1982 by William M. Gaines (*Crime Stories #22*)

G: Oh, well that's very probably the Code at work. I'll tell you an even funnier one. In *Psychoanalysis* we had a guy, who, one of whose problems was that he was Jewish. This was giving him problems. And we were not allowed to say he was Jewish. And we had to take out all reference to the fact that he was Jewish, thereby the entire story made no sense at all, because it was a story about a man with a Jewish problem and we're not allowed to say he was Jewish. This was the Code.

R: So you weren't allowed any kind of depictions of different ethnic backgrounds?

G: Not allowed to call any attention to it. My favorite story of all was where I finally challenged the goddamned Code because I knew I was giving up comics and I sent up my last issue, which was, I think, it was a science fiction . . . I forget the . . .

R: It was *Incredible Science Fiction #33.*

G: Probably. And the Code turned down this beautiful Torres story on mutants.

R: "An Eye for and Eye."

G: I don't even remember. Because it never got published until much later, maybe in a fanzine.

R: Yeah, I spoke with Angelo about that and he told me that you kept promising him that one way or another you'd get that story in print.

G: Well, we eventually did but I don't remember how many people saw it, it was just in a fanzine. But they wouldn't allow it to go through. So I wasn't about to go out and write another story because this was my last issue ever.

R: This was the very last color comic you were going to do?

G: The last color comic I was ever going to do. And, so I took "Judgement Day," which I thought was one of our very finest stories. Are you familiar with it?

R: Certainly.

G: And I sent that out. And they turned it down because there was a bead of perspiration on the black's forehead in the last panel. And on that basis, they turned down the story. And I said, 'If you turn down this story, I am going to take you to court, and I'm going to take it to the Supreme Court. You better let that story through.' So they did.

R: Do you think their objection was that the astronaut in the story was black?

BUT YOU DO NOT LOSE CONSCIOUSNESS. IT IS AS IF EVERY MUSCLE IN YOUR BODY IS PARALYZED. YOU LIE THERE, FACE DOWN, AND THE FISH-CREATURES STAND OVER YOU...SPEARS RAISED...

YOU WATCH...FASCINATED...WAITING FOR DEATH. AND SOMEHOW, EVEN THEN, THE PRIDE PERSISTS IN YOU. AT LEAST YOU DIE A *MAN!* YOU'RE NOT A *FREAK*...LIKE *THEM!* YOU LIE THERE, FACE DOWN IN THE RIVER BANK MUD, AND YOU *WATCH* AS THE SPEAR COMES DOWN...AND YOU DON'T EVEN *BLINK* YOUR THIRD EYE...

THE END

Copyright © 1972 by William M. Gaines (final panels of "An Eye for an Eye" in *Incredible Science Fiction #33*)

G: I have no idea what their objection was. I think they were just a bunch of fucking idiots, that's what their objection was.

R: I've seen the story that they wouldn't let you run, "An Eye for an Eye." It looked relatively innocuous.

G: It was a beautiful science fiction story. But they didn't like mutants. You have to understand. This thing was run by three or four old ladies who were shocked by almost anything. They were the ones who did the censoring. George Murphy ran it, but I don't think he read things. The staff of old ladies read it and it wasn't hard to shock them. And mutants are just something they don't understand.

R: Let's jump ahead then to the *Mad* days. Why did Irving Berlin try to sue you in the sixties?

G: Well, because we were making fun of his lyrics. And that in itself . . . We were saying, 'Sing to the tune of . . . ' And we were saying sing to the tune of songs that he and a number of other songwriters had written. And they had the feeling that if we're saying, sing to the tune of their song, they should get royalties. But of course, we didn't print their music and we didn't print their lyrics, so they really didn't have a leg to stand on and when it went to the Supreme Court, they lost.

R: I was reading Judge Kaufman's decision on the Berlin case, and basically what he said was that *Mad* had the right to engage in parody, that there was a social need, basically.

G: He put it very funny. He said that, "Irving Berlin does not own iambic pentameter."

R: Let's talk about the censorship climate in general, now. We currently have a very conservative Supreme Court. Do you have any fears about freedom of expression being abridged in any way by the current court?

AND INSIDE THE SHIP, THE MAN REMOVED HIS SPACE HELMET AND SHOOK HIS HEAD, AND THE INSTRUMENT LIGHTS MADE THE BEADS OF PERSPIRATION ON HIS DARK SKIN TWINKLE LIKE DISTANT STARS...

THE END 7

G: Well, we'll see. Most of these guys are very conservative, but I don't think they're idiots, and I don't think anybody in the Supreme Court seriously wants to abridge free speech, and I'm not too concerned about it.

R: What was your feeling on some of the recent things like the Robert Mapplethorpe case where they were trying to close down that photography exhibition in Cincinnati?

G: Well, I'll tell you. I'm glad I don't have to be a judge on that kind of thing because I tend to think that there's a difference between things that are done with public money and things that are done with private money. If part of the public was offended by this and they were paying for it, I can see their point. If it had been a private museum, they don't have a leg to stand on.

R: What's the story behind the visits the FBI made to the *Mad* offices?

G: Well, the FBI is a little touchy, and we were . . . We put out a three dollar bill which turned out to be making change at change machines in airports. And of course we had no such idea and this upset the FBI, I guess, with some justification. (chuckles) So they came in and insisted on taking our artwork and plates and whatever we had for these things, with the full consequences and a chuckle out of it.

R: Wasn't there another case when they spoke to you about something that had run in Mad which made a reference to a town called Mafia, Italy?

G: They were probably upset by the State Department, who for obvious reasons thought we were doing something that would cause an international incident.

R: Have you had any current censorship problems, or even legal problems, stemming from parodies, such as being sued by someone whose product you were making fun of?

G: Oh, not for years.

R: What about personalities, like show business people or politicians?

G: As I always like to say, it's been terribly dull around here, so we must be doing something wrong.

R: Did you ever think that you'd be part of the publishing establishment?

G: Well I'm not.

R: How do you see yourself?

G: Certainly not part of the publishing establishment. I don't even know any other publishers except Lyle Stuart, and he's certainly not part of the publishing establishment, either. Oh, and (Al) Goldstein, at *Screw*.

R: Didn't Lyle Stuart do the *Anarchist Cookbook*?

G: Yeah. He's still doing it.

R: How do you feel about your friend Lyle publishing a book for bombmakers?

G: I thought it was horrible. Lyle and I do not see eye to eye in many ways. And he's one of my dearest, probably my dearest, closest friend. But, over the years we have had many differences of opinion. I think it's a disgrace that he publishes the *Anarchist Cookbook*. On the other hand, I'm delighted that he can get away with it because that shows that this is a free country after all.

R: How would you describe yourself politically, Mr. Gaines?

G: I am a part-liberal, part-conservative. It depends on which part you're talking about. In foreign policy I'm a conservative. In domestic policy, in things having to do with sex, abortion, pornography, and what have you, I'm completely liberal.

R: So, I guess you feel that almost anything goes as far as publishing?

G: Yep.

R: What about something like child pornography?

G: I personally have no objection to it. They might arrest the guys for what they did to the kids, but I don't have any objection to the pictures they took.

R: Do you see any kind of censorship danger coming from special interest groups, such as gays, or the Women's Movement, or ethnic groups that might not like to parodied?

G: Yes, I see definite dangers from that. I'm not comfortable about it, but so far it hasn't bothered us too much. I know once a troop of very conservative Jews came up to the office and had a long discussion with my editor and ended up putting a mezzuzah outside of his door, where it remained until we changed editors. They were upset about something we had done, or allegedly done. I don't know. A lot of people misunderstand what we do.

R: Do you find that a lot of the people who criticize *Mad* and maybe criticized the E.C.s back in the fifties lacked a certain sense of humor?

G: Oh sure, absolutely. All our horror stuff was written tongue in cheek, and as horrible as it gets, it was all done tongue in cheek, in the spirit of black humor. And of course most of the people that didn't like it didn't understand that, and wouldn't understand any black humor, when you get right down to it.

R: Do you ever watch horror films?

G: I watch *Tales From The Crypt* every time they come on.

R: How do you like what they're doing with your stories?

G: I love it, I love it. They've done a splendid job.

R: Mr. Gaines, considering all the people *Mad* and E.C. have managed to offend over the years (Gaines breaks out into laughter at this point) is there anybody you consciously want to offend?

G: (Laughing) I must be mellowing, I can't think of a soul.

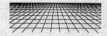

Glen Falls, NY Common Council voted to allow a theater group to string a banner promoting the musical *The Best Little Whorehouse in Texas*. Banning the banner "would almost be like putting a pair of pants on [Michelangelo's] *David*, if it came to the Hyde Museum, said Councilman-at-Large John Brennan.

POLITICAL CORRECTNESS:
GETTING THERE

Allan Sonnenschein

I can't define political correctness, but, thanking Justice Oliver Wendell Holmes, I know it when I see it. Indeed, political correctness is more than a term, but today's American political zeitgeist; a way of perceiving and defining the world. And while much of the debate over political correctness focuses on words, language is but its most obvious manifestation. What has been missing from discussions about political correctness has been any attempt to understand why and how it has become a social and political reference point for so many.

Great changes in ideas appear when the old thinking fails to come to grips with new realities. Much like in science when new observations of the universe could not be explained by Newton's laws. It took Einstein to explain them with his theories of relativity; hence, we began to think and speak differently about our world. All change comes form a need to make things work and conform to reality, and without that impetus the old saw holds true: if it ain't broken don't fix it. The birth of political correctness must be understood in that context.

Political correctness is the result of new political realities which began in the 1960s; the legislation of civil rights for the protection of minorities. We have had government mandated protection for minorities before the sixties, but with the exception of the Emancipation Proclamation in 1864, no act of government can be claimed to be more sweeping and total than the 1964 Civil Rights Act. This is not an overstatement of its significance because what it and subsequent legislation springing from it did was to turn morality into law. One could now find oneself in a courtroom for behavior which in the past, at worse, caused a guilty conscience and trip to the confession box.

Before there was political correctness, one consequence of civil rights legislation was the new political mythology; a tale acclaiming the political left as the legal champions of long suffering minorities. Like all good myths this one included reactionary monsters with names such as Goldwater and Nixon. History was divided into two periods: dark and barbaric days before 1960 and a new golden dawn brought to humanity by the House of Camelot and the landlord's heir from Texas. It was convenient to exclude from the history that it was one of the monsters, Richard Nixon, whom opened the doors to the White House to one of the myth's heroes, Dr. Martin Luther King,

and led the fight during the dark days for the 1957 Civil Rights Act. From this myth political correctness sprung.

The legislation to legalize minority rights through the dawn and days of the sixties, seventies and eighties kept elected officials busy writing and passing new acts. It seemed simple: Pass a law and get rid of a social ill. If one pill doesn't do the job, pass another and another; however, something was not happening. Civil rights for blacks, women, homosexuals, latins and all other subdivisions of humanity were legally established to welcome the new century on the horizon, but people's thinking and language were caught in a time warp somewhere in the 1950s. The law had changed, but we had not. There was a lesson to learn from this, but the political left chose to ignore it. Namely, if putting the right things on the books was enough to change behavior, we could have thrown out the printing press after Gutenberg published the Bible.

The political left knew something was wrong and had to be fixed. They recognized the two conflicting realities and asked themselves how it was possible after passing all those laws we had not arrived at utopia. My God, it was a failure of social engineering. It was not enough for them that the people obeyed the law, but they failed to share the left's religious belief in it. Something was wrong with the people. Something had to be done to help the people. They judged those who wished to send their children to schools of their choice as cross burners. They looked askance at those who chose to cherish a few thousand years of religious belief rather than support abor-

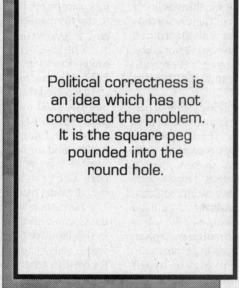

Political correctness is an idea which has not corrected the problem. It is the square peg pounded into the round hole.

tion on demand. Of course, they must be homophobes if they couldn't find it in their hearts to be sensitive to gays. Something was wrong with the people and it had to be remedied. The cure for them was going to be political correctness.

There is no exact date, but by the mid-eighties the left had written a new play on the old theme. If by passing laws they couldn't get you by the balls, they were going to get your hearts and minds with social and political reeducation. They used the media, schools, universities and whatever else was available, but it was one of the slickest and quickest jobs in social engineering. One can compare it to the French and Russian Revolutions to appreciate how a small group of elitists redid a nation; creating finishing schools for minds and manners. The champions of the myth came armed with the truth in their hip pockets, and they were not going to leave us alone until they got everybody together to hold hands and sing "We Are the World."

The left enjoys justifying political correctness by comparing racism to a form of social cancer; however, the language of metaphor is not always consistent with reality. Unlike physical disease, history records no "magic bullets" for societal woes, and a cursory observation will confirm that the syrupy palaver of political correctness has done little to revive this society. To belabor the medical metaphor, the political left have been little more than Dr. Feelgoods; getting us high on hyperbole, but leaving the disease untouched. Political correctness may leave one feeling good after telling one's secretary he understands she's not suffering from her period but her "regenerational life force," but I'll bet that pill won't stop sexual harassment in the workplace.

Political correctness is the brainchild of the left, and one that is a monster. Like a spoiled brat in the restaurant, banging his fork on the plate and spilling his milk; yet, his indulgent parents sit silently by and defy any diner to criticize. To criticize is to be insensitive; the buzzword of political correctness. It is the same spoiled brat we see on college campuses; reinventing language in the name of sensitivity. No right is greater than sensitivity for the monster's minority of the month and it is why the left has turned to censorship to get its way. Just look at the books and magazines you can no longer buy on college campuses because the monster has found them insensitive to women, blacks and, yes, animals.

The good news is that the little monster will not grow into adulthood. Political correctness is an idea which has not corrected the problem. It is the square peg pounded into the round hole. It's in there, but the fit is all wrong. One only has to look at Twentieth Century history to understand the failure of thought systems imposed from above. They last for a period of time, but they always crumble into the dust from where they were born. The Nazis enjoyed a run of 12 years and the Communists 70, and the political left in this country ought not to delude itself with thoughts of exceptions to the rule; especially, when they realize those systems were imposed with tanks and guns. To paraphrase the left, we shall overcome political correctness.

Politically Correct, and Unrepentant

William Rose

I have a recurrent nightmare. In it, I am confronting a seven judges wearing white robes and white hoods over their heads with slits for their eyes and mouths. I am standing in a circle of light and the rest of the room is dark, so I don't know who—if anyone—is watching.

I'm on trial, and the judge seated in the center points a long, bony finger at me and demands:

"Guilty or not guilty?"

"Guilty of what, Your Honor?" I quaver.

"Of being politically correct, of course."

"What does that mean, Your Honor?"

"You know perfectly well what that means," he roars. "Guilty or not?"

"I guess I'm guilty, Your Honor."

He looks at the other judges, all of whom respond by drawing the edge of their hands across their necks. He nods and says:

"Guilty as charged. Off with his head. Next case."

I wake up drenched in sweat, but still not sure what "political correctness" is. As far as I can make out it seems that it consists of diatribes against anyone who opposes racism, sexism and other forms of discrimination, focusing on their effort to use language that is not offensive to Blacks, Hispanics, Asian-Americans, Native Americans, women, etc.

What confuses me still more in this whole furor is that back when Blacks were "niggers," women "cute little chicks," progressives "dirty Commie bastards" and men were men (some of them, anyway), there was no such comparable furor. Why now?

For instance, the word "handicapped." Many people can't understand why the disabled would object to that term. Now, as I understand its etymology, handicapped in the sense of disabled is derived from the idea of a person with cap-in-hand, that is, a beggar. This, indeed, was about the only way a disabled person could earn a living in former times (and, unfortunately, is all too often the case today).

I didn't know the etymology of the word until a few years ago, but when I learned of its derogatory sense I determined not to use it, and use "disabled" instead. I had no intention of referring to a person with a disability as a beggar and, now that I'm disabled myself, I feel even more strongly on the subject. I know that there are those who believe that even the term "disabled" is derogatory, and in a sense it is (I have a physical problem and can no longer work in my chosen profession, but I'm hardly disabled—otherwise,

> Is it the belief that people who object to words like spic,nigger, guinea, dago, wop, greaseball,kraut, polack, kike, chink, gook, frog, cunt, handicapped and the like are nitpciking?

I couldn't write this article), and want to substitute the phrase "physically challenged." I don't personally chose to use it—even at the risk of being called "not politically correct" by some, but them's the breaks. There are contradictions in any new movement, but it's the fact that people who were formerly denigrated are now standing up and protesting is the important thing, in my opinion.

Some people object to the media and large corporations being attacked for derogatory remarks about various groups in our society. Truly, my heart bleeds for the poor media and corporate heads! For how many decades have they been perpetuating the most outrageous stereotypes and thereby fostering racism, sexism, ageism, etc.? Why is it that when a criminal is white this fact is rarely mentioned, but if he or she is Black or Hispanic, this juicy tidbit is usually mentioned in the first paragraph? And does anybody remember "skin-colored" Band-Aids which were only skin colored when the skin was white? Or simply sitting on a bus or subway and looking day after day at ads in which all the faces were white (affluent faces, that is—when the ad was about drug addiction or unwanted pregnancies the faces were usually any-

thing but white)? And who protested then?

So is this what being "anti-politically correct" is all about? Is it the belief that people who object to words like spic, nigger, guinea, dago, wop, greaseball, kraut, polack, kike, chink, gook, frog, cunt, handicapped and the like, are nitpicking? I don't agree that it's "just a matter of words." Doesn't language reflect culture, and isn't one of the ways to effect change to draw attention to the words we use to characterize and stereotype other people, thus dehumanizing them? Isn't that, in fact, why the otherwise silly debate over "political correctness" has stirred up such a storm? I guess we PCers hit a lot of people where it hurts, and if so, I'm glad of it. Maybe they'll begin to think about what they're saying and change, not just the words, but the way they view others in our society. God knows we need some change in that direction.

However, my real feeling is that, while some people use these derogatory terms unconsciously, there are others who have a hidden agenda. What they're really upset about are the efforts to combat racism, sexism and the like. For them, it's really a political question, a rather sneaky way for conservatives to attack progressives, for the unrepentant racist and sexist or whatever to continue the practice of perpetuating discrimination in our already lamentably divided society. It's the militantly "anti-political correctness" crowd who are nitpicking and hiding their true intentions (their own brand of "political correctness") behind a curtain of words—as though it were just words we're talking about, and not real people and their feelings and the way they're "kept in their place" in our society. Their place naturally being politically, socially and economically below the place of the vocal opposition to "political correctness."

If the debate were being conducted in a truly aboveboard fashion, we'd really be discussing the issues behind the words, issues like racism, sexism, ageism (yes, I'm also over fifty), and so on. But, not daring to discuss the pros and cons of racism, to take only one example, the "anti-political correctness" crowd chooses to ridicule efforts to change consciousness by changing language, that is, by changing the words with which we express our thoughts and feelings.

Lest this become too abstract, let me bring in a personal note. When I was a kid I lived in Georgia, after moving there from the North because of ill health. I went to Georgia because my family was from there, and I still feel my roots are in the South, despite all my contradictory feelings about the place. When I first moved there I was bewildered by a whole series of things. One of them was why my father always referred to Black men as "boys," even when they were sixty or seventy years old. And yet, white men were never "boys" after the age of seventeen or so.

Many years later I became a teacher, and taught for twenty-six years, until forced to retire by illness. For sixteen of those years I was privileged to teach Spanish and English as a Second Language at a branch of the City University of New York: Lehman College in the Bronx. My classes were a pretty heterogeneous mix of Hispanics, Blacks and Whites, Jews and Christians, men and women, etc. They were all survivors, some of oppression abroad and some of oppression right here in the good ol' U. S. of A. I soon discovered that an essential part of my work as a teacher—perhaps the *only* essential part—was to give these students a sense of their own self-worth, to teach them that there was nothing wrong with the way they were except that they didn't fit into the white mainstream's idea of what a worthy person should be. Some of us soon realized that the greatest block to learning which these students had wasn't the deficient educational background they'd received in ghetto schools, but the self-loathing those same schools had instilled in them over the previous twelve years of their lives (not to speak of the discrimination they'd suffered at the hands of the larger society). That any of

AT LAST, THE VOICE OF REASON!

them had reached college at all was a miracle and monument to basic toughness of many human beings.

So I tried to teach them that to value themselves adequately they had to value others in the same way, and to that end I fought anti-Black feelings among the Hispanics, anti-Hispanic feelings among the Blacks, anti-Semitic feelings in both groups, and anti-everyone feelings among the whites. Not that the whites didn't need a sense of self-worth themselves. These were Open Admissions students, working-class whites, the wops and greaseballs and hunkies and polacks and micks. They needed plenty of help, and I tried to give it to them. Now if that's being "politically correct," then I'm damned glad I'm "politically correct." I've tried to make a lot of other people "politically correct." I hope I've succeeded.

One last thing. My wife is Puerto Rican, and proud of it. A few years ago a man called her a "spic" in a supermarket line. I was about to punch him (yes, I was going to have recourse to naked violence, not rational discourse) when my wife grabbed my arm and said:

"Don't dirty your hands with him. He's just a crazy old man."

I didn't hit him, but I'd seen the pain in her eyes when she was called a "spic." I didn't really want to hit him. I wanted to kill him. Is that what we have to come to before people learn to respect each other as human beings?

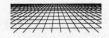

THE TOP 10
TAKE-THAT-BACK!!!-OR-I'LL-MAKE-YOU-WRITE-"NEW WORLD ORDER"-1000-TIMES-POLITICALLY-CORRECT-MEDIA-MOUTHS

Teri Wingender

The following list is not a complete one—I'm sure you've come across plenty more flickering across your TV screen or in the newspaper that nightly gets your hands dirty. These are the ones from various media that have most recently peeved me off and struck me as what is most nauseating about "political correctness."

I SUPPOSE TO PRACTICE POLITICAL CORRECTNESS PROPERLY, YOU SHOULD BE GENDERLESS AND KEEP YOUR MOUTH SHUT!

The selections are not listed by scale—in my view none are more dangerous or ridiculous than another. But together, they reveal the many faces of "political correctness" and its pervasiveness in the American media which I think is the real concern.

There are five criteria for these selections, with all or some of these characteristics:

(1) Profoundly hypocritical and stinking to high heaven of bad halibut—i.e. telling us what we should be saying or doing or thinking under the guise of open-mindedness.

(2) Abuses or obscures the English language.

(3) Claims to speak for the righteous or morally advanced among us, yet is often guilty (in reverse) of the very thing it claims to abhor—racism, sexism, ageism, etc.

(4) Censorious, ranging from the silly to the scary.

(5) Always, without exception, insulting to the intelligence.

1. Webster's College Dictionary
Random House

The first 'gender neutral' dictionary. Sol Steinmetz, executive editor says, "We wanted to emphasize the social consequences of language more than any dictionary before. Language is more than just a bunch of words," Steinmetz was quoted in Newsweek." Notations identify terms "commonly disliked," by adult females including "girl," "lady doctor," "honey," and "the fair sex." It also has an appendix entitled "Avoiding Sexist Language." But, hey, Sol, wait a cottonpickinminute! What about dames, dolls, broads, babes, chicks, bitches, skirt, pussy . . . perhaps these terms are not politically correct? Maybe you're just against censorship? Or are they still okay with you?

2. *Vanity Fair* August 5, 1991
"Demi's Big Moment."

Actress Demi Moore, maxi pregnant, stands in black lace and high heels holding her belly with both hands, her face cannily Madonna-like. (The Virgin, not the rock star, peculiarly.) In another pix, Demi holds a milk-filled breast, in another she is enrobed in an emerald green ball gown, the belly *avec* child exposed. All this visual stimulation seems to be trying to tell us, "Yes, Modern American Females, you too can be both knocked up and sexy, too (even if you can't afford Ungaro). Okaaaaay . . . (long thoughtful pause) Um, I'm almost positive I think I have a headache, honey.

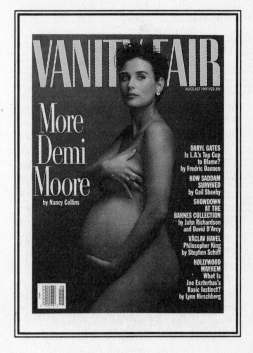

3. *Cosmopolitan*

Helen Burley Brown, ever at the fore of the women's liberation movement makes this offer to the politically correct sexual front: For the word "promiscuity,"she suggests "multi-friended" (I guess all the people we like but never slept with before better start holding onto their underpants). A cat by any other name still prowls in the alley, as far as I'm concerned. For "pornography" (*gasp!* Oh, the *horror* of it, Horatio!!!) she suggests "erotica." Very nice, very lady-like—I never knew Helen knew Latin. Now, this one really pisses me off—she wants to change "one night stand," which is probably one of the most wonderfully clear, elegant and tragically resonant phrases in the English/American idiom to "instant liaison" or "instant friendship." Sex as Lipton Soup. And again with the 'friend' thing. First of all, a "one night stand" to those of you who've had a couple or so, know that sex does not necessarily have the slightest thing to do with friendship. Which is fine, unless maybe you were expecting a ring. If you're in it for the sex, you'd rather have the Cracker Jacks and be proud of it. "One Night Stand" it stays, if I have anything to do with it.

4. *Lear's* (For the Woman Who Wasn't Born Yesterday)

They have this squirmy, condescending column called, "Good Men." Or sometimes they can find only one "Good Man" that month. Whatever. They show two or three pictures in black and white of good-looking, sensitive-looking males (I don't know if you've noticed, but this kind of look has a lot to do with the eyebrows). One issue has pictures of an architect, 43, a rancher, 55, and a vet from Bid-A-Wee, 37. In another issue, there is a quote (no source noted): "A good man aims to please but without expense to his dignity and separateness of self. That is his way of life." Besides beginning to laugh uncontrollably after saying this three times—go ahead and try it—can you IMAGINE if *Playboy* or *Penthouse* dared to show pictures of women (with or without pink parts showing, it doesn't matter) preceded by a quote of what "a good woman" should be?!?!?!? I honestly don't think Helen or Frances could take it.

5. *The Amsterdam News*

The publisher of the largest-circulation black newspaper in America called Tawana Brawley—a young New York woman who claimed to have been raped by white cops, but was found by a racially-mixed grand jury to have absolutely no basis for her accusation—an African-American princess." This statement, however politically correct it was for this particular black man to make, was a slap in the face to women who *have* been raped and to black women in general.

6. CNN

Ted Turner, probably since having married Jane Fonda, says his network can no longer use the word "foreign." The new word is "International." He presumably does not want to offend international-ers.

7. ABC

For fear of reprisal from stutterers across the nation, the network edited the movie *A Fish Called Wanda* to exclude scenes of ex-Monty-Pythoner Michael Paley's character, who stuttered uncontrollably. So, in effect, the poor character has been simply forbidden to speak *because* he stutters. We might call this politically correct backfire. Thank God Jamie Lee Curtis doesn't have freckles—we'd never get to see her half-naked again if ABC had anything to do with it.

8. *The Village Voice*

After the St. John's University case of

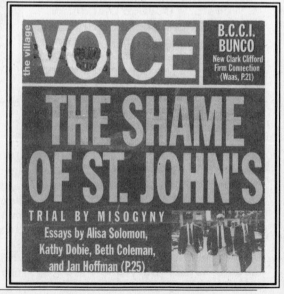

alleged rape had been decided and the young men involved found innocent of all charges, the *Voice* ran articles running their names and pictures again. This is a style of political correctness whereby a medium is so completely blinded by its own agenda, that when the innocent are found to be innocent, the only thing to do is find them guilty anyway, just like it was supposed to be from the first. Then again, maybe the *Voice* just had a lot of extra pictures they wanted to use up, so as to be environmentally conscientious.

9. ABC, CBS, C-SPAN, CNN

The Clarence Thomas/Anita Hill Soap of the Week. Our television media were so sensitive to the issue of alleged sexual harassment to a respected law professor and the possibly slandering of the vilest kind of a Supreme Court nominee that none of these networks could see the forest behind all those shady trees. While the sport of figuring out who was doing "best" for the Judiciary Committee (keeping score, that inalienable right of Americans everywhere) and who was the most "credible," not one of the networks entertained the possibility that BOTH of those bright, admirable people (I liked them, didn't you?) were LYING. He probably did harass her, he probably did say those things to her, but in BED.

The progression of this is: LAID, LIE, LYING. How *else* would a pubic hair get into his Coke? Am I the only one who noticed? I didn't think so. All you have to do is watch *Knott's Landing* to develop this skill.

10. *Playboy*

The magazine recently dropped its suit it had filed concurrently, but not in association with, *Penthouse* magazine against the American Family Association of Florida, which pressured distributors to stop selling "sexually explicit" publications. *Playboy* demurred, recognizing the AFA's right to protest (which was never the question—the issue was and is censorship) and stating that it was satisfied with the AFA's subsequent agreement not to engage in "extortionate conduct in the future." In return, the AFA recognized *Playboy*'s right to publish. Talk about strange bedfellows. *Penthouse* is still in litigation with the AFA.

Teri Wingender writes magazine articles on entertainment, celebrities, social issues and trends which have been published nationally and internationally. She is currently working on a book with Mitzi Shore, founder and director of the legendary Comedy Store in Los Angeles.

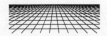

DON'T WORRY, HE WON'T GET FAR ON FOOT

BY JOHN CALLAHAN

DISTURBING IMAGES: THE CARTOONS OF JOHN CALLAHAN

Mike Baker

John Callahan is a cartoonist whose sense of humor, by his own definition, is rather black. His work pokes fun at things like death, physical handicaps and the KKK; subjects which some people fail to see humor in. And these people, in fits of political correctness, do what the narrow-minded have always excelled at: they complain. Letters are written to editors, and calls are made to special-interest groups as the righteous bemoan Callahan's lack of respect for the handicapped and his cavalier attitude toward the physically disabled.

At the age of 21, ten years before he started his career as a cartoonist, Callahan was involved in an automobile accident which severed his spine between the fifth and sixth vertebrae, rendering him quadriplegic; he still has almost full usage of his arms, but is otherwise paralyzed from the diaphragm down. Drawing is a two-handed job for him, as he has to exert pressure upon his hand to keep it closed around the pen.

Callahan doesn't go out of his way to draw attention to his handicap—he sold cartoons to *Penthouse* for two years before

IV. The correct way to approach a handicapped person.

" Sorry, mike, you just can't hold your liquor. "

they discovered that he was paralyzed—because he considers it irrelevant. "I reserve the right to draw gags about any group or individual," he said in his autobiography *Don't Worry, He Wont Get Far on Foot*, "especially about self-righteous assholes who presume to defend the disabled."

A good example of the above would be the person who wrote to *Vanguard*, the Portland State University student newspaper, about a Callahan cartoon featuring a man with hooks for hands being refused a drink because he can't hold his liquor. The letter writer, after calling Callahan insensitive, goes on to say that . . . "on this campus are a number of brave individuals who have refused to submit to their physical limitations . . . I applaud their courage and deplore the ugliness of spirit of John Callahan's mean cartoon" never realizing, until the paper's editors revealed the fact, that not only was Callahan paralyzed, he was also a long-time PSU student. It would have been interesting to see the letter writer's reac-

tion upon receiving that news flash.

Callahan poses a dilemma to the typical politically correct person; he makes fun of the so-called disadvantaged, a PC no-no, yet he is one of that group himself. An L.A.-based mental health organization encountered this dilemma, with interesting results. Upset about some of Callahan's cartoons, which had appeared in *The San Diego Union*, they called his agent, who informed them of Callahan's handicap. Opinions quickly shifted, and the group's spokesperson was soon praising Callahan and calling him a positive role model for the handicapped.

Euphemisms for the word handicapped—which, like cripple, is viewed by some as derogatory—have recently come into vogue as the politically correct seek kinder, gentler ways to describe that which they find offensive. In a recent newspaper article about this disturbing trend, Callahan mentioned that during a TV appearance to promote his new book *Digesting the Child Within*, he was referred to as handi-capable. "I rebel against any politically correct terms," Callahan was quoted as saying. "I'm paralyzed. Why mince words?"

Callahan is no stranger to controversy. In one of his earliest cartoons he drew a black beggar wearing a sign which read: Please help me, I am blind and black but not musical. With its publication came his first hate mail. He was called a racist.

Later cartoons identified him as sexist, agist, fascist and communist. But the truth of the matter, Callahan says, is that he's merely a cartoonist.

Mike Baker, a free-lance writer, is **Gauntlet**'s *West Coast correspondent*

P. C. RETROFIX

Rex Miller

Everyone remembers the days when you could tell a Polish airplane by the "hair under its wings", when a STINKBUG was "6 niggers in a Volkswagen", when GAY stood for Got AIDS Yet. But no one tells those jokes anymore. Well, maybe a few of us still do.

Take John Rousakis. Please.

In a weak moment John told this one during his recent mayoralty campaign in Savannah, Georgia, according to one newspaper account:

A rape victim was asked to identify her assailant. She said she couldn't but—"he must have been a Democrat—because she never had it so good." One imagines how this must have gone over with voters in a time when the pop song lyrics "when I say MAYBE I mean YES" are under attack for potentially contributing to date rape!

Consider the disadvantaged: in the 50s the word crippled was replaced by handicapped. That in turn became physically impaired, as retarded was phased out by special, developmentally-disadvantaged, and —most recently— a retarded person was said to be a "mental health consumer." A handicapped person has evolved or mutated into someone who is physically challenged. What in the name of the bleeding Christ does *physically challenged* mean? (You've been physically challenged, Sir Rupert. Choose your weapon!)

In time one expects to see a serial killer's lawyer describe him to the jury as behavioristically challenged, or to read of an insane mother killing her child in a severe attack of Post-Partem Depression and Extremely Premature Pre-Menstrual Stress.

Clearly media is in dire need of a P.C.—meaning Pop Culture—Retrofix.

Not even Pre-Menstrual Stress will be tolerated in our new patois excised of slurs, implications of inferiority, or stereotypical categorizing. Sanitized of all possible epithets based on race, religion, disability or status—not to mention sexual 'orientation',(itself a serious swipe at Orientals,) all vocabularies shall be cleansed of offense.

Chauvinist pigulation such as menage (for household) and its sexist cousin menage-a-trois will become menage/womynage depending on the dominant sex, numerically speaking. Women will be womyn and a girl will be a pre-womyn. Persin or persyn will have the son surgically removed. Womyn will endure womynstrual cycles, womynstrual cramps, womynstruation and—womynopause. Depending on their womyntality they may become eligible for WoMynsa membership.

Consciousness-raising begins with a retrofix at the supermarket, focusing on dastardly dual offenders whose insensitive names and titles are doubly-incorrect: SPIC AND SPAN , BONELESS CHUCK, RED MAN CHEWING TOBACCO, and the anti-corpulent BUTTERBALL TURKEYS. HOMOGENIZED MILK goes. AUNT JEMIMA, UNCLE BEN, and CHEF BOY-AR-DEE will be considered "forbidden fruit", (*Another* phrase containing a homophobic slur!) OREOS, APPLES, SQUIRT, TWINKIES all give offense, as does that politically inflammatory RECONSTITUTED KRAUT.

Driving home we'll change all the road signs reading *Slow*, insensitive slurs against the developmentally disenfranchised, to the larger but less offensive *"Road Impairment May Impose Disadvantageous Motoring Conditions."*

One persyn's SAMBO'S is another persin's *WHITE CASTLE*, but we must all work to expunge such overt race-bashing as the telephone directory with its *YELLOW PAGES*.

Native North Americans who take umbrage at the "chop", which they feel is degrading, want the Atlanta Braves to change their name, but why aren't they more offended by the Cleveland Indians considering that they've played so dismally for so long?

Heterosexual Native American-uities retrofixes this cereal premium that potentially offended both to lesbians/gays and Native Americans:

STRAIGHT ARROWS "INJUN-UITIES" INSIDE
NABISCO

(But aren't South Americans offended by the Indian usage "Native Americans"? Shouldn't the phrase be

> Female dogs must not be called bitches, children's books must have their gratutitous pussies, coons, and frogs removed, and similar vestiges of vanishing stereotypes must be eradicated.

NATIVE NORTH AMERICANS?) . . . And where does this leave the company that makes Eskimo Pies, out in the cold?)

Hardware stores give offense with spades, wasp repellent, and chink caulker.

B-repellent is what we need, as we cleanse the dark dictionary pages of blackballs, blackguards, blackheads, blackjacks, black markets, black-outs, black sheep, and blacktop that blackmails us with black widows of anti-Semantic and ethnic implications.

Female dogs must not be called bitches, children's books must have their gratuitous pussies, coons, and frogs removed, and similar vestiges of vanishing stereotypes must be eradicated. History books will become Herstory/History depending on the P.O.V. of the narrative's perspective. When no gender asserts itself numerically,history will be called theirstory.

Film titles such as *The Pope Must Die* and *How to Make Love to a Negro Without Getting Tired* will no longer be permitted. Even ironic titles such as the one bestowed by Whoopi Goldberg, (whose name is a multiple offender in itself!), on the renamed Spike Lee flick "Jungle

Beaver", will henceforth be censored. (Spike's name itself is offensive to addicts using syringes.) Country and Western libraries will have all references to the dually-bashing SPADE COOLEY deleted.

All motion picture titles will be reexamined and retrofixed. Take the seemingly inoffensive classic *Snow White and the Seven Dwarfs*:

SNOW is unacceptable, being a euphemism that tends to glamorize drug usage. (Coke, girl, white lady, toot, tootski, blow, the blowster, happy talc, God's dandruff, Columbian power-powder, nose candy, snort, snoot, sniff, whiff, dust, Bogota' Boogie, fun flakes, dynomite, Cloud 9, X.T.C., crack, whack, blast, snow et al.)

WHITE is a politically incorrect double-dildo of discomfiting disadvantageousness being both an epithet of supremacy and a drug term.

SEVEN is potentially offensive to obsessive/compulsive craps addicts, being of course the number associated with a 'natural' throw of dice. (Craps itself is scatological and offensive to the incontinent.) Seven is also a possible slur against Saturday Sabbath Adventists.

DWARFS and all references to teenieweenies, lilliputians, midgets, winklepickers, pee-wees, leprechauns, little people, Rooneys, dwarves, shorties, tiny li'l fuckers, etc., are verboten.

The retrofixed film title:

"TABULAR, COLUMNAR CRYSTALLIZATION OF FROZEN WATER VAPOR WITHOUT COLORATION AND A RANDOM NUMBER OF PERSONS WHO MIGHT OR MIGHT NOT BE PERCEIVED TO BE OF MORE DIMINUTIVE THAN USUAL PHYSICAL STATURE." By Walt Disney!

All aspects of life must be retrofixed, with the offending titles eliminated: Games (Old Maid), TV sit-comes (*That Girl, Golden Girls, Girl Talk, Leave it to Beaver*)—ad infinitum!

The comics are among the worse culprits of incorrectness run rampant. **Dick Tracy** is but one example with its stereotypes that have given offense to ethnic groups such as Latinos,(**Go-Go Gomez**), and Japanese,(**Jo-Jo Jitsu**), to name just two. But the Tracy strip is

loaded with characters who might potentially give offense: **Diet Smith**, an oblique jab at the overweight; **B.O. Plenty**, a dig at the homeless, disenfranchised, or otherwise 'fragrance free'; **Pruneface**, insensitive to elderly or the significantly-wrinkled; **Flat-Top**, a slur to those with cephalic defects; and of course the lead character whose name has a sexist connotation:

"Dick Tracy's G-Men" manages to offend three times: in referring to male genitalia, an allusion to an erotic zone, and a mention of a gender class.

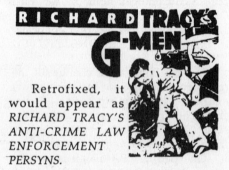

Retrofixed, it would appear as *RICHARD TRACY'S ANTI-CRIME LAW ENFORCEMENT PERSYNS.*

The music industry must clean up its act as well. Not only the genre of gangsta-rap bristles with epithets. What about **MICK** Jagger, **TOM** Waits, **QUEEN** and Don **HO**? Similarly all **HOOKERS**, including John Lee and Thomas, must be banned from the airwaves and libraries.

Scouts will no longer be permitted to go on **outings** and no films with Michael **Wilding** will be shown.

In deference to the animal rights advocates the euphemism for ecological militancy will no longer be **monkey**wrenching but merely wrenching.

Dyche Stadium, **Coit Towers, Love Canal**, and **Gay Court** will undergo a name change. Phyllis **Schla** will have her fly removed or zipped. Films imported from the U.K. will have all smoking scenes bleeped of "**fag**" mentions, all comics containing word balloons with impact onomatapoetics will have their "WOP!"s removed, and the phrase **bald-faced liar** will be retrofitted with a rug, if not a transplant. No more will one have a "**gay old time**" (Especially on the **Gay**

White Way!)

No more will we hear of the cops finding the body of "Irving Corleone, Godfather of the Jewish Mafia, his body riddled with doubt." Never again will Kingfish intone into Amos 'n' Andy's radio or TV mike: "We is gathered heah on dis suspicious Caucasian . . ."

No more snickering about the guy who was arrested for exposing himself in a porn theatre, ("I don't need a lawyer. I can get myself off!") Gone forever those serial killer refrigerators, ("the ones with more elbow room!") No more lesbian gags about the diesel dyke who was "hung like a donut!"

We must all pull together for a politi-cally correct future:

LET'S TAKE THE CONDOM OUT OF CONDOMINIUM!

Rex Miller, author of ten novels, makes his third appearance in Gauntlet, his wry humor underscoring a serious message. Miller's milieu is dark crime/suspense, with his next novel Chaingang due out in October 1992.

REX'S HOUSE DICTIONARY

The Random House Dictionary is but one authoritative source now making a conscious effort to avoid sexist verbiage. Smitten as one is by such "euphemizations" in the name of PC, the following is now included in the 1992 edition of *Rex's House Dictionary.*

Every effort should be made to employ linguistic usages—both in selection and grammatical construction—that eschew delineation of "gender offenders." Some specific suggestions:

1. Eliminate all words or expressions containing the word 'man,' such as substituting "foreperson" for foreman, or recasting the word by deletion:
> "Permanent" becomes "perent
> "Mandible" becomes "dible"
> "Emancipation" becomes "ecipation."

The rule of acceptable euphoniousness applies. Example: Demand will not be recast, as the resulting syllable "ded" sounds like and/or resembles dead or dead. In the case of such constructions substitute a synonym. In the case of words such as Germany, the deletion sounds too much like jury, and one would use Deutschland. Common sense should be employed in these determinations.

2. Use gender-neutral terms:

Instead of:	Consider using:
Anchorperson, etc.	Talking head
Businessperson, etc.	Greedmeister
Clergyman, etc.	Godster

Know why Jesus couldn't eat M & Ms?
Because they kept falling through his hands.

What do they call Venetian blinds in Ethiopia?
Bunk beds.

What do you call a black test-tube baby?
Janitor-in-A-Drum.

How do you fit four gays in a crowded bar?
Turn the stool upside down.

"Do you know how many animals had to die for that fur coat?" screamed the animal-rights activist to the lavishly dressed woman.
   "Honey," she replied, "do you know how many animals I had to fuck for this coat?"

POLITICAL CORRECTNESS BASHING:
Sleeping With The Enemy

John Edward Ames

No shit, I love offensive, 'tabu' humor like the above. That even includes the mean, sexist, homophobic and racist patter of Andrew "The Diceman" Clay or those totally tasteless cartoons in *Hustler*. When it comes to a good yuk, I'm so open-minded I'm usually the first one thrown out of respectable gatherings. You just can't offend me with a joke. I'll slam every ethnic group, "suffering minority," and sacred cow or cause known to man.

A joke's a joke. Nobody should be spared when King Laugh comes to town. But "the hand that whirls the water in the pool stirs the quicksand." Sometimes there's an ultrafine line between naughtiness and cruelty, between humor and hate.

Now we've got a new band wagon rolling through America, and the name that's on it is Political Correctness Watch. It's attracting those who have decided to make a stand against the well-docu-

If this guy's on **our** side,
like uh, who needs
enemies?

mented, holier-than-thou PC mentality. Unfortunately, some intelligent people who ought to know better are leaping on board a bit too quickly. Under their own self-righteous guise of defending free speech, they've helped to unleash a new form of meanness and intimidation.

Not that "political correctness" isn't a legitimate concept which underscores a valid problem: censorship and stifling of free expression. PC is a real enough enemy, all right. I remember getting tossed out of a party at a dog lover's house when I was in college. All I did was whip out a copy of *National Lampoon* which featured the cover satire "Dog Fishing in America" with an illo of a redneck fishing out of the back of his pickup, a cute little golden lab hooked on his line. And not too long ago I got soundly slapped across my smart mouth when, snockered on bourbon at a book-signing party, I yelled out, "Sure Jesus loves you—but will he swallow?" Damn, people can be *so* tight-assed.

Everywhere you go, there's some sanctimonious anal-retentive type or Oppressed Group of the Week eager to do dirt on free expression. That's why the critics of political correctness emerged in

the first place. But the original parameters of the concept have been pushed to distortion, the paradigm has shifted.

Especially among the young, the pressure not to be guilty of politically correct thinking has created a cruel irony: Somehow, in the desperate urge to be unflappable and cynically hip, it has become a greater sin to speak out against racism or sexism or homophobia, for example, than it is to actually be racist or sexist or homophobic.

I notice this trend especially among college students. Peer pressure is extreme in college, and students in the 1990s are under hellacious pressure not to appear "engage." An intelligent, charming young coed friend of mine has taken me roundly to task for casting the villain in my first horror novel as racist and sexist.

Never mind that this villain is a psychotic murderer. Never mind that most psychokillers *are* racist and sexist—this earnest young lass is on PC watch. Seldom in our conversations and letters has she mentioned the KKK or antisemitism or gay-bashing (this last being a very real problem right now on American campuses). Yet, several times she has alluded to lesbian college professors who unfairly lay guilt trips on white undergraduate males too naive to fight back. Anything is possible, but I have trouble processing that image. (In fairness, my friend doesn't like people who wear polyester, either, and even on my pauper's income I can appreciate that.)

The extreme reactionism against political correctness produces some odd arguments. Another college student, this one a senior at Boston College, wrote a review of *Dances with Wolves* ("Political Correctness on the American Frontier," Winter 1991 *Campus*) in which she archly noted that "*Dances with Wolves* is one of those transparent films in which it is easy to distinguish the good guys from the bad guys."

Well, cuss my coup! That's a rare trick for Hollywood, isn't it, keeping the villains distinct from the heroes? "One gets the impression," the reviewer added, "that Costner's motive is less to be historically accurate than to emphasize the inherent purity of the Sioux."

I write Indian point-of-view fiction myself (the CHEYENNE series under the pen name Judd Cole), and I'll eat my elkskin moccasins if this chick from Boston U. can name five Hollywood Westerns that don't grossly stereotype, trivialize, and insult Native Americans while depicting whites as the civilized Christian standard bearers. I wonder if she's ever written an indignant piece castigating director John Ford for wildly romanticizing the cavalry in *She Wore A Yellow Ribbon*. I doubt it. Those who are on PC watch seldom seem to get steamed about "historical inaccuracies" that glorify whites.

It's no coincidence, of course, that college campuses are hotbeds of PC watching. *Newsweek* and other corporate-profit publications have lately catalogued the threats, real enough if somewhat exaggerated, posed by various academic pressure groups who think being personally offended is worse than suppressing free speech.

But I've noticed that those who are most vigilantly on the qui vive for the politically correct mindset are the same Safeguarders of Democracy who clamor about the need for a "traditional core curriculum" to protect our cherished Western value system. Reading black history, studying Mexican literature or the biographies of radical feminists—all this somehow poses a grave danger to our "Judeo-Christian values," the cultural super-glue that keeps society together. It's much healthier for our sense of national identity, they argue, to study a fascist like Ezra Pound than a lezbo commie like Gertrude Stein.

I've spent ten years teaching university English and lived most of my adult life in college towns. Not once have I heard of a teacher being denied tenure for excessive loyalty to the "core curriculum" or for flag-waving. I have, however, witnessed the denial of tenure to radical political scientists and iconoclastic lit profs who occasionally visit gay bars. It's pure-dee bullshit and WASP paranoia to argue that a powerful, humorless minority of gays, feminists, ethnics and

> Everywhere you go, there's some sanctimonious anal-retentive type or Oppressed Group of the Week eager to do dirt on free expression.

other special-interest commandos wield such incredible power on college campuses. The most powerful coterie on almost any campus is the alumni organization, specifically the football-loving contingent. Not too many PCs in *that* crowd.

'Political correctness' is not a chimera. On the other hand, we have this instinctive tendency (aptly illustrated by the Desert Storm fiasco and the "ass-kicking" we gave Grenada and Panama) to overrate the enemy. And the PC crowd makes for a good enemy, especially from the point of view of the right wing. Because it's a "free speech" issue it naturally appeals to liberal intellectual types, who love to scream "Mea culpa" at every opportunity. But from its original, legitimate definition, 'political correctness' has broadened into a buzz phrase. It's main function now is to divert us from more substantial battles against more dangerous enemies. That's a shame. When the house is on fire, you shouldn't worry about a leaky faucet in the bathroom.

The PC watchers are launching a virulent, often mean-spirited assault on those who are mostly silly, irritating, and irrelevant. The right, which excels at cleverly creating diversions to divide and weaken their opponents, is lapping this shit up. Sure it's asinine to insist on calling blind people "visually challenged." Hell, I still refuse to call bums the "homeless." But it's even more asinine to make a federal case out of silly euphemisms while the Sierra Nevada is being stripped bare of timber and police brutality is on the rise and civil rights are being rolled back in the name of a holy jihad against drugs. I suspect that the ozone layer will be destroyed long before lesbian professors gain the power to force me to memorize *Gyn/Ecology*.

Okay, so I'm a hypocrite who shamelessly enjoys ethnic jokes. Still, I'm never going to forget how, as a young Marine in the late 60s and early 70s, I saw racial tension and insensitivity ruin lives and nearly destroy the Vietnam-era Marine Corps from within. Nor am I ever going to forget that it wasn't politically correct airheads who turned some of my friends into stew meat in Vietnam for the biggest zero in history.

And it wasn't white intellectuals—those who are now pissing and moaning the loudest about political correctness—who had their ass in the grass at Hue or the Que Son Valley or on Hill 881. It was Blacks, Puerto Ricans (the racial minority which suffered the highest rate of death in the Vietnam Marine Corps), Hispanics, Native Americans and poor whites. They were sent to die by the same white, greedy, upperclass politicians who now cynically exploit the murky issue of 'political correctness' to further divide Americans against themselves.

So here's a closing joke to politically balance the books:

What do you call a WASP who doesn't work for his father, isn't a lawyer, and believes in social causes?

A failure.

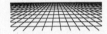

Ideas for a "PC" Christmas, courtesy of the *Philadelphia Inquirer*: wrap presents in colorful comics, exotic foreign newspapers, fabric and recycled paper. Decorate the tree with strings of popcorn and cranberries which can become bird and squirrel food after the holidays. Skip the card and just sign your name right on the box. The perfect "PC" gift—antiques—a high form of recycling.

G. Gordon Liddy in *Forbes* recounts being denied the use of a silhouette at a firing range in Dade County, Florida. Seems their *color* was deemed "insensitive."

Beware of Proselytizing Vegetarians

John Sutherland

At the beginning of their band's last tour, Paul and Linda McCartney made this totalitarian proclamation to their band members: "We will pick up the tab for your meals on this tour (a common practice among big-name performers) provided you eat only at vegetarian restaurants." No meat, no chicken, no dairy products. Just fresh pieces of roughage and gelatinous blobs of fried vegetable protein. Yum.

Few things are as self-righteous and bothersome as a celebrity vegetarian with an agenda, of which there is a growing legion these days. A few years back you would have expected this sort of culinary blackmail from, say, a vibrato-voiced folk singer, but not a major rock star.

Yet today it is the trendiest sort of rebirth one can go through, so politically-correct, so Yingy and Yangy, and usually described in the same terms as a religious awakening. It just may replace Buddhism as stardom's number one New Age attention-getter.

It seems that many Americans, famous and otherwise, have joined the vegetarian hayride. Some have simply forsaken red meat; more strident vegetarians will renounce chicken, fish, eggs and dairy products. That leaves only things that grow out of the soil.   Like most people, I have no problem with someone choosing vegetarianism, just as I have no problem with someone choosing a particular religion; it's a personal lifestyle choice. But should you ever find yourself in a room with a proselytizing vegetarian, you'll know what it's like to be handcuffed to Elmer Gantry. Conspicuous non-consumption has never been so noisy.

It's the zealots in any group that give it an extremist reputation and the vegetarian movement seems to have no shortage of them. So many veggies have become recruiters for the cause and their sworn duty is to convert the ignorant, bone-chewing masses.   To accomplish this they use guilt, fear and intimidation, coming in the form of dietary propaganda. ("That steak will clog your arteries like chicken fat clogs a drain . . . You know how they kill hogs? Pneumatic jackhammers! . . . How can you drink milk and still sleep at night? . . . Enjoy yourself; they don't have omelets in hell.")

For whatever reason, a lot of people seem to be suffering from sanctimonious self-deprivation. Perhaps it's a psychological reflex to the gluttony of the '80s, a form of self-loathing and denial, a personal penance. Some people immolate themselves, others become vegetarians.

You'll want to avoid the more evangelical vegetarians, not for fear that they may convert you but because you may end up striking one. Here are some hints that will help you recognize the real hardcores:

⬧ They genuflect at the sight of sirloin.

⬧ The women look like Emily Dickenson; the men look like Emily Dickenson.

⬧ They have the pallor and energy of someone who's been adrift in a raft for 50 years—until they start yelling at you for eating meat.

⬧ They will invite you to their homes to watch episodes of Marty Stauffer's "Wild America." Do not accept.

"I WONDER IF K.D. LANG REALLY LOVES COWS OR JUST REALLY HATES PLANTS!?"

⬧ If you do accept, bring your own snacks. Otherwise, you will be offered whole-bran hardtack and puffed rice patties, which are as tasty as styrofoam packing peanuts.

⬧ If, despite your best efforts, a preachy vegetarian ends up in your living room, tell him or her that a 12-hour football marathon is about to begin and you intend to watch it. Vegetarians are deeply opposed to violent land-acquisition games and will quickly leave.

None of this should be interpreted as an indictment of vegetarianism (pardon me—"cruelty-free eating"). It's fine if it's done quietly. I just happen to think it is wholly unnatural. Our primitive ancestors—pure of thought and instinct, unencumbered by moral dilemmas—ate other animals because something in their heads told them to. They obeyed the instinctive voice of nature, as all living creatures do, save for vegetarian man.

In fact, my philosophy on vegetarianism is probably consistent with the ancient troglodyte's—the moment I see a vegetarian dog, lion or shark, then I'll become one too.

ARE YOU POLITICALLY CORRECT?

DETERMINE YOUR "PC" QUOTIENT

I THINK I'LL EAT SOME NACHOS AND GET THAT AWFUL TASTE OUT OF MY MOUTH! I MUST SAY, I AM OFFENDED. THAT'S MY OPINION...OUGHT TO BE YOURS.

Richard Dominick

Questions! Questions! Questions!

Is it okay—or politically correct—to slap a slab of cheese in a mousetrap in your attic in hopes of breaking the neck of a harmless 2-ounce mouse, but wrong—or politically incorrect—to gas a mink and strip off it's pelt?

Well?

How about this? You're invited to a reception honoring an African Ambassador to the United States. You're thrilled, you're honored, you accept immediately—after all it's the politically correct thing to do. He's not "black" or a "Negro," and he's certainly not a "nigger." He's am African Ambassador to the United States, and you can't wait to see the photograph of you standing next to him in the society page of the newspaper tomorrow morning. So what happens when he leans over to you, unknowingly points at your daughter and whispers, "I'd like to pork that tight white ass."

Is it politically incorrect to punch him in the mouth?

Being politically correct is a tough job, but somebody has to do it. Are you man—(oops, I can't risk being labelled politically incorrect here)—or woman—enough to handle the job. Let's find out by taking this "ARE YOU POLITICALLY CORRECT? quiz.

The Quiz

Choose only one answer by circling the reaction you feel is politically correct. If you use a pen, try using all color inks.

(1) On her way to a rally demanding the Atlanta Braves ban their fans from doing the "Tomahawk Chop," your girlfriend is killed when her car is struck head-on by a pickup truck filled with drunken Indians. Do you . . .

A. bury her, then continue her fight to ban the "Tomahawk Chop".

B. continue her fight to ban the Tomahawk Chop, *then* bury her.

C. grab eight squaws and do a Richard Speck.

(2) It's your first day on your new job and boy are you excited! It's the position you've always wanted and the salary is great. Suddenly, your new boss walks into your office and says, "I'm gay—and I think I'm in love with you." Do you . . .

A. explain to him that you're not gay, but are very flattered, and if you were gay, he'd be the man.

B. tell him he's made you very uncomfortable and to never bring it up again.

C. drop your pants.

(3) You've just bought that $75,000 home you've had your eye on for the past five years. Two hours after your family has moved in, the doorbell rings, and you open the door. There stands a 400-pound black woman with no teeth and thirteen kids who says, "We's just hit da lottery and we be movin' next door." Do you . . .

A. congratulate her; welcome her in

B. congratulate her, then quietly put your home up for sale.

C. kill them all, then tell the police you saw some hippies in the neighborhood chanting "Acid is groovy."

(4) You're a white, upper middle class Lutheran. Your daughter, Becky, just eloped with a Brooklyn Jew named Murray. Do you . . .

A. throw them a surprise reception.

B. disown her.

C. feed Murray tainted lox.

(5) The new partner at the law firm is a woman. She scored the highest in her law school, was a successful public defender for three years, and academically and spiritually runs circles around you. She also has great tits. Do you . . .

A. disregard her physical beauty and look at her only as a colleague.

B. when she says things like "I'd like to see the facts in that case," reply back, "I'd like to see the facts in your case."

C. keep dropping your pencil in court and looking up her skirt.

(6) When your best friend says he believes Ted Kennedy is a good and honest man who cares about the people, do you . . .

A. respect his opinion.

B. laugh.

C. drop him off the Chappequidick Bridge.

(7) Your company is looking to hire someone for a specific job and asked you to pick the right candidate. After scouring over the resumes, you've picked the best candidate and set up an appointment. When he shows up, he is suffering from Muscular Dystrophy and is in a wheelchair. Do you . . .

A. hire him anyway despite his handicap.

B. interview other candidates before making the choice.

C. tell him you like all the Jerry Lewis movies, then wheel the crip out of your office.

(8) Your secretary breaks down one day and tells you her father used to sexually abuse her as a child. Do you . . .

A. comfort her.

B. act nervous and tell her you're late for an appointment.

C. call her dad to get "all the details."

(9) Your terminally ill father tells you he can't take the pain any longer and intends to commit suicide. Do you . . .

A. respect his dying wish and hold his hand until the end.

B. act nervous and tell him you're late for an appointment.

C. respect his dying wish, hold his hand until the end—then go through his pockets.

(10) Your best friend confesses that not only is he gay, but he tested positive for AIDS. Do you . . .

A. make sure his remaining days are spent happily

B. hide your shock, and stop calling him.

C. call him a "queer" and hit him with a baseball bat.

Give yourself 10 points for all your "A" answers—20 points for all your "B" answers and 30 points for all your "C" answers.

100-140 points: Congratulations! You are so politically correct, Willie Horton could marry your daughter and I doubt you'd even blink. In fact, you've probably still got a poster of Magic Johnson hanging somewhere in your house.

150-220 points: You're trying to be politically correct, but you still don't have the knack for it. Wash a few lepers, kiss a few AIDS patients, throw some paint on a dame in a mink, then come back and try again.

230-300 points: You're David Duke!

The National Federation of the Blind claimed responsibility for the cancellation of the low-rated ABC comedy *Good and Evil*. The group picketed ABC's New York headquarters and other affiliates because of the insensitive portrayal of a blind character. In one episode, the group objected to the blind character entering a laboratory wildly wielding a cane. He practically demolished the lab, fondled a man he thought was a woman and made a sexual pass at a coat rack.

Jil McIntosh

Recently in the comic strip Ernie, character Sid Fernwilter remarked that women are somewhere between men and chimpanzees. The cartoonist included a panel explaining that the remark was only made because Sid was a sleaze. Of course, that didn't stop some readers from complaining.

The problem was that the cartoonist used a perfectly acceptable line; unfortunately, the wrong person said it. Had a woman remarked that men were between women and apes, there probably wouldn't have been any outcry at all.

Why is it that slurs against some—but not all—groups are intolerable? For instance, it's currently acceptable in advertising to show women excelling at small tasks, such as making instant bouillon or ordering cream cheese instead of butter, while men stand by, clumsy and inefficient. No ads show a woman playing the dummy instead.

If there's a character running around aimlessly, such as the fellow who is virtually ignored by everyone until it's time to get his muffler fixed, it's always a man. It simply isn't correct to portray a woman as addled as these men.

Women definitely have the upper hand in the media right now. They can select a mate on the strength of the whiskey he drinks, without being considered shallow. They can proudly inform others that they own a company, without being boastful. They can walk in on men who cannot run their business properly and, with a few suggestions and a telephone line, make everything work. Would an advertiser show two confused women saved by a man?

The Merchant of Venice is banned because a Jew is portrayed as money-hungry. Yet the cheapest product in many model lines is called the "Scotsman," and there's nothing wrong with using a Scot in your ads if you want people to know that the product is economical.

A comedy can't portray blacks as happy-go-lucky simpletons, but there's nothing wrong if these same idiots are farmers from rural (Canadian) Maritime provinces, or those from the rural South. Native people must never be shown intoxicated (unless they later rise above it to become Noble Savages) but Germans, who are just as prone to alcoholism as any other group, are constantly shown at festivals with huge mugs of beer even thought these festivals occur no more fre-

> Either everyone is in on the joke, with open season on everyone, or the joke is abandoned altogether.

quently than Christmas.

Racist remarks should be unacceptable no matter who utters them, or who they are leveled against. It's difficult enough for most adults to figure out the pecking order. What about children? How can we expect them to understand that Scrooge McDuck is okay, but old Looney Tunes cartoons aren't because they portray minstrel shows?

How do we teach where to draw the line? The only way is by redrawing those lines. Either everyone is in on the joke, with open season on everyone, or the joke is abandoned altogether.

Jil McIntosh is a freelance Canadian journalist.

Looking for job announcements, Ernie sits down with the last dozen issues of *The Chronicle of Education*.

CONTRADICTIONS

Darryl Hattenhauer

For the first time, instead of turning directly to the job announcements, he reads the the articles.

He reads that the courts have ruled that professors can be fired for swearing in class. He reads about the President of Rexall College of Pharmacy, who was fired for sexual harassment after patting a woman's knee.

He reads about a spokesperson for minorities who says that Blacks and Hispanics have higher rates of AIDS, and that therefore Blacks and Hispanics should be the ones hired to spread the word about prevention. He reads that a white is a racist for saying that one has a higher risk of contracting AIDS from Haitians, hemophiliacs, central Africans, heroin addicts, American inner-city Blacks, homosexuals, and Hispanics.

He reads about racist white universities, where blacks are constantly reminded of their race. He reads that blacks should go to all-black colleges so they can be constantly reminded of their heritage.

He reads that racism denies black athletes the educational background to become sports managers. He reads that an official with the Los Angeles Dodgers was fired for saying that black athletes lack the educational background to become sports managers. He reads about a college president who was fired for writing privately, "I am not sure how many under-represented students are ready, emotionally, and intellectually, for a university experience." He reads about a minority spokesperson who states, "Most black students, unless they come from a very affluent family, don't know anything about graduate school."

He reads an article called "Colleges Try New Techniques in Fierce Competition for Black Students." The article says Dartmouth, whose conservatism Ernie hates, has given up trying to recruit bright black students from the ghetto and now concentrates on finding them in the middle-class suburbs.

He reads that Miami University of Ohio has been trying to hire minorities, but the most qualified candidates were still generally white, so the university eliminated whites from its searches.

He reads that after the Bakke

> He reads a complaint that journalists mention the race of blacks but not whites. He reads that journalists should point out when athletes are black so blacks will have role models to look up to.

decision, WASP male students who would formerly have been admitted are now being denied, even if they are more qualified than some of the members of the "protected classes" who are admitted. He reads that a black student has complained about those who "imply that we're taking the places of more qualified whites." He reads that the University of California's higher admission standards for Asians is not discrimination but "an administrative goal."

He reads an article about a movie called *Soulman* that is racist because it features a black woman as a single mother and because it encourages the audience to laugh at racism. He reads an article about *Soulman* that mentions the director is black. He reads that the racist media ignore the plight of the black single mother, and he reads about a new edition of Langston Hughes' *Tales of Semple*.

He reads a complaint that journalists mention the race of blacks but not whites. He reads that journalists should point out when athletes are black so blacks will have role models to look up to. He reads about racist white journalists who present athletes as role models.

He reads about a white boy who was

beaten by blacks and becomes a racist. He reads about a black who was mistreated by whites and developed a "cognitive schema."

He tries to stir himself from his stupor by looking at the job announcements. After much futile searching he finds a composition job: " . . . Teaching load will consist of courses in spelling, grammar, basic English, and English for automotive curriculum students." The job is at Carmel Community College. *Well why not, Ernie?* he thinks to himself. *If you've got to be miserable, it might as well be in a nice place.* So he writes to them. Another hour lost. Another five dollars bet.

Carmel Community College writes back. They send an application form. And they tell him he must fill out; sign, and return the voluntary anonymous affirmative action form, on which it states that in the California Junior College system, "no one will be hired who has been accused of a sexcrime." Well, he hasn't been found guilty of anything. Then he reads the notice again.

Darryl Hattenhauer teaches at Arizona State University West. He is a writer of literary criticism and is currently working on a novel.

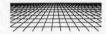

Shopping for a "PC" book?: *Shopping for a Better World* (Ballantine) rates 2000 products as to which perform animal testing and which don't. It also rates products on whether manufactures give to charity, advance female employees and minorities, are not involved in South Africa and support the environment.

Black or African-American—which is it to be if you want to be "PC"? The next time a "person of color" takes offense at not being labeled African-American, refer them to a 1991 Temple University poll by political science professor Michael Hooper, in which he found just 40% of Philadelphia's black community prefers the term African-American. This begs the more general "PC" question: when groups *demand* they be identified in a certain fashion, are they supported by those they claim to represent?

The Top Ten Most/Least PC of 1991

Bill Paige

Well, it seemed like a good idea at the time.

That's what the Children of The Sixties are saying about today's use—let's call it abuse—of the phrase "Politically Correct."

(William Safire says Karen DeCrow, a former president of the National Organization for Woman, coined the phrase in a 1975 speech; DeCrow says Mao Tsetung used it long before she ever did.)

In the good old days of rage, Political Correctness simply meant being on the right side (that is, somewhere left of center) of such issues as racism, feminism and gay rights. It meant accepting the notion that for far too long, "History" has really only been the history of white males.

For those progressives who actually thought about changing the world (and for a while, did), being PC meant working to neutralize policies and politicians that were obviously wrong-headed about life's most important elements: Sex (free love, not possessiveness), Drugs (pot and acid, not heroin and speed) and Rock 'n' Roll (Grateful Dead and Jefferson Airplane, not Perry Como and the Lettermen). For the passive majority, it meant giving brothers and sisters enough space to find their own identity.

Things are different today. The PC lines have become smeared by the sweat of special interest groups and extreme factions within mainstream organizations looking to convert (pervert?) as many as possible to their way of thinking, regardless of how many truths they distort. In fact, the concept of Political Correctness has become so corrupted that conservatives and traditionalists now use it as a term of derision against liberals whose attitudes on equality for women, gays and minorities (they say!) shadow other fundamental rights, especially free speech.

The most obvious examples of this blurring can be seen on the nation's college campuses:

✧ A 1989 survey by the American Council on Education and the National Association of Student Personnel Administrators showed that 60 percent of the colleges and universities polled had written policies on bigotry, racial harassment or intimidation.

✧ An orientation handout at Smith College rhetorically asked students if they had ever been guilty of *ableism* (prejudice based on someone's physical ability); *ageism* (prejudice based on a person's age); *classism* (prejudice based on social and/or economic class); *Eurocentrism* (prejudice toward anything having to do with Western culture) or *lookism* (prejudice based on the way people look).

✧ Derek Bok, retiring president of Harvard University, told a group of newspaper editors that the PC phenomenon doesn't really exist.

And so the worm turns.
The watershed event of this

Republican doublespeak (what else to call it?) occurred at the University of Michigan's graduation ceremony in May 1991; President George Bush's commencement address attacked the very notion of Political Correctness, claiming that it had led to "inquisition" and "bullying" on some college campuses.

"Ironically, on the 200th anniversary of our Bill of Rights, we find free speech under assault throughout the United States," Bush told the school's 8,300 graduates and 55,000 others gathered in a football stadium. "And although the [political correctness] movement arises from the laudable desire to sweep away the debris of racism, sexism and hatred .. . It declares certain topics off-limits, certain expressions off-limits, even certain gestures off-limits. What began as a cause for civility, has soured into a cause of conflict and even censorship."

Really? George Bush said all of that in favor of free speech? The same George Bush who, following the lead of his predecessor, Ronald Reagan, has appointed Supreme Court justices who ordered doctors and nurses to stop talking about abortion in federally-funded family-planning clinics? Who vetoed a rigorous civil rights bill? Who was forced to accept a compromise version of that bill only after his status among women voters was damaged by the Senate Judiciary Committee's flagrant humiliation of Anita Hill during Clarence Thomas' Supreme Court confirmation?

The prime-time Hill vs. Thomas broadcast (what else could keep Americans glued to the tube other than repeated references to porn films and penis size?) was not only 1991's most visible public debate on sexual harassment, but also a startling display of how seriously a pack of rabid white males are willing to take charges of sexual harassment from the most credible black woman.

The not-so-subtle message conveyed by Senators Alan Simpson and Howell Heflin was that Hill lived in "a fantasy world."

Politically Correct? *Not!*
So while the temptation is great to simply list the members of that disgrace-

ful panel as the year's greatest PC offenders, it would leave too little room to expose those who prefer to promote their narrow agenda in relative obscurity.

Here, then, are "my" nominations for the **Most Politically Correct** and **Least Politically Correct** people and events of the past year. For purposes of this exercise, consider the MPC group as those special interests who squawk the loudest about injustice and the spineless wimps who bend over to appease them; the LPC as those who refuse to hide their version of the truth under a barrel, regardless of who they know it's going to piss off.

There are others, of course; you can find candidates in any newspaper any day of the week. Also, beware of wolves in sheep's clothing. There are heroes and villains perched on both sides of the fence.

Donald Wildmon

1991's Top Ten Most Politically Correct

1.) The **American Family Association**, headed by the **Rev. Donald Wildmon**, is considered too PC by most people—even other fundamentalist Christians. Each month, Wildmon's AFA *Journal* (published and mailed out of Tupelo, Mississippi, birthplace of Elvis Presley, with some of the group's $6 million annual budget) urges the AFA faithful to protest and boycott sponsors of entertainment Wildmon doesn't like. Television is Wildmon's prime focus, via the spinoff group CLeaR-TV (Christian Leaders for Responsible Television). CLeaR lashes out against the advertisers of programs like *Northern Exposure, Murphy Brown, Roseanne, L.A. Law, Married, With Children, Anything But Love*, and other shows obviously designed to trigger the downfall of Western civilization. Wildmon particularly dislikes episodes that dare to take serious social issues out of the closet—AIDS, homosexuality, pregnancy, abortion, etc. His venom extends to the secular news media, which to Wildmon's way of thinking runs far too many anti-religion stories; school sex education programs and K-Mart (because subsidiary Waldenbooks sells *Playboy*

and *Penthouse*).

The AFA *Journal* recently took the Disney empire to task for being "taken over by the 'politically correct' crowd that gives big money exclusively to leftwing (sic) politicians and supports all the chic causes—especially when it comes to environmental issues." Another article lamenting the presence of PC themes on prime-time TV stated, "Conspicuously absent from prime time's laundry list of 'socially responsible' images are portrayals of such middle American concerns as religious faith, old-fashioned patriotism and even occasional respect for authority." Do people actually believe this stuff? You bet they do.

Wildmon claims he's simply making America safe for "decent" people; most people think he's simply crazy.

2.) Another group seeking to "greenmail" corporate America into removing ads from certain "objectionable" shows, **Concerned Viewers for Quality Television** of Wilmington, Delaware, was forced to admit defeat last fall when its highly-publicized "Turn Off Your TV Day" failed to influence any change in television viewer-

> The *New York Times* criticized the dictionary's editors for "sanctioning the jargon of special interest groups," particularly feminists who successfully lobbied for the inclusion of such words as "womyn," "herstory" and "waitron."

subordination" of women through pictures or words as a progression that ends with "snuff" photos and films, in which women are killed as part of the sexual experience. Despite failed efforts to turn MacKinnon's radical views into legal ordinances in Minneapolis and Indianapolis (strong opposition came from the Feminist Anti-Censorship Task Force), there are constitutional theorists who believe she eventually will succeed in making pornography, which has no legal definition, exempt from First Amendment protection.

4.) **Beverly LaHaye**, president of the conservative **Concerned Women for America**, gets the nod for challenging a People for the American Way report on book censorship in American schools, accusing PAW of being "outside the American mainstream and totally out of touch with parents." Talk about the pot calling the kettle black! The PAW report showed that among the books attacked were John Steinbeck's *Red Pony* and *The Grapes of Wrath; Adventures of Huckleberry Finn and Tom Sawyer* by Mark Twain and Webster's Ninth Collegiate Dictionary. We can't have Johnny looking up how to spell dirty words, now, can we?

5.) Speaking of dictionaries, the new **Random House Webster's** College Dictionary prided itself on having vanquished a wide range of sexist stereotypes, advising users to substitute "housekeeper" for "cleaning woman" and "bellhop" for "bellboy." *The New York Times*, however, criticized the dictionary's editors for "sanctioning the jargon of special interest groups," particularly feminists who successfully lobbied for the inclusion of such words as "womyn," "herstory" and "waitron." The editors, who themselves might be persuaded to call their critics Grundys ("narrow-minded conventional" people) convincingly argue that the more than 180,000-entry dictionary is "descriptive" rather than "prescriptive."

6.) Is it courage or cowardice that keeps the **City University of New York**

ship. Overnight ratings from A.C. Nielsen showed that 61.8 percent of households tuned into prime time on October 29, compared with 61.5 percent that watched one year earlier. The organized protest was countered by "Turn On Your TV Day," sponsored by the New York chapter of the Gay and Lesbian Alliance Against Defamation.

3.) While it's relatively simple to dismiss the repugnant doctrine of Andrea Dworkin (i.e., all sexual encounters between men and women constitute rape), consider the more appealing agenda of **Catherine MacKinnon**, a tenured professor at the University of Michigan Law School. "MacKinnon stands as a sort of polestar at the apogee of feminist law," writes Fred Strebeigh in *The New York Times Magazine*, "exerting a pull that seems magnetic, influencing even those who steer divergent courses . . . " It was MacKinnon who wrote the book on sexual harassment in the workplace in 1979. It was MacKinnon who pioneered the concept of "hostile environment," upheld by the Supreme Court in 1986. Her current campaign against pornography portrays the "graphic sexually explicit

(CUNY) from firing **Leonard Jeffries, Jr.**, chairman of the school's Afro-American Studies Department? CUNY board officials have been urged to take action against Jeffries because of a speech he made last July in which he accused Jews of financing the African slave trade and conspiring with the Mafia to demean blacks in movies. Further, Jeffries has distributed booklets in classes that maintain that the skin pigment melanin gives black intellectual superiority; he also refers to those of European descent as greedy, materialistic "ice people," and to Afro-Americans as humanistic and communal "sun people." Chief among Jeffries' critics are Governor Mario Cuomo and Senator Alfonse D'Amato, who calls the chairman's support via taxpayer dollars "an outrage." CUNY trustees have refused to remove Jeffries from his position citing academic freedom.

7.) The **Philadelphia Inquirer** showed its sensitive side by apologizing for an editorial that suggested poor black women should be given free Norplant contraceptive implants. "Ironically, the apology kicked off a second round of mail criticizing the newspaper for wimping out on a stand that was rare in its boldness and candor," observed syndicated columnist Clarence Page. The Inquirer's embattled editorial page editor, Dave Boldt, urged readers to accept the fact that newspapers make mistakes. "We're writing the first draft of history," Boldt said. Maybe Dave should just take a poll of some focus groups to see how history should turn out.

8.) In another bizarre pressure groups confrontation, **Sears** Roebuck discontinued sales of a line of stuffed animals because of protests by **The Wildlife Legislative Fund of America** and **National Rifle Association**. Both groups called Sears insensitive to hunters because eight percent of the wholesale price of the toy animals (ranging in price from $13 to $325) was being donated to the Humane Society of the United States. The Wildlife Legislative Fund described the Humane Society as "a hard-line animal-rights organization." A Sears spokeswoman told

The New York Times, "We're eating 67,000 stuffed animals." Any of 'em crows?

9.) The aforementioned People for the American Way report, which cited a 20 percent increase in attacks on the freedom to learn, also exposed the anti-*Impressions* group **EXCEL15** (Excellence in Children's Educational Literature). PAW President Arthur Kropp blamed "far Right or religious Right" groups for 45 challenges to the *Impressions* reading series, which its foes claim expose children to violence and witchcraft and encourage them to question authority. EXCEL15 says some 1,500 U.S. school systems use *Impressions*, which includes works by A.A. Milne, Martin Luther King, Jr., Maurice Sendak, Dr. Seuss, Rudyard Kipling and C.S. Lewis. The controversy has prompted dozens of parents to run for school board seats, even though most board officials agreed that "single-issue" candidates are not helpful in making the broad range of decisions facing schools.

10.) **Illinois Republican Congressman Henry Hyde** sponsored the Collegiate Speech Protection Act of 1991, which would ban schools from punishing any student for speech protected by the First Amendment. But Jay Miller of the Illinois ACLU, who has known Hyde for 20 years, remarked: "[Hyde] wants to protect the kinds of speech you hate: racist, homophobic and sexist kinds of things. He represents a right-wing group and they're coming out for free expression for themselves." Perhaps Hyde would have had more luck sabotaging the efforts of fellow Illinois lawmaker Sidney Yates. Yates engineered the so-called "corn for porn" deal that effectively killed Senator Jesse Helms' proposed anti-obscenity restrictions on grants issued by the National Endowment of the Arts.

✦

1991's Top Ten Least Politically Correct

1.) "Like her hero the Marquis de Sade, **Camille Paglia** considers herself an independent thinker who shocks." That's how *Playboy* introduced an interview with this Yale Ph.D., who is currently an associate professor of humanities at the University of the Arts in Philadelphia. Paglia's *Sexual Personae: Art and Decadence From Nefertiti to Emily Dickinson* is a preposterous 700-page deconstruction of feminist rhetoric that has infuriated academics and feminists alike. "It was intended to please no one and to offend everyone," Paglia says of the book. "Art history as written is completely sex free, repressive and puritanical. I want precision and historical knowledge, but at the same time, I try to zap it with pornographic intensity." Paglia also has attacked the concept of Political Correctness, telling Celia Farber of *Spin*: "Liberal, conservative—those words are now meaningless. They belong to a vanished era. Most liberals today are utterly incoherent. Liberalism has generated nothing but a bunch of push-button feel-good emotions. It is not a political system." All this and she loves heavy metal. Wow.

2.) Although it may be hard to imagine anyone surviving in politics carrying around as much hate baggage as **David Duke**, nearly 700,000 Louisianans supported him for governor last November. Think about it: Hundreds of thousands of people surrendered their precious vote to a former grand dragon of the Ku Klux Klan who, during his college years, peddled anti-Semitic literature while wearing a Nazi uniform. Duke really bought into the Third Reich's "big lie" strategy. He thought that by constantly characterizing his bigotry as "youthful indiscretion" others also might see it that way. His critics countered with the argument that Duke expressed racist views well into his 30s and that his opposition

> "It was intended to please no one and to offend everyone," Paglia says of her book.

to affirmative action and welfare are thinly veiled examples of racism. Fortunately, concern about Duke's ability to attract new business to the state (especially another Super Bowl, which NFL officials had said would never go to New Orleans if DuKKKe was in office) forced residents to choose between the lesser of two evils and re-elect former Governor Edwin Edwards, an alleged gambler who was acquitted on federal racketeering and fraud charges in 1986.

Unfortunately, Duke has decided to enter a number of Republican Presidential primaries, "to help keep George Bush in line." Feminists note: In 1976, Duke co-wrote a guide for women called *Finderskeepers*, which included this advice on dating older men: "You don't want a man to be great in bed one night but unable to recognize you on the street the next day because of rapidly advancing senility."

3.) Former *Out Week* editor Michelangelo Signorile helped found **Queer Nation** (dubbed "the angriest, nerviest in-your-face gay-rights group" by *Newsweek*) because he disagreed with ACT UP's continued focus on AIDS-related issues. Picketing, "kiss-ins" and political lobbying, specifically for a hate-crimes bill in New Mexico, are just a few of QN's aggressive tactics. In 1991, Tennessee-based Cracker Barrel Old Country Store fired a dozen gay workers because their "sexual preferences fail to demonstrate heterosexual values which have been the foundation of families in our society." QN/Atlanta responded by regularly picketing Cracker Barrel restaurants, and staging a sit-in on Mother's Day. "Queer Nation makes everybody else look reasonable," says gay San Francisco journalist Randy Shilts. The group is having trouble remaining PC within its own ranks, however, as minorities and women encourage a louder voice for their own agenda. Still, the fringe group has raised the temperature on gay rights issues with its catchy slogan, "We're here. We're queer. Get used to it."

4.) It's a sure bet you won't see David Duke attending a Queer Nation rally with "gangsta" rapper **Ice Cube**? Released last fall, Ice Cube's vicious hate opus, *Death Certificate* (Priority Records), featured an unconscionable stream of racist, misogynistic and homophobic street invectives. The album entered the Hot 100 at No. 2 and generated outrage upon outrage, even from *Billboard* magazine. "[Cube's] unabashed espousal of violence against Koreans, Jews, and other whites crosses the line that divides art from the advocacy of crime," the normally timid trade magazine editorialized. "Each of us must decide whether or not Ice Cube's record is fit to sell or purchase." Granted, kids are buying Ice Cube's bleak vision of the truth and the majority of hate crimes are committed by youth. But those who would make a connection between rap music and gang violence are going at it backwards. When will they start trying to solve the real problems of a government and culture that has produced the anger of an Ice Cube?

5.) **Dinesh D'Souza**, a former domestic policy analyst in the Reagan administration and current fellow at the American Enterprise Institute, ruffled academics' feathers with his book, *Illiberal Education: The Politics of Race and Sex on Campus*. D'Souza blames campus affirmative action policies for lowering academic standards to increase minority enrollment. He argues that college campuses often are forced to establish a PC agenda to keep the peace among minority groups who feel disillusioned and alienated because they cannot live up to academic expectations. "All of this because universities want to keep conversations about preferential treatment [for minorities] out of the public eye," D'Souza says.

6.) **Prodigy Services Company**, a joint venture between I.B.M. and Sears Roebuck, got an earful from the Anti-Defamation League of B'nai B'rith when it permitted anti-Semitic messages to appear on its computer bulletin board. Prodigy claimed that the most offensive communication—including the line, "Hitler had some valid points too . . . Remove the Jews and we will go a long ways toward avoiding much trouble"—was never posted for viewing by all 1.1 million Prodigy users. "The fact that some of the ideas expressed are not correct as defined by any one group does not mean that they should be denied a forum," said Prodigy President Ted Papes.

7.) Any organization that gets Jane Weidlin (ex-Go-Gos) into her skivvies to protest the wearing of fashion fur has my vote of approval, but officials in the fur, meat and cosmetics industries are wondering if they'll ever awaken from the nightmare called **People for the Ethical Treatment of Animals**. PETA lashes out at anyone and everyone promoting the sale of fur coats, from American Express to the daytime soap opera "As the World Turns."

The group also trots out (hope I don't get in trouble for that pun!) highly-charged language to campaign against horse-drawn carriages in Washington, D.C.; the consumption of turkey at Thanksgiving dinners (45 million slaughtered last year!); animal experimentation by cosmetics companies, especially L'Oreal and Gillette; automobile safety tests by General Motors that use ferrets and pigs; educational programs that utilize live animals and any Hollywood production that depicts animals in a negative light. PETA *News* lauded Elvira, Mistress of the Dark, for turning down $10,000 to work with an elephant on "Circus of the Stars." For just $10, however, you can order PETA's own video, *Cheap Tricks*, which shows examples of mule diving, pigeon bowling, lion taming and ostrich racing. We're sure that it's not exploitative, however. Nope. No way.

8.) What was **Barbara**, a waitress at Bette's Ocean View Diner in Berkeley, California, trying to accomplish by refusing service to a male customer who was reading Nat Hentoff's article, "The State of Freedom: Looking for Vital Signs in the Bill of Rights" in *Playboy* magazine?

Did she think that her moral outrage would result in a *Playboy* "read-in" at the restaurant a few weeks later? Did she think Bobby Lilly of the National Organization of Women's East Bay chapter would say, "I'm concerned about the way . . . feminists are playing into the hands of the religious right"? Did she think a pack of radical lesbians would scream and throw hot dogs dipped in catsup at supporters of the First Amendment? Did she think at all?

9.) This list wouldn't be complete without **Ted Turner and fans of his Atlanta Braves**, for doing the "Tomahawk Chop." While many people considered the Chop (as well as such sports team nicknames as the Braves, Indians, Seminoles, Blackhawks and Redskins) a tribute to the fighting spirit of Native Americans, not everyone shared that perception. Aaron Two Elk of Atlanta, regional director of the American Indian Movement, called the Chop "dehumanizing, derogatory and very unethical." The love of Turner's life, Jane Fonda, refused to do the Chop after Native American groups protested that it constituted offensive racist mimicry (although Jimmy and Roselyn Carter kept chopping away). The bottom line is that we'll probably never see a revival of retired Braves mascot, Chief Nok-a-homa, who, in the 1970s, did a war dance whenever a Brave hit a home run.

10.) Finally, this hot flash from our Food Bureau: **Tofu**, once considered the world's most nutritionally correct edible, has been revealed as having more fat than white-meat chicken! OK, Linda McCartney, so it doesn't have a face or a heart, is low in sodium and a great source of calcium and protein. But according to *The New York Times'* Marian Burros, "A 4.2-ounce piece of tofu has 5 grams of total fat and a gram of saturated fat. Four ounces of a white-meat broiler [chicken] without skin has 1.7 grams of total fat and half a gram of saturated fat." Is nothing sacred?

So for better or worse, there are the nominees. No doubt other, more deserving characters have escaped our attention, but they'll just have to wait their turn (we'll get to you next year, Don Henley; that's a promise). Readers are invited to submit names and the good and evil PC deeds attached to them in care of this publication. Unless something drastic occurs in society, there will be enough to do another list next year.

---

*Bill Paige is **Playboy** magazine's public relations manager and a freelance writer covering music and First Amendment issues for Chicago's alternative **Heartland Journal**.*

AMERICA:
A Great Place
To Raise Your Kids

Ken Rand

Thousands, even dozens, of people from Mexico and other Latin American countries, not all with governments sympathetic to American interests, enter the country each day, except Sunday and Halloween, without proper credentials. Some are poor. Some don't even have pockets in which to carry proper credentials. Some talk funny, look funny, smell funny, and can't change a 20. Few can name the Chicago Cubs starting lineup.

"Wetback Crossing—Drive Muy Slowamente" signs dot freeways throughout the American southwest.

In the Caribbean, anything that will float—bathtubs, CIA weapons shipments, bales of marijuana or laundered money, rubber duckies, you name it—is used to transport jillions of Cuban axe murderers north to Florida every day, except Columbus Day and Popeye's Birthday. "Mon, we be tired ob de boss, de bananas and de loco Gringo touristas," they say.

Thor Heyerdahl proved the Pacific can't be crossed east to west by rubber duckie, but the Yellow Hoard still manage to reach our shores. Some sell their daughters to Arab harem merchants in the personal ads in the backs of American tabloids to afford passage on Qantas to LAX, where they are greeted by swarms of relatives who, while they know the casts and plots of 27 daytime soaps, still talk funny, look funny, smell funny and can't change a 20.

And now that the ex-evil empire is sub-dividing, and maps of the USSR are printed on toilet paper, expect a new surge in Soviet emigration and a shot in the arm to our potato soup, fur hat and orthopedic shoe industry.

The last straw: Bing Crosby's granddaughter has been replaced by a Klingon as weapons officer on the Enterprise

What's going on? Since the people who really know are too busy stealing hubcaps, we are forced to guess, just like economists.

Immigrants, fleeing war and poverty in bombed-out, disease-ridden foreign ghettos, come to live in war and poverty

> But immigration reform is not the answer to our missing pet problem. If we extinguish our Lady Liberty's noble flame, who will pick our lettuce, kick our field goals and get shot when our drug addicts rob our 7-11s?

in bombed-out, disease-ridden American ghettos. They sleep (as best they can, given the deteriorating quality of the average appliance carton, now mostly made in Korea) in our gutters and alleys, highway underpasses and freeway culverts, abandoned low-income housing projects and jails. They reject our nuclear family-unit way of life. They take advantage of our world-renowned kindness to strangers, including those from oil-rich countries, by over-burdening our welfare system. They steal our pets and eat them. They don't speak no American.

Cultural exchange groups (the Croatian Machinegun Folk Ensemble, the Sri Lankan Singing Goat-Herders, the Salvadoran Militia Chorus and Orchestra) infiltrate our gymnastic events, drive-in theaters, video game arcades, discos and roadside attractions, corrupting our artists with foreign ideas (peace, freedom, democracy). The Western movie has subtitles. Sports commentators rhapsodize over the swarthy sinew of athlete's whose names contain too many consonants. Our country's adversaries steal the spotlight on Arsenio, Oprah, Letterman and Larry King.

But immigration reform is not the answer to our missing pet problem. If we extinguish our Lady Liberty's noble flame, who will pick our lettuce, kick our field goals and get shot when our drug addicts rob our 7-11s?

Moreover, our sacred Minorities are not all imported. To achieve the lofty, coveted status of Minority, domestic-bred handicapped, vegetarians, gays, lesbians, animal rights activists, feminists, downwinders, pro-choicers, pro-lifers, environmentalists, creationists, single welfare mothers with AIDS and bad backs, savers-of-the-critter-of-the-week, honest politicians and real fiscal conservatives need not be unintelligible when they riot—only loud.

Is there a Final Solution to the Minority Question?

Consider: the existence of Minorities implies a majority. The Right tried to legitimize a majority, and thus contain the burgeoning Minority, by declaring the existence of a Moral, Silent Majority. That didn't work, not because nobody believes the Right, which nobody does, but it failed because the Right didn't understand the majority is outnumbered by the Minority.

You don't need CNN or Peter Jennings to understand this seeming paradox: Demonstrator = Minority = good. Demonstratee = majority = bad. That's it. One isn't a card-carrying Minority until one has been audited or arrested for trespassing or parading without a permit. One cannot riot in a three-piece suit.

No, homogenization of America's Minorities into a distinct majority can't happen. The American melting pot is a myth. Minorities in America will grow in number, diversity and volume until we all are a Minority, and deaf.

Then, with any luck, the Indians will go on the Warpath and kick us all out for good.

Ken Rand is a radio news director in Kemmerer, Wyoming and a free-lance writer. He will be writing a regular column for Factsheet Five.

If everyone that we Protestant, straight, male, anglos have ever made angry suddenly retaliates . . . then minorities will lose their leverage of guilt over us.

FROM LIP SERVICE TO FORKED TONGUE

Teri Wingender

It's not too often that a word or phrase comes along that makes me want to double cross my legs. Ever since Henry Miller posed the word 'fuck' in front of a proper noun, nowadays having an effect inasmuch as hanging pictures of naked cherubs in churches, there isn't an epithet I could say I'd renounce on the face of it. There is a far more detestable formation now in our lexicon than any other word I've heard. This is the concept known as *Politically Correct.* I know, it sounds obscene, especially after having to live with *new world order* for a terribly long time, but bear with me while we explore the etymology of it.

Like all fascist phraseology, this ideological hook for all of those dedicating themselves to a knee-jerk life of unexamined hyper-sensitivity has ordinarily been attached to "thinking," but is likely soon to be applied to "bedwetting," "fellatio," "dinner parties," and "memo writing." That's ordinarily how these things go. To be "politically correct" is yet another way to further dilute the English language and provide a cheap, bargain basement vocabulary to those who cannot on their own decide what is right and what is wrong to the exclusion of context, common sense and intent. Which, is of course, why "politically correct thinking" is a contradiction in terms. Words are not inherently bad, George Carlin once told us when he had more hair—it's how we use them that matters. Knowing what words are not nice to use at say, the Thanksgiving dinner table, but OK on your honeymoon night is pretty

> A little sense of
> humor goes a long
> way in dealing with
> political correctness.
> So does common
> sense.

much a matter of socialization, not soul-searching.

So now we have a growing body of words and phrases which are no longer acceptable according to special interest groups, social organizations and media organs (oops, that sounds dirty, doesn't it? Maybe "limbs" is better. No, wait a minute. Wouldn't want to offend any horizontally disadvantaged trees. Trees are people, too). In any case, it doesn't matter that you already *know* some words are not nice words, these other people in the groups aforementioned are now going to itemize them for you and make sure you do not use them. At least not at the charity balls. And to make up for the loss of some very vivid verbs and tremendously tactile terminology, they give us wish washy mean-nothings which I personally am not taking very well.

This new age of saying the right thing is different from the "do your own thing" period in our social history when *"consciousness raising"* and *"needing your own space"* were the parameters of a socially acceptable (at least in the suburbs) life. Then, it was at least funny. A 20-year old veteran detective of New York City's police department tells about the time he

was forced to take what the city called a *sensitivity training program*. Unfortunately, he did not call in sick. Among the generally known racial epithets at the time, this officer, who thought he'd heard them all, also discovered in the official written materials a cornucopia of words he had never encountered before in all the years of working the exquisitely dirty streets of the Naked City.

Among the instructions and information these officers received was a recommendation (for white officers) to acknowledge that "black people are human beings, too." The officers of color, however, could presumably skip this part, although they were likely informed of the *homo erectus* of ugly white women. Says the detective, "Most of the cops handled this new information fairly well, though anxious that they were going to be required to use endearments and touch each other." The detective, however, considering himself to have been a man of the world, asked his fellow officers about the condemned epithets and found that no one knew which "sensitivity training" officer had had enough insensitivity once to even *know* words like that.

Sand-up comic Paul Mooney has never been known for being "politically correct" though he has been observed to be correct about politics. Among his pithy predictions: "I was telling people Richard Nixon was a maniac *way* before he fucked up. *Waaaay* before he fucked up." Or: "Didn't I say Patty Hearst, when it was all over, was going to write a book, become a white woman again and go on Johnny Carson?"

Mooney, who is black, was furious the day Richard Pryor told his audiences he was not going to use the word "*nigger*" anymore. Pryor had recently returned to the United States from Africa and, says Mooney, "walking the sands of Egypt." The next time Mooney took the stage, at the legendary Comedy Store on Sunset Boulevard in Los Angeles, he raved to the black members of his audience, "Well, I been right here all this time Richard was in Africa and all of you are still niggers to me and I'm saying "nigger" and I'm not going to stop saying "nigger" so you can pay me five million dollars and maybe I'll stop saying "nigger" too. But for now, "niggerniggerniggerniggernigger . . . " Black people walked out of the room. Says another black comic, Dave Tyree, "I was amazed when they did that. They were storming out of the room and I'm saying, "Aw, you people don't understand *nothing*. I was so ashamed of black people, then." The point was, of course, all words are powerful, some words are ones only *you*, personally, privately and intimately have power over and no one can tell you that you don't. No one can take these words away from you. Not anybody, not any way, not any how. Says Paul, "It's like when a whore calls another whore a 'whore.' She can do that, but you call her friend a 'whore,' she's gonna run across the street and rip your eyes out."

A little sense of humor goes a long way in dealing with political correctness. So does common sense. If you are an inherently kind person, you do not ever need to know what is politically correct. If you are a mean and creepy person (i.e. a rectal gap) it's probably better that all us genuinely nicer people (those of us who only use the word "asshole" when ab-

solutely necessary) know that up front. Because if you have all the acceptable lingo written down for you, I won't know you're a rectal gap until you've already gotten what you want from me.

In the seventies, it was the liberals conjuring up "needing space" and "consciousness-raising." We were trying to be sensitive to our own injured psyches, and we weren't making anybody crazy but ourselves. In the nineties, the au courant sensitivities are neither liberal nor conservative, but simply fascist—we must be hypersensitive to everybody and often limited to only one correct phrase that simply obscures the meaning of whatever the hell we were trying to say in the first place. Which is sad and scary and makes me more claustrophobic than elevators ever will. Politically correct speech is another reason for just shutting your mouth when you don't have anything to say, nice or no. Silence is a lot more dignified. And if you can't get your tongue around exactly the perfect word that expresses how you really feel, look it up in your dusty old dictionary—one that was written before 1990, please.

The Association for Retarded Citizens of the United States voted to change its name to "The Arc" (an acronym for Association for Retarded Citizens). The group's president said parents of children with brain disorders would join the group if it changed its name. Following this logic the NAACP (National Association for the Advancement of Colored People) should change its name to the NAAAA or N4A (National Association for the Advancement of African-Americans) to boost membership.

THE "RAP" OF THE POLITICALLY CORRECT

Patrick Lawless

Recently in one of the small "giveaway" papers here, there was an editorial by a member of the staff which accused one of Kansas City's radio stations of being racist because their ads say they do not play "rap music." The ad in question also said that they don't play "sleepy Top 40" or "loud screaming rock," but this evidently didn't bother the columnist. What we have here, of course, is yet another example of the Politically Correct Thought Police in action. They look for racism, sexism, ageism, lookism, etc. everywhere and see it whether it is there or not. Their main concentration would seem to be on college campuses, where they do things like passing rules against what they call "inappropriate laughter," but as can be seen by the radio example, their numbers are increasing and so is their "Thought Patrol Area."

Most of us would agree that a radio station has the right to choose its format, and that they also have the right to tell people what their format is. Country stations play country, classical stations play classical, all news stations have all news, etc. But when a station specifically mentions that they do not play rap, it's suddenly "racist." I suppose the columnist would also accuse anybody who doesn't like rap music of being racist, ignoring the fact that different people have different preferences and that it has nothing to do with racism. Of course, a large part of the PCTP's missions seems to be to try to deny people the right to make choices, whether in music, literature or whatever. And if you choose "wrong" then you are found guilty of racism, or sexism or whatever "ism" they are looking for at the time.

Part of the solution to the problem of the PCTP is to show how ridiculous they are, as the comic strip Tank McNamara did recently, when some characters were concerned about "heightism" in basketball and demanded that the coach use a short basketball player.

Beyond that, we must continue to make our own choices in literature, music and all other areas of our lives. If we do not, other people will decide for us how we should think and act, until this is a nation where everyone thinks correctly, where everyone thinks alike.

Patrick Lawless is a freelance writer

My Dinner with the Politically Correct

Richard Dominick

Dinner was slated for eight. Being unfashionable and hungry, I arrived at the Tudor mansion early. Marilyn met me at the door.

"Richard, how nice of you to join us tonight," she said through enough white porcelain to make a bathroom sink. "How did you get here?"

"I took a cab."

"Was the driver Croatian?"

"Yes."

"Thank God. Last week I had a Yugoslavian driver, I almost died. I prayed Lena next door didn't see me."

We walked into the massive living room. The rug was Persian, the furniture Greek, the cook black.

Marilyn's husband, Kenneth, was behind the bar mixing vodka and tonics. He was a corporate lawyer, wealthy, loved golf, art, and was one of the few people left in America who thought Woody Allen was a genius. He waved when he spotted me.

"Richard. How do pussy cat."

I shivered at the sight and sound of him, but I smiled back. "Hi Kenneth."

"So glad you can spend the evening with us. After all, we are funding your next writing project. Drink?"

"Whiskey. No ice."

"Sorry kid," Kenneth said. "They'll be no corn mash products in this house tonight. Another corn farmer in Iowa blew off his banker's head, his wife's head, his two kid's heads and then his own head because low corn prices forced him to lose his farm. We're in mourning. Vodka?"

"Sure."

"Great."

Kenneth finished mixing the drinks, while Marilyn pulled me aside. "I hope you're not offended that our cook is black."

"Of course not. Why should I be?"

"Well, it was okay to use them as butlers, cooks and maids when they were called Negroes, but it wasn't right to hire them as servants when they were called Afro-Americans, what with all that 'Soul on Ice' stuff and all, but when they became blacks it was okay to hire them as servants again as long as you paid them a few dimes and quarters over minimum wage, but now that they're African-Americans we're supposed to be hiring them as literature professors at community colleges and things like that, not servants."

For some reason I asked, "So why did you hire him?"

Marilyn smiled sheepishly. "Well, his younger sister gave birth to a crack baby, and his older brother died in a homeless shelter. That makes him a little more desirable then just some black African-American, so I figured what the hell, it's okay."

"What did you do when you just called them niggers?"

"Hired them for one square meal a day and gave them a cot in the garage."

Kenneth joined us now and handed me my drink. I sat on one side of the loveseat, Kenneth and Marilyn sat on the couch.

"Mind if I smoke?" I asked.

"We're against smoking, of course," Kenneth said, "but we respect your heart and lungs, so please burn 'em up."

"Thanks."

"It's a good thing you're sitting where you are," Marilyn added.

"Why?" I asked.

"The loveseat's our smoking section." She slid an ashtray across the coffee table. "Enjoy."

I lit up and blew out a thick cloud of bluish smoke.

"Hors d'oeuvres will be out shortly," Marilyn informed me.

"Great," I said. "I'm starved."

"They're deviled eggs," Kenneth added. "After all, once you break an egg

> "After all, once you break an egg you're actually aborting a chicken baby, so we feel we're making a statement by serving them."

you're actually aborting a chicken baby, so we feel we're making a statement by serving them."

"And we have them deviled to show our openness to all religious beliefs, even the satanic."

I just nodded and continued smoking. It was then I heard the sound of a motor from behind the kitchen door.

"What's that sound?" I asked.

They both laughed. "It's a long story," said Kenneth, "but I'll shorten it for you. It's our butler."

"You have a mechanized butler?"

"No, no," he laughed. Well, in a way, I guess we do, yes. You see, we hired a—"

"Don't be shocked," Marilyn interrupted.

"Thank you dear," Kenneth cleared his throat and took a long drink from his vodka. "We hired a refugee from Bangla Desh as our butler."

"Forgive us," pleaded Marilyn.

"Forgive you? Why? I think it's great."

"Great? Haven't we taught you anything, Richard," Marilyn snorted. "Bangla Desh is a third world country. We should have taken him in, sponsored him, paid his way through Princeton."

> "We bought six paper place settings and keep washing them. We planted an evergreen in the back to replace the tree cut down to make the plates."

"Bought him a Volvo," added Kenneth.

"Taught him art, music, how to use a toilet," Marilyn said.

"So why did you do it?" I asked Marilyn.

"He lost his legs in a typhoon."

"He was pinned underneath a pig cart," Kenneth added. "For three days. It made him crazy."

"Emotionally distraught," corrected Marilyn.

"Yes. Emotionally distraught. He thinks he's a sitar. So when he comes out, pluck at his shirt."

"So no Ivy League university wanted him and you hired him instead."

"Yes," said Kenneth.

"But don't forget," added Marilyn. "Minimum wage is $4.20. We pay him $4.90 . . . with dental."

"And his teeth are very bad," Kenneth chimed in proudly.

We sat, drank and talked some more. Their legless Bangla Desh butler and his motorized wheelchair shot out of the kitchen door. He held up in his hand the silver tray of deviled eggs and spun around serving us. Kenneth was right, his teeth were very bad. I plucked at his shirt.

He smiled and made various sitar noises. I was impressed. Eventually we moved to the dining room, sat at the table and got ready for dinner. The table was set with silverware and paper plates."

"No china," I asked.

"Heavens no," Kenneth shrieked. "After their tanks ran over those students we threw all our china away. Democracy will always come before a proper place setting in this house."

Marilyn added, "We bought six paper place settings and keep washing them. We planted an evergreen in the back to replace the tree cut down to make the plates."

I nodded and smiled. I also looked down at my watch. "What's to eat?" I asked over the growling of my stomach.

"Can you guess?" Marilyn asked.

"I doubt it."

"Let me give you a hint. It's the only meat we'll eat because of this particular animal's overpopulation. If we didn't eat them, they would overpopulate and starve. In fact, already they've started starving and even killing themselves. Can you guess?"

"Deer? Venison?"

"No," Kenneth smiled. "Mexicans."

"You mean Mexican people," I said astounded.

"Yes. Babies to be exact. Female babies. The meat's whiter and much more tender. You have to kill and eat the females because they're breeders. We tried teenage girls at first, but by that age the meat was filled with knife wounds and bullet holes and tasted bitter from all the drugs and alcohol. But babies are fresh."

"What are you? Crazy? You can't eat human Mexican babies!"

"Sure we can," Marilyn chimed in. "If we didn't kill and eat them, they would only suffer and die. They would live in poverty, be hungry, sleep with rats and eventually either kill of be killed. There's just too many Mexicans. By killing some of them, it thins the population and the others live a better life. It's the right thing to do."

"Besides," added Kenneth. "It's not the Mexican's fault. It's those damn Catholics. They tell them to have babies or go to Hell. We're only doing the right thing. We're killing Mexicans, so that other Mexicans can live and live better. Everybody's doing it, Richard. Where have you been?"

It was then I stood up and looked down at my guests.

"Here's where I draw the line," I shouted. "It's one thing to be politically correct, but like anything else, once you begin taking it too seriously, start molding your life around your beliefs, it becomes a religion. And once there's enough people, it becomes an organized religion, and then you end up with a doctrine that tells you 'yes, it's okay to kill and eat Mexican babies!' Well you're not God! And you have no right to eat humans! And I refuse to join in! Goodnight!"

I headed towards the door, but Kenneth's voice stopped me.

"Dear boy, let me just say this. I can afford to be politically correct. Since I'm in a position of wealth and power, any opinions I have or decisions I make concerning others doesn't affect me—just them! That's the beauty part! When you're in the position I am, money talks buster. You may laugh at my political correctness, but I believe it pays your bills. After all, I'm funding your next writing project. Without my money and my beliefs, you'll have to get a job and pay your own way. You'll have to decide just how important your art is. Important enough to work all days at a meaningless job to support it?"

I stood facing the solid oak door which led outside.

"Well, boy?" He said. "What will it be?"

I turned around and looked at Kenneth. I planted both feet squarely on this plush carpeting. I put both hands on my hips. "I'll have a leg," I said heading back to the table.

Richard Dominick is a freelance writer.

SHOW US YOU'RE NUTS

Mental Health Group Dictates What Is And Isn't Funny

Duane Swierczynski

Mark Davis' office at the Philadelphia Mental Health Care Corporation (PMHCC) is covered with buttons.

And ribbons, and bumper stickers, and miniature posters—all emblazoned with every motivational slogan imaginable. "Go For It." "When Life Gives You Lemons, Make Lemonade." Even though Mark Davis seems to appreciate a good slogan, there was one slogan he discovered last summer while driving down I-95 that he *didn't* enjoy.

"I was kind of numb at first," recounted Davis. "You see this all the time, you hear this all the time. . . . then I got angry and I felt assaulted and basically, almost like that billboard was made for me personally, more or less. I though about all the people out there affected by a message like that."

The message was an ad for local radio station Eagle 106's (WEGX-FM) new morning show. The offending slogan: "Show us you're nuts."

"It sounded to me that it wasn't [sexual] nuts he was talking about," said Davis.

WEGX began the campaign to attract attention to their new morning show, the "Nut Hut," a four-hour mix of phone pranks, listener call-ins, song parodies, and music. "The idea was that people would call up with a bunch of outrageous things to do," described David S. Noll, the station's general manager. "It was meant to be tongue-in-cheek, not offensive." Such "Nut Hut" gags included getting viewers to shave their head and parade around Veteran's Stadium. These gags were meant to get the city talking about the show, spread a little laughter, get ratings up — not insult the mentally disabled.

Nevertheless, what was meant to stir a little talk about the "Nut Hut" stirred the ire of the Philadelphia Mental Health Care Corporation and Project SHARE, a mental health advocacy group. "I felt slapped in the face," said Sandra J. Walton of Project SHARE. "It's bad enough I have to fight stigma everyday. These signs are not small. They're big. Just to say 'You're Nuts' and they don't even know us! They did apologize, saying that they didn't mean to be offensive to the mental health field, but I'm sorry, I just felt that it was."

Advertising with slogans like "Show Us You're Nuts" and "Warning: Crazy People Are Coming" (from the 1989 Dudley Moore dud, *Crazy People*) contribute to a stigma about the mentally ill, according to Davis. "The stigma is rooted in fear, fear of catching a mental illness, fear of developing a mental illness, fear that or friend may have a mental illness. It was harder overcoming the stigma of mental illness than it was overcoming the actual mental illness itself. There's a deep history of this throughout the centuries."

Surprisingly, Davis is free with jokes

> "... when it's on a billboard, or used as the title of a show, it's offensive, and it's very much a violation of *our* rights."

delayed by lack of new advertising art, and eventually remained up along I-95, the Schuylkill Expressway, Roosevelt Boulevard, and Admiral Wilson Boulevard as late as December. Noll and WEGX have taken a "tightrope" approach to offending the PMHCC, never wholly apologizing for their campaign, yet recognizing that their campaign may have been offensive to the group. The PMHCC, however, sees the protest as a major victory for mental health "consumers," (rather than "patients"), writing in the fall issue of *Vision*, the group's newsletter: "Consumers ruffle feathers of 'Eagle 106.'"

Davis originally claimed to have been offended not so much by the show's concept but by its advertising, but later commented differently. "I really do object to the show's content," said Davis in retrospect. "We ourselves, people with mental illnesses, joke amongst ourselves. Only a person who's been through something can really have a sense of humor about it, truly understand what they're laughing at. It's healthy for us to have that kind of humor, but when it's on a billboard, or used as the title of a show, it's offensive, and it's very much a violation of *our* rights."

Ironically, Mark Davis' meeting with Eagle 106 didn't just give him the opportunity to define to *Gauntlet* what was funny and unfunny, and it didn't just earn him public affairs spots and an internship opportunity for the PMHCC. There were other perks. Like the tiny sticker reading "The Nut Hut, Eagle 106," on his slogan-plastered wall. The promo package of "Nut Hut" peanuts on his desk. And draped over his chair, a bright yellow "Nut Hut" t-shirt. How did Davis explain keeping offending promotions around his office? Again, by his own definition of humor.

"I think it's kind of funny," admitted Davis.

about the mentally ill, mostly consisting of self-deprecation. Why can he laugh about the mentally ill where others can't? "When we joke amongst ourselves, it's one thing, but when someone takes those jokes and puts them in a series of jokes, like Polish jokes, it hurts to hear those things about your ethnic background, disease, or illness."

Even though WEGX's advertising campaign wasn't designed to have anything to do with the mentally ill, both Davis and Walton complained to Noll and WEGX and demanded a meeting with the radio station after written requests were "ignored," according to Walton. As a result of the 75-minute meeting, WEGX promised to accept an intern from the PMHCC, prepare public-affairs spots on mental illness, and, according to Walton and Davis, apologize on-the-air.

Officially, morning host John Lander never apologized. Noll commented that the issue would be addressed on the air, but he wouldn't call it an on-the-air apology. The "offending" billboards were to be taken down in a month (then August), but not in response to the PMHCC complaint. "It was time for a new campaign," said Noll. The billboards were further

Duane Swierczynski is a free-lance writer, whose work has appeared in **Philadelphia Magazine**.

HEY, I GOTTA YOU "P.C." ... RIGHT HERE!

art by Alfred Klosterman

Don Vito Corleone

as told to

Thomas F. Monteleone

"So . . . " he says to me over a gilt-edged cup of steaming *capuchino*, "you're a writer . . . and a Siciliano?"

I nod, manufacturing a small smile.

"Good. That's-a good. We don't have too many of our boys grow up to be writers, you know. There was Mario, of course . . . And Frankie— Frankie Coppola. And now . . . (he pauses to sigh dramatically with a little shrug) . . . and now, we gotta *you*"

"You got me," I say firmly, but with *rispetto*.

"You got any idea why I ask you to come here today. . . ?" He leans back in his chair, bathed in the shadows of a long afternoon.

It is my turn to shrug (thankfully, I know all the right moves). "You always told me—someday you might ask even *me* for a favor."

"That's right, Tomasso. As you know, it doesn't matter to me how a man makes his living—even if he's gotta write in-a *Inglese* to make-a the money."

I smile, nod, but say nothing. It is obvious he plans to continue.

"You see, I was reading in *Time* magazine that everybody's gotta be more Politically Correct these days, and this article, it takes care of *everybody*! Everybody but us!"

"'Us' . . . ?" I ask tentatively.

He nods slowly, more with his eyes than his entire head. "*Us*," he says in that familiar half-whisper.

"Okay," I say softly. "*Gabeesh* . . . what can I do to help."

"I want you to write a—whaddya call it?— an article? An essay? for *this* rag here." He gestures diffidently at a thick publication with a garish cover depicting a multi-armed monster emerging from a living room television set.

"You mean *Gauntlet*?"

"Whatever it's called . . . it doesn't matter to me. What's important is that you deliver my message to *la pecora* —to the sheep."

"I think I can do that, no problem."

"Good. That's-a good." He steeples his hands as he leans forward on his polished desk. Leaning close to a desk intercom, he keys it, whispers into it: "Send 'im in . . ."

A door open in the shadows of the far end of the office and a forty-ish guy enters. He's dressed conservatively, a spare tire where his waist used to be—just a sport radial at this point, but if he doesn't watch the linguini, he's going to have himself an all-weather job. His face is round and he's doing a good job of looking like a candidate for Rogaine.

"This is Johnny 'the Scribe' Di-Ciancia," says Don Vito, as the man takes a seat to the left of the desk. "He's been helping me with this 'PC' thing."

"Nice to meet you, Johnny," I say, shaking hands.

Johnny is shy, I can tell by looking at him. He smiles thinly as he pulls out some papers from a folder he's carrying. "Okay, here's what we have in mind," he says, with a deferential look towards the Don.

I pull out my notebook computer, ready to type in any key phrases.

"First-off, we gotta get rid of these references to anything 'mob-related'."

"Okay."

"From now on," says Johnny, "it's gonna be '*large, frenzied, crowd-related*' . . . you got that?"

"Got it." I'm not crazy about it, but I definitely got it.

"And the ethnic slurs," says the Don. "No more guinea-goombah stuff, okay? No more wops, dagos, greaseballs, or spaghetti-benders."

"I covered all that, boss," says

> "That's good, but we're not done yet. What about when we need to whack somebody? The only hits I wanna hear about are the ones at Yankee Stadium."

Johnny. "If they wanna call us anything from now on—other than 'Sons of Italy' or 'Italian-Stallions'—I came up with '*pasta sculptors*'."

Inwardly I wince, but I look across the desktop which looms as large as strike force carrier. Don Vito's eyebrow's are arched as he considers this sobriquet.

"Not bad," he says after a moment. "Sounds kind of artistic—like Michelangelo, eh?"

"No question about it," I say.

"Okay, what's next?" He looks at Johnny the Scribe, gestures for him to continue.

"Why don't you let me just run down the list, boss . . . ?"

Don Vito nods. "I'll stop you if something grabs me the wrong way."

"All right," says Johnny. "Instead of 'muscling in,' it's now *increasing a market share*; a bookmaker: *short term investment broker*; prostitution: *analog dating service*; pimps: *affirmative action officers*; Protection: *neighborhood improvement contributions*; and bribes, which are now called *political action donations*."

Johnny the Scribe looks pleased with himself. He looks over at his boss, who is chewing on a piece of marzapan candy.

"That's good, but we're not done yet.

What about when we need to whack somebody . . . ? The only hits I wanna hear about are the ones at Yankee stadium."

"Okay,"says Johnny. "How about *waste management decision?*"

"I can live with that," says Don Vito.

"And hit-men could be *personnel termination actuators.* Victims: *the lethally challenged.*"

"Sounds like a great idea to me." Don Vito smiles, then finishes off his *capuchino* with a flourish and a raised pinky finger. "Whaddya think, Tommy?"

"Hey, this stuff is great," I say with mustered enthusiasm (okay, so I'm a chicken . . .). "A whole new era in media relations."

"Okay," he says to me. "You write this up, pretty-like, you know, so people'll like reading it. And make sure you let all these media-assholes understand—they've got a new vocabulary now. And they better *use* it."

"Or else they'll be *exploring alternate marine habitats,*" says Johnny.

"Huh?" Don Vito and I say simultaneously.

"Sleeping with the fishes," says 'the Scribe' with a sly grin.

"I like that," says the Man.

I add it to the list on the screen of my notebook, start going through the motions of finishing up. "Well, looks like I'm about ready to get to work," I say.

Don Vito looks at me, his eyebrows furrowed. "Haven't you guys forgotten something?"

I feel the sweat bursting out of me. Have we pissed him off? Are we *really* supposed to kiss his ring?

"Ah, what's that?" I manage to say weakly.

"The most important thing—and you two *mamalukes* don't *know*?!"

"Sorry, boss," says Johnny. "It's this middle-age thing—you know how it is. Sometimes I can't even remember what I had for breakfast . . . "

This last remark seems to strike a sympathetic chord in Don Vito. He nods gently, with genuine feeling.

"We need a new name for the organization," he says. "This 'mafia' thing . . . it's gotta go."

I look at Johnny the Scribe and he has this helpless look on his face. It's a desperate look that says:*I'm fucked, compaesano . . . I forgot all about this one . . . I got nothin' . . . "*

I suddenly feel this— this *absence* in my gut. It radiates outward like the blown-off ring of gases from a supernova, threatening to absorb me into its nothingness. *A New name!* He wants a new name and we got a big Zero here.

"So whaddya have for me?" asks the Man.

I'm staring at him, caressed by the shadows, when it comes to me.

I smile and gesture with my hands like I'm describing the size of a caught fish. "The new name," I say, "is *The Mothers And Fathers Italian Association.*"

Don Vito stands up, walks around the desk and hugs me with his usual style. "That's-a nice," he says. " . . . has a nice *family* ring to it."

Thomas F. Monteleone's latest novel is **The Blood of the Lamb**, *in hardcover from Tor Books, July, 1992.*

D-d-d-don't delay.
D-d-do your Holiday
shopping today!

The National Stuttering Project, which decided the Howard Stern Show was not offensive to stutters (see below) found the Warner Bros. Holiday merchandise catalog offensive with Porky Pig pitching holiday gifts. The same Ira Zimmerman, who was so fascinated by Stern's humor, found Porky Pig's s-s-stuttering "demeaning" and "in poor taste," while admitting Porky cartoons did not bother the group, the *USA Today* reported. True to its "PC" form Warner Bros. said an apology was sent to Zimmerman and the Porkmeister would not be included in the next catalog.

The National Stuttering Project called off its boycott of Howard Stern's radio show, in Los Angeles, after listening to 35 hours of his morning "shock-jock" program, which features a Stern sidekick "Stuttering John" Melendez. NSP spokesman Ira Zimmerman, in calling off the boycott said, "Stern's humor challenges all standards of civility. Stuttering is a small part of that. The Howard Stern show is funny and repulsive, and fascinating all at the same time. It's like watching a toilet overflow."

To accommodate pressure groups when *A Fish Called Wanda* aired on ABC-TV, the network edited all scenes involving a character stuttering . . . at the behest of the National Stuttering Project.

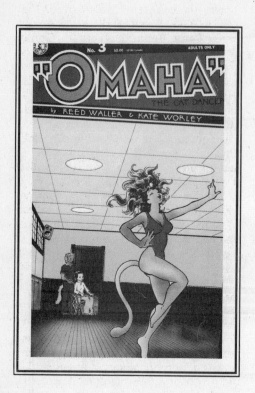

FINDING THE COST OF FREEDOM

Kate Worley

I write a banned comic book.

In fact, if you look at the record of obscenity trials involving comics, I write one of the most universally filthy comic books in the history of the medium. As I look back through the clippings file, several comics appear more than once (*Cherry, Weirdo, Elektra Assassin*), but one appears on almost every bust list since 1986. . . *Omaha, Omaha, Omaha*.

The sexual content of the book is proportionally small. I didn't realize how small until one zealous New Zealand defending attorney actually counted all of the panels in the first 3 volumes of *The Collected Omaha*, and found the percentage of sexually explicit material to be about 4 percent. There is little or no violence, sexual or otherwise. There have been issues with *no* sex in them whatsoever. What's the problem, then? Well, all the sex in *Omaha* is totally explicit, including penile erection and full penetration. We have also included homosexual acts, both male and female. And sex involving more than two persons. Not to mention fully nude dancing. According to some people, this is all made worse by the fact that our characters are funny animals.

I never expected that by writing this little black-and-white, adult funny-animal soap opera, I would learn about the history of obscenity law throughout the English-speaking world, but it's working out that way. And the cost is

comic "offended against current standards of propriety" and as such demanded "condemnation" under the 1876 Customs Consolidation Act. As "condemned" books, the comics were destroyed. The cost to Knockabout of these lost books was, Tony Bennett wrote to Denis Kitchen, "around $700 in various ways (not regretted)."

At the time that letter was written, in October of 1982, the police were also holding approximately $20,000 worth of stock for Knockabout, pending hearings.

Cut to May of 1990. Kitchen Sink Press publisher Denis Kitchen receives a letter from Titan Distributors Ltd. of the UK, explaining apologetically that they will no longer carry *Omaha*, since, with the recent increase of "adult" comic titles, Customs is being extra vigilant in their search and seizure activities, and it makes no sense, economically, to import a book they will never receive because the "Adults Only" label will cause it to be seized. *Omaha* is not, as of this writing, being imported into Great Britain.

I don't mean to cast aspersions on Titan, who carried us for many years. They were only dealing with the ugly reality of British Customs. You can see the nature of the Customs problem here:

about as high as a law-school education. For the comic book retailer, higher.

As I write this, several comic book shops in Toronto are up to their ass in alligators, fighting obscenity charges on a number of titles they carry, including the one I write, *Omaha The Cat Dancer*. The Canadian comic retailers have been under fire since 1985's *R. vs Wagner*, the court case that inculcated "feminist" principles into obscenity law in Canada. This gave rise to a slew of local cases throughout the country. This is a new and fascinating development in *Omaha*'s ongoing obscenity troubles in the Commonwealth countries.

We never got that far before. All the way into the country, wow!

Traditionally, *Omaha*'s difficulties in the Commonwealth countries have begun when the Customs people first opened the boxes. *Omaha* was initially published, as *Bizarre Sex #9*, in September of 1981. In October of that year, a shipment of 100 copies was seized by Customs and Excise in England. The case against the importing distributor, Knockabout Comics, was heard in October of 1982. Magistrate Audrey Frisby ruled against Knockabout owner Tony Bennett, agreeing with prosecuting solicitor David North that the

Seizure of material, long delay till hearings, economic loss, either through condemnation and subsequent destruction of material, or simply through unavailability for sale of the materials in question. (Anecdotal evidence also suggests that in at least some of the cases, the material is destroyed by Customs before a hearing takes place.)

This pattern is the same throughout the Commonwealth, and has in fact been repeated with regard to *Omaha* in Canada, Australia and New Zealand. In most of these reviews, most notably the 1990-91 case in New Zealand, *Omaha* itself has been completely vindicated. Which I'm

sure is much comfort to those importers whose seized material has already been destroyed. Okay, so the Brits (and Aussies and Canucks and all) have a set of antiquated laws preventing controversial material from even getting into their countries, at the whim of the government (actually, the whim of the individual government official).

Things are better here, right? Here we deal with things at the local level, and the people have an input . . . "community standards" and so forth. We have a First Amendment which at least permits argument in the courts, and that makes a difference. It is different here, isn't it? No, not very. And when it comes to the impact on the pocketbook, it may even be worse.

The most famous case involving comic books in this country (thus far), is the case of Friendly Frank. Frank Mangiaracina (now you know why they call him Friendly Frank) is an independent distributor of comic books in the upper Midwest, who also owned several retail comic book stores. On December 10,1986, the store in Lansing, Illinois was entered by six policemen who proceeded to arrest manager Michael Correa on charges of intent to disseminate obscene material. The store was then closed, by authority of

the building inspector, on a zoning violation which states that it was a violation to sell adult material with 1200 feet of a residential area.

While the store managed to reopen a few days later, Michael Correa remained under the charge of intent to disseminate obscene material, a Class A misdemeanor in Illinois. The arrest report, by Officer Anthony Van Gorp, reads as follows: " On November 28, 1986 Officer Zeldenrust and I west to Friendly Frank's Comic Shop. . . As we looked through the comics we noticed comic books depicting various sex acts, lesbianism, homosexuality etc. . . Officer Zeldenrust and I also observed youths looking through the comics. We also noticed that none of the comics were in a separate viewing area for adults. On December 3,1986 I went into the shop and purchased $41.10 of comics while Sgt. Hoekstra observed my actions from across the street. While I was in the store I observed a youth looking through a magazine with the words "The adult illustrated fantasy magazine" [presumably *Heavy Metal* - KW] on the cover. The store clerk made no attempt to stop the youth although he left the store after he noticed

. . .there was no civilian complaint against the store.With the exception [of one], all the cases involving comic books have been initiated solely by law enforcement officers.

I was watching him. The comics were brought to Markham Court and on the advice of the States Attorney's Office arrest should be made. At 1332 hours (1:32 P.M.) Michael Correa, store manager, was arrested on obscenity charges."

The books found obscene in writing were *Bizarre Sex #5* (featuring Omaha), *The Bodyssey, Heavy Metal, Murder* (#2 or #3 or both), *Omaha the Cat Dancer #1-3,* and *Weirdo #17-18*. In later affidavits, some books were added, then dropped, references to "satanically influenced" material were added, then dropped, and references to "youths" reading the material were dropped.

Note also that there was no civilian complaint against the store. This is true in most of the cases since 1986. With the exception of a recent case in Gainesville, Florida, all the cases I can find documented involving comic books have been initiated solely by law enforcement officers. Most statutes (including the one in Illinois) refer to material "the average person, applying contemporary, adult, community standards" would find as appealing to prurient interest. In practice, however, it appears that the persons applying such standards (whatever those are) is the average law enforcement officer.

Michael Correa was found guilty in a finding tendered January 13, 1988. He was fined $750 and put on one year's probation. The judge who presided at the bench trial, Paul T. Foxgrover, gave Correa a warning, telling him that he would be charged much more seriously if he were ever brought up in a similar case. Correa, having been reviled in some local press, including the paper in his home town of Gary, Indiana, resigned his position as manager of Friendly Franks, which he had held for two years.

In September of 1989, the Lansing store closed, having lost its lease. Frank sold off the stock cheap, having no where else to put it, selling from 20,000 to 30,000 comics, most of them brand new (therefore, with cover prices between 75 cents and $2, probably) at 10 to 15 cents each. Using the most conservative figures, this means Frank lost about $15,000 on the stock.

Michael Correa's conviction was overturned by the First Appellate Court in November of 1989.

Frank, through his attorney, Burton Joseph, later brought suit against the city of Lansing for having improperly closed his store in the original arrest. They won, receiving damages of about $15,000, of which some $5000 went for attorney's fees.

The defense on the obscenity charges had, in total, cost approximately $25,000, for both the original case and the appeal. Not of course, including the loss Frank suffered because of the lost lease. And we're just talking money, here. What price can be put on the loss of Michael Correa's job, his pain and humiliation at being branded a pornographer, and the impact on the public mind of comic books being branded "obscene"?

Of course, it could have been worse yet.

On November 18, 1987, a Virginia jury decided that Dennis and Barbara Pryba were subject to the forfeiture

provisions of the Racketeer Influenced and Corrupt Organizations Act (RICO) for selling merchandise, valued at approximately $105, that had been judged obscene. For this, they forfeited approximately $1 million in businesses, including all stock and personal property in the 3 bookstores and 8 video clubs they owned and operated, nine bank accounts, five vehicles and a warehouse. If they had had a partridge in a pear tree, no doubt it would also have been forfeit. And all before sentencing even took place on the obscenity charge, for which both received serious sentences.

This was the first application of the RICO statute in an obscenity prosecution. Most of the assets seized were in no way obscene. The jury never had an opportunity, in applying the RICO forfeiture, to consider the legality of the vast majority of the publications and tapes seized. In fact, not all of the materials brought to trial were judged obscene. But that some were was enough to have the Pryba's convicted as "racketeers," and thus make all of their assets subject to forfeit.

Defendants of RICO (which was originally targeted at organized crime), will point out that Dennis Pryba was convicted under the federal anti-obscenity statute, making him subject to federal RICO. But 27 states have state RICO laws, as well, which presumably would apply to state statute (although I don't know this for certain, and have been unable to find current information). RICO apologists might also point out that in Congressional hearings on RICO reform, the point was made repeatedly that one instance of violation was not enough for RICO prosecution: For that, a pattern must be shown. What shows a pattern of violation enough to call one a "racketeer" (under the "reforms" of the Act, they would now simply be called a "criminal")? *Two* violations.

Frank told me this is one of the reasons they fought the obscenity charge. If they had accepted one conviction for obscenity, they would have been vulnerable to RICO prosecution if another such charge was levied.

So retailers are at terrible risk, if they

> So while the creator is not personally liable in an obscenity case, charges of obscenity do affect the creator's ability to make a living.

choose to carry adult material. But is the risk or the reality of economic hardship for the retailer enough reason for the artist to cry "Censorship!"? I think so, if the end result of this situation is that an artist cannot get work distributed and sold, and ultimately, must give up doing work containing adult themes (at least, sexual themes) in order to eat.

How this hits us personally, with regard to *Omaha* is easy to document. Even before the local obscenity cases arose, Reed and I felt the economic impact of *Omaha's* controversial sexual content. Until 1987, Diamond Distribution refused to carry *Omaha* because of it's sexual content. Diamond at the time controlled about 40% of the national distribution of comics. Any comics store which used Diamond as its exclusive distributor could not get *Omaha*. Westfield, the largest comic subscription service in the country, also refused to carry *Omaha*, until 1988. This essentially cut *Omaha* off from those who get their comics by mail. Both of these services, largely because of retailer and consumer pressure, finally changed their minds, and began carrying *Omaha*. Another possible reason for their decision was that, during this period, the sexual content of *Omaha* went down. Not deliberately, simply because the extremely heavy plot got in the way. Whatever the reasoning, it looked like perhaps, at last, we would have widespread distribution, with consequent increase in royalties, and improvement on macaroni and cheese dinners.

At the same time, however, retailers looked at the Friendly Frank case . . . and cringed. Some quit carrying the book altogether. Some put it under the counter, available only on request. Some bagged it, or shrink-wrapped it. None of these strategies are good for sales. They went up . . . but not very far.

The busts have gone on. Canada . . . New Zealand . . . and, most recently, Florida. As the cases piled up, some retailers who had carried the book, quit. And then our British distributor gave up, which cost us about 10% of our sales. Back to the mac and cheese.

Fortunately, we both like mac and cheese. Also fortunately, I was able to get other free-lance work (most notably for Disney's new comic line) that allowed us to continue to pay rent. Otherwise, at least one of us would have had to find a day job. While it is not impossible to produce comics while working a 40 hour week, it is extremely difficult. Comics are highly labor-intensive, especially the way we do them, using the old-fashioned 7 to 9 panel page. A page, counting both my and Reed's time, takes about 8 to 10 hours of work. An issue of Omaha is 30 pages long. With full distribution, including Commonwealth countries, we each can make about as much as a full-time secretary. With restricted distribution, it's Burger Whoopee wages.

So, while the creator is not personally liable in an obscenity case, charges of obscenity do affect the creator's ability to make a living. I can understand any creator who therefore chooses to censor themselves in order to gain sufficiently wide distribution of their work to get paid decently for their work. And I certainly can understand distributors and retailers being reluctant to carry a work with the history of *Omaha*. They have economic considerations too, and the consequences of a bust affect them directly, and with infinitely more severity than they do us. But if we knuckle under, the risk is increased for all of us.

Robin Snyder, the editor of Murder, put it most elegantly in a commentary in *The Comics Journal*: "When any individual is robbed, cheated, mugged or is the victim of any force or fraud, he turns to the Law for help, the Administration of the Law being one of the functions of Government. But, where does one turn when the mugger is the Law itself?"

Well, there is somewhere for comic retailers to turn, at any rate. Immediately after the Friendly Frank's bust, our publisher, Denis Kitchen of Kitchen Sink Press, founded the ComicBook Legal Defense Fund, to support the First Amendment fights involving comic retailers. Monies received over and above the costs of Frank's case were put into an interest-bearing account for other fights. But any long battle will need more than the Fund currently has, and the recent Florida cases have seriously depleted it. Retailers are fighting on the front lines for all of us, but they can't do it without support. If you want to help ensure that comics receive their proper protection under the First Amendment, you can send money to: Comic Book Legal Defense Fund, P.O. Box 501, Princeton, WI 54968.

Oh, and if you want to see more of our filthy comic, check your local comic store, or write to Kitchen Sink Press, No. 2 Swamp Rd., Princeton, WI 54968

Kate Worley has been the writer of **Omaha the Cat Dancer** *since 1986. She wears her "I write banned books" button with pride.*

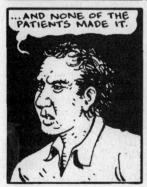

AND ON TOPPA THAT HE LATER CLAIMED THAT ABC'D USED HIS COMMENTS OUTTA CONTEXT AND HE'D TRIED TO MAKE A RETRACTION BUT THEY WOULDN'T LET 'IM... I READ THAT IN THE REPORT: IT'S A PUBLIC DOCUMENT.

AND LIKE HOW ABC SHOWS A RENOVATION AREA AND CLAIMS THAT PROVES NO CLEANING GOES ON HERE, LIKE THE CONSTRUCTION CREWS ARE SUPPOSED TO SWEEP UP THE SAWDUST EVEN THOUGH THERE'S NO ONE AROUND... SHIT, THE HOSPITAL'S CLEANED EVERY DAY!

'AY, MAN, THAT LYING ENRAGES ME. I'M NOT SO MUCH TAKIN' UP FOR THE HOSPITAL— IT'S FAR FROM PERFECT, BUT THAT REPORT WASN'T EVEN JOURNALISM, IT WAS A DRAMA ABC USED TO BOOST ITS RATINGS.

FUCKIN' AIRHEAD DIANE SAWYER... SHE WORKED FOR NIXON, PROB'LY STILL IDOLIZES 'IM, AN' YET PEOPLE BELIEVE EVERYTHING SHE SAYS...

I WANNA FOCUS ON THIS THING NATIONALLY! I AIN'T THROUGH WITH IT!

I GOT INDICATIONS THAT ABC DELIBERATELY STAGED AT LEAST ONE SEQUENCE... THE ONE WHERE THEY CLAIMED THE PATIENT WASN'T FED, WHERE THEY WERE SUPPOSED TO HAVE FILMED WITH A HIDDEN CAMERA FOR SEVENTY-TWO HOURS...

WHEN THE NURSE BRINGS IN THE GUY'S FOOD IT'S ON A BLUE TRAY. AFTER HIS BUDDY SUPPOSEDLY HAS FED HIM, THE TRAY HAS MIRACULOUSLY TURNED WHITE AND THERE'RE MORE FOOD CONTAINERS ON IT THAN WHEN IT WAS BROUGHT IN. PLUS THE CAMERA ANGLES CHANGE IN THE SCENE. OBVIOUSLY THERE WAS SOME STAGING GOING ON...

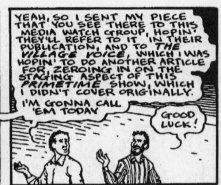

YEAH, SO I SENT MY PIECE THAT YOU SEE THERE TO THIS MEDIA WATCH GROUP, HOPIN' THEY'LL REFER TO IT IN THEIR PUBLICATION, AND TO *THE VILLAGE VOICE*, WHICH I WAS HOPIN' TO DO ANOTHER ARTICLE FOR, ZEROING IN ON THE STAGING ASPECT OF THIS *PRIMETIME* SHOW, WHICH I DIDN'T COVER ORIGINALLY.

I'M GONNA CALL 'EM TODAY

GOOD LUCK!

LATER

BOB, HARVEY PEKAR, 'JA GET MY ARTICLE?

YEAH. PRETTY GOOD STUFF.

WELL, C'N YA USE ANY OF IT?

UH, IT'S KIND OF A LOCAL STORY

LOCAL, WHADDAYA MEAN, LOCAL? IT WAS BROADCAST NATIONALLY. IT GOT ALL KINDA NATIONAL POLITICIANS ALL UP IN ARMS. WHY IS IT LOCAL, BECAUSE IT HAPPENED IN CLEVELAND AND NOT NEW YORK?

MAYBE THE A-BOMBING A' HIROSHIMA WAS LOCAL TOO, 'CAUSE IT WASN'T TOKYO!

I MEAN, I KNOW THIS ISN'T THE GULF CRISIS, BUT IT'S AS CLEAR AN EXAMPLE OF NETWORK NEWS IRRESPONSIBILITY AS YOU'RE GONNA FIND. I DON'T SEE HOW YOU CAN IGNORE IT

YEAH, BUT IF WE REPRINTED IT, IT'D TAKE UP FORTY PER CENT OF OUR PAPER

I'M NOT ASKIN' YOU TO REPRINT IT, ONLY TO REFER TO IT... PLUS I GOT NEW EVIDENCE REGARDING ABC STAGING PART OF THE SEQUENCE.

PLUS YOU SAID SOME RIGHT-WING MEDIA WATCH GROUP HAD PRAISED THE *PRIMETIME* REPORT, ACCEPTED ALL THE LIES AT FACE VALUE. HOW COME THEY CAN WRITE ABOUT IT AND YOU CAN'T

WELL, I'LL TAKE ANOTHER LOOK AT IT...

YEAH, SURE YOU WILL. NEVERMIND, I'LL TRY T' PURSUE IT ON MY OWN.

BLIND, PROVINCIAL MOTHERFUCKER.

SIGH... WELL, I'LL TRY *THE VOICE*. FAT CHANCE... WHAT A GLUTTON FOR PUNISHMENT I AM. MAYBE I'LL GET LUCKY, THOUGH. WHAT'S TO LOSE BUT MY TEMPER?

YEAH, ED. LOOK, I GOT A NEW ANGLE ON THAT *PRIMETIME* STORY: ABOUT THEM ACTUALLY STAGING ONE OF THE SCENES.

I'M VERY BUSY NOW, HARVEY. I'M DOING AN EDIT. WHY DON'T YOU JUST WRITE IT AND SEND IT TO ME?

BECAUSE IT WOULD PROBABLY BE A WASTE, YOU PROBABLY WOULDN'T WANT IT NO MATTER WHAT IT WAS. I'LL WRITE IT, BUT I GOTTA AT LEAST TALK TO YOU ABOUT IT AND TELL YOU WHAT I GOT, SEE IF THERE'S AT LEAST A CHANCE YOU C'N USE IT.

4

" . . . THERE'S A WAY"

Dori Seda:
An Appreciation

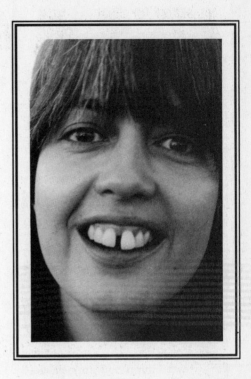

Leslie Sternbergh

Nobody was really expecting Dori to die . . . with the possible exception of Dori herself. Now that is not meant to imply that Dori Seda had anything like a conscious death wish. This was not the case; in 1987, when her friends would mention the D-word to her as potential consequence of her "bad girl" behavior, she would laugh out loud and say, "Y'know, hyuk-hyuk-koff-koff, you're probably right!"

Hyuk hyuk, koff koff. She'd graciously acknowledge that you had a point, albeit not one she felt was worth taking too seriously.

Even her willfulness was conveyed with such warmth—the wild smile with those in-your-face gap teeth, big vivid flashing dark eyes under an evanescent thoughtful frown—and her hands, waving to underscore, to reaffirm, in one hand always that smoldering Barclay, a gestural censer, trailing smoky postscripts to her flourishes.

Dori knew how to make an entrance, too. She could appear on the scene like a veritable weather system, people turning to get a look at this larger-than-life glamour that she had, a sort of ingenuous coruscation, partly elegant, party goofy . . . and way too soon extinguished, damn it. Way too soon gone from us all.

There's this phrase Dori liked to use—she'd say some thing was "not very pleasant"—and the way she'd say it, she'd be sort of leering, but in this really appealing way, rubbernecking like an avid kid at life's rich weird lewd funny pageant of pathos . . . So now Dori's gone. Flu, on top of chronic lung problems, on top of injuries from a minor car accident—she came home from the emergency room of Marin County Hospital with an unnoticed lung puncture and a fear of incurring more medical expenses. She quit smoking those three packs a day. She was finally talking to her boyfriend Don Donahue, about which hospital she

> It seemed incredible that Dori's warm, funny work . . . [was] being regarded as pornography that should not see print by her own mother.

should immediately check into, when she simply stopped breathing, and died. Not very pleasant indeed.

Dori Seda was a great cartoonist. Her work was admired and appreciated by many readers. Before her death in February 1988, she'd been working on a second issue of her comic book, *Lonely Nights* (subtitled "stories to read when the couple next door is fucking too loud"). There were plans to include her work in an upcoming anthology of underground comix by women cartoonists, a book called *Twisted Sisters* (subtitled "a collection of bad girl art"). Dori knew the editor of the book, Diane Noomin, and the title's co-creator, Aline Kominsky-Crumb; she and Aline and Diane often had their stories published in the same comic books—books like *Weirdo* and *Wimmen's Comix*, one issue of which was co-edited by Dori with her best friend, cartoonist Krystine Kryttre.

Dori was a valued member of a kind of small press community of cartoonists, friends, artists, writers, editors and publishers, working in a realm where friends and acquaintances are often as close as family. Dori really loved this closeness, this familial feeling. She gave gifts to people. She threw a big wild party when *Lonely Nights* was published. She corresponded with people, by phone or by mail.

She made herself lavender writing paper with a letterhead that read, "Dori Seda—Cartoonist", next to a comic image of five people with word balloons that poked fun at cartooning, the Bay Area where she lived, at herself, and human nature in general. And on this satirical stationery, six days after her thirty-sixth birthday, Dori wrote a curious, serious letter. Three dozen weeks before her death, she wrote her will.

"TO WHOM IT MAY CONCERN," the letter begins. "This is sort of a contract and sort of a will (although I don't plan on dying soon,)" . . . What a thing for Dori to've said, even in jest, all the worse in retrospect. The text continues. It goes on about different things she felt it necessary to say, in a firm but rather funny voice, unmistakably Dori. She makes one point clearly, and several times reiterates it— that Don should have her artwork. Twice later she uses the phrase "in the event that I drop dead," qualifying it the first time— "which I don't expect to happen"—both times concluding that Don should have her artwork. Those references made to her surviving family are all negative. This odd contract was at her insistence witnessed by two friends, Kryttre and Dan O'Neill. For whatever reasons, she wanted a legal document.

This letter is now a matter of public record. Nobody rushed off to file it when it was written— or even when Dori died. In fact, after Dori's unexpected death there was a lot of sadness and regret and a big wake and more than a little shock that her self-destructive tendencies had so suddenly and so overwhelmingly succeeded. Nobody really thought about the will. In fact, when Dori's mother came to Berkeley to collect some of her few possessions, the letter was informally honored anyway; she agreed that Don Donahue should keep the artwork itself, pages and pages of it. And so it went for some time as everyone faced the prospect of there being no Dori anymore. There seemed to be no need for the contents of the letter to be called into question.

From 1988 through 1990, there was talk of a "Dori book" being done, a new collection to feature unpublished work she'd finished for that second issue of *Lonely Nights*, among other things. Dori'd done a lot of comics in different titles—some out of print—and other kinds of artwork, from larger paintings to small ceramic sculptures, wonderful little

The author and Dori Seda

cartoon scenes in three dimensions, each one about a foot square. Photographs of some of these were to be included in this book, too. Such a volume would be representative of the body of work that Dori had produced as a cartoonist and artist.

Then the rumors started; I can't even quite remember when or from whom I first heard of problems encountered by a publisher interested in including one of Dori's stories in an anthology of comics. The story, as I heard it, was that Dori's mother had the right to give or deny access to the publication of her daughter's work. The rights had legally gone to her as Dori's next of kin, according to California estate law. Since Dori's will had not been filed she was considered to have died intestate, without a will, and the rights had gone to her mother, automatically. Nobody had thought about Dori's mother not wanting the work published. It seemed incredible that Dori's warm, funny work—raunchy and ribald but leavened by its sweetness, by a drawing style as rudely cute and winsome as the one who produced it—that these works were being regarded as pornography that should not see print, by her own mother. This was hard to believe.

I spoke with various friends about this issue, one of them being Mitch Berger. Mitch has worked in his capacity as a

lawyer on behalf of many people in the field of comics. It was during one of these conversations with Mitch that I mentioned the letter Dori wrote, and her insistence on the signatures of her two friends as witnesses. Dori liked to do many things; she'd even insisted on a contract for *Lonely Nights*, something many people working in underground comics might not have done. To file this will, though, seemed a drastic measure, by no means ideal. With all these things in mind, I contacted Dori's mother, and went to Chicago to talk to her. That—and what happened afterward—is what this comic is about.

Those interested in the work of Dori Seda may find it in underground comic books, many of which are currently still in print. She is featured in *Gap-toothed Women*, a short film by Les Blank for which she also did the poster art. *Twisted Sisters*, edited by Diane Noomin, was published in November 1991 by Viking Penguin and is currently available in many bookstores. The book is dedicated to Dori.

Leslie Sternbergh is a cartoonist, who lives in New York City. Some of her most recent work appears in **Twisted Sisters**. *She is also the artist for* **Gauntlet**'s *back cover.*

OH, GOOD—YOU'RE A SMOKER! YEAH, Y'KNOW IN NEW YORK YOU CAN'T SMOKE IN CABS OR PUBLIC PLACES ANY MORE—THEY PASSED A LAW—

—YEAH—DORI WAS SO FUNNY--SHE'D MAKE THE *NON*-SMOKERS GO OUT ON THE BACK PORCH AT HER PLACE—!!

THAT'S DISGUSTING --I THINK IT'S A PERSON'S OWN BUSINESS IF THEY WANT TO SMOKE!

—NOW LISTEN—I THOUGHT WE'D GO HAVE DINNER, AFTER THIS—DO YOU LIKE CHINESE?

—OH, YEAH!—BACK IN NEW YORK WE GO TO THIS PLACE ON MOTT STREET—THEY HAVE THE BEST *SEAFOOD*—!!!

GOOD! WE'LL GO FOR SOME CHINESE, THEN ....

SO, UH—I GUESS MAYBE PEOPLE HAVE SPOKEN TO YOU ABOUT THE--POSSIBILITY OF SOME OF DORI'S WORK BEING PUBLISHED—? YOU KNOW, SHE WAS WORKING ON A BOOK WHEN SHE DIED—

WELL—I SPOKE TO THAT *ERICK* FELLOW, FROM LAST GASP--HE'S *HORRIBLE*

OH—WELL, HE'S *FRENCH*...DORI REALLY LIKED HIM... THEY USETA *WORK* TOGETHER—UH—

I MEAN, HE'S A—A *CHARACTER*—THE PEOPLE AROUND COMIX, ARE—*LIKE* THAT...HE LIKES TO GET TATTOOED...

D'YOU KNOW WHAT HE SAID TO ME? WHEN I SAID I'D OKAY ANYTHING THAT GETS PRINTED, HE SAID "THAT'S NOT VERY LIKELY"—— CAN YOU *IMAGINE* THE *NERVE*?!?

OH—SO YOU WOULDN'T MIND THINGS GETTING PUBLISHED?..

I DIDN'T SAY *THAT*—WE'LL TALK ABOUT IT--WE'RE ALMOST THERE

HERE—I NEED TO DO THIS FIRST-- HOLD THIS OTHER BOTTLE FOR ME... -- THE GRAVE'S NOT FAR FROM HERE—

HERE WE ARE

.Seda

Dori

1988

YEAH --WOW

AND HERE'S HER *FATHER'S* ...

YES -THESE FLOWERS NEED WATERING ...

YES—I WANTED MATCHING HEAD-STONES—SEE, THIS ONE HAS A NICE FLORAL HOLDER BUILT IN... BUT WHEN I GOT HERE AND SAW IT, THEY'D GIVEN ME THIS PLAIN ONE—THEY SAID THEY DON'T MAKE THEM NOW

I HAVE PICTURES OF DORI'S GRAVE, FOR *KATE*—AND I'D LIKE TO HAVE YOU TAKE A PICTURE OF ME BY DORI'S GRAVE —I'LL GET A SHOT OF YOU THERE ALSO

YES, KATE SENDS HER LOVE—SHE SAID I'D ENJOY MEETING YOU— SHE'S A SWEETHEART--I'LL SEE HER IN SAN DIEGO IN AUGUST

SHE'S VERY NICE... HERE— I'VE WANTED TO DO THIS FOR A WHILE

THERE.

③

WELL, *I* DON'T AGREE WITH THAT--!!

--YOU DON'T AGREE WITH FREEDOM OF SPEECH--?!

NOT LIKE *THAT*!! HALF THE PEOPLE WHO READ THAT STUFF WILL *DIE OF AIDS*!!!

WHAT?! THAT'S NOT TRUE! YOU REALLY THINK THAT?!?

LISTEN--THERE'S AN ANTHOLOGY OF WOMEN CARTOONISTS IN THE WORKS--DORI *KNEW* ABOUT IT, AND SHE WAS LOOKING FORWARD TO BEING IN IT WITH OTHER "BADGIRL" ARTISTS WHO WERE HER FRIENDS-- WHAT ABOUT *THAT*? IT'S CALLED "TWISTED SISTERS"--

UH-HUH... MM-HM...

NOPE. I DON'T THINK SO--NO. SORRY.

WHY'D I GO AN' SAY THAT *TITLE*-SHIT!

...LISTEN--I'M SORRY TO HAVE TO DISAPPOINT YOU LIKE THIS, AND I KNOW THIS IS WHY YOU CAME TO SEE ME--BUT DORI ENJOYED HER RECOGNITION WHILE SHE WAS ALIVE, AND NOW SHE'S DEAD. DORI WAS *OURS*.

DORI WAS *DORI'S*.

LET'S GO--WE'LL FIND SOME NICE CHINESE PLACE TO HAVE DINNER

UH--YOU DIDN'T HAVE ONE IN *MIND*? UH--

OH, THERE'RE *LOTS* OF 'EM AROUND HERE!!

GULP

WHAT'S GOING ON OVER THERE? JUST LOOK AT ALL THOSE PEOPLE...

I DUNNO...LOOKS LIKE A FEW YUPPIES... FEW FLOWERS, BUT THERE'RE *BALLOONS*--HEY, I'LL BET IT'S A BABY'S FUNERAL--LIKE A STILLBORN...

BUT THERE'S NO *MINISTER*--

WELL, SOMETIMES PEOPLE DON'T HAVE A SERVICE FOR THAT...

THAT'S NOT *RIGHT*!

HM--WHAT TIME IS IT?

LISTEN--COULD WE EAT NEAR THE HOTEL? MY RIDE COMES AT *SIX*--AN' I'M NOT SURE IF WE--

--IT'S ONLY FOUR THIRTY--WE'VE GOT *PLENTY* OF TIME--*GET IN*!!

HEY--WE COULD EAT *IN* THE HOTEL--MY TREAT! THEY'VE GOT A NICE--

OH, NO--I'LL TREAT! --WE'LL HAVE GOOD *CHINESE* FOOD--!!!

THINGS WERE STILL PRETTY TENSE--WE DROVE FOR WHAT SEEMED LIKE A VERY LONG TIME, FOR *MILES*...

YES, I'LL BUY US SOME DINNER...YOU SAID YOU LIKE *SEAFOOD*...WE'LL GET YOU BACK ON TIME...

...OKAY...

COME TO THINK OF IT, I RE-MEMBER *DORI* OFTEN GETTING ALL *FEISTY* AN' *ARGUMENTATIVE* AT DINNER TIME--DÉJÀ FUGGIN'VU!

IT TOOK US A GOOD TWENTY MINUTES TO FIND THAT CHINESE PLACE--*THEN*--

IT SAYS THAT THEY'RE *CLOSED* FOR *VACATION*!! Y'KNOW THERE'S A DINER BY THE HOTEL--THE *TIME*--COULDN'T WE MAYBE--

I'M IN HELL.

NO, NO--LET'S SEE IF WE CAN'T FIND *ANOTHER* CHINESE RESTAURANT

LISTEN--COULDN'T WE JUST GO TO THAT PLACE RIGHT NEXT DOOR TO THE HOTEL? I MEAN, IT'S REALLY GETTING KINDA *LATE*!!

WELL, I'M *SURE* THAT THERE'S ANOTHER CHINESE PLACE AROUND HERE *SOMEWHERE*!

--ARGH--

BUT WE DON'T HAVE *TIME*--

--BUT--

--*PLEASE*?

WELL... ALL RIGHT--

GOOD GRIEF--THIS REALLY IS LIKE BEING WITH THE LESS PLEASANT SIDE OF *DORI*--!!!

-CAN I TAKE YOUR ORDER--?

IN A DINER...NO APPETITE--HM--I THINK I'LL JUST HAVE A B.L.T.--

SHIT--SHIT, SHIT-!!

OH--I'LL HAVE THE ... *SEAFOOD SALAD*--AN' A COKE...

OH NO!! THAT'S NOT ENOUGH! YOU SAID YOU LIKE *SEAFOOD*--WHY, THERE'S LOTS HERE--

--AND I'LL HAVE--

MY MEAL ARRIVED--AN' IF A DISH COULD LOOK ANY MORE LIKE ONE OF DORI'S CARTOONS THAN THIS ONE DID, WELL, I'D LIKE TO SEE IT--THE THING WAS *ABSURD*--

RANCID SHRIMPS

STALE SARIMI

A COUPLE OF FAKE SCALLOPS

IN A CARVED-OUT PINEAPPLE GARNISHED WITH ITS LEAVES (THEY TRIED!)

I FELT AS IF DORI MIGHT BE OUT THERE SOMEWHERE, LAUGHING AT THE WHOLE THING...

THAT LOOKS GOOD! HOW IS IT?

OH, IT'S *YUMMY*

GOOD--MINE'S GOOD TOO

...SO YOU REALLY DON'T THINK--

NO, WHY, WHAT ABOUT *US*--HER FAMILY--

--BUT NOTHING LIKE THAT EVER HAPPENED WHEN--

--SHE *WAS* ALIVE, AND WITH THE WAY NOW SHE'S *DEAD*, AND WITH THE WAY THIS COUNTRY'S GOING I CAN JUST SEE THE HEADLINES...

OH COME ON--THAT'S *RIDICULOUS*--

NO YOU'RE BEING RIDICULOUS--SHE'S *DEAD* AN' THERE'S NO POINT.

UH--WHAT *TIME* IS IT?

6

OF NICE AND MEN
Russ Miller

"If animals had reason, they would act just as ridiculous as we menfolks do."
—*Josh Billings (Henry Wheeler Shaw)*

The problem with "causes" is they can become too convenient a couch upon which to refuge our personal fears. Animal rights is, I think, such a cause . After all siding with animals is too safe and easy a thing to do . It takes much less courage or effort to coddle a pet than it does to be a good friend, or rehabilitate a human being. In actuality I don't have a problem with animal rights people per se, until they begin to impose their value system on the rest of us. Granted, there are people that inflict cruelty on animals as a kind of sick expression of their own insecurities and I believe that to be wrong. But, when a fundamentalist mind set occurs that forbids any kind of dignity to animals or their caretakers out of sheer ignorance, this also, is very wrong.

Making animals the recipients of an anthropomorphic fantasy is wantonly denying the animal its nobility, and the animal steward his or her earned integrity as one who has become skilled in domestication and prolonging of animal life and species life. This is creatively ignoring the facts and missing the point of responsible animal care altogether.

Just to propose that you "love" animals is hollow at best. Every year, at least twice I see a news report of a house or apartment that has been forcefully entered because of an overwhelming stench, only to discover hundreds of cats living there in squalor. Often the owner's response is simply, "I just LOVE animals."

Selective animal love is another odd splinter of the animal rights movement. There are those that promote the idea that certain (usually "cute") animals are deserving of preferential treatment. These people are not vegetarians, they wear leather products, but will throw paint or spit on people wearing furs . What this action is saying of the assailant is "I have the right to express myself and you don't." This is like a child throwing a tantrum. Argued to its end, we should tolerate throwing manure on someone eating a salad, because vegetables have a right to live too. After all, they produce oxygen. No one ever seems to picket the annual rattlesnake round up held in Texas and Oklahoma.

Indignation is a perfectly reasonable human reaction to illogical and senseless behavior, especially if it is behavior born of ill will or corrupt motivations. However, like most emotionally spurred responses, zealots can be misdirected, or at least misinformed. There are plenty of things in this world to be indignant about. Some, I think would produce monumentally more important long term benefits for us as a race than worrying too much about how a farmer chooses to kill his livestock.

My sense of indignation rises when I read a quote by an animal activist that says, "A rat is a pig is a dog is a boy" Come on, animals are not people. Sitting Bull once said, "When there was nothing left but mice to hunt, we would hunt mice because we are hunters." I suppose we're to believe when we have nothing but each other to hunt people become prey. In the context of fundamentalist animal rights, and paint throwing, this may be coming to pass.

> I guess I just don't understand why, when we face so many problems crucial to our very survival, there is so much energy poured into a superficial "cause" like trying to equate animals with humans.

I guess I just don't understand why, when we face so many problems crucial to our very survival, there is so much energy poured into a superficial "cause" like trying to equate animals with humans. For instance, nowadays, small businesses have little or no chance of ever getting a start. Hard working middle class people cannot afford to give themselves or their children medical attention because the medical profession has priced itself out of reach. Our educational system is obscenely deteriorated.

Recent statistics show that more children in third world countries are being immunized for disease than children in many of the large cities here in the United States. AIDS research is still only receiving a trickle of financial interest and little support. And, AIDS is an epidemic.

The world is a tough place to navigate. Living is, and always has been, hard. There are many things to fear and injustice seems commonplace. These are not difficulties of a few, these are common to all people. As humans, especially here in the United States, we have the right to speak out when we become indignant. The freedom to speak our truth, to

debate issues in a public forum is our right. Our founders knew that words spoken with passion and intelligence can sway an opponent or at least lead to an agreed upon impasse. Speaking truth as opposed to assaulting with an aerosol paint can leave both parties with their dignity and honor intact. Anyone can humiliate an opponent, but what does that say about your belief?

As a part time college professor, I've had the privilege of observing our young people coming up and I am beginning to believe that as a nation we are losing the ability to debate. A majority of my students cannot argue the truth articulately enough to posit a notion in the hearer's mind. Link this inability to think and use language to academic laziness and you've designed a person worthy of "causes". This produces bandwagon jumpers, not leaders, not free thinkers, not even courteous individuals.

A case in point. Recently, in our area, because of the lack of small game being taken by hunters, the predator population (coyotes) has risen at an alarming rate. This increase in coyotes threatens the antelope population which will be birthing soon. A local college proposed on the front page of the local paper, the solution to the problem was not to decrease the number of predators as the Game and Fish Department had originally decided, but rather, that the student body surround the antelope herd, hand in hand and keep the coyotes at bay. Considering the skittish nature of antelope, it would be interesting to see them try! At its best this is misdirected energy and a sad commentary on our times.

In an age of "political correctness" (which in itself is a choice of non-choice, or a kind of spineless non-commitment) there are basics of which we are all too quickly losing sight. Saying, "we should be kind to animals" is like saying "I'm against nuclear warfare". Or, as a recently read bumper sticker says: MEAT IS DEAD. My response: DUH!!

> "All our knowledge merely helps us to die a more painful death than the animals that know nothing."
> —Maurice Maeterlinck

OF NICE AND MEN

WELCOME TO THE I.M. SENSITIVE SHOW. I'M YOUR HOST, I.M. TODAY'S TOPIC IS INDEED SENSITIVE... WE'LL CONCERN OURSELVES WITH ANIMAL RIGHTS, AND WHO BETTER QUALIFIED TO DISCUSS THIS MATTER THAN THE ANIMALS THEMSEVES?

(THANKS, BOZE.)

OUR FIRST GUEST IS BUN E. RABBIT.

ART AND STORY-- RUSS MILLER
LETTERING-- JOHN CLARK

PLEASE BE SEATED, MIZ RABBIT.

THANK YOU, BUT THAT'S *MISSUS* RABBIT.

OH, I'M SORRY, HOW INSENSITIVE OF ME.

OH, THAT'S OKAY, I'M USED TO IT. YOU SEE, NOBODY CARES ABOUT <u>MY</u> INDIVIDUAL RIGHTS.

HOW SAD. TELL US ABOUT IT.

FIRST OF ALL, EVERYBODY EATS US! AND I MEAN ANY-THING THAT HUNTS, BITES, KILLS OR EATS MEAT EATS US RABBITS!

GET SERIOUS! I'M A *WOLF!*

WHAT ABOUT THE PUPFISH, THE MOUNT GRAHAM RED SQUIRREL...

FINE, FINE, THEY'RE ALL ON MY DIET! MORE "COMIDA" FOR ME, I SAYS!

ALL RIGHT, ALL RIGHT. PERHAPS IT'S TIME FOR OUR NEXT GUEST. A "GLASNOST" KINDA GUY, MISHA MINK!

HELLO COMRADES... OOO...I MEAN, WHAT'S SHAKIN' DUDES?

WELL, I'M SHAKING A BIT AFTER THAT EPISODE WITH THE RABBIT...

OH, GET OVER YOURSELF! RABBITS HAVE NO RIGHTS... THEY HAVE LOUSY FUR, AND THEY EAT THEIR YOUNG, YOU KNOW...

AGAIN WITH THE CANNIBALISM!

NOW YOU TAKE YOUR DOMESTIC RABBITS, THEY *ARE PRIME!* GOOD EATING, AND THEIR FUR IS RIVALED ONLY BY...WELL....ME!

SLAUGHTER

WHY IN GOD'S NAME DID YOU DO THAT?

TOO COCKY! PLUS IMPORTED FOODS ARE RARE FOR ME, I COULDN'T PASS UP THE OPPORTUNITY...

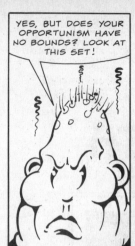

YES, BUT DOES YOUR OPPORTUNISM HAVE NO BOUNDS? LOOK AT THIS SET!

LOOK HERE, AMIGO, YOU DON'T THINK YOUR ANCESTORS ATE MY ANCESTORS?

PERISH THE THOUGHT!

MY POINT IS, YOU HUMANS TOUGHED YOUR WAY TO THE TOP OF THE FOOD CHAIN... COULD BE YOU'LL WIMP YOUR WAY OUT!

I THINK IT'S TIME FOR A STATION BREAK. WHEN WE RETURN, OUR GUEST WILL BE ENVIRONMENTALIST GREEN SLACKWITT FROM W.E.A.C., "WOEFUL ENVIRONMENTALISTS ALIENATING CIVILIZATION..."

WHEW! WHAT A SHOW!

THAT'S JUST GREAT! WHAT'S THE BAD?

UH...I'VE GOT SOME GOOD NEWS AND BAD, BABY.

GREEN SLACKWITT WAS JUST RUN OVER BY A HUMANE SOCIETY TRUCK ON AN EMERGENCY CALL...HAD TO SPAY A CAT.

OH, SWELL!

THE GOOD NEWS IS, OUR RATINGS ARE THROUGH THE ROOF! THE BUNNY EPISODE KICKED US UP BY TEN MILLION VIEWERS, AND THE RUSSIAN MINK PEAKED US TO THE TOP RATED SHOW ON THE NETWORK!

YOW-ZA! SAY, WOLFY...HOW WOULD YOU LIKE TO BE MY ED McMAHON?!

OH, HA HA HA HA HA!

THE END

Interview With

Joe Coleman

Carlo McCormick

It's Wild! It's Weird! It's... BLAB!

Original uncensored cover for *Blab!*

G: Most of the problems you've encountered, in terms of censorship, have been as a performer and not so much for your work as a visual artist.

C: I've had some censorship with the comics too. For instance, in a recent issue of *Blab*, which has an interview with me and a comic strip I did on Carl Panzram on the cover, that comic you see is not the original cover, which was "The couple that slays together stays together," and was censored. Dennis Kitchen didn't want to print it because he thought his distributor would not pick it up. Another case that was mentioned before in *Gauntlet* was the painting that I did for the film "Henry: Portrait of a Serial Killer." It was supposed to be the movie poster and was commissioned by the director of the film, John McNaughton, but the distributor prevented it. Instead they did a new poster that's very similar except that it's a photograph instead of my art work.

G: In both instances it's a case of self-censorship, out of fear, rather than any outside voice of authority actually interceding in the project.

C: Yeah, it was them coming to me, asking me to do something, and then thinking that it was too strong.

G: This sort of self-censorship within the "creative" community has become increasingly prevalent as an alarming trend in the arts today. However, it's been your work as a performance artist that's been subject to direct censorship of people in authority trying to stop, or persecute you for your shows.

C: Yeah, that's almost like part of the performance now. It's gotten to the point where I do the show, but then the show itself has a life of its own and tells me a story that I didn't even plan. One of the earliest ones which is really full of irony is the famous movie-trial here in New York, where Bob Barker had me arrested for eating mice. What's incredible about it, is the guy's name is Barker, which is slang for the side show pitch man who would introduce freak acts. One of the most famous freaks is the geek, and here he is coming out in the press saying, "Here's this horrible man that eats live rats," just like a barker would do. The guy's a real classic barker, too, because he does TV shows like "Truth or Consequences" in which he exploits people's greed by making them do the most humiliating things in order to win stupid prizes. Then he refused to be the host of the Miss America pageant, which he'd done for a long time, because they were wearing fur coats. But meanwhile, their advertisers, like all those cosmetic companies, systematically use animal biproducts, so it's kind of phony at the same time.

G: Bob Barker became aware of you through your part in the movie *Mondo New York*. Didn't that film have distribution problems because of its content?

C: That was one of the first that had that rating problem, which "Henry" also had. Both were released un-rated, because if they'd been released with one it would have been an X, and those days it wasn't like in the '60s or '70s where movies like *Clockwork Orange* were rated X, but still played all the theaters. You can't play an X-rated film at a normal theater these days, which cuts out your distribution. Some of my performance nights, like the one in Boston, have been real interesting in the way that events surrounding the shows transform them into something else. That show, which was pretty personal to begin with, had to do with my mother's death which occurred just four days before it. She died of cancer and had been suffering from it for a long time. The performance was sort of a tribute to her, starting out with my collection of old, grainy pornographic films of fucking and sucking from some unidentifiable period of old hard-core pornography.

After about 20 minutes the lights came on and I burst through the screen hanging upside down from a cable, swinging over the audience, screaming and exploding. Fucking and sucking is what created me, from some time in the distant past, that's what my parents were doing. Here, I am exploding—I thought the big bang theory of creation was the appropriate one—and hanging from the ceiling because you come into the world upside down attached to an umbilical cord.

There was also a goat—the placenta, hanging upside down next to me. The explosions were extinguished with cow's blood. After the rope was cut, I went into the audience, sat with them, and introduced them to Mommy and Daddy. In this case, they were two rats I had christened Mommy and Daddy.

I bit off the head of Daddy because I had a lot of problems with my father, but I swallowed my mother and that has a lot to do with my Christian background—eating the body and drinking the blood of Christ. When my mother met my father, she was excommunicated, and her priest, who she was really into, told her she was going to burn in Hell for all eternity because you were not allowed, at that time in the Catholic church, to get a divorce. She was so afraid of Hell, she denied her death until the end, and just would not accept that she was going to die.

So then I set off all the fires in the theater, the fires of Hell. The effigy of me was on fire. Everything started exploding, the place filled with smoke and all the fire alarms went off. That's what brought the fire department there. The biggest thing they charged me with was "possession of an infernal machine." That's something that I never intended to put into it, something the outside world picked up and made into its own thing. Whether it has to do with legend, with Jules Verne, or whatever, it's like what Barker did: it's like I'm playing a game with my life, I'm doing things, then the world does things back to me, and then I react to it.

G: You had similar problems with the authorities when you performed in Los Angeles?

C: The show itself got closed down. The cops and the ASPCA were there the whole time and let Stephen Holman and Charles Schneider, the other two acts, do their shows, but when I was supposed to go on they shut the place down. The cops were looking for me, but they weren't very well informed, so they stopped every-one leaving the building who looked weird, asking them if they were Joe Coleman, and I just walked past them.

Anyway, I told a few friends that I'd do the performance at Venice Beach and to meet me there. So then it turned into this trek, where as many people who found out about it through word of mouth drove out to Venice Beach and somehow got organized enough in one spot so that by the time I got there, they were all waiting. I went to this lifeguard station that was about 20 or 30 feet up and had the cars surround it to use their headlights to light it. I did the whole performance on top of this lifeguard station, putting out explosives by diving into the ocean at the end. Fire and water were a real nice combination. It's something that I wouldn't have planned, but happened through circumstance. Another thing was that the police had these helicopters with spotlights circling the theater. It was this great special effect I could never have afforded.

G: There's this attitude in the art world, and even society as a whole, that certain transgressions of law and social order are, if not acceptable, at least pardonable, if they're committed in the name of art. What do you think of today's art?

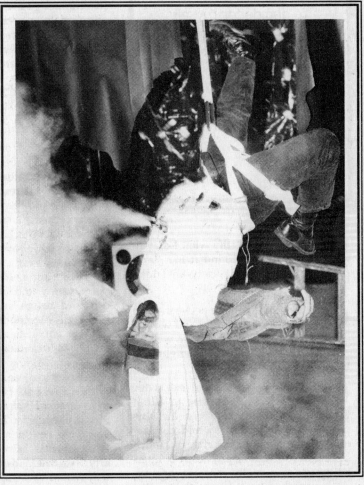

C: I don't have much respect for what's termed art today, which seems to do more with fashion and commodities than with personal expression. To me, I have to do what I do and you can call it art, or crime, or abnormal psychology—whatever you want—it's still something I've got to do. The word art has been used too easily, to make an investment, or as a game for sophisticated bourgeois people in power. I'm not interested in that, it has nothing to do with what I'm after. I'm doing this stuff for me, not for

> I can't trust laws to tell me what to do. I have to decide for myself what's right and wrong. In law it doesn't matter if you're right or wrong, it only matters how good you can bullshit.

is no longer this little thing—instead you're supposed to have allegiance to a tribe that is the whole United States. How can you look at it like that? I can only trust what I call my family, the people I let into my life. I can't trust the rest of the world the same way that early man couldn't trust outsiders. I can't trust laws to tell me what to do. I have to decide for myself what's right and wrong. In law it doesn't matter if you're right or wrong, it only matters how good you can bullshit. It has more to do with semantics than morality.

G: Coming from this position of extreme social alienation, it's perhaps your determined stance as this outsider which is what our culture finds so threatening and is unconsciously reacting to in your work.

C: But it's threatened unnecessarily. How am I really a threat? I'm not killing anybody. Take someone like Richard Speck, a guy who I believe is trying to communicate pain, but to a point where it's self-destruction. The act of stabbing someone is the most desperate act of communication. It's trying to make a point, trying to connect, trying to reach out and touch someone, but it's a desperate attempt, the one where there's nothing left. If he didn't communicate, he'd be killing himself.

I'm not doing that. I'm coming up with a way to communicate my most horrible rage and frustration. I think everyone felt at some point in their life like they just wanted to explode. Well, what if you could explode and still be there after? What a release that would be. How do you articulate that kind of pain and frustration that would cause someone to go into a McDonald's and start slaying people? I'm not trying to say murder is the right way. I'm trying to point out that there's feelings like that, and those feelings need to be communicated, to be able to be allowed to be expressed. That's where censorship comes into play: if you're not allowed to express those things, then you're going to turn into a Richard Speck.

G: Would you say that your work functions on either that psychiatric construct of catharsis or the more

anybody else. If to justify what I do you have to put labels around it like "art" that's okay for you and society, but I don't care.

G: In terms of that line between what is licensed or licit as art and what is criminal, you've said that if you weren't painting and performing you might well be out there killing people.

C: I think that potential exists for everyone. People refuse to admit that the killer is inside. Man has this pretense of sophistication and civilization, but he really hasn't changed much since the cro-magnon; physically or internally. We're actually more savage because now man has the potential to wipe out the entire planet and has developed far more savage ways to torture his fellow man. He threatens the very host, the planet earth, that he lives on. Maybe man has always been like that. Maybe anytime this kind of life develops on a planet, the thing that is man is like a cancer. Man's need to kill is basic and hasn't changed. Men were supposed to kill and hunt for food, and to kill and die to protect the family or the tribe. Now you're not supposed to do that anymore. Now your tribe anthropological one of shamanism some sort of healing force through a shared, ritualistic release of darker, deeper human emotions?

C: The forces that are at work are the ones that are personal, the ones that motivate me. I can't say that I'm doing this for you or the community, but I don't know if that changes it in this regard. I do it for myself, but in doing so I'm trying to communicate, to connect with other people, and it's up to them to get from it what they can, which in some cases may be cathartic or shamanic in its effects.

G: As much as your work is about communicating this kind of pain, frustration and alienation, doesn't it be-come a sort of private self-fulfilling prophesy if the horror, revulsion and fear you're trying to express are the things that draw a line between you and your work and its audience's instinctive recoil from it?

C: No, because I can communicate my pain and you can really feel it; you can find those things in yourself. I'm part of this culture and I'm not so very different than you or anyone else. These same pains that are in me are in you. Whether you have the same life or not really doesn't matter. You're a human being within this particular culture right now. And it seems like this particular culture is full of pain and fear, and all those things that need expression and release.

(Continued from p. 85)

What can you do? Glad you asked. Why not inundate Mr. Berdella with cutting edge or alternative reading material (*nothing* dealing with illegal activities, nothing obscene or pornographic and no hate literature) and force the repressive forces at Jefferson City Correctional Center to scrutinize and respond to each and every piece confiscated? Send reading material to Mr. Berdella at the Jefferson City Correctional Center, P.O. Box 900-167208, Jefferson City, MO 65102-0900. Mr. Berdella requests you send *one* stamp with any material, so he will be required to sign for all material. He will use the stamp to let you know if the material has been accepted or seized.

We'll let you know what happened in the next issue.

Texas scrutinized *Gauntlet* from cover to cover and found the following: "Pages 162 and 239 contain depiction of sado-masochism (bondage). Page 248 contains graphic depiction of men engaging in homosexual activity [editor's note: this was from a mailing sent by Donald Wildmon and the AFA]. Page 343 contains graphic depiction of necrophilia. Pages 170, 171, 242, 243 and 245 contain material of a racial nature which could lead to prison disruptions if distributed on [sic] the units."

This last from a prison system that allows the Ku Klux Klan to disseminate *their* literature in Texas prison facilities.

On the other hand, *Gauntlet* found its way into prisons in Pennsylvania, Colorado, Arizona, Minnesota, Illinois and, damn, if it didn't slip through the cracks into Missouri and Texas *after* its confiscation and ban.

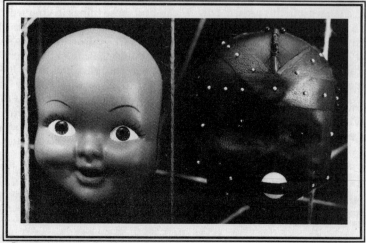

Photography copyright © 1992 by H.E. Fassl

FREAKBABIES

A Play in One Act by

Nancy A. Collins

List of Characters:

Jessica Knight, a photographer
Harry Cabrini, a retired carnival man
Fallon, a human pincushion
Rand Holstrum, the World's Ugliest Man
Sally Holstrum, wife of the World's Ugliest Man
A Roustabout
Col. Smidgen, a midget
The Freakbabies

SCENE ONE

The set is a freak tent. While JESSICA KNIGHT is outside, the flaps of the tent are closed. When she enters the tent, the curtains pull back to fully expose the interior of the "ten-in-one." There should be a banner for the world's ugliest man on prominent display. The sounds of the midway should be audible during the early part of the scene. Jessica Knight enters from stage right. She is carrying camera equipment. The sound of two men arguing comes from inside the tent. As Jessica Knight draws near, HARRY CABRINI and FALLON make their appearance from inside the tent. Fallon gives Cabrini the bum's rush, knocking Jessica Knight on her ass by accident.

FALLON

Gawd damn *pre-vert*! I don't wanna see your ugly face again, unnerstand? Go peddle your monsters somewheres else!

Cabrini picks himself up and dusts off his leisure suit. His Toupee is slightly askew. He is angry, but also frightened of Fallon.

CABRINI

You'll be sorry, Fallon! How much longer you reckon Holstrum'll be round? Once your meal ticket's gone, you'll be coming round beggin' for ole Cabrini's help!

FALLON

Not fuckin' likely! Now git for I call the roustabouts!

Cabrini stalks off, pretending to ignore Jessica Knight sprawled on the ground.

KNIGHT

What th' hell . . .? Fallon, what's going on?

FALLON

(helping her back on her feet)

Sorry bout all that, honey. Didn't realize
you was on the other side of the tent. Come
on in, I'll tell you all about it.

They enter the freak tent. There are several raised plat-
forms with chairs on them. Each has a banner attached,
such as "Col. Smidgen, World's Smallest Soldier", "Jolly
Jenny, World's Fattest Sexpot", etc. The midget is sitting
on his platform, smoking a cigar and reading the paper
In his undershirt. Fallon has his own platform with a table
and chair set on it. There is a bottle of whiskey and a
couple of glasses on the table, along with Fallon's needles. Fallon climbs up on the platform and pours them
both drinks, all the while talking to Knight.)

FALLON

I reckon you'd like to know what that hoo-
ha was all about. Seeing how's you got
knocked ass over tea kettle, can't says I
blames you. What you just saw was none
other than Harry Cabrini, one of th'
sleaziest items found in the business,
which is, believe me, sayin' something!

KNIGHT

Cabrini? What's he do?

FALLON

He sells freaks.

KNIGHT

What do you mean?

FALLON

Exactly what I said. How d'ya think they
find their way into th' business? They
drive out on their own when they hear a
circus is in town? Well, some do. But most

freaks don't have much say bout where they end up. Most get sold by their folks. That's how Smidgen got into showbiz. Hasn't seen his folks since Eisenhower was in office.

>   (to Col. smidgen).

Ain't that right, Smidge?

SMIDGEN
(not looklng up from his paper)

Fuckin' A!

FALLON

See? Sometimes they get sold by the doctors that was lookin' after 'em. That's how Rand got into it. Before he was th' World's Ugliest Man, he was laid up in some gawd-forsaken hell-hole of a hospital. Then this intern heard about me lookin' for a head-liner and arranged it so's I could meet Rand. I paid him a good hunk of change for the privilege, and I ain't had cause to regret it since. I'm sure they don't think of it as 'selling'. More like being a talent scout, I reckon.

KNIGHT

You've *bought* freaks?

FALLON

Fallon finishes his drink and begins systematically piercing his lower lip, ears, upper arms, etc. with long needles.

Don't make it sound like slavery, girl! It's more like payin' a finder's fee! I give my folks decent wages and they're free to come an' go as they see fit! The slave days are long gone. But Cabrini . . . Cabrini is a whole other kettle of fish. Cabrini ain't no agent. He's a slaver . . . At least, that's *my*

opinion. Maybe I'm wrong. But the freaks
Cabrini comes up with . . . there's something *wrong* with 'em. Most are feeble-
minded.Or worse. I made the mistake of
buyin' a pickled punk offa him a few years
back, and he's been houndin' me ever
since. Wants me to buy one of his live'uns.
Buyin' trouble is more like it! Here, look
an' see if I ain't right.

He produces a Polaroid picture from his back pocket
and hands it to knight.

He left one of his damn photos, "In case I
changed my mind".

KNIGHT
(stares at the picture in sick fascination)
My God!

FALLON
Y'see? Where'd he come up with a freak
that young? Most of 'em that age are either
in state homes or special schools,
nowadays. Where's it's mama? And how
come he's got more then *one* of 'em?

While Knight ponders this question, Rand Holstrum and
his wife, Sally, enter from stage left. Rand is dressed in a
smoking jacket. The left side of his face is hideously
swollen and deformed. His hands are arthritic. Rand
sounds like John Hurt in *The Elephant Man*. He breathes
noisily and has difficulty speaking. Sally is carrying a
rolled length of chicken wire and a hammer.

RAND
Jessie!

KNIGHT
(Turns to greet Rand and Sally)
Rand! Good to see you! It's been what? A
year?

RAND
More like two! You remember the wife,
don't you?

While Rand talks to Knight, Sally begins unrolling the
chickenwire and nailing it up in front of Rand's platform.
She waves hello to Knight without looking away from
what she's doing.

KNIGHT
Of course. Hi, Sally!

FALLON
(removes needles from his flesh)
Look, I gotta go check on Jolly Jenny. She's
fallen in love again and is off her feed. If I
ain't careful I'm gonna end up with an
anorexic fat lady! It's bad for business!
Make yourself at home!
(exits stage right).

KNGHT
Thanks, Fallon! Catch ya later!

RAND
(takes out his wallet and shows Knight snapshots)
Got some new ones for you . . . Randy's a
dentist now . . . Got a practice in . . .
Sheboygan . . . Here's one of June with her
husband and little Dee-Dee . . . She can say
her A-B-C's now . . . Smart as a whip . . .
KNIGHT
Time flies. Oh, I happened to, uh, run into
some guy named Harry Cabrini today . . .

SALLY
(stops hammering and looks at Knight)
Cabrini's here?

KNIGHT

He was, but Fallon threw him out. I don't
know if he's still around or not . . .

SALLY

He better not be hanging around!
(shakes hammer at Knight for emphasis.)

If I find that slimeball skulkin' round this
tent again, I'll show im where monkeys
put bad nuts!

RAND

Now, Sally . . .

SALLY

(resumes hammering)

Don't you 'now, Sally' me, Rand
Holstrum! The trouble with you is that
you're too damn nice! Even to people who
don't deserve more'n what you'd give a
dog on the street!

Rand shakes his head and takes his place on the platform, behind the chickenwire.

You know what I caught that crazy
motherfucker doing? I come back from the
Burger King and found the nutcase taking
measurements of Rand's skull!

RAND

I've been . . . measured before, Sal . . .

SALLY

Yeah, but by *doctors*! What business does
some screwball like Harry Cabrini have
doing shit like that?

She finishes her hammering and steps back to view her
work.

Whaddaya think?

KNIGHT
Looks good to me.

SALLY
Looks ain't the point. Hand me that bottle.

She points to an empty beer bottle laying on the ground.
Knight hands it to her.

You ready, honey?

RAND
As I'll ever be . . .

Sally parodies a baseball player winding up for a pitch
then hurls the beer bottle at her husband. It bounces
harmlessly off the chickenwire.

RAND
(mimicking an umpire)
Yer out!

A roustabout enters from stage right carrying a take-out
bag full of hamburgers.

ROUSTABOUT
Got them burgers you wanted Miz
Holstrum.

SALLY
Thanks hon! You're a lifesaver!

She takes the burgers and hands the roustabout some
money. Roustabout exits the way he came.

Rand! Go change your clothes, honey. You
don't want to get that nice smoker June
sent you for Father's Day dirty!

Rand gets off the platform and retires stage left. Sally
busies herself with setting up a card-table and a cuisinart.

KNIGHT
Uh, have you known Cabrini for long?

SALLY

I remember back when he used to run his
own ten-in-one during the Korean War.
He retired a few years back after his head-
liner Pengo the Penguin Boy died of a
stroke. Pengo was a class act; he played
piano with his face! Real trooper. Cabrini
on the other hand . . . Let's just
say no one was heartbroke when he folded
his tent. All I know is the creep lives in a
trailer park on River Road.

While Sally talks she takes the burgers and dumps them
in the cuisinart. She liquifies the burgers and then pours
the mess into a tall glass.

You interested in hanging around for
lunch?

Rand reappears minus his smoker. Sally hands him the
glass.

KNIGHT

Not this time Sal. Thanks for the invite
though. See you later Rand!

She exits stage right.

SALLY

Such a nice girl! If only she would find a
man and settle down!

RAND

Now Sally, not everyone can be as lucky as
you . . .

Rand drinks the burger slush as scene ends.

SCENE TWO

The set is the front room of a mobile home. It's filthy, full
of empty fast-food sacks and discarded burger wrap-
pers; the waste basket is full of empty liquor bottles,
most of them cheap if not generic manufacture; the

ashtrays are piled full of butts. On the walls are faded posters from Cabrini's carnival days, while scattered about the parlor are 10-gallon pickle jars housing malformed fetuses floating in formaldehyde. Most of the jars are shrouded, although there should be one or two left exposed. The front door is stage left, while the rest of the trailer is stage right. As the lights come on, the sound of someone pounding on the front door can be heard. As it grows louder, a muffled mewling sound joins in. Cabrini enters, dressed in an ill-fitting polyester leisure suit that looks like it came from the Goodwill. He is balding and has bad teeth.

CABRINI

Hold your horses, dammit! I'm comin'!

He turns around and hisses into the room he just left.

Hush! I don't wanna hear another peep outta y'all!

Cabrini hurries over to an old steamer trunk, rooting through the drawers, tossing jockstraps and socks everywhere, until he retrieves a one-size-fits-all toupee. Cabrini slaps the toupee on his head without looking in mirror.

KNIGHT

Mr.Cabrini? Hello? Is anyone there?

CABRINI

I *said* I'm comin', goddammit!

He opens the door the the length of the chain.

Who th' fuck are you?

KNIGHT's VOICE

Mr. Cabrini? Mr. Harry Cabrini?

CABRINI

Yeah, I'm Cabrini — what's it t'you, lady? I ain't in the market for no Girl Scout Cookies!

KNIGHT'S VOICE
Mr. Cabrini, my name is Jessica Knight. I
was told by a Mr. Fallon that you had . . .
something I might be interested in.

CABRINI
(opens the door and lets Knight in)
C'mon in, dammit! No point in lettin'
every skeeter in the county in with you!

Knight enters the room, eyeing the place with distaste.
Cabrini watches her closely.

You're that gal what takes pictures of
freaks. Flippo the Seal Boy told me bout
you.

KNIGHT
And Fallon told me about you.

CABRINI
Oh yeah? Well, what d'you want, lady? I
ain't got all night . . .

KNIGHT
(showing him the Polaroids he got from Fallon)
A picture. I'll pay you.

CABRINI
Okay. Hunnert bucks. Otherwise you walk.

Knight gives him the money. Cabrini is pleased with
himself. He digs through the clutter and comes up with
a couple of glasses and a bottle of cheap booze.

CABRINI
(continued)
I don't get much in the way of visitors. And
I reckon you deserve a free drink for your
money.

Cabrini pours the drinks. Knight takes a sip and grimaces.

Cabrini gulps his with gusto.

> You know, I've run cross a few of your
> type in the business. Fellers who take pic-
> tures. But yer the first woman I ever met.

KNIGHT

I'm a professional photographer, and I've
been collecting shots of . . . carnival performers for the last ten years. I'm hoping
to get a book published . . .

CABRINI

Save the talk for someone else, sister! A
fish's a fish and a peek's a peek!

KNIGHT
(changing the subject)
How did you find them?

CABRINI

None of yer fuckin' business! All you want
is a picture. What's it matter where they
come from? They come from normal, god-
fearin folk. Like they all do. Just like you
an' me.

He pours another shot for himself.

> The freak business is dyin' out, y'know.
> Been dyin' since the War. People learned
> more bout what makes freaks. Folks used
> t' think they was th' sins of th' parents made
> flesh. That they didn't have no souls on
> account of that. That they weren't like real
> people. Hell, now that the March of Dimes
> has got rid of most that what used to reel
> th' fish in! An' if that weren't bad enough,
> lots of states passed laws classifying freak-
> shows as *obscene*! Like there weren't no
> difference between some whore shaking
> her titties and a freak showin' hisself for a

living! Don't get me wrong, now. There'll always be folks wantin' t'look. I think it's cause it makes 'em feel good. No matter how fuckin' awful things might be, at least you can walk down th' street without makin' folks sick, right? But who wants to pay to see dwarfs? Midgets? Fat Ladies? Pinheads? Sure, they're gross, but you can see 'em for free at th'Wal-Mart any day of th'week! No, to really get somewheres nowadays, you gotta have something that really *scares* 'em. Something that shocks 'em! Something that makes 'em forget they're lookin' at another human! Tall order, ain't it?

KNIGHT

Uh, I, well . . .

CABRINI
(warming to the subject)

I got t'readin' about how there used to be these here guys back in Europe. During them Dark Ages. Anyway, these guys was called Freak Masters. Got a nice ring to it, don't you think? Anyways, these Freak Masters, when times was tough an' there weren't no natural freaks to be had, they'd kidnap babies . . .

The mewling and bumping grows louder

. . . . and they'd put 'em in these here special cages, so's they'd grow up all twisted-like. And they'd make 'em wear these special masks so's their faces would grow a certain way, what with baby meat bein' so tender and all . . .

The mewling grows even louder, Cabrini loses his temper and bangs on the door.

Dammit! I told y'all to quiet down! I got company out here! Where was I . . . ? Oh, yeah . . . Sometimes they'd turn babies into mermaids by skinning the inside of their legs and then binding them so's they'd graft together, creating a tail like a fish. Others they'd skin alive bit by bit, replacing human skin with pieces of hide cut off dogs. Then they'd cut out their voiceboxes and disconnect their joints so's they had to run on all-fours, like an animal! Anyway, these freakbabies come out kinda brain-damaged, those that didn't die, that is. But the kings and popes and shit back then didn't care. They bought freaks by the truckloads! Pet monsters!

Cabrini laughs and starts taking swigs out of the bottle.

Them was the days! Yes sir! They didn't have no freaktents back then. But it don't matter. There'll always be freaktents. We carry 'em with us wherever we go.
(taps temple and grins drunkenly).

KNIGHT
(fidgeting)
Mr. Cabrini, it's getting late.

CABRINI
I reckon you want to take your picture and get. That's th'trouble with th'world t'day. People always in a hurry. You stay put; I'll see if I can't drag one of'em out where you can take a picture.

Cabrini opens the door to the freakbabies' room and ducks in. The mewling sound turns into frightened squealing, as if he's trying to corner a piglet. You can hear Cabrini bumping around and swearing. While this is going on, Knight pokes through some of the garbage strewn abound the living room, coming up with a baby-sized s & m mask. She stares at it with both distaste, horror and fascination.

CABRINI'S VOICE

Damn it, hold still you little fucker! GET
BACK HERE YOU LITTLE—Watch the door!
The little mother bit me!

Cabrini reappears, his clothes disheveled, his toupee
askew, sucking on his wounded hand.

What can I say? They're fuckin' morons.
Just like animals! Don't clean up after
themselves. Don't talk. Shit whenever the
mood strikes 'em . . .

Knight turns around, staring in horror at Cabrini. Cabrini
takes a soiled handkerchief from his pocket and mops
his face.

KNIGHT

That's alright, Mr. Cabrini. I'll come back
sometime later, when they're not so . . .
upset.

CABRINI
(advancing on Knight)

What's the matter, girlie? Don't you want
your picture no more?

KNIGHT

Of course I do . . . It's just that it's late and
I, um, have to be somewhere . . . I'll come
back later if that's alright with you.

CABRINI

I don't give refunds!

KNIGHT

(backing towards the door)
No that's okay! You can keep
the money . . . I don't mind, honest!

CABRINI

You know, you're kinda pretty. Too pretty
to be spendin' your time takin' pictures of
ugly things. Why do you wanna do some-

thing like that for?

KNIGHT

Like I said I'm trying to put together a book
. . .

CABRINI

Naw that ain't it. I know what you are and
what you're *really* interested in! You're all
the same no matter how much education
or money you got! Some of you are doctors
or newspaper men. Others are art-teests.
(smirks)
Like you. Thought I was dirt but you still
paid me for the honor of lookin' at my
freakbabies! Y'all treat me like I ain't no
more than a brothel-keeper. But what does
that make *you* Little Miss Art-teest?

KNIGHT

Look, all I want is to leave . . .

CABRINI

Lookin' at freaks gets you all hot don't it?
It makes you all hot and slick lookin at 'em
and knowin' you're beautiful. Is that it?

He moves closer until he is towering over her.

KNIGHT

No! No you're wrong! You're wrong about
everything!

CABRINI

Am I?

Cabrini grabs Knight's hair trying to pull her forward so
he can kiss her, his other hand grabbing at her breasts.
Knight kicks him in the shins and scratches his face. He
staggers backward wiping at the blood on his cheek with
his sleeve.

You goddam freak! Goddamn freak bitch!

Before Cabrini can launch another attack, Knight grabs

one of the pickled punk jars and brings it down on Cabrini's head. The jar shatters, sending liquid and the preserved fetus flying. The freakbabies squeal and mewl in fear. Knight stands over Cabrini's prone figure for a few seconds, gasping and trembling. She looks in the direction of the freakbabies' door then back down at Cabrini. After a moments hesitation, she bends down and takes the hundred dollar bill she gave Cabrini out of his wallet and flees the scene of the crime. It is uncertain whether Cabrini is dead or unconscious. The sound of a car peeling out can be heard offstage. The lights dim, although there is still enough light for the motionless figure of Cabrini to still be seen. After a few beats the door to the freakbabies room opens and a couple of small, twisted, hairy forms emerge. These are the freakbabies. They are hesitant and mewl and whimper in hushed tones. They stroke and prod Cabrini experimentally, then haul the body back into thelr room, yammering wordlessly amongst themselves. The door slams shut behind them.

CURTAIN

Nancy A. Collins is the author of the Bram Stoker Award-winning **Sunglasses After Dark***. Her most recent novel is* **In the Blood** *(Penguin/ROC). She is currently the writer for DC Comics* **Swamp Thing***.*

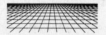

LOVE I$ WHERE YOU BUY IT

Brian Hodge

I always feel like a voyeur, sitting in my chair.

But the girl didn't notice. They never do. This one was blond, too thin, wearing only a G-string. She was allegedly dancing, but

that was a stretch of the imagination. Swaying while occasionally tossing her shoulders were her limits. Just for me, though. And about four dozen other guys.

The place was named Mount Venus. Far from being Tampa's top night-time entertainment mecca, but it did the job for me. These places all look much the same on the inside. A runway stage, focal point for ninety percent of the building's lights. Tacky glitz. Bouncers with swollen muscles and ample bellies. Small round tables and stray chairs, and at the outlying borders, darkened booths. Wall-to-wall pop and an overhanging smoke bank thick enough to shut down an airport.

All the same, instantly recognizable. Like a painting by Dali or an Ansel Adams photo, there's a rhythm there, an essence more than the sum of parts. Lifeblood.

"Hi there." Another girl, off-duty from the stage, up for something else. She knelt at my left, cocking an arm on my thigh. "How 'bout a private dance?"

I studied her a moment, barely long enough to draw breath. But long enough to know she wasn't the one for tonight.

"Not right now." I smiled gently, swirled a watery seven-and-seven, sipped. "Maybe later."

She'd heard the line before, undoubtedly, and knew precisely how to react. She was wearing a filmy teddy that barely reached her thighs and gapped to reveal no bra. She arched her back, scarcely noticeable unless you were expecting it, but enough to accentuate the gap. A firm hand slid up my leg, fingers drumming lightly. A hurt pout, and oh, she was *good*.

"You're sure about that? Just one dance?"

I shook my head, said nothing this time. She gave a practiced sigh, pushed herself up to try elsewhere. But just before moving along, she delivered the coup de grace: a quick over-the-shoulder glance, eyebrows arched, that was supposed to make me feel like a faggot.

The dancers in these places are like buses, always another coming along in a few minutes. No rest for the wicked. They patrol the exclusively male audience like panthers looking for an easy kill, eyeballing and separating wheat from chaff, men from boys. Forget the crazies, who sit

> It was the look on her face. The look of someone who knows she's being watched, and loves every second of it.

alone and don't blink and let their mouths hang open. Forget the ones going apeshit with friends, because it's hard enough to make yourself heard over the music as it is. Use your own judgment on the drunks. But definitely zero in on the quiet ones, the normal guys who sit and watch. And like what they see. Easy pickings.

Fortunately for them, we normal ones were the majority, sitting in that promenade between stage and booths. Up near the stage was a group of five guys who were especially noisy. Businessmen on the prowl, by their look, down in Tampa for a convention, out for fun and games. Bolstered by too much booze and that I-won't-tell-if-you-won't pact reserved for their wives back home in Terre Haute or wherever.

The song changed, and so did the dancer. Now a tall redhead bumped and ground. One of the businessmen pounded their table, then tipped his head back and howled. He chugged beer and laughed when it foamed onto his jacket via his chin. Call him Mr. Happy.

You'll always find his kind, no matter where you go. They're everywhere, all the same, interchangeably obnoxious. Devoid of class. I knew my share of them back home.

Tampa wasn't my town any more than it belonged to him, or the rest of the quintet making shambles of their suits. It belonged to my sister, and she granted visitation rights. She was a nurse on night shift and I slept late, and so far we'd not seen much of one another. That was okay, and the nights were mine alone.

A stranger in a strange land? Not me. Maybe I was an unknown here, a nobody. But at least I knew the lay of *this* land.

I'd turned down six more offers of a private dance by the time I found her, the *her* I'd been looking for, whom I would know upon sight . She was one *of* two dancing to an R.E.M. song. Michael Stipe's voice, This one goes out to the one I love, and I knew I needn't look further.

Her height was average, her dancing better. No stranger to exertion, a distinct contrast to most of her predecessors. Her black hair had been cultivated into a messy look, and it worked well for her. She danced in heels and garter belt and stockings, a nicely erotic ensemble, but that wasn't what did it for me.

It was the look on her face.

The look of someone who knows she's being watched, and loves every second of it. Some dancers looked as if the moment they hit the stage, they tuned out everything but lights and music. Sent thought whirling into the ozone for four minutes so they wouldn't have to contend with the notion of sixty guys watching, with little left to imagination. But she was different, this one. A palpable love of all those eyes crawling across her body, over the sheer clothing, *beneath* the clothing until they skimmed her body itself. She would deeply get off on the fantasies she *knew* were in progress over her.

Hips undulated, tummy muscles flexed and rolled. She twirled over to a fireman's pole and rode the shiny chrome up and down with orgasmic delight. Then spun away, licking both thumbs to in turn wet each pert nipple. Knowing full well that every eye in the place was fixed on her, and for every dropping jaw scraping a tabletop, she was the cause.

She was in control, as firmly as if ruling us with whip and chair. And when her tongue peeked out to wet her lips and she smiled at us, I knew she did this for more than money. She did it for the love of it.

I once heard one of the more sensible pop psychologists state that men fall in love through their eyes, women through their ears. If so, there could be no more perfect arrangement than this, men watching women who synced themselves to their music. And if the urgency of the night precluded love, then there was always lust.

She left the stage when the song ended, worked her way along the crowd on the opposite side of the room. I watched as she knelt beside some big dopey guy, surely a college football player. Teeth like My Friend Flicka. She made her pitch and he enthusiastically bobbed his head. Again, equine, another word and she'd have him pawing the ground to count. They stood and she led him back to the welcoming shadows of the booths. A romantic corner getaway.

But I could wait. Sometimes I have the patience of a saint.

I watched her, still. Watched her weave those sinewy muscle for her private audience of one. Such an unlikely *menage a trois* we made.

I had known the joys of the eye ever since I was twelve and had seen my older sister and her boyfriend, how they behaved on the sofa when they thought they were alone. Such lessons they taught . . . anatomical, spiritual, and libidinous.

Watching the unaware is surely the ultimate violation of the soul, if not the body. A secret gaze cannot be fought, nor stopped from glimpsing those stolen moments when a soul is laid out as naked as a body, in all its imperfections and glories.

Before my erection raged too fierce, too early, I headed to the bathroom to void away an earlier drink. I was just zipping up again, alone, when I was joined by Mr. Happy. His walk had become an unsteady lurch, and an alcohol flush had bloomed all the way up into his receding hairline. He gave me a sloppy grin and fumbled with his zipper, its operation elusive, and he laughed and balanced against one of the toilet stalls.

"Whoa! Gonna get me a piece of tail toooo*night!*" he cried. "Gonna ride, ride, riiiide!"

"Yeah?" I returned the grin, cheerful as ever. "That's pretty good for one more flaming asshole who's way out of control."

His face clouded over a moment, as if the words had to swim upstream for comprehension.

"Hey now justaminute, you sumbitch, you—" He frowned. That cheery grin of mine really had him perplexed. "I mean—" He upturned his palms, hunched his shoulders. "Look, you pays your money and you gets your show. Right? Right?"

I never could stand guys like him. And so as Mr. Happy wavered before the stall, wanting me to like him or something, I cold-cocked him. He stumbled backward into the stall, each eye rolling independently of the other. I stepped forward and caught him, seated the poor slob on the toilet so he wouldn't fall and hurt himself. Down for the count, he slumped against the wall. I shut the stall door. Goodnight, sweet prince. Make a spectacle of yourself no more this night. Some things should *not* be seen.

I flexed the dull throbbing out of my wrist on my way back to my chair. Sat quietly tending the watery drink. Waiting, for her, love of my nightlife.

It took her another twenty minutes to make it around to my side of the room. Sidetracked by two more dances, but she was as inevitable as that proverbial next bus. When she was within range, appraising us *en masse*, I baited the trap. The briefest flicker of eye contact and the faintest of smiles were sufficient summons.

"Feel like a dance?" she asked, squatting before me, her elbows resting on my knees. She was no disappointment up close, as they sometimes are. Strip away the veneer of lights and motion and music, and they don't always hold up. You see the desperation up close, the various prices paid for being the focal point of all those eyes.

"Ummm . . . I might." Being coy, that's part of the game I play, *we* play. Along with the questions. A lapdance veteran, I know the answers, but ask anyway. "What exactly do we do?"

Her eyes lit up, she had a live one here. "Well, you see, we head off over to one of the booths for a couple songs, and we get nice and comfy . . . and I make you feel *real* good."

"How much?"

"There's a ten dollar dance and a twenty dollar dance."

"What's the difference?"

"How good you want to feel."

She was great, an answer for everything, forever at tonguetip by virtue of sheer repetition. You pays your money and you gets your show, absolutely. Mr. Happy should be so lucky now.

"What's your name?" I finally asked.

" . . . Lori." This one came a bit slower. Probably wasn't asked her name very often, her business encounters ruled by anonymity.

"Okay, Lori. You just got yourself a twenty dollar dancing partner."

She smiled with the satisfaction of a Fortune 500 exec closing the biggest deal of her life. Lori took me by the hand, led me back, past the other spectators, back, further from the range of the stagelights, back, into the waiting shadows of the booths. A romantic getaway of our very own, all eight minutes worth, or whatever it would turn out to be. Then she asked for the money.

Private dance may have been the term of choice, but its choreography was older than time. After I settled into the cracked vinyl of the booth, scuffed and stained and pocked with cigarette scars, Lori began by straddling my lap. She ground herself down upon me, teased her breasts into my face. Wiggled around and over me to a rhythm heard mostly in her head, dry-humping, riding the bulge in my lap.

I responded as would any healthy male with breath in his lungs. I ran my hands over her, gliding one way, then another, slipping my fingers into that moist cleft you could only dream about while she was onstage. At least until she shooed my hands away. Maybe afraid a bouncer might see us and decide I was having more fun than my twenty bucks allowed.

Lori groaned and cooed at me, planted tiny light kisses on my cheeks and ears. I guess so it might be easier for me to pretend that she was enjoying this as much as she thought I was.

But it wouldn't have taken much on her part to square us even. Not that an attractive woman in her early twenties squirming on your lap is unpleasant. But the sights, sounds, sensations . . . merely foreplay. I always want more. Need more.

"Lori? Do you have a boyfriend?" I asked. Again, part of the game, and I *so* love to play. To ask the questions for which they have no ready, pat answers.

"Sometimes." She was straddling me again, this time facing away, riding my knees like a rocking horse.

"Does he know you do this?"

Lori spun around on my lap to face me, rhythm faltering, then lost altogether. This time the eye contact wasn't transient.

"Look, it's my job. I'm a dancer. I'm *not* a whore." Slowly, with greater deliberation, she began to regain her rhythm.

I'm not a whore. Maybe not, maybe so. In a world where magazine covers quote Jessica Hahn saying, "I am not a bimbo," you learn to question credibility. *I am not a whore. I am not a bimbo. I am not a crook.* All pretty much the same. The only difference lies in motives, whether it's done for love or for money.

The lapdance continued, two songs' worth, and after the second ended Lori slid off in dismount and sat beside me in the booth. I watched her watch the dancers onstage as she gnawed at a fingernail. Hair still attractively messy. She noticed my stare and gave me a smile, an uneasy but genuine one this time, not the Fortune 500 smile of before. The facade of buyer and seller between us had somehow been cracked. It's what I crave most, I think. Watching facades strip away as thoroughly as clothing.

"I was wondering," I said. "Do you do any private dancing after hours? You know . . . after this place closes down?"

Lori's gaze flicked from the dancers to me, back again, then to the floor. Was *she* playing coy now? How's that for a twist. Or maybe she was feeling the pangs of being caught in a lie.

"Yeah," she finally said. "I do that too."

Facade dissolved, the core revealed. And the voyeur triumphant. We made our arrangements; simple plans, really. All I had to do was hang around swilling overpriced drinks until two in the morning, and off we would go. Ride, ride, ride, as some wise sage had earlier forecasted.

I kept to the background for the rest of the night, set a new record for how long a seven-and-seven can be made to last. You have to pace yourself, retain that edge of control. Or else you degenerate into Mr. Happy, and all manner of misfortune may befall you. It happens.

I sat, watching the dancers but not really seeing them anymore. Except when Lori danced. Swaying, kicking, twirling . . . absorbing all that undivided attention and locking it deep within herself. The one thing she lived for, loved. The one thing she could steal from this place and make her own. Far more fundamental than some five dollar tip slipped into a garter belt.

I wondered, not for the first time, what led me back to places such as Mount Venus, women such as Lori, time and again. It wasn't like I *had* to pay for it; I had, in advance of my thirtieth birthday, accumulated an impressive roster of two ex-wives and numerous ex-girlfriends. Fulfillment of some crazy rape fantasy hardly seemed likely, not with a wallet suddenly lighter by fifty or sixty dollars. And forget the reassurance of a sure thing at the end of the night. You can always find a bar where the investment of a few hours of your time and a few drinks and some banal conversation secure the same goal.

The more I thought about it, the more I realized that the answer would always elude me so long as I looked only at myself. Or only at Lori, all the Loris preceding her. They were of a definitive type, every one, and you had to look at us together, what we made. A man who's mastered the art of watching eroticism, and a woman who's mastered the art of being watched.

Two of a perfect pair.

Closing time seemed to roll around a lot quicker after that. When the lights finally came up, murky through the stale cloud of cigarette smoke, Lori sought me out and said to give her a few minutes. She then disappeared through a door near the restrooms; when it opened I caught a glimpse of wall-to-wall female flesh before it slammed shut. I amused myself by watching the bouncers strolling about, herding out stragglers and looking like bullfrogs puffed up for mating season. One of them came toting Mr. Happy from the john in a fireman's carry. Maybe a cab would be called. Or maybe they would just toss him onto a scrap heap in the back with others of his ilk, and wait until Mrs. Happy came to claim him.

Lori emerged from the dressing room several minutes later. She still wore the same heels, but the garter belt and stockings were gone in favor of jeans and a Spuds MacKenzie T-shirt, stylishly knotted over one hipbone. Her face looked washed and her hair had been arranged into fresh disarray. She looked as if she belonged on a college campus. Maybe, by daylight hours, she did.

"Do you have a car?" she asked.

"Yeah," I said, and she bid farewell to a couple bouncers at the door. They watched us leave and I could feel their glares at my back. They were the most humorless men I'd ever seen. The cancer of unrequited love, perhaps.

When we were getting into my rental, courtesy of the airport Avis, Lori told me she always took a cab to work.

"Do you have to take one home very often?"

"Not when I don't want to." She was getting better at this game. A legitimate answer, and it divulged little. I admired that.

She played navigator, giving directions on how to reach her apartment. The trip took us on a scenic tour of Tampa by night. It's a far different kind of city than, say, Miami, Orlando, and so on. It feels older, earthier. More real. As if less of a veneer covers what goes on in its streets, buildings, shadows.

When we arrived, the place I parked wasn't much better than an alley, and I had no idea where I was. Good luck trying to drive a straight line back to my sister's once I left.

Lori lived in a building that, from outward appearances, looked like a warehouse. Probably subdivided into lofts. I followed Lori past a row of over-burdened garbage cans, into a recessed doorway framed by bricks darkened with decades of grime. Half a block away two cats screeched in heat or fury, and more trash cans clattered. Much farther, sirens wailed desolate unease. By the light of day, this place would no doubt resemble a dungeon which lacked the decency to stay hidden underground.

Her keys jingling, Lori led me up a creaking stairway, steeper than a climb up Kilimanjaro and as narrow as a sewer pipe. Another door met us at the top. And on the other side, boom, there was the bed, unmade, barely three steps to the right of the doorway. It was all I could see, given the lack of illumination. The bed was lit from above, a few weak moonbeams filtering through a skylight directly over-head. The rectangle of light was cut into sharp squares by a grid framework over the skylight, and the bed looked like a cage.

As we began to shed our clothes, I

> When I touched the bed, I recoiled. The sheets, instead of soft and cool, felt brittle. They even crackled.

had the sense of a vastness of space, that the room was huge. Even though the bed was all I could see, plus an adjacent nightstand. Attribute it to that peculiar radar that lets you know whether the pitch-black space you're occupying is the size of a phone booth or a cathedral.

Our clothes were limp heaps on the wooden floor, and I looked at Lori. Some-thing seemed to be missing from the moment. Business.

"Don't you want me to throw some cash on the nightstand?"

She shrugged. "Whatever. I don't care."

Certainly not the answer I expected. I felt disappointed, in a vague way. As if I owed her something else now, besides money and undivided attention. Some-thing I'd be unable to deliver.

My eyes were beginning to get used to the dim light, my field of vision ex-panding. Points of light seemed to glint in the air. Like reflections on angled planes of glass. A moment later I thought I could sense faint movement, beyond the limits of sight, rustling in the thick of shadows.

Lori gasped and pulled me down with her, toward the bed, reclining and gripping my wrist and tugging me to her. And when I touched the bed, I recoiled. The sheets, instead of soft and cool, felt brittle. They even crackled.

Overhead lights blinked on then. After the near-darkness they were almost blinding. I recalled scenes from various movies, dead stadiums suddenly flooded with banks of lights. No hiding place.

I'd been right, the room *was* enor-mous. While my range of motion was limited. Only as far as the walls of plate glass set a few feet beyond each side of the bed. With the brick wall behind us, we were enclosed as neatly as an exhibit in a zoo.

Complete with spectators, as well.

They lined the entire span of glass walls, far too many to count in a glance. All eyes trained on Lori and me, glazed stares nailing us to the bed. All ages, all shapes, all sizes. Male and female and some that looked somewhere between.

"I *can't* do it alone," Lori said, still on the bed, now parting her legs. Moist and beckoning. "It feels as sad as *dancing* alone."

I couldn't look at her yet, still transfixed by the sea of eyes beyond the badly smeared glass. On one side, a preteen girl pressed her mouth to it, leaving streaks of vivid lipstick to frame a squirming pink tongue. On another side, a grossly obese man, hydrocephalic, sat picking his nose. Elsewhere, an ancient wrinkled man stroked himself; his release was immediate and premature, dribbling down the glass. In the background, I thought I recognized a bouncer from Mount Venus, sorting through a huge fistful of green green cash.

"I just want to be noticed," Lori told me, and when I finally looked at her, she implored me with her eyes. "I just want them to see me for what I am."

So far as I knew, the door was still unlocked. But that was the furthest choice from my mind. No longer a viable option. And there she lay before me, waiting, willing, stretched out atop her bed, the wretched sheets crusted with the residue of a thousand prior late-night trysts.

You pays your money and you gets your show.

Featuring two of a perfect pair.

So I closed my eyes, very very tightly, and lowered myself the rest of the way into her.

Because . . . the show must go on.

Brian Hodge is the author of **Darklife** *and two prior novels.* **Deathgrip**, *his new novel is due for release in May 1992.*

PELTS

From a One-Act Play
by F. Paul Wilson

CARESSED IN THE DARKNESS OF THE JERSEY PINE BARRENS, JEB AND HIS SON GARY FINISH THEIR EVENING'S SKINNING TASKS AS WELL AS A CROCK JUG OF HARD CIDER.

GOOD! A GOOD DAY'S WORK! AIN'T THEY BEAUTIES?

THEY SURE ARE. MOST BEAUTIFUL PELTS I EVER SEEN. BUT WHAT ARE THEY? THEY LOOKED A LITTLE LIKE RACCOONS, BUT I AIN'T NEVER SEEN--

RESCRIPTED FOR COMIC BOOK FORMAT AND ILLUSTRATED BY RUSS MILLER--LETTERED BY JOHN CLARK

DON'T VEX ME WITH POINTY-HEADED QUESTIONS, BOY! WHO *CARES* WHAT THEY WERE? WE GOT US THE BEST-LOOKING PELTS IN THE PINES! LITTLE THANKS TO YOU!

AW, DADDY--

THE HEAD, BOY! YOU GOTTA MAKE SURE TO GET 'EM IN THE *HEAD!* COUPLA TIMES THERE YOU ALMOST MESSED UP THE PELTS WITH BODY SHOTS! THE HEAD, THE *HEAD!*

I WAS TRYIN', DADDY, BUT ITS HARD TO GET A BEAD ON THE LITTLE SUCKERS!

GOTTA LEARN, BOY. GOTTA LEARN TO TAKE YOUR TIME. THEM THINGS IS JUST SITTING DUCKS WHEN THEY'RE IN THE LEG TRAPS. PRETTY DAMN NEAR TUCKERED OUT FROM STRUGGLIN' ALL NIGHT LONG TO PULL FREE. NO HURRY. THEY'RE NOT GOIN' ANYWHERE!

WELL... WE DID ALL RIGHT!

THAT WE DID. NEVER SEEN ANYTHING LIKE IT. THE WHOLE LINE OF TRAPS, AND EACH AND EVERY ONE WITH SOMETHIN' SQUIRMIN' IN IT.

YEAH. AN' AFTER WE WAS FINISHED AND PACKED UP ALL THE ANIMALS, I LOOKED BACK AS WE WAS LEAVIN' AND THERE WAS A BRIGHT RED SPOT ON THE SNOW BY EACH AND EVERY TRAP. LOOKED TO ME LIKE A BLOODY-FOOTED GIANT HAD STOMPED THROUGH THE FIELD.

I BEEN THINKING. ARE YOU SURE THESE THINGS AIN'T GONNA BE CAUSIN' US TROUBLE?

TROUBLE? WHAT THE HELL'S THAT SUPPOSED TO MEAN?

WELL, I MEAN, WE DID POACH 'EM OFF OLD MAN FORSTER'S LAND. YOU KNOW WHAT THEY SAY ABOUT HIS PLACE.

GARBAGE! SUPERSTITIOUS GARBAGE. I HEARD ALL THEM STORIES--HUNTERS GOIN' ONTO HIS LAND AND NEVER COMIN' OUT, STRANGE NOISES, WEIRD LIGHTS. *GARBAGE!* OLD MAN FORSTER SPREADS THEM TALES HISSELF, JUST LIKE HIS DADDY 'AFORE HIM! WANTS TO KEEP EVERYBODY OFF HIS ACREAGE. FINE. LET THE OTHER CHICKENSHITS BELIEVE THAT STUFF, BUT IT AIN'T GONNA STOP ME! HELL, WE TRAPPED THAT LAND TODAY AND GOT AWAY SCOTT FREE WITH A GOLDMINE, DIDN'T WE, BOY? DIDN'T WE?

YEAH, WE SURE DID, DADDY. KIND OF A STRANGE GOLDMINE, THOUGH, DONTCHA THINK? I MEAN, WE AIN'T EVEN SURE WHAT KIND OF ANIMALS THEY WAS.

WHO CARES! LONG AS THEY GOT GREAT FUR. LOOK HOW THOSE PELTS SHIMMER. AND WINTER THICK! SO CELEBRATE, BOY! CELEBRATE!

UNNOTICED, AS GARY AND JEB CHATTER INTO THE COLD MORNING HOURS, THE PELTS BEGIN TO SQUIRM ON THEIR STRETCHING BOARDS...

I DUNNO, DADDY. THEM THINGS GIVE ME A WEIRD FEELING. FOR SOME REASON I BEEN THINKIN' 'BOUT HOW IT'D FEEL TO HAVE YOUR HAND CAUGHT IN A TRAP SO'S YOU'D HAVE TO LIE IN THE FREEZIN' SNOW ALL NIGHT. YOU THINK ANIMALS FEEL MUCH PAIN?

NOT IF YOU HIT 'EM RIGHT. ONE GOOD WHACK WITH A LOUISVILLE SLUGGER OUGHT TO DO IT EVERY TIME. AIN'T GOING SOFT ON ME, ARE YOU, BOY?

NO, DADDY. IT'S JUST THAT WHEN WE WAS BUSTIN' THEIR HEADS THIS MORNING, A COUPLE OF THEM... WELL, SORTA HELD UP THEIR PAWS LIKE THEY WAS BEGGIN' ME NOT TO HURT THEM. IT WAS ALMOST LIKE...HUMAN.

SPEAKING OF PAWS, LOOK AT THIS. FOUND IT STUCK IN ONE OF THE TRAPS.

HEY! LOOKS LIKE A FRONT PAW TO ONE OF THEM BEASTIES.

YEP, THE THING HAD JUST FINISHED CHEWIN' IT OFF WHEN WE GOT THERE, BUT I NAILED IT AFORE IT GOT AWAY.

Y'KNOW, I SENT JAKE THE FURRIER A PIECE OF THE PELT YOU STRIPPED. HE CALLED AWHILE BACK. TRIED TO ACT COOL, BUT I COULD TELL HE WAS ALL EXCITED. WE'RE GONNA HAVE US SOME SPENDING MONEY, BOY. MAYBE WE OUGHTTA CATCH A COUPLA THOSE BEASTIES ALIVE, STICK 'EM INNA CAGE...MATE 'EM...GET INTO THE FUR FARMIN' BUSINESS.

AS PA NODDED OFF, THE PELTS BEGAN TO MOVE...

HEY! WHAT THE...

GARY FOUND HIS BODY RESPONDING TO ANOTHER WILL. HE APPROACHED HIS FATHER...

KRACK! KRACK!

THEN GARY TURNED THE BAT ON HIMSELF.

NO! NO!

SMACK! SMACK! SMACK! SPLAT!

THE NEXT MORNING, JAKE THE FURRIER AND SHANNA, A VACANT BUT SUCCESSFUL MODEL ENTER A DISTURBING AND PUNGENT SCENE.

EEEUUUH! JAKE, LOOKIT ALL THE BLOOD!

WHAT DID YOU EXPECT, SHANNA? I'M A FURRIER. THIS IS ONE OF THE PLACES I GET MY PELTS. FUR DOESN'T GROW ON TREES. IT GROWS ON LITTLE ANIMALS. AND IT'S GOTTA BE PEELED OFF THEIR BACKS BEFORE YOU CAN WEAR IT.

PLEASE. I HAVEN'T HAD BREAKFAST YET.

WONDER WHERE JEB AND THE KID ARE? WEREN'T UP AT THE HOUSE. *WHEW!* JERSEY LIGHTNING! PROBABLY WAKING UP WITH ONE HELLUVA HEADACHE.

I DON'T KNOW WHY I LET YOU TALK ME INTO COMING HERE. IF THIS IS ANOTHER ONE OF YOUR DUMB SCHEMES TO TRY AND GET INTO MY PANTS--

SHANNA, GIVE ME A BREAK. WE'VE HAD A GOOD PROFESSIONAL RELATIONSHIP THE LAST FEW YEARS, HAVEN'T WE? I TOLD YOU, THIS IS BUSINESS. THE MODELING BUSINESS.

SO, WHY ARE WE HERE?

BECAUSE OF THIS. IF OLD JEB'S GOT A STACK OF PELTS THAT ARE ANYTHING LIKE THIS...

LOOK AT THEM! *LOOK* AT THEM! WHERE ON EARTH DID THAT OLD FOX GET THEM? THEY'RE MAGNIFICENT! EXQUISITE! WHAT A COAT THESE'LL MAKE! LOOK AT THE COLOR! I'VE NEVER SEEN SUCH A PERFECT MATCH! THEY WON'T NEED TO BE DYED! SHANNA! LOOK AT THESE!

AND JUST WHAT WOULD IT TAKE TO CONVINCE JAKEY THE FURRIER THAT HE'S FOUND THE RIGHT MODEL FOR THE JOB?

OH, I DON'T KNOW. YOU SHOULD USE YOUR IMAGINATION, MAYBE.

CONVINCING...VERY CONVINCING.

I CAN BE EVEN MORE CONVINCING IN THE CAR. COME ON, I'LL SHOW YOU.

YEAH, YEAH, LEMME SEE IF I CAN FIND A BLANKET BACK HERE.

ALL RIGHT, BUT DON'T BE LONG.

YO, JAKE, I'M WAITING! HURRY UP!

YEAH, HURRY UP AND GET THIS OVER WITH! MY GOD, WHAT A COAT THESE'LL MAKE! YOU'RE A SCHLUB-AND-A-HALF, JAKE, BUT YOU DO KNOW YOUR FUR. AND SHANNA'S GOING TO WEAR THIS ONE.

UNABLE TO FIND A BLANKET, JAKE RETURNS AND CHECKS A CLOSET.

MAYBE THERE'S SOMETHING IN--

OH, SHIT, OH MY GOD, IT'S JEB! OH, THIS IS TERRIBLE. WE GOTTA GET THE POLICE, WE GOTTA GET SOMEBODY! WHAT ARE WE GONNA DO?

THEN GARY BURSTS THROUGH THE OUTSIDE DOOR, A BLOODY RUIN!

DADDY! YOU FOUND DADDY! YOU *KNOW!*

FIGHTING BACK PANIC, JAKE GRABS A KNIFE FROM THE SKINNING TABLE.

THE PAIN! THE *PAIN!* OH, GOD, STOP THE PAIN!

STAY BACK, KID. I'M WARNING YOU--STAY BACK!

WITH AN ALMOST EAGER LUNGE, GARY HURLS HIMSELF ONTO THE KNIFE, IMPALING HIMSELF AND SLUMPING TO THE FLOOR, DEAD.

OH GOD! LET'S GET OUT OF HERE!

I'VE GOT TO TAKE CARE OF SOMETHING FIRST. GOT TO MAKE SURE NOBODY WILL KNOW WE WERE HERE. DON'T WANT TO LEAVE ANY EVIDENCE...

...AND I DON'T WANT ANYBODY ELSE TO GET THESE PELTS.

AS SHANNA RUNS TO THE CAR, JAKE METHODICALLY DRAGS THE CORPSES OF JEB AND GARY AWAY AND SYSTEMATICALLY BEGINS CLEANING UP THE EVIDENCE. IN HIS FERVOR TO BE THOROUGH AND MOP UP ALL OF THE EVIDENCE, JAKE DOES NOT NOTICE THE SQUIRMING PELTS, UNTIL...

HEY! WHAT THE HELL *IS* THIS?... WHAT THE HELL'S GOING....ON?... WHAT'S...HAPPENING?

HE REALIZES WHAT THEY WANT FROM HIM...

NO!

JAKE? WHAT'S HAPPENING? WHERE ARE YOU? JAKE?

SHANNA RETURNS A FEW MINUTES LATER...

MADE YOU A GIFT, SHANNA...

JAKE! OH MY GOD, JAKE! WHAT'S HAPPENED TO YOU?

MADE... IT...FOR YOU...

GET AWAY FROM ME, JAKE! MY GOD! GET AWAY FROM ME WITH THAT!

A MUTILATED JAKE HOLDS OUT A VEST MADE FROM HIS OWN FLESH AS AN OFFERING TO SHANNA.

IN HER FRENZIED HASTE TO GET AWAY, SHANNA ACCIDENT-ALLY CATCHES HER HAND IN A HANGING FOOT-RESTRAINT TRAP.

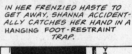

SNAP

EEEEEKK!

GET AWAY!

OH, GOD! GET BACK! GET BACK, DAMN YOU!

SHANNA, COME BACK...YOU'LL CATCH YOUR DEATH...OF COLD...

CLANKITY

END

ohlysaek 91

HESTER

Dave Swartout

"Your clitoris or penis is as wonderful as your fingers and ears, toes and elbows," Miss Hester said a couple years back, telling my fifth grade class why our sex organs were as good as the rest of our bodies, terrific when used responsibly.

She didn't know that last day of school, after wishing all of us a great summer, was her last day as a teacher.

Stored from sight like a rain-damaged old book, even though she was young, they made Miss Hester the grade school librarian across town: forcing her to exhort children to whisper for the rest of her professional career.

OBJECTS

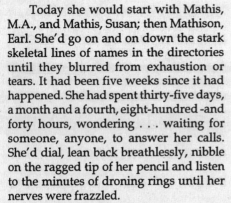

Ron Leming

Today she would start with Mathis, M.A., and Mathis, Susan; then Mathison, Earl. She'd go on and on down the stark skeletal lines of names in the directories until they blurred from exhaustion or tears. It had been five weeks since it had happened. She had spent thirty-five days, a month and a fourth, eight-hundred -and-forty hours, wondering . . . waiting for someone, anyone, to answer her calls. She'd dial, lean back breathlessly, nibble on the ragged tip of her pencil and listen to the minutes of droning rings until her nerves were frazzled.

But nobody ever answered...

So she crossed off the name and the number she had just dialed, and she would say to herself, softly, "Now this one is dead, too." She didn't question why the phone lines still functioned, why there was still power, why gas still flowed through pipes. Computers, she assumed, accepted, and held on to her acceptance as a source of hope. Parts of the world still worked, so there had to be *people* at the dials and motors and switches and valves that controlled the lifeblood of the city. At night, though, standing on the balcony and gazing at the city below, she could see that it was dying, going dark, street by street, block by block, piece by piece.

Having reached a stage where she was intentionally trying to trick herself into smiling whenever she could, she wondered what her employees would think of her, now . . . if they could see 'Iron-ass-Codey', sprawled on the unmade hotel bed, clad in nothing but the briefest of crotchless panties, phoning numbers of names she had never heard before . . . of *strangers*.

But they weren't there to see and be shocked by her. They mightn't be anywhere at all . . .

The first day she'd been in Hollywood, she'd taken a taxi to Frederick's and bought the sexiest thing she could find; a pair of blindingly pink panties, trimmed in black and red lace, with a mouth-like split crotch. She would wear them for her man, James, when she got back.

When she got back . . .

Her mood was strange today, she realized. Instead of crying again she began to caress and hold her small breasts, trying to see and feel in them what James felt and saw. The soft nipples began to wrinkle and rise and grow sensitive. They tingled with her touch, a tingle that reached into her belly, and she closed her eyes, squirmed until she could dangle her legs off the bed and touch the floor with her feet.

James, a confirmed breast man, had spent hours loving her breasts before he'd moved on . . . as she did now. Her hand found the slightly damp split in the panties and, thinking of James as *him*, she masturbated quickly, desperately. Her orgasm turned to sadness and little whimpering noises escaped her throat. They sounded like the noises a new puppy, lonely for its mother, might make in the middle of the night searching for the home tit. But for her, an alarm clock would not assuage the loneliness of missing another heart beating beside hers.

When it was over and she had gone to the bathroom and washed, she told herself that it was true, she was real, she was still *alive*.

She didn't know what had happened.She would probably never know. She had flown to Los Angeles from Florida for the annual theatrical supply and design convention. But the morning after her arrival, when the activities were scheduled to get under way, she had awakened to silence. Not a lack of speech and normal human activity; to a total absence of sound of any kind.

Half asleep, she'd begun wandering the pink and red and gold corridors, calling for somebody, *anybody*, to answer. All she found in reply were echoes, her own footsteps and bizarre sensations of emptiness. All her eyes witnessed was an enduring, unendurable look at human bodies. Bodies which, for some reason over time, neither smelled nor rotted . . . nor moved nor went away. They just looked peacefully permanently, silently dead.

She'd gone downstairs, through bodies sitting up, lying down, one or two *leaning*, as if they were just pausing before going for coffee and a newspaper and business calls. Bodies huddled against one another, on floors where they'd fallen, in lobby chairs holding burnt out pipes and crumpled newspapers, flat gin and tonics on dusty tables next to them. Bodies stretched over the reception desk. There might have been others behind the desk, but she didn't look.

There was one old woman, especially. She had been pressed like a bookend against the hotel's front door. It was half open and the old woman's arm was outthrust, as if attempting to clutch fragments of *outside*. Her cheek was flattened against the glass, her lips spread wide in a gasp for air or, possibly, sudden surprise. Dentures were skewed, sideways, in her mouth. The soft silence of death had left her no pride or dignity.

Right after that, Sarah had grabbed the register from the phone table and run upstairs to hide in her room. For a while she shook. She didn't cry, didn't scream. Just hugged herself and trembled. Then, confused and unbelieving, she called down for a drink. But no one answered in the bar. She'd gone to calling bars, professional associates in the hotel, the police department, hospitals, a newspaper and a television station, all the people registered in the hotel and, finally, to each name listed in the city's phone directory.

It had taken her five weeks to reach the M's in the first thick book.

"Hello?"

✧

Sarah's eyelids began blinking uncontrollably. Her hands shook and her voice came out, not a whisper, but a quiet shriek. "You . . . you're *somebody*!"

For an instant he didn't reply and she thought she might have reached a recorded message, only half played.

Then, "Well, *I* like to think so."

One hand clutched the phone and the other clutched her breast as she looked at the directory trying to remember who she had called. But her eyes were misted with tears and there were so many names.

"I've called and I've called," she said, "and *nobody* . . . but now you! You aren't dead like the others."

"Where are you calling from?"

"Why, I'm at . . . " She hesitated. His voice was calm and interesting. It sounded cold, or murky. No . . . smokey, she decided.

"I asked *where* you *are*."

Flustered, she had to retrieve her roomkey from the bedside table, squint at it through a teary cloud of relief and gladness.

"It's the Beverly Hills Hotel. Room 113."

Nothing in reply but a queer, half-stifled breathing. "I'm coming," he said. And then he hung up.

When the connection was broken, she sat and stared, wishing he hadn't hung up. Could she have just believed he was alive. Did she need human company so badly she had merely *imagined* the voice?

But that couldn't be, she assured herself, deciding to dress. Of course, she laughed. She was half-naked. She couldn't meet anyone that way. Jumping up from the bed, she hurried to the dresser. But her eyes glanced down, into the wastepaper basket, at the newspaper she had thrown away after the tenth fastidious reading. And she remembered the headline . . . HOTEL RAPIST CLAIMS VICTIM FIVE . . . remembered the story of violation and mutilation.

For a timeless few moments, the shivering claimed her. *I'm going crazy,* she thought. *He wouldn't have survived, not in a city filled with millions of people. That's just stupid.* She didn't know what a world of silent dead would be like, what her future would be. But, she thought, *maybe this has rid us of some things we're better off without.* Like frightening newspaper headlines and the people who make them.

She gazed into the closet. Her clothes were all so . . . competent. It was how she coped, by being methodical, by being

She remembered the headline . . . HOTEL RAPIST CLAIMS VICTIM FIVE

willing to do with cool, calm efficiency, whatever had to be done to keep her shadows at bay and her life on a balanced heading.

She looked in the three-quarter length mirror on the closet door. Hair down, she knew a few people, at least, considered her beautiful. Her hair was brown with a little gray and curled in all the right places. At 34, she was still in good shape. 5'3" and thin, muscular, softly rounded. Her breasts were small, her hips prominent, her skin mapped with freckles and moles by the hundreds that James, a big man, had loved. Yes, she was attractive.

Bra-less, she donned a green mini-dress and soft white blouse. She'd bought them north of Titusville, when she'd gotten a little tipsy at lunch. She'd never worn them before. No nylons, her legs were attractive by themselves. Sarah chuckled at her attempts to dress seductively. After all, half an hour ago, she'd thought the last man on Earth was a woman.

❖

The sudden *rap!* on the door made her jump, produced instantly the strange chills people sometimes get when there's no good reason and only their bodies are terrified. When her mind had taken over, denying the apprehension, she put on a wide smile and threw the door invitingly open.

He was dressed well enough. Slacks, a white polo shirt. brown shoes. He seemed very neat and all of a piece. Middle class, suburban, her business mind evaluated. His was a face in the crowd,

nondescript. But he could perhaps be attractive, were he not scowling so grimly.

"Hi!" she said, brightly.

He surged forward and his hands were on her, *touching* her, *roughly groping*. He grabbed her and flung her out into the corridor. Her back slammed against the wall, her hip ricocheted off a small table. He shoved her against the wall, steadied her with a hand pinching her left shoulder, and then he *hit* her.

She blinked once. There was no pain yet, but she felt something loosen in her mouth. His hand had cracked into her cheek, and now he was reaching for her once more. It was a shock, a sudden fissure in her hastily erected reality. *Why?* she wondered. *What have I done to him?* His hand, when she winced, caressed the place where he had struck. Then, with the palm only, it drifted below her jawline.

Such *madness* in his eyes, she thought. But a hungry kind of sadness, too, trying to break through the fury. It failed.

The man required his other hand to rip her blouse open. Then he used both hands on her breasts, kneading and twisting and pulling them as if she were a machine which — prodded here, probed

there, kicked in the slats the way you would kick a recalcitrant animal — or the way *he* would — might provide him with the performance he so desperately sought.

Stooping, he pressed his tongue against her right nipple, shoving it off-course, moaning as if had found paradise. Sarah's nipples were elongated, engorged and angry-red, her body charged with adrenalin.

She knew a plant rested atop the table he had her wedged against. Without taking her eyes from the man, she reached out, grabbed the plant, quickly raised it up and brought it down on his head. Neither the plant nor the man's skull broke, but he did stand up straight, yowling and rubbing his head. She instantly shot her arm out on a straight line below her waist, as hard and with as much strength as she could muster. He gurgled deep in his throat and, looking down, she saw the blow had caught him where she'd aimed, exactly in the balls. And she saw, a little surprised, that the plant was a wickedly-thorned cactus. Her knee came up the way his arms had, automatically, and she felt the way it sank into his injured softness. She smiled and the man stumbled back, into her room, where he fell. She followed him, brought one sharp heel down onto his face. She shifted balance and her other heel followed the course of the cactus and her knee. The man was hurting so badly that even screams wouldn't rise from his twisted mouth. Sarah kicked him once more in the ribs, and then she slammed the door shut— with her on the outside, in the corridor— and dashed awkwardly to the elevator.

Did she imagine him back there, thrashing around, trying to get up? Or was he already coming, angrier than before?

The elevator door sighed unhurriedly shut. She jabbed randomly at a button and the machine began to rise. Breathing hard, half sobbing, she slipped the torn blouse back over her now-tender breasts, tried to pull it together. When the elevator stopped, she pressed all the buttons so that it would continue moving as long as possible and he wouldn't know where she had gotten off. Then she hobbled down the corridor and into a room.

Against the wall with the picture window she saw them. Man on top of woman, seemingly frozen in joyous orgasm. One of the dead woman's hands still clutched his buttocks. Her long red nails had left four tracks of dried blood. Sarah turned and left them to their eternal lovemaking.

The next room found the silent dead watching a hissing TV. Mom in nightgown, dad in shorts and undershirt holding a beer. Junior in cotton pajamas, an expression of "Aw, can't I watch just one more show," frozen on his face. Sarah walked in and turned off the TV. "Time to go to bed," she said.

It was the same in all the rooms she tried. Grotesque masques, life seized but frozen. It had been quick. The end had come to most so stealthily and silently that there had been no time to weep or pray or even take a final step. They died where they stood or sat or lay.

Sarah kicked her shoes off and waited again for the elevator. When it came, she rode down to the lobby, the ran outside. She ran senselessly, then she realized she didn't know the city at all. Scarcely moving, flatfooted, she was conscious only of the silent dead on the sidewalks, in doorways, in stalled and wrecked cars.

She began running back, watching in case the man had followed her after all. Sooner or later, she knew, he would, and all she had to call home was the corner where the hotel stood. She ran behind the hotel, found the pink and white bungalows which were its true heart and history. Humphrey Bogart and Lauren Bacall had stayed in one of these tiny bungalows. Maybe, just maybe, the lingering spirit of Charlie Alnutt or Sam Spade would hide her.

Inside the bungalow she chose, it was dark. She hurried through it, checking for the dead. Only at the last second did she stop herself from flicking on the light.

Exhausted, she slipped into the bedroom and sank to the mattress, softly crying. All her clothes, everything she had in this unknown world to remind her of who she was were left behind in her room. She was left with nothing.

No, not nothing . . .

She had *something* left. Something *he* wanted. She had the one thing that, ultimately, all men wanted. It made her feel that all she had done, the strength she had developed, everything she'd accomplished to tell herself she was an object, was not only meaningless, now, but so obstinately, obdurately regressed to an inescapable reality that there was no chance at self-deception left to her at all. However much generation after generation of so-called civilized people had tried to deny it, it had always been this low, ugly primal struggle between men and women.

How could he be so mad that he couldn't *see* what he was doing? Or was he mad at all? Was he merely liberated now, to behave openly as he had always dreamed of behaving. Angry men had told her often enough that they felt violently victimized by women. She had seen the same madness in their eyes, the same trembling rage.

She knew she didn't dare, but she lay back on the unmade bed. She didn't want to, but she slipped into sleep.

And she awoke. To footsteps, weirdly and distantly muffled. They drew closer. Somehow, she could tell that he was angry, thwarted and, by God, man enough to *do* something about it. Sarah curled in upon herself.

He *couldn't* know she was in the bungalow. There were no lights, she'd made no sound . . . unless she'd cried out in her sleep. She covered her mouth with her hands, afraid to breathe, lest he hear her. He would realize any second the bungalow was deserted, abandoned as everything good or decent he'd ever believed. He'd give up. No one was *here!*

It was quiet. Almost unendurably quiet. Then the bedroom door caromed off the wall it struck in opening. The being framed by the distant light was *not* caring, was *not* friend or lover.

He has a knife.

Sarah's mind bruisingly accepted the fact. *It shines from his clenched fist*, she thought. *Oh, please don't cut me. Don't slice me up. Don't take me apart.*

Scars of old wounds throbbed as he walked over to the bed.

Leaning, he kissed her forehead, then her lips with a kind of violent tenderness. The knife was absently gripped, a negligent flicking, as he moved it past her cheeks, her eyes. She tried to keep her eyes on it. He poked her with it and, as she gasped, he stuck his tongue in her mouth, wallowed it around.

He used the knife, *the knife*, to cut the remnants of her blouse the rest of the way off, and was careless enough, or cruel enough to leave a ruby red droplet of blood glistening against her soft breast. Reaching his head down, he drew the blood in, lapped where it had been.

His fingers squeezed, closed in on her breasts, kept the knifepoint pricking her bare belly. Her hand moved and he squeezed his legs together. *Fight or flight*, she told herself, feeling her nipples erect. They didn't write about *that*. They never said that it was so violently humiliating because women, too, had honest flesh that could become aroused against the mind's will. That your own body could betray you and that there were people who were glad to send it on its way until your sense of self was shattered into bloody bits.

He shoved her flat down on the bed, put his hand on his dick. *When had he gotten it out. Had it been out when he'd burst into the room.* He stroked himself while he cut her panties off. She reached down, covered herself with her fingers. He thrust his dick between them and tormented her, made her hold him and stroke him. Then he thrust his face between her legs, cramming it into her. She felt horribly betrayed when she felt her hips thrust forward, felt the sensations that were the natural reaction to his damnable licking, slobbering, invading tongue.

He exchanged positions, grabbed a handful of her hair in his knotted hand and forced, yanked her head down. The gleam of the knife blade was shining in her left eye. His unoccupied hand reached between her legs, well taught, knowledgeable. When she began to heave and buck, she cursed her body, her own now-hated passion. The passion that was destroying her against her will.

He forced his dick into her mouth, yanked her head back and forth on it. She gagged as he prodded more deeply and filled her throat with that which he hated so much that he had to do *this* to her to remember his own, unneeded identity.

He released her and she curled into a fetal ball on the bed, alien to her own body. Repulsed, sore, she looked up in time to see the peculiarly wistful expression in his eyes as he lifted the knife above her. It was the way he drooled and labored for air that made Sarah look dully away.

But the knife didn't fall, and when she looked up again, she saw that the look in his eyes was not now one of total madness, but of momentarily banked hatred and dawning awareness. And so she performed the most devastating and wisest trick of womankind . . . she said what *he* was thinking.

"That's right, you *asshole*. They're *all* dead and I'm all that's left. If you murder me, then it's over . . . for you, too. You can never do it again. If you kill me . . . " she yawned and stretched lightly, " . . . then you kill *yourself.*"

He walked away from her. At the bedroom door, he spun to face her, the knife used to slice small cuts in his forearm. All the madness was back in his eyes.

"We *always* win, in the end," he said, then. Growled. "That's the way it is. You destroy us, over and over again, never letting us free. But in the end, we always rip you up." He sighed, and his face looked pained as he absently sliced his arm. "You *women*," he spat. "You plan and scheme and think you're so clever. You find our worst weaknesses and think that's what we are. You never see the strengths, just judge us by our failures. You save every mistake we make, you save it all up and you hit us with it all at once, when we need you the most, when you've used us up and drained us and want to get rid of us. But not this time, bitch. You won't get rid of me this time, you won't hide from me. I can *smell* you. I'll hide in empty places and shadows . . . like the lives you leave us when you abandon us. I'll watch you and I'll be more patient than you can ever imagine being. I'll *plan* and I'll enjoy every moment of it. I'll wait a year, ten years, fucking forever if I have to. But then . . . I'll be *there* and you'll be mine again. To *destroy*."

✧

When she came out of the bungalow at last, it was dark. Unhurriedly, deciding to walk, she headed inside the hotel, for the curving stairway. It was necessary at each landing to step over the silent dead. She saw the marks of *his* passing. He had torn some of the dead to pieces, bloodlessly. Sarah ignored them, ignored their open-eyes stares at her nakedness. *Don't speak to strangers.*

She would have to kill him, she supposed, but it would be difficult. Not impossible, but she felt she lacked the temperament for all that would involve. She wouldn't stalk him she decided. She would simply be ready and wait for him. He would come, sooner or later.

Once back in her room, feeling reminiscent, she took a quick shower, washing the feel of him off and out of her, the smell, and then she put on the plain white cotton panties James had always teased her about.

She wore them now because they made her feel like *Sarah*. They were undeniably *hers*.

Making herself comfortable on the bed, she pulled the telephone across the sheets, reached for her pencils and the directory. Now, where had she been before . . .

She would call everywhere. If she was alive, and *he* was alive, then others must be alive, *too. He* would stalk her, harass her, lurk and play idiotic male games and tricks on her, just the way *he* had promised. Men were good at determination, at patience, at mindless, blind persistence.

But *she* was competent.

He might kill her someday, and *he* might not. She just might kill *him*. In the meanwhile, what mattered was finding life, keeping the silent dead from becoming objects, too. She marked off another name, another number, and licked the tip of her pencil. Who else would keep the silent dead remembered unless she, competently, methodically, in gathering quietude, registered and remembered them?

And then the phone rang . . .

Ron Leming's artwork has appeared extensively in the first two issues of **Gauntlet**. *His first person account of sexual abuse as a child, that has haunted his life ever since (issue #2), was one of the most commented upon pieces in that issue.*

INTRODUCTION to "Limits of Fantasy"

In the summer of 1974 Michel Parry, an old friend, complained to me that nobody was sending him tales on sexual themes for his black magic anthologies. Aroused by the suggestion, I wrote "Dolls", which enabled me both to explore what happened to the supernatural story when the underlying sexual theme (not always present, of course) became overt and to write a long short story that was stronger on narrative than atmosphere, a useful preparation for writing my first novel. Michel hadn't expected anything quite so sexually explicit, and I was amused when his publishers, Mayflower, felt compelled to show "Dolls" to their lawyers for advice. They were advised to publish, and over the next two years Michel commissioned several more such tales from me, including two for a short-lived series of anthologies of erotic horror which he edited as Linda Lovecraft, who was in fact the owner of a chain of sex shops and who is one more reason why asking for Lovecraft in a British bookshop may earn you a dubious look. Perhaps the anthologies were ahead of their time, because More Devil's Kisses, the second in the series, was pulped shortly after publication, apparently in response to objections from Scotland Yard. Rumour had it that the problem was a tale reprinted from National Lampoon, involving a seven-year-old girl and a horse. I confess to being more amused than irritated by the ban, much as I felt upon learning that my first novel had been seen (in a television documentary) on top of a pile of books for burning by Christian fundamentalists—something of a compliment as far as I'm concerned. On reflection, though, I think I wasn't entitled to feel quite so superior about censorship. Though my sexual tales had been, on the whole, progressively darker and more unpleasant, I'd suppressed the third of them, "In the Picture." It was the initial draft of the story published here.

At the time (May 1975) I believed I had decided not to revise and submit the story because it wasn't up to publishable standard, and that was certainly the case. However, the reasons were more personal than I admitted to myself. All fiction is to some extent the product of censorship, whether by the culture within which it is produced or by the writer's own selection of material, both of which processes tend to be to some extent unconscious. Perhaps the most insidious form of censorship, insofar as it may be the most seductive for the writer, is by his own dishonesty. For me the most immediate proof is that it wasn't until Barry Hoffman asked me if I had any suppressed fiction that I realized, on rereading "In the Picture", that my dishonesty was its central flaw.

One mode of fiction I dislike—one especially common in my field - is the kind where the act of writing about a character seems designed to announce that the character has nothing to do with the author. On the most basic level, it's nonsense, since by writing about a character the writer must draw that personality to some extent from within himself. More to the present point, it smells of protesting too much, and while that may be clear to the reader, for the writer it's a kind of censorship of self. I rather hope that "In the Picture" is the only tale in which I succumb to that temptation.

"In the Picture" follows the broad outline of "The Limits of Fantasy", though much more humorlessly, up to the scene with   Enid Stone, and then Sid Pym begins to indulge in fantasies of rape and degradation which I believe are foreign to his sexual makeup and which are contrived simply to demonstrate what a swine he is—in other words, that he is quite unlike myself. Of course nothing could be further from the truth. In response to Barry Hoffman I treated "In the Picture" as the first version of the story and rewrote it exactly as I would any other first draft, and I had the most fun writing Pym's boarding-school fantasy, which is at least as much my fantasy as his. For me his presentation of it is both comic and erotic.

It seems to me that even the most liberal of us employ two definitions of pornography: the kind that turns ourselves on, which we're more prone to regard as erotic, and the kind which appeals to people with sexual tastes unlike our own and which we're more likely to condemn as pornographic. In my case the absurdity is that the group of scenarios which I sum up as the boarding-school fantasy (which is obviously as much fetishistic as sadistic) is the only species of pornography I find appealing, and it was therefore especially dishonest of me to include no more than a hint of it when I collected my sexual tales in *Scared Stiff*. I suppose, then and in my original suppression of "In the Picture", I was afraid of losing friends, but that really isn't something writers should take into account when writing. I suspect I was assuming that my readers and people in general are squarer when it comes to erotic fantasy than is in fact the case. Since the publication of *Scared Stiff* I've heard from readers of various sexes that they found parts of the book erotic, and a female reader gave me a copy of *Caught Looking*, a polemic published by the Feminist Anti-Censorship Taskforce, in which one of the illustrations (all chosen by the FACT designers on the basis that they themselves found the images erotically appealing) is a still from a spanking video made in Britain before such videos were banned outright under a censorship that is fast overtaking the equivalent glossy magazines. (The Spankarama Cinema in Soho, rather unfairly chastised in the Winter 1982/83 *Sight and Sound* and touched on by association in *Incarnate*, is long gone; perhaps I should have had a publicity photograph taken under the sign while it was there.) Incidentally, perhaps one minor reason for my reticence was the notion that this sexual taste is peculiarly British, but a day in Amsterdam proved me wrong.

So I trust this hasn't been too embarrassing. I haven't found it so, but then I may sometimes lack tact in these areas: I once greeted a friend I met in a sex shop, who immediately fled. Still, I'm committed to telling as much of the truth as I can, as every writer should be. If we can't tell the truth about ourselves, how can we presume to do so about anyone or anything? Secretiveness is a weakness, whereas honesty is strength.

—*Ramsey Campbell*

Copyright © 1992 by Ron Leming

The Limits of Fantasy

Ramsey Campbell

As Sid Pym passed his door and walked two blocks to look in the shop window, a duck jeered harshly in the park. March frost had begun to bloom on the window, but the streetlamp made the magazine covers shine: the schoolgirl in her twenties awaiting a spanking, the two bronzed men displaying samples of their muscles to each other, the topless woman tonguing a lollipop. Sid was looking away in disgust from two large masked women flourishing whips over a trussed victim when the girl marched past behind him.

Her reflection glided from cover to cover, her feet trod on the back of the trussed man's head. Despite the jumbling of images, Sid knew her. He recognized her long blonde hair, her slim graceful legs, firm breasts, plump jutting bottom outlined by her ankle-length coat, and as she glanced in his direction, he saw that she recognized him. He had time to glimpse how she wrinkled her nose as her reflection left the shop window.

He almost started after her. She'd reacted as if he was one of the men who needed those magazines, but he was one of the people who created them. He'd only come to the window to see how his work shaped up, and there it was, between a book about Nazi war crimes and an Enid Stone romance. He'd given the picture of Toby Hale and his wife Jilly a warm amber tint to go with the title *Pretty Hot*, and he thought it looked classier than most of its companions. He didn't think Toby needed to worry so much about the rising costs of production. If Sid had gone in for that sort of thing he would have bought the magazine on the strength of the cover.

The newspapers had to admit he was good, one of the best in town. That was why the *Weekly News* wanted him to cover Enid Stone's return home, even though some of the editors seemed to dislike accepting pictures from him since word had got round that he was involved in *Pretty Hot*. Why should anyone disparage him for doing a friend a favour? It wasn't even as though he posed, he only took the photographs. There ought to be a way to let the blonde girl know that, to make her respect him. He swung away from the shop window and stalked after her, telling himself that if he caught up with her he'd have it out with her. But the street was already deserted, and as he reached his building her window, in the midst of the house opposite his rooms, lit up.

He felt as if she had let him know she'd seen him before pulling the curtains—as if she'd glimpsed his relief at not having to confront her. He bruised his testicles as he groped for his keys, and that enraged him more than ever. A phone which he recognized as his once the front door was open had started ringing, and he dashed up the musty stairs in the dark.

It was Toby Hale on the phone. "Still free tomorrow? They're willing."

"A bit different, is it? A bit stronger?"

"What the punters want."

"I'm all for giving people what they really want," Sid declared, and took several quick breaths. The blonde girl was in her bathroom now. "I'll see you at the studio," he told Toby, and fumbled the receiver into place.

What was she trying to do to him? If she had watched him come home she must know he was in his room, even though he hadn't had time to switch on the light. Besides, this wasn't the first time she'd behaved as if the frosted glass of her bathroom window ought to stop him watching her. "Black underwear, is it now?" he said through his teeth, and bent over his bed to reach for a camera.

God, she thought a lot of herself. Each of her movements looked like a pose to Sid as he reeled her towards him with the zoom lens. Despite the way the window fragmented her he could distinguish the curve of her bottom in black knickers and the black swellings of her breasts. Then her breasts turned flesh-coloured, and she dropped the bra. She was slipping the knickers down her bare legs when the whir of rewinding announced that he'd finished the roll of Tri-X. "Got you," he whispered, and hugged the camera to himself.

When she passed beyond the frame of the window he coaxed his curtains shut and switched the room light on. He was tempted to develop the roll now, but anticipating it made him feel so powerful in a sleepy generalized way that he decided to wait until the morning, when he would be more awake. He took *Pretty Hot* to bed with him and scanned the article about sex magic, and an idea was raising its head in his when he fell asleep.

He slept late. In the morning he had to leave the Tri-X negatives and hurry to the studio. Fog slid flatly over the pavements before him, vehicles nosed through the grey, grumbling monotonously. It occurred to him as he turned along the cheap side street near the edge of town that people were less likely to notice him in the fog, though why should he care if they did?

> In his darkroom he watched the form of the blonde girl rise from the developing fluid . . .

Toby opened the street door at Sid's triple knock and preceded him up the carpetless stairs. Toby had already set up the lights and switched them on, which made the small room with its double bed and mock-leather sofa appear starker than ever. A brawny man was sitting on the sofa with a woman draped face down across his knees, her short skirt thrown back, her black nylon knickers more or less pulled down.

Apart from the mortar-board jammed onto his head, the man looked like a wrestler or a bouncer. He glanced up as Sid entered, and the hint of a warning crossed his large bland reddish face as Sid appraised the woman. She was too plump for Sid's taste, her mottled buttocks were too flabby. She looked bored—more so when she glanced at Sid, who disliked her at once.

"This is Sid, our snapshooter," Toby announced. "Sid, our friends are going to model for both stories."

"All right there, mate," the man said, and the woman grunted.

Sid glanced through the viewfinder, then made to adjust the woman's knickers; but he hadn't touched them when the man's hand seized his wrist. "Hands off. I'll do that. She's my wife."

"Come on, the lot of you," the woman complained. "I'm getting a cold bum."

It wouldn't be cold for long, Sid thought, and felt his penis stir unexpectedly. But the man didn't hit her, he only mimed the positions as if he were enacting a series of film stills, resting his hand on her buttocks to denote slaps. For the pair of colour shots Toby could afford the man rubbed rouge on her bottom.

"That was okay, was it, Sid?" Toby said anxiously. "It'd be nice if we could shoot *Slave of Love* tomorrow."

"Wouldn't be nice for us," the woman said, groaning as she stood up. "We've got our lives to lead, you know."

"We could make it a week today," her husband said.

"They look right for the stories, I reckon," Hale told Sid when they'd left. "I'm working on some younger models, but those two'll do for that kind of stuff. The perves who want it don't care."

Sid thought it best to agree, but as he walked home he grew angrier: how could that fat bitch have given him a tickle? Working with people like her might be one of Sid's steps to fame, but she needed him more than he needed her. "I'll retouch you, but I won't touch you," he muttered, grinning. Someone like the blonde girl over the road, now—she would have been Sid's choice of a model for *Spanked and Submissive*, and it wouldn't all have been faked, either.

That got his penis going. He had to stand still for a few minutes until its tip went back to sleep, and the thought of the negatives waiting in his darkroom didn't help. He would have her in his hands, he would be able to do what he liked with her. He had to put the idea out of his head before he felt safe to walk.

After the fog, even the dim musty hall of the house seemed like a promise of clarity. In his darkroom he watched the form of the blonde girl rise from the developing fluid, and he felt as if a fog of dissatisfaction with himself and with the session at the studio were leaving him. The photographs came clear, and for a moment he couldn't understand why the girl's body was composed of dots like a newspaper photograph enlarged beyond reason. Of course, it was the frosting on her bathroom window.

Having her in his flat without her knowing excited him, but not enough. Perhaps he needed her to be home so that he could watch her failure to realize he had her. He opened a packet of hamburgers and cooked himself whatever meal it was. The effort annoyed him, and so did the eating: chew, chew, chew. He switched on the television, and the little picture danced for him, oracular heads spoke. He kept glancing at the undeveloped frame of her window.

By the time she arrived home the fog was spiked with drizzle. As soon as she had switched on the light she began to remove her clothes, but before she'd taken off more than her coat she drew the curtains. Had she seen him? Was she taking pleasure in his frustration at having to imagine her undressing? But he already had her almost naked. He spread the photographs across the table, and then he lurched towards his bed to find the article about sex magic.

By themselves the photographs were only pieces of card, but what had the article said? Toby Hale had put in all the ideas he could find about images during an afternoon spent in the library. The Catholic church sometimes made an image of a demon and burned it to bring off an exorcism . . . Someone in Illinois killed a man by letting rain fall on his photograph... Here it was, the stuff Tony had found in a book about magic by someone with a degree from a university Sid had never heard of. The best spells are the ones you write yourself. Find the words that are truest to your secret soul. Focus your imagination, build up to the discharge of psychic energy. Chant the words that best express your desires. Toby was talking about doing that with your partner, but it had given Sid a better idea. He hurried to the window, his undecided penis hindering him a little, and shut the curtains tight.

As he returned to the table he felt uneasy: excited, furtive, ridiculous - he wasn't sure which was uppermost. If only this could work! You never know until you try, he thought, which was the motto on the contents page of *Pretty Hot*. He

pulled the first photograph to him. Her breasts swelled in their lacy bra, her black knickers were taut over her round bottom. He wished he could see her face. He cleared his throat, and muttered almost inaudibly: "I'm going to take your knickers down. I'm going to smack your bare bum."

He sounded absurd. The whole situation was absurd. How could he expect it to work if he could barely hear himself? "By the time I've finished with you," he said loudly, "you won't be able to sit down for a week."

Too loud! Nobody could hear him, he told himself. Except that he could, and he sounded like a fool. As he glared at the photograph, he was sure that she was smiling. She had beaten him. He wouldn't put it past her to have let him take the photographs because they had absolutely no effect on her. All at once he was furious. "You've had it now," he shouted.

His eyes were burning. The photograph flickered, and appeared to stir. He thought her face turned up to him. If it did, it must be out of fear. His penis pulled eagerly at his flies. "All right, miss," he shouted hoarsely. "Those knickers are coming down."

She seemed to jerk, and he could imagine her bending reluctantly beneath the pressure of a hand on the back of her neck. Her black knickers stretched over her bottom. Then the photograph blurred as tears tried to dampen his eyes, but he could see her more clearly than ever. By God, the tears ought to be hers. "Now then," he shouted, "you're going to get what you've been asking for."

He seized her bare arm. She tried to pull away, shaking her head mutely, her eyes bright with apprehension. In a moment he'd trapped her legs between his thighs and pushed her across his knee, locking his left arm around her waist. Her long blonde hair trailed to the floor, concealing her face. He took hold of the waistband of her knickers and drew them slowly down, gradually revealing her round creamy buttocks. When she began to wriggle, he trapped her more firmly with his arm and legs. "Let's see what this feels like," he said, and slapped her hard.

He heard it. For a moment he was sure he had. He stared about his empty flat with his hot eyes. He almost went to peer between the curtains at her window, but gazed at the photograph instead. "Oh no, miss, you won't get away from me," he whispered, and saw her move uneasily as he closed his eyes.

He began systematically to slap her: one on the left buttock, one on the right. After a dozen of these her bottom was turning pink and he was growing hot—his face, his penis, the palm of his hand. He could feel her warm thighs squirming between his. "You like that, do you? Let's see how much you like."

Two slaps on the left, two on the right. A dozen pairs of those, then five on the same spot, five on the other. As her bottom grew red she tried to cover it with her hands, but he pinned her wrists together with his left hand and forcing them up to the dimple above her bottom, went to work in earnest: ten on the left buttock, ten on its twin . . . She was sobbing beneath her hair, her bottom was wriggling helplessly. His room had gone. There was nothing but Sid and his victim until he came violently and unexpectedly, squealing.

He didn't see her the next day. She was gone when he wakened from a satisfied slumber, and she had drawn the curtains before he realized she was home again. She was making it easier for him to see her the way he wanted. Anticipating that during the days which followed made him feel secretly powerful, and so did Toby Hale's suggestion when Sid rang him to confirm the *Slave of Love* session. "We're short of stories for number three," Toby said. "I don't suppose you've got anything good and strong for us?"

"I might have," Sid told him.

He didn't fully realize how involving it would be until he began to write. He was dominating her not only by writing about her but also by delivering her up to the readers of the magazine. He made her into a new pupil at a boarding school for girls in their late teens. *"Your here to lern disiplin. My naime is Mr Sidney and dont you forgett it."* She would wear kneesocks and a gymslip that revealed her uniform knickers whenever she bent down. *"Over my nee, yung lady. Im goaing to giv you a speling leson." "Plese plese dont take my nickers down, Ill be a good gurl." "You didnt cawl me Mr Sidney, thats two dozin extrar with the hare brush . . ."* He felt as if the words were unlocking a secret aspect of himself, a core of unsuspected truth which gave him access to some kind of power. Was this what they meant by sex magic? It took him almost a week of evenings to savour writing the story, and he didn't mind not seeing her all that week; it helped him see her as he was writing her. Each night as he drifted off to sleep he imagined her lying in bed sobbing, rubbing her bottom.

At the end of the story he met her on the bus.

He was returning from town with a bagful of film. She caught the bus just as he was lowering himself onto one of the front seats downstairs. As she boarded the bus she saw him, and immediately looked away. Even though there were empty seats she stayed on her feet, holding onto the pole by the stairs.

Sid gazed at the curve of her bottom, defining itself and then growing blurred as her long coat swung with the movements of the bus ploughing through the fog. Why wouldn't she sit down? He leaned forwards impulsively, emboldened by the nights he'd spent in secret with her, and touched her arm. "Would you like to sit down, love?"

She looked down at him, and he recoiled. Her eyes were bright with loathing, and yet she looked trapped. She shook her head once, keeping her lips pressed so tight they grew pale, then she turned her back on him. He'd make her turn her back tonight, he thought, by God he would. He had to sit on his hands for the rest of the journey, but he walked behind her all the way from the bus stop to her house.

"You're not tying me up with that," the woman said. "Cut my wrists off, that would. Pyjama cord or nothing, and none of your cheap stuff neither."

"Sid, would you mind seeing if you can come up with some cord?" Toby Hale said, taking out his reptilian wallet. "I'll stay and discuss the scene."

There was sweat in his eyebrows. The woman was making him sweat because she was their only female model for the story, since Toby's wife wouldn't touch anything kinky. Sid kicked the fog as he hurried to the shops. Just let the fat bitch give him any lip.

Her husband bound her wrists and ankles to the legs of the bed. He untied her and turned her over and tied her again. He untied her and tied her wrists and ankles together behind her back, and poked his crotch at her face. Sid snapped her and snapped her, wondering how far Tony had asked them to go, and then he had to reload. "Get a bastard move on," the woman told him. "This is bloody uncomfortable, did you but know."

Sid couldn't restrain himself. "If you don't like the work we can always get someone else."

"Can you now?" The woman's face rocked towards him on the bow of herself, and then she toppled sideways on the bed, her breasts flopping on her chest, a few pubic strands springing free of her purple knickers like the legs of a lurking spider. "Bloody get someone, then," she cried.

Toby had to calm her and her suffused husband down while Sid muttered apologies. That night he set the frosted photograph in front of him and chanted his story over it until the girl pleaded for mercy. He no longer cared if Toby had his doubts about the story, though Sid was damned if he could see what had made him frown over it. If only Sid could find someone like the girl to model for the story . . . Even when he'd finished with her for the evening, his having been forced to apologize to Toby's models clung to him. He was glad he would be photographing Enid Stone tomorrow. Maybe it was time for him to think of moving on.

He was on his way to Enid Stone's press conference when he saw the girl again. As he emerged from his building she was arriving home from wherever she worked, and she was on his side of the road. The slam of the front door made her

> He felt as if the words were unlocking a secret aspect of himself . . . was this what they meant by sex magic?

flinch and dodge to the opposite pavement, but not before a streetlamp had shown him her face. Her eyes were sunken in dark rings, her mouth was shivering; her long blonde hair looked dulled by the fog. She was moving awkwardly, as if it pained her to walk.

She must have female trouble, Sid decided, squirming at the notion. On his way to the bookshop his glimpse of her proved as hard to leave behind as the fog was, and he had to keep telling himself that it was nothing to do with him. The bookshop window was full of Enid Stone's books upheld by wire brackets. Maybe one day he'd see a Sid Pym exhibition in a window.

He hadn't expected Enid Stone to be so small. She looked like someone's shrunken crabby granny, impatiently suffering her hundredth birthday party. She sat in an armchair at the end of a thickly carpeted room above the bookshop, confronting a curve of reporters sitting on straight chairs. "Don't crowd me," she was telling them. "A girl's got to breathe, you know."

Sid joined the photographers who were lined up against the wall like miscreants outside a classroom. Once the

> "You're here to learn discipline," he said soft and slow.

reporters began to speak, having been set in motion by a man from the publishers, Enid Stone snapped at their questions, her head jerking rapidly, her eyes glittering like a bird's. "That'll do," she said abruptly. "Give a girl a chance to rest her voice. Who's going to make me beautiful?"

This was apparently meant for the photographers, since the man from the publishers beckoned them forwards. The reporters were moving their chairs aside when Enid Stone raised one bony hand to halt the advance of the cameras. "Where's the one who takes the dirty pictures? Have you let him in?"

Even when several reporters and photographers turned to look at Sid he couldn't believe she meant him. "Is that Mr Muck? Show him the air," she ordered. "No pictures till he goes."

The line of photographers took a step forwards and closed in front of Sid. As he stared at their backs, his face and ears throbbing as if from blows, the man from the publishers took hold of his arm. "I'm afraid that if Miss Stone won't have you I must ask you to leave."

Sid trudged downstairs, unable to hear his footsteps for the extravagant carpet. He felt as if he weren't quite there.

Outside, the fog was so thick that the buses had stopped running. It filled his eyes, his mind. However fast he walked, there was always as much of it waiting beyond it. Its passiveness infuriated him. He wanted to feel he was overcoming something, and by God, he would once he was home.

He grabbed the copy of the story he'd written for Toby Hale and threw it on the table. He found the photograph beside the bed and propped it against a packet of salt in front of him. The picture had grown dull with so much handling, but he hadn't the patience to develop a fresh copy just now. "My name's *Mister* Sidney and don't you forget it," he informed the photograph.

There was no response. His penis was as still as the fingerprinted glossy piece of card. The scene at the bookshop had angered him too much, that was all. He only had to relax and let his imagination take hold. "You're here to learn discipline," he said soft and slow.

The figure composed of dots seemed to shift, but it was only Sid's vision; his eyes were smarting. He imagined the figure in front of him changing, and suddenly he was afraid of seeing her as she had looked beneath the streetlamp. The memory distressed him, but why should he think of it now? He ought to be in control of how she appeared to him. Perhaps his anger at losing control would give him the power to take hold of her. "My name's Mr. Sidney," he repeated, and heard a mocking echo in his brain.

His eyes were stinging when it should be her bottom that was. He closed his eyes and saw her floating helplessly towards him. "Come here if you know what's good for you," he said quickly, and then he thought he knew how to catch her. "Please," he said in a high panicky voice, "please don't hurt me."

It worked. All at once she was sprawling across his lap. "What's my name?" he demanded, and raised his voice almost to a squeak. "Mr. Sidney," he said.

"Mr. Sidney *sir*," he shouted, and dealt her a hefty slap. He was about to give the kind of squeal he would have loved her to emit when he heard her do so—faintly, across the road.

He blinked at the curtains as if he had wakened from a dream. It couldn't have been the girl, and if it had been, she was distracting him. He closed his eyes again and gripped them with his left hand as if that would help him trap his image of her. "What's my name?" he shouted, and slapped her again. This time there was no mistaking the cry which penetrated the fog.

Sid knocked his chair over backwards in his haste to reach the window. When he threw the curtains open he could see nothing but the deserted road boxed in by fog. The circle of lit pavement where he'd last seen the girl was bare and stark. He was staring at the fog, feeling as though it was even closer to him than it looked, when he heard a door slam. It was the front door of the building across the road. In a moment the girl appeared at the edge of the fog. She glanced up at him, and then she fled towards the park.

It was as if he'd released her by relinquishing his image of her and going to the window. He felt as though he was on the brink of realizing the extent of his secret power. Suppose there really was something to this sex magic? Suppose he had made her experience at least some of his fantasies? He couldn't believe he had reached her physically, but what would it be like for her to have her thoughts invaded by his fantasies about her? He had to know the truth, though he didn't know what he would do with it. He grabbed his coat and ran downstairs, into the fog.

Once on the pavement he stood still and held his breath. He heard his heartbeat, the cackling of ducks, the girl's heels running away from him. He advanced into the fog, trying to ensure that she didn't hear him. The bookshop window drifted by, crowded with posed figures and their victims. Ahead of him the fog parted for a moment, and the girl looked back as if she'd sensed his gaze closing around her. She saw him illuminated harshly by the fluorescent tube in the bookshop window, and at once she ran for her life.

"Don't run away," Sid called. "I won't hurt you, I only want to talk to you." Surely any other thoughts that were lurking in his mind were only words. It occurred to him that he had never heard her speak. In that case, whose sobs had he heard in his fantasies? There wasn't time for him to wonder now. She had vanished into the fog, but a change in the sound of her footsteps told him where she had taken refuge: in the park.

He ran to the nearest entrance, the one she would have used, and peered along the path. Thickly swirling rays of light from a streetlamp splayed through the railings and stubbed themselves against the fog. He held his breath, which tasted like a head cold, and heard her gravelly footsteps fleeing along the path. "We'll have to meet sooner or later, love," he called, and ran into the park.

Trees gleamed dully, wet black pillars upholding the fog. The grass on either side of the path looked weighed down by the slow passage of the murk which Sid seemed to be following. Once he heard a cry and a loud splash—a bird landing on the lake which was somewhere ahead, he supposed. He halted again, but all he could hear was the dripping of branches laden with fog.

"I told you I don't want to hurt you," he muttered. "Better wait for me, or I'll—" The chase was beginning to excite and frustrate and anger him. He left the gravel path and padded across the grass alongside it, straining his ears. When the fog solidified a hundred yards or so to his right, at first he didn't notice. Belatedly he realized that the dim pale hump was a bridge which led the path over the lake, and was just in time to stop himself striding into the water.

It wasn't deep, but the thought that the girl could have made him wet himself enraged him. He glared about, his eyes beginning to sting. "I can see you," he whispered as if the words would make it true, and then his gaze was drawn from the bridge to the shadows beneath.

At first he wasn't sure what he was seeing. He seemed to be watching an image developing in the dark water, growing clearer and more undeniable. It had sunk, and now it was rising, floating under the bridge from the opposite side. Its eyes were open, but they looked like the water. Its arms and legs were trailing limply, and so was its blonde hair.

Sid shivered and stared, unable to look away. Had she jumped or fallen? The splash he'd heard a few minutes ago must have been her plunging into the lake, and yet there had been no sounds of her trying to save herself. She must have struck her head on something as she fell. She couldn't just have lain there willing herself to drown, Sid reassured himself, but if she had, how could anyone blame him? There was nobody to see him except her, and she couldn't, not with eyes like those she had now. A spasm of horror and guilt set him staggering away from the lake.

The slippery grass almost sent him sprawling more than once. When he skidded onto the path the gravel ground like teeth, and yet he felt insubstantial, at the mercy of the blurred night, unable to control his thoughts. He fled panting through the gateway, willing himself not to slow down until he was safe in his rooms; he had to destroy the photographs before anyone saw them. But fog was gathering in his lungs, and he had a stitch in his side. He stumbled to a halt in front of the bookshop.

The light from the fluorescent tubes seemed to reach for him. He saw his face staring out from among the women bearing whips. If they or anyone else knew what he secretly imagined he'd caused . .

His buttocks clenched and unclenched at the thought he was struggling not to think. He gripped his knees and bent almost double to rid himself of the pain in his side so that he could catch his breath, and then he saw his face fit over the face of a bound victim.

It was only the stitch that had paralyzed him, he told himself, near to panic. It was only the fog which was making the photograph of the victim appear to stir, to align its position with his. "Please, please," he said wildly, his voice rising, and at once tried to take the words back. They were echoing in his mind, they wouldn't stop. He felt as if they were about to unlock a deeper aspect of himself, a power which would overwhelm him.

He didn't want this, it was contrary to everything he knew about himself. "My name is—" he began, but his pleading thoughts were louder than his voice, almost as loud as the sharp swishing which filled his ears. He was falling forwards helplessly, into himself or into the window, wherever the women and pain were waiting. For a moment he managed to cling to the knowledge that the images were nothing but the covers of magazines, and then he realized fully that they were more than that, far more. They were euphemisms for what waited beyond them.

Ramsey Campbell's novels have drawn acclaim from both sides of the Atlantic. His most recent book, waking Nightmares, appeared in late 1991.

The Night Seasons, J.N. Williamson, Zebra

Adapted from Williamson's World Fantasy Award-nominated novella, of the same name (which originally appeared in *Night Cry*), *The Night Seasons* is a refreshingly original horror novel about a very strange prison and some even stranger characters. Williamson has a knack for well-crafted prose and bizarre themes, and he combines the two in *The Night Seasons*.

MONSTERS

Jay Owens

"iT'S OBSCENE MATERIAL," THE
DIRECTOR DECLARES,
HIDING THE LATEST ISSUE OF *BOY
TOY* IN HIS BRIEFCASE.

"i CAN'T BELIEVE THIS KIND OF
BRUTALITY EVEN EXISTS,"
REMARKS THE MAN IN THE
BROOKS BROTHERS SUIT
AS HE SQUIRMS IN HIS LEATHER
JOCK STRAP.

"iT'S SELF INDULGENT CRAP,"
MUTTERS THE GENTLEMAN IN
THE PRESSED WHITE SHIRT,
SLOWLY JACKING OFF UNDER THE
MAHOGANY TABLE.

tHE MALE WITH THE GUCCI
WATCH AGREES.
"tHERE IS NO DOUBT THAT IT
PORTRAYS UNNATURAL ACTS,"
HE SAYS, FIDDLING WITH THE
VIBRATOR IN HIS POCKET.

"oNE WORD SAYS IT ALL,"
BACKS UP THE BACHELOR IN THE
PATENT LEATHER SHOES.
HE SMILES AS HIS WARM PISS
TRICKLES DOWN HIS THIGH.
"dISGUSTING, DISGUSTING, DIS-
GUSTING."

"aND YOU, mCcONNELL. . . . i SUP-
POSE YOU DISAGREE AGAIN?"
ASKS THE DIRECTOR.

McConnell perks up at the mention of his name.

"Yes, Sir," he replies. "It's just art."

"jUST ART?!" REMARKS THE DIREC-
TOR.
"aND WHO SETS THE GUIDELINES
FOR WHAT CONSTITUTES ART
AROUND HERE???"

"You do, Sir. Of course."

"aND YOU STILL DISAGREE?
ONLY ONE WEEK BEFORE YOUR
REVIEW . . .
AND YOU STILL DISAGREE??"

"Yes, Sir."

"wELL . . . WE'LL HAVE TO TAKE A
VOTE ON IT.
THOSE IN FAVOR OF MY POSITION,
RAISE YOUR HANDS."

"lOOKS LIKE YOU'RE OUTVOTED
AGAIN, mCcONNELL . . .
sURE YOU DON'T WANT TO MAKE
IT UNANIMOUS?"

"Yes, Sir."

—BUT WAIT! Is he? He could swear he saw his hand move. Just for an instant. No, he tells himself . . . It was only a twitch. Just a slight muscle spasm. Nothing more.

—But how long can he hold out? Week after week of disagreeing only to lose . . . not just the votes and the freedoms . . . but his job.

"And for what?" he asks himself.

He knows there is a reason somewhere . . .

✧

McConnell tucks his daughter into bed at night.

"Daddy?" she asks, as he smooths the covers.

"Yes, dear."

"Will you leave the light on when you leave?"

"No," he insists kindly. "I have told you time and time again that there is no monster under your bed."

"But I'm scared. Do monsters really exist, Daddy?"

He pauses as he considers the question.

"Yes," he answers. "I suppose they do."

"What if they get me?"

McConnell sits down on the edge of his daughter's bed.

"Let me tell you something about monsters. If you fear something, then you're safe. It's the people you trust to protect you that turn out to be monsters."

"But I trust you, Daddy," whispers the daughter.

"I know, darling, that's what scares me."

McConnell gets up to switch off the light on his way out.

"Daddy?"

"Yes?"

"Then if you're scared, you're OK."

He smiles sadly as he flicks the switch.

He pauses outside her room after he closes the door. He leans his head against the wall, glancing at his trembling hand. He struggles hard to steady it. It's something he's been working on lately.

And he heads toward his bedroom, his hand resting solidly at his side.

He knows that there won't be another "twitch" . . . another "tremble." He'll see to it that as long as he's alive, the vote will never be unanimous.

And his reason is lying in bed.

THE PROCESS

Steve Rasnic Tem

His brother the lawyer used to tell him that writing tales of horror was a rather self-indulgent thing to do. He might have replied that attempting to get criminals off whom you knew were guilty was self-indulgent as well, but that would have been mean, and he knew his brother hadn't intended cruelty in his own comment. His brother was one of his biggest fans.

His brother might have replied, however, that even when you knew the probable outcome of the trial, it was the process that was important. And he, the writer, might have said that even when the story was predictable and derivative, the process was the essential element. It was in the process where horrors were encountered, dealt with or ignored.

He began his own process with his eyes closed, looking for the thing that disturbed, that agitated, that made all the shadows take on a life of their own.

Most evenings, staring at the screen, he would think about his grandfather. His grandfather had been a concentration camp survivor. Saying it that simply— and how else could he say such a thing?— seemed brutal. During adolescence he'd wanted to talk with friends about his

> ... he attempted to grab onto their basic fears and shake until something—a whimper, perhaps just a sigh of anxiety—broke loose.

him, so that in his everyday life he was eventually able to see how he slept like a madman, ate like a murderer, made love sometimes like a sadist, sometimes like a werewolf. He made a poor demon—he hadn't the faith. But as vampire he was unsurpassed. And all his life he lived in his house like a ghost.

But always it began in front of the blank sheet of paper, or later the blank screen. There was where he'd see the face of darkness, the face of horror.

When his ambition was at its lowest ebb, he attempted to *frighten* people with his fiction; he attempted to grab on to their basic fears and shake until something—a whimper, perhaps just a sigh of anxiety—broke loose.

But at its best, horror described the spectrum of emotions— awe, terror, compassion, fear—which people experienced when faced with the darkness of their existence. The fear was simply the easiest to write about. Sometimes, however, he thought the awe and compassion were most threatening; many writers—himself included—might like to pretend these responses to the darkness did not exist. A kind of self-censorship occurred, an attempt to avoid the love and the terror and the awe that could shake you to your bones, and make you doubt everything you had learned about the forces which surround, and move within, us all.

But what did he really know of darkness? He discovered that words possessed both magnetic and gravitational properties. He sometimes used these qualities when he was trying to begin a new story. He'd write down the words and phrases which he thought were key to the story. Then he'd set his alarm for the middle of the night, and when it went off he'd get up and jot down some more words and phrases, syllables even, for the story. Sometimes he'd do this for several days. Eventually the words and phrases would betray their natural linkages, often in surprising ways. Often the words and concepts which were drawn into the web of other words, concepts, and syllables greatly disturbed him. But by this method he discovered that, among other things, adults tended to treat children as if they were either dolls or vegetables, and

grandfather and his experiences, but they always changed the subject. His grandfather, too, was reluctant to discuss the camps, except when he had been drinking, or after something had upset him, reminded him. Then he would tell the stories, and they would be like a myth of creation; even then the writer in him recognized the truth in these tales.

His grandfather had worked hard all his life, acquiring real estate a piece at a time. Before he died he owned four nursing homes. His nursing homes were sad, smelly places—the people received only the most minimal care. When the writer was old enough to ask about these homes, to challenge his grandfather, his grandfather would stare at him and say. "How *dare* you? What do you know of suffering?"

What *did* he know? Of suffering, or of darkness of any kind? The writer could only pretend, and do the unthinkable, which was to search for a darkness inside himself which heretofore had never shown itself. He had to *pretend* to be the madman, the murderer, the sadist and the werewolf, demon, vampire, ghost. And strangely enough, over time these disguises felt increasingly comfortable on that the ties which bound him to his wife consisted as much of mutual sorrow as of love.

----

body   kiss   sorrow   loss   shit
nourish   corruption   sweetheart   eat
assault   fetus   sausage   rip   enter
soil   meat   dirt   worm   dismember
intercourse   night   malformations

But what did he know of darkness? Were all his stories destined to be like his grandfather's nursing homes, blind to their own particular forms of horror? Gazing now into that bottomless screen brought him back to a night several years ago when he'd been sitting there trying to stare his way through a plot problem. It was a vampire story, involving a highly stylized blood sipper who needed to suddenly turn ugly and butcher several people. Along with this particular story he'd been pondering a question he'd been asked to answer for a fan magazine: "Why spend your time imagining more horrors to bring into the world when we already have so many?"

He knew his answer would have something to do with the safety involved in fearing something as rare and inaccessible as a vampire.

In the next room, his five-year-old daughter Alice had been screaming and pounding the floor for some time. The tantrum was because his wife had told her that she couldn't go somewhere or other—he couldn't remember the exact details—and now she was hysterical. He could imagine her little pale face turning red as a tomato as she belted out "Hate you! Hate you all!" His temptation, as always, was to go to her and sit her on his lap, whisper to her and try to soothe her, seduce the scarlet heat out of her face. His wife had insisted that was the wrong approach, but he saw no reason why his daughter should have to suffer that way. But that night, that night he was busy trying to solve this writing problem and wondering how he was going to explain to a readership of starry-eyed fans that most horror fiction had nothing to do with real horror but instead was a complex

game by which real horror was avoided. So he didn't go into Alice's room that night even though she'd been screaming for almost an hour. And eventually she did stop, just as that smug therapist had always said she would. And he had some peace for a time until his wife started screaming from Alice's room.

He jumped away from the keyboard then as if it were hot, as if he'd suddenly remembered something terrible and the keyboard had seduced the memory away. He ran into the next room and there was his wife pounding the floor and screaming hysterically. And there was this sharp smell of shit in the air and he was thinking

CUPEC '91

maybe that Alice had messed her pants on purpose she'd gotten so mad at them, and was that why his wife was so upset? And he looked around the room for Alice thinking he'd ask her about this—he wouldn't lose it like his wife that was no good he'd just, calmly, ask Alice about this. And there was Alice lying facedown in the floor on the other side of his wife and he turned her over and his sweet Alice wasn't red as a tomato anymore. His poor child was dark as eggplant.

The doctor at the ER found a little plastic block lodged in her small throat that she'd choked on. He'd asked them if she'd put things like that in her mouth before and they'd both said not in a couple years and they'd agreed on that and wondered what she'd been thinking of like this was some idle discussion of parenting at the PTA and not this awful debriefing following the death of their only child. And he would always wonder if she'd tried to swallow the thing simply because she was mad at them and because

> And there I am under the ice, looking up at you with my cold fish eyes.

they'd told her Never NEVER NEVER put foreign objects in your mouth, Sweet Alice.

So now besides his grandfather's nursing homes *that* was what he thought about every night as he gazed into the endless blankness of his computer screen. And listened for noises coming from the other room.

And it was during this time following his daughter's death that he began to acknowledge the other fictions in his life, the fictions which were too ephemeral or too dangerous to put down. For months after Alice's death he'd have dreams about a huge black car pulling up in front of the house and the quick footsteps of a child bounding up the steps. Alice hadn't died at all but had simply been taken somewhere and it all had been this terrible misunderstanding and his wife was begging him to open the door and let their sweet child in but he couldn't, he didn't dare, and he hated himself that he didn't dare.

He would attempt to write this story of his child's arrival in that huge black automobile but he never could. This was the fiction he felt compelled to withhold, the fiction he knew he must censor. In-stead there were stories about child zombies and child vampires but never that one true story of his own child's return in that terrible black car.

Just as he was never able to write down any of the other special fictions which floated in and out of dreams and daydreams and dreary hours staring wide-eyed at the empty screen.

There was that story when as a teenager he had found the rotting corpse of his own mother underneath their front steps. In this particular version of the tale she had died because he'd been having sex with her for years. In other versions she had committed suicide because of her own desires for him.

There was also that ongoing adventure in which he wandered for mile after mile in a vast underground world composed of all the basements in his old neighborhood linked one to the other by means of muddy tunnels and passages hung with curtains made from pee-stained sheets and doors that were actually the door to his bathroom, the door to his parents' bedroom, the door to the bar down the street, the door to the funeral home where they'd taken his little Alice. The ceiling of this underground world was made up of his own shit-stained underwear, his mother's underwear he used to steal out of the hamper, a quilt made up of used tampons, aborted fetuses, and diseased skin sewn together and blended so that he could not distinguish the individual pieces.

Then there was the censored love affair he had for years with his sister, who as he grew older became his next door neighbor, then became his daughter Alice all grown up, not dead anymore, but in her face she looked dead, and sometimes her eyes were missing, the sockets stuffed with cotton.

And none of these stories could he ever bring himself to write down. These were his dearest, his censored fictions.

But beyond them all was the continuing fictions he maintained about a future life for his dead child, a life in which she grew older, dated, went to college, became a doctor and gave him numerous healthy and wonderful grandkids, with only occasional lapses in which her skin looked torn, her ears bled, or her face took on that unnatural color of darkness.

He felt guiltiest about these last fictions, although he wasn't sure why. The only life Alice could have now was this life within and informed by his imagination.

This was what the writer knew of darkness, of horror.

Sometimes, when it seemed he had nothing more to say, he would interview his characters, who knew far more of the story than he did and who would reveal their deepest secrets if he only asked them in the right way, as if they'd simply been waiting all this time for the right question. Many times he had had intimations of just how independent a thing one's own imagination could be, as if a spirit or god who lived inside you, possessed you and used you as its vehicle. You could never be completely responsible for your imagination, nor justifiably take all the credit for its accomplishments. You were simply lucky enough to be mounted. It *rode* you.

MAXWELL: Why don't you tell the folks how much I secretly enjoy smelling nasty smells: garbage and sour milk, sour armpits and shit and pee and decaying bodies. Especially the latter. Oh, yeah.

WRITER: People don't want to read about that stuff. Besides, it isn't relevant. This is a story about a love affair gone bad. You've grown bored with her, at least she thinks you've grown bored with her. Now she's somewhat afraid of you because she thinks you're some kind of sadist. Late at night she hears what she thinks may be the cries of small animals in pain.

MAXWELL: What do you mean not relevant? I spend hours each day in the stink of other people, smelling those smells, daydreaming about those smells, so how could it not be relevant? Besides, I never got bored with her. I've grown obsessed with the stink of her. It makes me want to go ahead and do other things with her in the celebration of that stench. I want to cut off her head and make love to her corpse.

WRITER: I can't write that down! That's not what I want to write about

here—that's not where my process is taking me. (And in his fiction, this is not the sort of story he'd want his beautiful grown up daughter Alice to read.)

MAXWELL: More often than not your "process" is simply an avoidance of the things which disturb you most, because you consider those things impolite.

WRITER: Sometimes just living day to day is a difficult balancing act, a hard skate across transparent ice . . .

MAXWELL: And there I am under the ice, looking up at you with my cold fish eyes.

WRITER: Why cut off her head, anyway?

MAXWELL: Because if I see her face I'll *know* that it's her and that she's thinking and dreaming somewhere inside there but at the same time she stinks, with every breath she decomposes, so that at some point this person I love will be dead. With just her corpse I have the dying part of her to make love to. Her head, the dreaming part is off somewhere else dreaming its dreams where I won't have to look at it and remember what it is I'm losing. You can't fool me, you know. You smell that smell, too. I can see it in your face. You smell it good and well. So what does it smell like?

WRITER: It smells like I'm dying.

MAXWELL: Don't feel so bad—everybody else smells it, too. You've seen pictures of Hitler, the way his nose looks like he's sniffing, as if he's smelling this awful smell . . .

Sometimes when the words simply refused to come the writer would spend his afternoons in the malls and in the carefully-manicured parks, eavesdropping on other people's conversations. This was easy; privacy increasingly appeared to be the unnatural state. When he listened in to this talk between people, he often found an appalling ugliness, so ugly in fact that it finally made him understand why the people in fiction seldom spoke so harshly. And why other writers seemed compelled to sanitize the speeches their characters made. His job, he had always thought, was to find the ugliness and explore it, describe it, and yet how could he quote such ugliness without being contaminated? His characters' mouths were but an extension of his own and how could he say such things? And who would want to listen? What bothered him most was that the ugliest of the statements he overheard were all by men, bad enough at times that it shamed him to be a man, bad enough that when he went home at night with a notebook full of ugliness he would examine himself in the mirror, trying to find the darkness among the lines and planes of his face.

"So I told her either we were going to fuck or it was all over."

"It's all pink on the inside."

"Ugly dykes should have their cunts sewn shut."

"I heard somebody fucked her in the ass with a pipe. Guess she'll be big enough for me now."

"When I see a pretty face I just want to mess it all up."

"You should have seen the look on her face when I bit off her nipple!"

"What I like to do most is have her blow me while I'm pounding her head against the floor. If she bites even a little, she gets it worse."

There was a time when coming home and reading Dr. Seuss to Alice was a good antidote to this terrible task of notetaking. After Alice died there seemed no relief. Sometimes in his censored and unwritten fictions Alice would grow up and encounter some of these ugly male voices. And he would be filled with such rage his stories could barely contain it all.

So what did he know of shame? What did he know of darkness? It surprised him sometimes how the events in both his own life and in his fictions resembled the plots of classic works he had read as a young man. His courtship, marriage, education, and periodic loss of confidence could be traced through books like *The House of Seven Gables, Billy Budd, A Farewell to Arms, A Separate Peace,* and *Siddhartha.* The details of his own life were less interesting than these, but perhaps truer to some unknown, ideal fiction. Certainly the same patterns were there, and in his own books, although perhaps expressed a bit less artfully.

He made notes concerning this phenomenon in hopes of developing a UTF (Universal Theory of Fiction), which

might aid him in his career. But he eventually realized that the truly important events of a life *occurred in the head,* and were not so easily written down.

He began to worry about how much he had censored of his own everyday life because it didn't fit any acceptable pattern.

And how much essential darkness had he kept out of the plot? There were times, after he'd spent a period of months doing what he often called "elaborative" work, fiction which was heavy on language, fictive essays on small objects such as bells, balls, and cereal box toys, words spun out like cotton candy at a moment's notice—so pretty the reader might simply stop and admire rather than *read*—when he'd feel a need to spend a few days writing purely about the essentials of his experience. He assumed that most writing which came out of an *urge,* however vaguely defined the urge, must naturally be *about* these essentials, although oftentimes in a determined disguise.

If the need for essentials became too great, he found he could not write long fiction. A proposed novella about a haunted hotel became a vignette about a man who dies late in his life, crushed under the weight of his memories. A screenplay concerning the demonic possession of a small New England town became a list of the ways in which the mind becomes the enemy, with serious speculation that perhaps his *own* thinking processes might be considered deranged. A novel about a family's confrontation with a thing at the bottom of their backyard well became a short, hysterical paragraph screeching out his fear of dying.

Although none of these items was ever published, he continued to think of them as his essential work.

It always came down, finally, to the matter of his self-indulgence. Why would such a nice fellow say/write such terrible things?

The writer, ultimately, was a mirror. It was the writer's job to reflect the ideas, scenes, and images that came floating through the ether of both the conscious and subconscious minds. And for some unknown reason his particular portion of that material was the ugly, distasteful, frightening, possibly even immoral part. He supposed that different writers developed different sorts of mirrors, better able to catch creatures of a particular species.

It fell to others to debate, praise, decry, god knows even *ban* what had been retrieved. He supposed that writers can and possibly should be part of those "others," but their original job was to catch the material in the first place. And perhaps that original function of theirs was basically amoral. So depending on the stage of creation the writer could be either amoral or moral.

When the writer reflects the immorality of the times is the writer immoral? If a mirror is truly required by the society, then the answer is certainly no. But what happens when there is a multitude of mirrors all reflecting essentially the same thing? Did this perpetuate the immorality? At what point does a deeper exploration of immorality (its origins, its processes) make a work moral as opposed to a *celebration* of that immorality? Writers seemed the least likely to know the answers to such questions, so deeply involved were they in the process of mirroring, of excavation. And certainly it was important for such excavations to continue, else some important knowledge about the human condition and its possibilities might be lost.

He distrusted anyone who offered easy answers for such questions.

It always came down to a blank sheet of paper, or a blank screen, and his steady fall into that blankness. What to say and what to withhold. What to censor and what to lay bare.

And what did the writer know of darkness? What did he know of suffering? What did he know of horror?

In his secret and unwritten fiction his dead daughter grabs him on either side of his shaggy head and shakes him to the core of his dying being. And tells him.

---

*Steve Tem's "Back Window" (***Gauntlet** *#1) was a Bram Stoker nominee, and generated the most mail of any piece in that issue. A collection of his non-fiction* **Regions of the Strange: Essays on the Art of Horror Fiction** *will be published in 1993.*

Introduction

I am a German, and when I mention this I hope you don't say, "Hey, why does a Kraut write in an American magazine? He should write for German magazines, that old Nazi!"

I fear some Americans at least think something like that when they hear I am German, and I've come to that view because I listen to Americans visiting Germany and they think the Third Reich is still alive. And they're surprised to find out it's not.

I agree the Third Reich was an abomination, but we have learned from our history. Yet, it seems there are people in foreign countries who can't or don't want to acknowledge this fact.

I am a twenty-one year old chemistry student and didn't live during the Third Reich, but I must justify myself all the time. Because I am German, many still see the devil in me today. At the University, I learn chemistry for the good of mankind, not to build new and more effective gas chambers.

We have learned! We are not all Nazis! We are proud to belong to NATO and be a part of the Western World. And the majority of Germans, including me, love Americans!

Yes, fifty years is not much time to get rid of the past. The Third Reich was a great mistake, but it's over (let us hope that something like that will never return). Yet, I know that "old" soldiers, like in the following story, cannot forget the time they were tortured or hurt by Germans. With time, though, everything changes, and that includes the Germans of today's Germany.

—Oliver Zschenker

BLIND
HATRED

Oliver Zschenker

He sat behind the windowpane of the sitting room and looked straight across the street to the opposite house. The new neighbors lived there and with them the nightmares came back . . .

Alec Dawson sat with other prisoners of war in a camp near Cologne. Two SS-officers came once a day to the camp and carried away at least ten soldiers. Nobody knew where they were brought. There were rumors that the Nazis tortured the Americans, the English, the French and Russians slowly and cruelly until they welcomed their death. The taller of the SS-men spoke something in German to the other. Dawson didn't understand one word of that damned language, but he knew they were discussing who would be led to their death. They might be gassed or torn up by animals. Their "selection" was random—it was just for fun.

The smaller man, with the Hitler-moustache, took his machine gun and pointed it at the squatted crowd of foreign soldiers. They kneeled on the cold concrete ground and stared at the fat devourers of Sauerkraut who played Gods with their lives.

Suddenly the SS-officer fired. The loud noise of the machine gun echoed in the camp, echoed, echoed . . .

The Nazis began to laugh as the first heads of some American soldiers exploded in fountains of red blood and splinters of bone . . .

Alec Dawson opened his eyes again and watched the man who came out of the house across the street. The man was followed by his wife. She gave him a short kiss on the cheek and he got into his black Mercedes (a *German* car!) and drove away. The woman went back into the house, and Alec rose out of the rocking chair. His short gray hair was uncombed, and his wrinkled face showed its seventy years. But in his eyes, you could still recognize Alec Dawson the prisoner of the Nazis. Those eyes were cold and hard.

He'd been fortunate. The Allies rescued him, but many others died senselessly; killed by the Germans just for fun or pleasure. He was allowed to leave the Devil's land in Fall 1945. He had endured much; he was an ill, nervous, eccentric and lonely man, all because of the Germans. The *Germans* . . .

Michael locked the automobile in the garage and went into the house. It had been his lifelong dream to live in the USA. When he'd been allowed to work there at a chemical company, his dream had become reality. It was completely fulfilled when he met Carol in a department store in Chicago. He married her and finally they had *their* house, near Chicago, in the USA!

Yes, he'd managed it and he was very happy.

Michael used his key to unlock the front door, then opened it, entered and shouted for his wife. She did not answer. He shut the door, laid his briefcase on the bureau and went looking for her. He looked in the kitchen and shouted for her again.

Once more there was no answer.

He went to the stairway and cried for his wife one last time. Already there was fear in his voice. Nothing!

He went slowly upstairs, saw the door to their bedroom shut and went to open it. He turned the handle, pushed the

> As Michael moved his head, he saw a gray-haired old man standing in the corner with a sawed-off shotgun.

door open and saw . . .

. . . his wife laid strapped down and gagged on their bed; her eyes full of fear. As Michael moved his head, he saw a gray-haired old man standing in the corner with a sawed-off shotgun.

"Friendly wife you've got there. She let me in the house," he said, with a malevolent grin on his face.

"What do you want?" Michael asked slowly.

"I think the more important question is what a pig like you seeks here in the United States!"

"I don't understand," said Michael, looking with compassion at his wife. "Why are you pointing a weapon at my wife?"

"Don't be afraid. Nothing will happen to the woman. You're the person I'm interested in. What is your job?" The old man bared his teeth like a vampire before biting its victim.

"I'm a chemist!" Michael answered. Beads of sweat appeared on his forehead, although it was not hot in the house.

"After you've lost the War, you are *now* going to kill us with your chemistry-shit, right?"

Michael knew the man was dangerous. Anything could happen; with just one wrong word. "I don't know what you're talking about, sir."

"Oh, I can hear your German accent quite well. You Germans are all *Nazis* and damned fanatics. I know it! I lived through it. I know it! I'm not as stupid as our politicians you can buy with your dirty money. You're very clever, you Krauts! I know it, but nobody listens to me. N O B O D Y! . . ."

"I'm not a *Nazi*. There are only a few Nazi's in Germany, now. We learned! Can't you understand. I didn't even live during that damned time. I'm only thirty-six years old, man!" Michael said desperately.

"Didn't you have parents? Do you think I'm an imbecile?" shouted the old man.

Michael began to shout, too. His entire life he'd had to justify being German. He was fed up with it. He had been born in Germany. There was nothing he could do about that.

"Have you been in Germany since the War?" he asked, his voice rising. "Have you spoken with the people? Do you think this mad Hitler still has power in our country? If so, you are an imbecile!"

At that moment the old man fired, hitting Michael in the chest, killing him instantly.

But Alec wanted to be sure and fired a second time. Michael's head disappeared under a fountain of blood. Splinters of bone flew across the room and into the hall. The old man grinned, satisfied. He went to the bed and freed the weeping woman from her bonds.

"Why the hell did you marry a German?" he asked as he took off the gag.

"Because I loved him!" she yelled and spit in his face.

"And *I will* have *his baby*, Father!"

He was shocked. His daughter fucked by a *German*! The faces of the grinning SS-officers appeared before his eyes. They laughed at him, in his mind. *At the end evil always prevails!*

But not this time, he swore.

Alec Dawson saw in his daughter's face the face of the SS-man with the Hitler mustache, pointed his weapon at the crying woman and fired twice.

DEATH AT ELEVEN

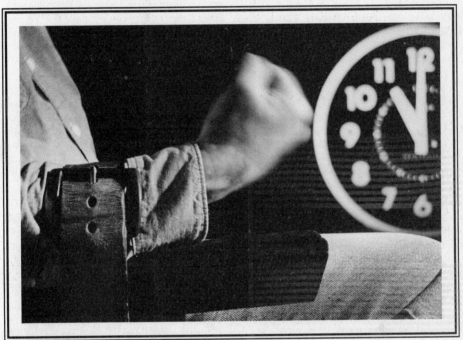

Elizabeth Massie

(For AIUSA Group #157, with love)

It took Joe Williams seven minutes to die. The first jolts, totaling two minutes, weren't enough. The doctor checked his heart and it was still beating. Perturbed and embarrassed, the executioners tried again. More volts were sent into Joe's body.It was said that with the second attempt, Joe's hand, balled into a shiny fist, beat a spastic rhythm on the chair's arm. One witness, ashen-faced before the television cameras outside the prison when it was over,said she could read a Morse message in the rhythm.

N-O, N-O.

Other witnesses laughed her off with nervous chuckles.

Joe's execution had drawn the usual crowds outside the facility. Death penalty opponents held hands and lit candles and sang with strong voices. Death penalty advocates had picnic suppers on truck tailgates and waved homemade posters showing a black man being shoved into an electric oven by a smiling guard. "Poppin' Fresh Joe", read the captions.

Other signs read "You made Ricky die, now you're gonna fry",and "Let's watch that next one, warden!"

Henry was the next one. He had been on death row for six years, and in the legal lottery of failed appeals, he would die in January. Thursday night the twelfth. Eleven o'clock. And not long after Joe's death, the District Court decided that preventing the televising of executions would constitute censorship.

And so the next execution would come live into the living rooms of the entire country.

With the consent of the condemned, of course.

Bruce sat in the car, engine running, staring out through the foggy windshield at the wall of the prison. There was a little snow on the ground. It was gray and wet, full of gravel and dirt. Heat from the vent caught Bruce's eyelashes and made him squint. The radio was on, blowing soft strains of an indistinguishable country tune through the air, tangling with the heat, making Bruce feel at once overwhelmed and alienated.

He had been waiting in the parking lot for over an hour,cutting off the engine sporadically to save gas, hopping out and stomping about in the cold occasionally to keep his legs from cramping. Soon after one p.m., while he was standing outside, it sleeted, and he turned his face upward and held still, eyes closed. Icy rain coated his face and beard. It was cold, but it was real.

After a few minutes, he climbed back into the car and turned on the engine and the heater.

Again, he let the music jumble his thoughts of Henry.

Little brother Henry. Two years younger than Bruce, a little taller, a little thinner. His eyes were the same dark brown as Bruce's, and at one time, his wavy brown hair had been to his shoulders. Bruce wondered what Henry looked like now that his hair was cut short.

It had been three months since Bruce had visited Henry in prison. For the first years, Bruce had gone to see him. He had vacuumed his car each Saturday morning, picked up his mother and sister from their homes in Draper Country, and driven the additional forty two miles to the maximum security facility in Stocksburg. There, the three of them would spend the afternoon passing the phone receiver back and forth before the grease-iced window that kept them from Henry.

Every Saturday. Rain or sleet. Summer or winter.

Bruce's wife knew of the arrangement when she had married him five Augusts ago. But Bruce knew that it pissed her off more often than not now. The couple never had late Saturday mornings with coffee and newspapers. They never accepted invitations from friends for quick weekend trips to the beach. They never shared lazy Saturday afternoons with spontaneous passion. Saturdays were for Henry.

But that was what Bruce had wanted. It was his choice. Guilty or not, ex-drug addict or not, Henry was Bruce's little brother.

But even though he still drove his mother and sister to Stocksburg, Bruce did not visit Henry anymore. Henry wanted to go public. Against Bruce's pleading, he would face the camera. Bruce hated him for it, would have beat the shit out of him if he could have reached through the visitor's window.

The sleet stopped. Bruce turned the car off once more,and listened to the ticking of the engine. He watched several people, hunched under thick winter coats, scuttle across the lot to their vehicles. He could not see their faces, and did not want to. There would be nothing more than weariness there, and resignation, and desperation. All these were friends and family of death row inmates. How could they look any other way?

At three fifteen, while leaning against the door and staring beyond the high fence to the woods to the west, the passenger door popped open. Bruce jumped.

> Eleven days, and the
> first public execution
> would take place since
> a hanging in Kentucky
> in 1936.

His mother, Meg,slid in beside him. She dropped her heavy purse on the floor beside her feet. She pulled off one shoe and bent to massage her toes. Marty, Bruce's sister, climbed in behind Meg.

Bruce turned the key in the ignition. The motor,recently revved, kicked in immediately. Meg sucked air as her fingers found a blister.

Before they had driven as far as the first gate, Meg said, "Who'll call David tonight?"

Neither Marty nor Bruce said anything. The guard in the guard house gave a cursory nod as the car passed. Bruce steered onto the main road and pushed it up to fifty.

Meg patted her hair. Little sparkles of water disappeared into the gray. She wiped her hand on her skirt and said, "Who'll call David?"

Bruce felt the muscles in his neck tighten. Marty said,"I called last week."

Meg sniffed. She looked out of the window. From the corner of his vision, Bruce could see her jaw working.

"I can't talk to him tonight," she said. "It's too hard on me. I can't, you know that. Not now. Everything's too close."

Marty said, "Mom." Her hand came

over the seat and gently squeezed her mother's shoulder.

After a moment, Meg said, "Henry asked about you,Bruce."

Bruce nodded slowly. *'Don't tell me. I don't want to know.'*

"He was hoping you wouldn't have to work today so you could come with us. He wanted to see you." Meg turned away from the window. She slipped her foot back into her shoe.

Marty, in the back, dug through a paper bag. Bruce knew she was after her small bottle. Her coping aid. The top came off with a muffled crack. In the rearview, Bruce could see her taking a long sip. Then she said, "Will you call Dad, Bruce? Henry had some things to tell him."

Bruce slowed at an intersection, then stepped on the accelerator. Mobile homes and tar-bricked houses flew by,the smoke from their chimneys holding low against the sleet-heavy winter air.

"It's less than two weeks," said Marty. "We have notes. Please?"

"Dad doesn't want to know," Bruce said. "He never calls. He never comes to Stocksburg."

"You don't come in no more," muttered Meg.

"He's three hundred miles away," said Marty. Bruce could smell her breath now, the cloyingly sweet smell of oblivion on its way.

"Right," Bruce said.

Meg dug in her purse. She brought out a piece of folded note paper. "I have the notes for David. I wrote it all down." She put the paper into Bruce's coat pocket. He did not take it out. He would call Dad, or would at least make a pretense. There was no arguing at this point. Not with eleven days to go.

Eleven days, and the first public execution would take place since a hanging in Kentucky in 1936. But many more than the paltry 20,000 spectators of the hanging would have the privilege this time. Anyone with a set, cable hookup or a satellite dish, could pull up their La-z-boys, open a bag of microwave popcorn, and tune in. Free press at work. Black and white or color. Death at eleven.

The next ten minutes were driven in silence. A turn on Route 782 brought them

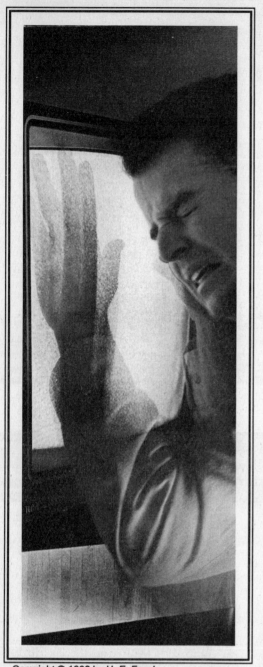

to Meg's driveway, and the single-story white house. Meg's dog, Tinker, bounded out of his house and hopped around at the end of his chain.

Meg collected her purse and opened the car door. Before she got out, she said, "Will you come in with us next week,Bruce? How could we tell him you had to work again? Next week, Bruce. Listen to me."

Bruce did not look at his mother. His teeth ground against each other. His tongue felt as gritty as the filthy snow outside. His eyes stung.

"It's the last week. Your last chance to see him. Bruce?"

"Why did he consent?" Bruce paced his breathing. Anger rushed up his throat.

"I don't want to talk about it no more."

It was all he could do to keep from driving his hand through the window beside him. "Why did he consent?"

Meg got out and slammed the car door shut. Through the glass, he could read her lips. "He don't know why anymore than we do!"

And she was gone in a flurry of black winter coat and heavy purse. In the back, Marty sighed, then nursed the bottle again.

On Tuesday, one week and two days before Henry was to be executed, the press decided to pull out all the stops. It was as though local as well as national television stations decided to throw one large, spectacular pre-execution party. News each night began with clips of what was to come— interviews with the warden, police officers, man-on-the street bits. Footage of Henry's trials were thrown in along with still shots of the waiting chair. With a first in their midst, the networks weren't going to miss their chance to make social comments. But with the newly gained permission to broadcast Henry's death, they weren't going to slit their own throats. All coverage, outside the prison and in, grimly pointed to the need for the guilty to pay the ultimate price, regardless.Bruce went to work, came home for dinner, and avoided the television. His wife, Becky, tried to talk to him but it was hard to respond. All he could give her were one word answers. Everything else was tied up in painful knots,blocking his vocal chords.

Thursday night, Becky put the newspaper beside Bruce's supper plate. It was opened to an editorial, blasting the networks' blatant railroading of public opinion. Bruce skimmed the commentary.

"The only reason television has decided to have such a field day with their ground-breaking telecast," wrote the editor, "is because Henry Huffman is a white man. In fact, if the next man scheduled to be executed had been black, this writer believes either it would have been approached with less pomp and circumstance, or they would have delayed until a more appropriate executee came around. Although capital punishment is handed down with unequal frequency when the criminal is black and the victim white, the networks have no need to share this kind of information. It has nothing to do with their show, and they do have a show to put on. Henry Huffman has become their protective pawn. They are watching their step. Why risk cries of racism when so much exposure and money is on the line?" "They made a good point," said Becky.

Bruce threw the paper across the table. "There are no good points," he said.

Becky's lips made a thin line across her face.

"There are no fucking good points," Bruce said. "Henry consented. He's bringing this on himself."

Becky went into the family room to watch television. She turned the sound down low.

Friday night, Bruce woke from a nightmare. He had been a child; Henry had been a child. Henry was locked in a car, and Bruce was trying to find the key to get him out. The car had begun to sink into the ground, and people were gathered around, watching and pointing and laughing. Some had flash cameras, and bent close to the glass to get a good picture. Bruce searched the weeds around the car, trying to get the key to free Henry. But he could hear Henry calling from the car, "It's my fault, Bruce. I'm sorry. Good-bye." Bruce covered his eyes as the car was

sucked under the dirt.

Becky said, "Bruce, are you all right?"

Breathing hard, Bruce lay without answering. He wiped his sweating forehead. His temples pounded.

Becky rolled over and put a cool hand on his naked, fevered chest. Bruce was aroused, but made himself turn away.

Through the parted curtains, he could see a tiny, cold moon. He watched until the moon was gone and a cold sun had taken its place.

"This is the last chance," said Meg. She stood by the open passenger door. "If you don't come now, you'll have no more chances to see him."

Bruce gripped the steering wheel. The snow on the parking lot was gone, leaving only puddles in the low spots in the blacktop.

"He'd pleaded for us to get you to come. He wants to see you."

Bruce said, "I can't."

Marty stood several yards away from the car, her hands in her pockets. Her face was worn and her hair was not brushed. She stared at the ground.

"He betrayed us," Bruce said. He turned on the radio. A country song was playing.

"He didn't," said Meg.

"Just go see him. Get out of here."

"He didn't," said Meg. She was crying now.

"I'll even call Dad. You won't have to beg. That good enough? Now go on."

He knew it wasn't good enough, but Meg and Marty went on.

Bruce didn't go to work the day of the execution. He did not want to see the faces of his co-workers. He could not fathom sitting in his office. He considered going out alone for a while, but once in the car, he could not remember how to drive.

He fixed a simple lunch, but the first bite made him nauseous. He took a nap in the afternoon, and could not sleep.

Becky came home at six-thirty. She

offered dinner, and Bruce refused. She asked him if there was anything she could do. He told her it might be best if she visited friends that evening. She left. Bruce sat in the family room, staring at the blank television screen.

"He betrayed us," he whispered, and the words were loud and terrifying in the empty room. They echoed and taunted.

Bruce put his hands over his ears. He cried, "He betrayed us!" The scream twisted above and around him, until the words themselves became a lie.

The words were a lie.

Bruce caught his heart and sat upright. '*Dear God,*' he thought. He tried to remember Henry's face, but couldn't. He tried to imagine Henry's voice, even the pinched voice over the receiver in the visitors' cubicle. He couldn't remember. Yes, there was betrayal, but the lie was in the blame.

The betrayal was not Henry's. It was Bruce's. Henry's choice, which Bruce could never understand, had been made in the insanity and claustrophobia of death row. Bruce's choice had been a futile exercise in punishment, a denial of the life which would soon end.

And he would never again see his brother.

At ten fifty six, Bruce turned on the television set. He knelt before the screen, keeping his eyes downcast, and put his hand on glass. Glass, the great separator, the great dehumanizer.

He wished it was a dream, and he could find the key in the weeds.

There was only one way to see Henry again.

"I love you, man," he said. Tears streaked the dust on the television screen. "Forgive me."

At eleven o'clock, the private moment between two brothers was cheered by millions of enthralled onlookers.

Beth Massie won a 1991 Bram Stoker Award for Superior Achievement from the Horror Writers of America, Inc. for her novelette, "Stephen."

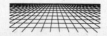

LINES FROM A DIARY

Trina Robbins

December 16

He turned me in, but I do not blame him. I know that they have terrible methods of producing confessions. I would have done the same as he. As it was, I didn't wait to be forced; I confessed instantly. I have such fear of pain!

First they burned my paintings, while I was forced to watch. In a happier time, it might have been performance art —the oils bubbling and steaming, the threads of canvas blackening and curling up. I saw rounded breasts darken and shrivel, pubic hair burst into flame. Bodies, fat and skinny, pink and brown, became black smoke, floated up to the ceiling and dissipated. And all the while they patiently explained to me how I had offended and why I must be punished.

I'm in serious trouble. I didn't need my public defender to tell me what I already knew—obscenity is punishable by death. He thinks that if I plead temporary insanity he can get me off with just a forced re-education. Perhaps I was *not* in my right mind when I painted those pictures; I no longer know.

> I saw a picture of a woman, and she was naked. I awoke feeling disgusted . . . I must have done something terrible in my previous existence

January 21

Today is the first day of the rest of my life! My memories begin with waking up in my hospital cot last night. That is good, because I don't want to remember my previous existence. I only know that I did something very bad—something that hurt the State. I certainly don't want to hurt the State anymore, so I'm glad that the electroshock treatments were so effective.

The State is so good to me! They have given me a name—Joan—and a closet full of dresses in pretty pastels, pinks and yellows, all trimmed with ruffles and lace at the necks and wrists. I even have a job waiting for me when I am released, which my doctor tells me will be soon, because I am such a good patient. I'll be starting at the Kwik-Kow fast burger shoppe, washing dishes. But if I'm good, my doctor promises that I'll be promoted to a place behind the counter, taking orders. I've gotten very good at taking orders.

February 19

My new-found happiness has proved fleeting. I am almost afraid to say it—fragmentary memories are resurfacing. They usually come back to me while I'm at work, washing dishes. A rainbow-filled bubble will rise from the sink and burst before my eyes, leaving in its place another thought. I know now that my name was not Joan, but something more interesting. I am afraid to remember what it was. And I *never* wore pastels! I used to wear only black. But how could I? Black is such an ugly color!

Last night I had a terrifying dream. I saw a picture of a woman, and she was naked. I awoke feeling disgusted. Of course I undress in the dark, just like everybody else. Where did the picture come from? I am afraid to tell my doctor; he'll think that my re-education was faulty, and possibly it was.

I must have done something terrible in my previous existence!

March 5

Things are getting worse instead of better. I have started to draw pictures! At first I sketched them out with my finger on the surface of the wet sink, hastily rubbing them out before anyone else could see them. Then I bought some stationary; lined paper decorated with bunnies and ducks. I paint on it with cosmetics and nail polish. I know I'm not supposed to be drawing—after all, the Bureau of Re-education made me a dishwasher, not an artist!—so I don't dare get caught buying art supplies. I am creating miracles with Helena Rubenstein!

A new man came to work today, sweeping the floors at Kwik-Kow. I think he was sent, like me, by the Bureau of Re-education. He seems serenely happy, just sweeping the floors. I remember how happy I was at first, washing dishes. He seems strangely familiar, as though he, too, was part of my old life.

I think I remember my name.

March 8

This morning I told him my name, hoping it would interest him. "My name is not Joan," I said, "It's Rain. And I paint." He grunted a noncommittal reply and turned to his sweeping, but as his eyes shifted away from mine, I caught a flicker of fear in them. Now he stays away from me. When his sleeves ride up, I see the scars on his arm.

In the evening, upon my return from work, I carefully drew the blinds. Then I peeled off the hateful pastels and bravely stood naked before my full length mirror. The reflection showed me full breasts, a rounded belly, dark hair between my legs. It didn't look like those plastic dolls with the long yellow hair that the Department of Play gives young girls on Christmas. But to me it seemed beautiful because it was my body. I reached for my lined stationary and my perfumed colors. With smears of Midnite Blu, Frostee Peach, Scarlet Mist and Copper Luv, I copied the image in the mirror.

Will they catch me? It doesn't matter, "My name is Rain," I told the nude, "And I paint."

Trina Robbins is a comics artist and editor of **Choices,** *reviewed below.*

CHOICES: A PRO CHOICE BENEFIT COMIC
Edited by Trina Robbins
Angry Isis Press
$5.50

Trina Robbins has been extensively involved in the world of comics for over twenty years. Although an accomplished cartoonist in her own right, her shining strength has been utilized as a editor of two worthwhile publications: *Strip AIDS USA* in 1988, and more recently *Choices*, from which "Burning Issue" is reprinted on page 32.

Calling upon her many friends and co-cartoonists, Trina has solicited donations of artwork from a veritable Who's Who in cartooning to create publications that benefit AIDS research through the San Francisco-based Shanti Project and NOW's fight to ensure reproductive choice for all women everywhere.

In *Choices* the reader will find a thought-provoking selection of subject-related cartooning from newspaper strip artists Gary Trudeau, Cathy Guisewrite and Nicole Hollander. Comic book cartoonists contributing to these pages include Steve Leialoha, Steve Lafler, Reed Waller and Kate Worely, Diane Noomin and Howard Cruise to name but a few.

Both publications are highly recommended for comics fans due to the wide and varied roster of artists they showcase. The contribution made by purchasing these books and thus furthering two important causes is an added plus.

(*Choices* can be ordered from Angry Isis, 1982 15th Street, San Francisco, CA 94114 for $5.50.)

—*Kate Kane*

Vampire

Richard Christian Matheson

Man.
Late. Rain.
Road.
Man.
Searching. Starved. Sick.
Driving.
Radio. News. Scanners. Police. Broadcast.
Accident. Town.
Near.
Speeding. Puddles.
Aching.
Minutes.
Arrive. Park. Watch.
Bodies. Blood. Crowd. Sirens.
Wait.
Hour. Sit. Pain. Cigarette. Thermos. Coffee.
Sweat. Nausea.
Streetlights. Eyes. Stretchers. Sheets.
Flesh.
Death.
Shaking. Chills.
Clock. Wait.
More. Wait.
Car. Stink. Cigarette.
Ambulance. Crying. Towtruck. Bodies. Taken.
Crowd. Police. Photographers. Drunks. Leave.
Gone.
Street. Quiet.
Rain. Dark. Humid.
Alone.
Door. Out. Stand. Walk. Pain. Stare. Closer.
Buildings. Silent. Street. Dead.
Blood. Chalk. Outlines. Middle.
Inhale. Eyes. Closed.
Think. Inhale. Concentrate. Feel. Breathe.

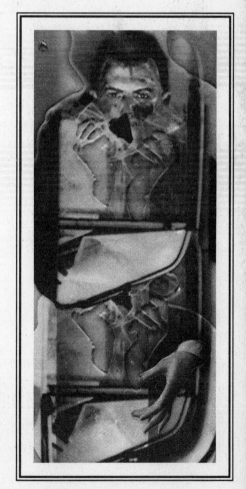

Copyright © 1992 by Harry O. Morris

Flow.
Death. Collision. Woman. Screaming. Windshield.
Expression.
Moment. Death.
Energy. Concentrate. Images. Exploding.
Moment.
Women. Car. Truck. Explosion.
Impact. Moment.
Rush.
Feeling. Feeding.
Metal. Burning. Screams. Blood. Death.
Moment. Collision. Images. Faster.
Strength. Medicine. Trance.
Stronger.
Concentrate. Better.
Images. Collision. Stronger. Seeing. Death.
Moment. Healing. Moment.
Addiction.
Drug. Rush. Body. Warmer.
Death. Concentrating. Healing. Addition. Drug.
Warmth. Calm.
Death. Medicine.
Death.
Life.
Medicine.
Addiction. Strong.
Leave.
Car. Engine. Drive. Rain. Streets. Freeway. Map.
Drive. Relax. Safe. Warm. Rush. Good.
Radio. Cigarette. Breeze.
Night.
Searching. Accidents. Death.
Life.
Dash. Clock. Waiting.
Soon.

Originally appeared in Cutting Edge, edited by Dennis Etchison. Copyright © 1988 by Richard Christian Matheson. Richard Christian Matheson is a screenwriter/producer/director who works extensively in television and feature films. His first novel Created By will appear in 1992.

LAUGH TRACK

Brian Riordan

Servants to mother machine
Nursed by video screens
   —"Mental Slavery," Kreator

"Yo, man. C'mere."

"Whasa problem?"

"I can't laugh at this show no mo."

"Say what?"

"I can't laugh at this show no mo. It don't got no laugh track."

"What da fuck you talking bout?"

"Well, I ain't exactly sure. I mean, in my *mind*, I know dis show is all funny and whatnot, and I *feel* like I'm laughin, but I'm really not. Am I losin you?"

"Little bit."

"Aright, see, a couple of weeks ago, I was watchin dis show, an I noticed I wudn't laughin a *peep* through da whole damn thing. But da show was funny as *shit*, you know? An I felt I was laughin my head off straight out all da time it was on. But I really *wudn't* man, it was all in my *mind*. Honest to God it wud da weirdest shit I ever felt. You gettin all dis?"

" . . . yeah, think so."

"Cool. Now, I wud watchin da same show again tonight, right? An I finally realized why I wudn't laughin no mo while it wud on. *The show ain't got no laugh track*."

"What?"

"Dammit, ain't you heard a thing I said?"

"Yeah, but . . . "

"But what? What don't ya un-nerstand?"

"Well . . . Ya shittin me. You gotta be."

"I ain't shittin you."

"Yeah, you *all* fulla shit today."

"Fuh Chrissake, *I ain't shittin you*."

"C'mon. Dis is crazy."

"I know. Thought I was goin crazy da first time I noticed it, too. But it's true."

"Really, man? Dis ain't just some bad joke?"

"No joke."

"Shit, dat's scary."

"Said da same thing myself."

"So . . . so what ya gonna do bout it?"

"Well, what *can* I do bout it?"

"I dunno."

"I mean, you can't exactly go to a doctor fuh dis sorta thing."

"Damright. You be put in some fuckin padded room."

"Mmm-hmm."

"Shit, dis is weird."

"Tell it."

"Man, you an me got to get our minds off dis."

"Huh?"

"What ya watchin on TV here?"

"What? . . . Uh *Doogie Howser*, I think."

"Dis any good? I heard it was."

"Shit, yeah. One a da funniest god-damn shows I seen all year."

"So why ain't ya laughin?"

"Well, I would, but dis one ain't got no laugh track."

"Oh."

Brian Riordan is a part-time writer, living in New Jersey.

Flesh-Eating Muthas

© M.A. VICKERY 91

James Kisner

It was a big mother. A comet. Curtis and Reggie sat on the roof watching it as it whizzed overhead, tearing the sky a new asshole.

"Curt, my man," Reggie said, "that was one mean comet.

My eyes still hurting from looking at it."

"Shit, man, you weren't supposed to look right *at* it! Didn't you read in the papers it could burn your eyeballs right out of the sockets? It's like looking at a piece of the goddamn sun!"

Reggie blinked and rubbed his eyes. "Curtis! Where are you? Curtis! I can't see you!"

"You dumb sumbitch.I told you. . ."

"Reggie doubled over like he was going to throw up, then pointed at his friend. "You bought it, man. Ain't nothing wrong with my eyes."

Any other man with a degree of sense would not josh Curtis—who weighed two-forty and was six-four—and had almost made the final cut for the Cleveland Browns, but skinny little Reggie, had been his friend since childhood, and could get away with just about anything with the bigger man.

"You are one dumb muthafucker," Curtis said, tensing his massive shoulders.

Reggie was an inch shorter than Curtis, but of considerably less mass. He was also less educated than his friend, who had a good chance at a scholarship at Ohio State next fall. Reggie was considering going to technical school to learn to be a welder—that or an Amway distributor.

Curtis sighed and watched the tail of the comet trail away, slowly fading into the night sky. "That's one comet the scientists didn't know nothin' about," he said in his explanatory, but non-patronizing way. "It just come out of nowhere. Maybe like the one that killed the dinosaurs."

Reggie stuck a Salem Light between his lips and lit it. He puffed and blew smoke through his nose. "What comet killed the dinosaurs?" he inquired.

"Don't you know shit?"

"I know shit when I see it, so I don't step in it, brother, but what the hell you mean a comet killed the dinosaurs?"

"Every 25 or 30 million years something happens that wipes out most life on the earth. Some scientists think a comet — one nobody knows about for sure—came out of nothing and smacked the earth, making tidal waves and filling the air with dust and all kinds of other shit fall-

out like a friggin' atomic bomb and that, my little man, is what snuffed the thunder lizards."

"No shit?"

"No shit, Sherlock."

Reggie's face evidenced genuine fear. "You think that comet going to smack the earth and snuff *our* asses?"

Curtis smiled. "Hell, it missed us by a million miles. Probably cause somebody's hair to fall out somewhere or make dumb fucks like you go blind. It'd have to *hit* us to do anything bad.

"Reggie laughed nervously. "I knew that."

"Sure you did, brother."

"You sure are smart, Curt. If I had your brains and your body, I'd be king of fucking Cleveland."

Curtis grabbed his friend by the shoulder and squeezed him affectionately. He'd probably be bruised for days, but the big man's affection was worth it. "Now why the hell would I want to be king of Cleveland? Let's go get a beer."

Curtis and Reggie passed the next few hours drinking beer and watching the Linnea Quigley movie festival on Cinemax in Curtis' living room. They both passed out and didn't awaken till late the next morning.

Curtis was not only a smart man, but also a cautious one. He had learned that being black meant he had to be right when he said something, so he rarely said anything he didn't know for a fact to be an absolute or damn close.

He was, however, wrong about the comet. Of course, there was no way he could have known what it would do. No one could have predicted the effects it would have.

Not even Curtis.

He awoke Reggie, who had fallen asleep on the floor in front of the TV, then staggered out to the kitchen. "Hey, Mom?"

"Don't talk so loud!" Reggie said, sitting up slowly. "I got M.C. Hammer himself hammerin' inside my head."

"What a pussy. Can't even handle beer."

"Fuck you too, brother. You can't even handle pussy." Curtis ignored him. "Mom?" Curtis opened the refrigerator and took out a plastic jug of milk, then pulled down a large box of Wheaties and two bowls from the cupboard. "Get your ass in here, Reggie-Boy, and eat your friggin' Wheaties."

Reggie lurched in and sat at the table. "Ain't you got any Cheerios? I like them Honey-Nut kind—you don't have to put sugar on them."

"Wheaties got Michael Jordan on the box."

"Oh." Reggie started spooning cereal into his mouth, chewing quite vigorously considering how much his head hurt. "You know, I can hear my teeth hitting each other. Sounds like a sledge hammer."

"I thought it was M.C. Hammer."

"Ooooh, sheee-it. I need aspirin."

"Finish the Wheaties."

Reggie stood up. "You ain't my mother." He went back into the bathroom and searched the medicine cabinet for aspirin. He returned with three tablets which he downed with a glass of milk. Then he belched loudly. "Goddamn, that's nasty!"

"What?"

"A beer-Wheaties-aspirin-and-milk belch."

"Want another bowl?"

"Fuck no." He sat down and picked a cigarette out of the pack. It was half-broken, so he had to pinch it together to light and smoke it. "Where's your mother?"

"I don't know. It's almost noon. She could be anywhere. It's Saturday—her getting-out day."

"Shit, is it Saturday already?"

"Well, it was Friday last night."

"Let's get out of here and go see what's shaking in the street. We'll take your car."

"Could that be because your car's out of gas?"

Reggie looked sheepish.

Curtis shook his head, tucked in his shirt, farted and belched. "Oooooh, nasty," he said, and the two of them left the apartment to cruise Euclid Avenue in Curtis' Chrysler.

"Streets ain't too lively seems to me," Reggie said.

"It's too hot today. Everybody staying in to watch cable TV. Cable TV has ruined our society. I believe it is the White Man's opiate of the people."

"What the fuck does that mean?"

"A paraphrase of Mr. Karl Marx, the German Jew who thought up Communism, socialism and a couple other 'isms."

"You ain't no Communist..."

"Hell, no, bro."

"I gotta get some smokes. Let's stop at...hey, Curtis! Your mama!"

Not even Reggie could say that to Curtis. "What you mean my 'mama'?"

"Not like that, man. Look over there? Ain't that your mama?"

"Where?"

"Over there, Curtis. Ain't that your mama—chewing on that ham?"

"That ain't no goddamn ham!"

✧

Curtis slammed on the brakes, riding up over the curb. He jumped out of the car and ran to his mother, a short, gray-haired black woman in her late sixties.

She watched him come yet she didn't move.

She didn't even say, "Hi, sonny," or "Hi, Curtis," or anything. She was too busy eating.

"Mama!" Curtis yelled. "Oh, God, I was right."

She cocked her head. Her eyes were more yellowish than normal; she didn't seem to recognize her son. Since she didn't recognize him, she continued with her meal.

She was chewing on a human arm, taking big bites out of it and pumping her jaws up and down like an animal. Her mouth was covered with blood, as was her old flowered dress. Next to her, in her old canvas shopping bag, was another arm, a leg, and— Curtis stopped taking inventory when he saw what strongly resembled someone's *johnson*.

He grabbed his mother by the shoulders and shook her. Her head rattled but her eyes stayed fixed on him.

"What's happened to you, Mama?"

She stopped chewing briefly. "Why, Curtis! I wondered when you was going to get up. I couldn't wait forever. I got too hungry—and, of course, I was tempted—Lord knows—but I just couldn't eat your good old friend Reggie. I bet he tender, though, not like this 'un."

Curtis' jaw dropped. Had his mother gone crazy during the night? Had she gotten a bottle of bad wine?

Bile crawled up the back of his throat, dragging along bits of breakfast and last night's beer and dinner and maybe even some leftover lunch. Curtis swallowed hard.

Then he made a big mistake. He tried to take the arm away from his mother. She wouldn't let it go. In fact, scary as it was for him to realize, she had acquired new strength and he *couldn't* pry it from her skinny old hands.

"What you doing, trying to steal my food! Go get your own! You're bigger and stronger than me. You ought to be able to get some fine eatin'."

"Mama, you are NOT a cannibal!"

"'Course not. Cannibals cook they meals. I eats 'em raw."

Reggie, half-crazed with curiosity, left the car and came over. His eyes doubled in size when he saw the hand on the end of what he thought was a ham. Then he lost several day's worth of meals when Curtis' mama started nibbling on the fingers.

After he was finished heaving, Reggie turned around to Curtis and said, "I can't help it, man. That comet must've done something to my eyes. It look like your mama eating somebody's arm . . ."

"That's the strangest thing," Mama said, spitting out a fingernail, "after that big old light went over I woke up with this craving for eating people. And I just couldn't get over it. I just had to get out of the apartment and get me some human meat. It's good too. Y'all want some ribs?"

Reggie fainted.

Curtis, always the man of action, hauled back and hit his poor old Mama in the face. She collapsed, and he took his

> Curtis stopped taking inventory when he saw what strongly resembled someone's *johnson.*

belt off and tied her arms behind her and put her in the back seat of the car on her side. Then he set his unconscious friend in the passenger seat, got in and roared down the street.

For a couple of blocks.

He screeched to a halt when he saw a bunch of wiry old women, tearing bodies apart, having a flesh-eating picnic right in the middle of the street. They were carrying on and laughing just like it was the most natural thing in the world.

His Mama had said something about the "big old light" in the sky. She meant the comet! Maybe this was the one that came every 25 or 30 million years, only this time it was going to wipe out humanity by causing everybody to eat everybody.

Except it was only women doing the eating.

In fact, it was only people's gray-haired Mamas out there eating people.

Maybe there was hope.

Curtis heard sirens. Of course! Somebody had called the police. He edged his car over to the curb and just watched.

Two Cleveland Police cars approached from the opposite end of the street. Out of them emerged several black officers, and one white one. After they all got sick, one had the presence of mind to use the bullhorn:

"Ladies, this is the Cleveland Police. You are to stop —stop eating—you are all under arrest!"

"What's the charge," a woman who was picking a rib cage clean yelled.

"What's the charge?" the man with the bullhorn whispered to an older officer. "Those bodies are fresh. So I guess it's murder. Or accessory to murder or something. Goddamn it, people just can't go around eating other people."

"Yes, sir. I mean, no, sir." He put the bullhorn to his lips again. "You are under arrest for suspicion of murder with probable cause."

"Fuck probable cause, whatever the fuck that is," a woman answered.

"Probable cause being," the officer continued, "that you are consuming freshly dead human beings."

"Course they're fresh. You want us to eat spoiled meat?"

The rest of the women laughed.

"Put up your hands, goddamn it."

"Fuck you," came from several directions.

"Put up your hands or we'll fire."

The women totally ignored the police, until one of them turned and noticed the white officer among them. "Look, Tonya! White meat!"

All the women turned and advanced towards the police, apparently intent on sampling this rare delicacy — rare in this neighborhood anyhow.

The police tried to push the women back. One broke a billie club on a woman's head. Her skull split open but she laughed and took a huge bite out of his arm.

The women were not only cannibals, they were dead!

The police opened fire. They had .44 magnums and riot guns. They blew holes in the women big enough to let sunlight through. One woman's head exploded.

But they kept coming.

They pulled the officers away from the cars, then pulled them apart. The white man was the last to go.

They all shared him—at least the women who still had faces and teeth did.

The couple whose heads had been blown off wandered around aimlessly, their hands clawing at the air. One fell to the ground and reached out to get a foot. She tried to stuff it where her mouth had been.

Curtis, a man who had rarely known fear, watched and was suddenly terrified. This was beyond understanding. Society was totally fucked now: cigarettes, booze and sex were dangerous.

Radon could kill you in your own home. Drinking water was polluted. The ozone layer was like swiss cheese. Now, the last holy thing left—your Mama— was dangerous.

While Curtis was reflecting on the irony of just plain being alive, he hadn't noticed how the crowd of women had grown. There were twice as many, drawn by the cries of "fresh meat," as they ate the police officers.

Now he heard the call of "fresh meat" again. The walking dead mothers were advancing towards the car.

He jerked Reggie awake. "Roll up the windows and lock the doors, then hold on tight. It's lunch time and we're the cold cuts!"

"Sweet Jesus!" Reggie said, coming quickly to his senses.

Curtis started the car, put it in reverse and slammed his foot on the accelerator. He traveled backward half a block, then rammed into a group of flesh-eating mamas coming from the other direction. Two or three of them flew through the air, bounced off parked cars and got back on their feet, apparently unharmed.

Curtis floored it again, spun the car in a semi-circle, then spotted an alley. He roared down the alley between two buildings, knocking over trash cans filled with freshly-cleaned human bones. A head landed on the hood, its single eye staring at him momentarily.

"Shit," Reggie said, "they got Snake-man."

Snake-man, so called because he had a snake tattooed on his dick, seemed unhappy. Or his head did. The car hit a chuck hole and Snake-man's head hit the windshield, and part of his neck bone lodged between one of the wipers.

"Get him off there!" Reggie

screamed.

Curtis turned on the wipers. They wiped Snake-man's head back and forth, mangling its frowning visage further, but not shaking it loose.

Curtis reached the end of the alley and made a hard turn onto another street. Women were running up and down it fighting each other over pieces of flesh.

"What the holy fuck is going on?" Reggie said.

Curtis kept rolling, just running over any one that darted out in front of him and explained his theory about the comet and how its radiation might have changed the mothers into cannibals.

"Ain't that a bitch. What we going to do?"

"The police tried to shoot them. You can't kill them." He headed the car towards an old woman biting the nose off a ragged head. She bounced off his bumper. Reggie looked back and saw her get up, retrieve her head and continue eating. "See? Man, I watched the cops pump them old ladies full of holes and they still kept coming. They ate the cops, man. They ate the fucking cops!"

"But why don't it make us cannibals? We saw the comet."

"I guess it only affects women."

"Jesus, everything affects pussy, don't it?"

"This is no time to be talking about pussy."

"Sorry, brother. But you don't see me chewing on no arm."

"I wonder if it's women everywhere—I mean all over the world? Think of that, Reggie-Boy. There's more women than men!" Reggie shuddered, watching a man and two children running away from a woman who looked to be about a hundred.

Curtis kept driving. He wanted to stop and help, but he knew he was no match for the women.

"What we going to do?"

"I don't know . . . get back to the apartment . . . turn on the TV . . . see what's happening . . ."

"Goddamn! Curt . . ."

Curtis had forgotten about his mother in the back seat. She had come to and grabbed Reggie around the neck, pulling his head back and taking a big bite out of the top. Blood gushed out. Curtis elbowed his mother in the face, feeling sick as he heard the cartilage in her nose crack. She reached for *his* arm. He stopped the car, turned around and hit her real hard this time, knocking her senseless again.

"Reggie?"

His friend was holding the wound on his head. "I guess I'll make it, man. Let's just get out of the mean motherfucking, mother-eating streets!"

By the time they reached the apartment building, it was deserted. The mothers were apparently sweeping through the neighborhood, taking all the meat, then moving on.

They were sloppy eaters, Curtis noted as he went up the stairs, carrying his inert mama over his shoulder and helping to hold Reggie up. They'd left pieces everywhere. Bones. Ears.

Toes. It was ironic that the women who had told generations of youngsters to clean their plates were themselves so slovenly.

Curtis opened the door, laid his mother on the couch temporarily, and then went back to deadbolt the door. He bandaged Reggie's wound, then found some rope and bound his mother to a kitchen chair and carried her into her bedroom. He nailed her door shut, then returned to the living room where Reggie was watching the cable news channel. He had a beer and was smoking the butts left over from the night before from the ashtray.

Curtis grabbed a beer and sat down next to his friend.

" . . . hordes of women, primarily older women, have been transformed into rampaging beasts, attacking men and children and allegedly eating . . . "

"'Allegedly' my ass," Reggie snorted.

"Shut up and listen."

" . . . the phenomenon is confined to North America. No official explanation has been given for the cause of this outbreak of alleged cannibalism . . . "

The newsman prattled on a few more moments belaboring the obvious until even a zero-I.Q. moron would know what was happening, until he touched his earphone. "Ladies and gentlemen, I've just been informed of a startling new development. We take you now live to our White House correspondent, Juanita Chong, for an on-the-spot report."

Juanita Chong's oriental-chicano face filled the screen. Behind her could be seen the White House and several military vehicles parked out front. "Thank you, Dan. This report is not yet totally confirmed, but an inside source at the White House has leaked to our sources..."

"Get on with it, woman!" Reggie yelled.

Curtis elbowed him.

" ... the First Lady has eaten the President and the White House Chief of Staff. Secret Service Men have her..."

"That's a relief," Curtis said.

"Say what, bro?"

"At least it's not just black women. We don't have to take the rap for this one."

"Much of Washington is in chaos as gangs of women descend on men and children and—it's so hard to put this into words—kill and *eat* them. A Pentagon source has cited possible water contamination, perhaps by terrorists from a Third World nation ... "

"Yeah, blame it on the Middle East," Curtis snorted.

" ... but no one is confirming or denying anything at this stage. Wait, Dan, I'm getting a report—yes, a man on the inside said he saw the First Lady eating the President. The Vice-President has already been notified and..."

Juanita suddenly lurched forward, her face filling the screen. There were muffled sounds, the scratching of metal on concrete as a microphone dropped. Something shattered. Then Juanita came back in focus.

She was holding a hairy leg. "Really, Dan, I don't see what the fuss is about." She took a bite from the leg. "This seems perfectly natural to me ... "

She was abruptly cut off.

The scene shifted back to the anchorman. "That was our live report from Washington." His face was white. "We now take you to New York, where ... "

> She was holding a hairy leg. "Really, Dan, I don't see what the fuss is about." She took a bite from the leg. "This seems perfectly natural to me ... "

Curtis grabbed the remote control and flicked the TV off.

"Hey, man..."

"It's getting the younger women now. That Juanita Chong is only about thirty-five. She just had a baby."

"It's mothers, man," Reggie said. "Just mothers."

"Maybe you're on to something, there, my man."

"Damn straight I am. The mothers of the world—hey, dig it. I saw a movie once. They're *zombies*. You know. They go around eating people. I saw lotsa movies like that."

"This ain't a movie."

"In the movies, you blow off their heads or burn them alive and that stops them. Not like vampires where you put a stake in the heart. You got to get their heads."

"Bull-fucking-shit, man. I saw them get their heads blown off and they still kicking."

"But ... "

"The movies ain't real life, Reggie. Real life is what's happening out in the streets. Like it's always been."

"You think they'd get full. That's a funny thing in them movies. The bitches keep eating and never get full, and you tell me there's more women than men. They going to come back through again and again till they get all of us. We're fucked." Reggie picked through the butts in the ashtray looking for one long enough to smoke. "We outnumbered. They eat us all alive. And I ain't even got any smokes. Shit."

"Wait a minute, Reggie," Curtis said. "That's the answer."

"Say what?"

"You're smarter than you think, except you let them movies jam up your thinking machine."

"What'd I say?"

"More women than men!" Curtis got up and ran to the phone. He thumbed through the blue pages till he found the local F.B.I. number. He punched it in and waited. Thankfully, a man's voice came on the line.

"Now, listen up," he began. "I know how to end this. It ain't going to be pretty but . . ."

Curtis was right again. His mind, developed with the cunning that comes with dealing with the reality of the streets, had come up with a simple solution. It wasn't elegant, but it worked.

The F.B.I. didn't buy it at first, but they promised to get it through to the new President and he approved, especially since his own wife had already eaten one of the kids, and had to be restrained with chains.

So they corralled the cannibal mothers in heavily-secured camps throughout the country, placed them in fenced-in compounds surrounded by high walls with electrified barbed wire on top and just sat back and waited.

Since they were more women than men it would have happened eventually anyhow, but Curtis' plan hastened the inevitable. Once the women ran out of men, they had no choice but to eat *each other*. That was something that never happened in the movies. Because movies were mostly written by white people who had no street smarts.

It wasn't long before the problem was under control. The population in the camps reduced quickly, leaving only the meanest mothers surviving. In some camps, the population actually got down to only two.

At that point, the military had orders to use flame-throwers. Total incineration had proven the only effective means of destroying them.

Fortunately, not all the women had to die. The comet passed back over the earth going the other way and ninety-nine percent of the remaining women reverted to their former selves with no memories of having been cannibals.

As for the other one percent . . .

Curtis couldn't be expected to turn in his own Mama. He kept her in her room so the government men wouldn't find her.

He kept her well-fed. Every night he came home with fresh food for his dear old Mama.

But he sure was beginning to miss his friends. Especially Reggie. But his Mama kept saying how tender-looking Reggie was, and—well, hell, he couldn't deny his *Mama* anything.

James Kisner is a novelist and short story writer whose latest work is featured in the prestigious **Dark Harvest #9** *anthology.*

LYRICS OF ABUSE FIND AUDIENCE

Steve Lopez

If there was any doubt left in America that popular music isn't what it used to be, along comes a hit album to erase any confusion.

The first two weeks out, it sold a million copies, flying all the way to the top of Billboard magazine's pop album chart. Now at No. 18, the album is in its 10th week on the chart, with sales still brisk.

The happy and successful musicians, who are rolling in dough these days, call their rap band N.W.A. This stands for Niggers With Attitude. And the songs on their hot new album, songs that have captured the imagination of so many fans, cover a number of topics.

Roughing up girlfriends. Raping women. Killing prostitutes. Beating women who don't submit to oral sex. Robbing and thieving. Killing cops.

Yes, in just one album, you can find not just inspiration for a life of crime and violence, but helpful tips on how to make the grade.

On the oral sex part, for instance: "Punch the bitch in the eye, and then the ho will fall to the ground . . ."

While the *ho* is helpless, perhaps semiconscious, you can have your way. If there's still a problem, you might refer to the song "One Less Bitch" for pointers.

She was the perfect ho, but wouldn't you know, the bitch tried to gag me, so I had to kill her. Listen up and let me tell you how I did it.

He did it with a .44.

What a man.

Fortunately, you don't have to listen to her plead for mercy, like the woman who is shot three times in the song "To Kill a Hooker."

One less, one less, one less bitch I gotta worry about.

Personally, I'd like to have one less, one less, one less band we gotta worry about. N.W.A. makes rappers 2 Live Crew, who beat an obscenity rap last year, seem like choirboys.

"We're in a sad state when a group like this can flourish," says Carol Ray, chief of Women Against Abuse in Philadelphia, whose 61-bed shelter has been filled since June.

The sickest thing, she says, is that one million people couldn't wait to run out and buy the album, which is called *Efil4zaggin*. (Niggaz41ife spelled backward.) Once every 12 to 15 seconds in America, Ray says, a woman is battered.

> Even if you burned all the albums and tapes today, there'd still be more than a million morons out there who like tapping **their** toes to the idea of slapping women around and shooting anything that moves.

And lyrics such as N.W.A.'s are an endorsement.

The same conclusion was reached by Dee Barnes, host of a Fox TV rap show called *Pump It Up*. And she has an interesting perspective, when you consider that she filed a suit against a member of N.W.A. who allegedly picked her up by the hair, smashed her face into a wall, kicked her in the ribs and stomped on her fingers in a Hollywood club.

Barnes said Andre Young, 26, who was charged with battery, was upset about the way the TV show handled a piece on N.W.A.

"My lawsuit is not just about one 5-foot-3-inch woman getting slapped around by a 6-foot-2-inch guy," Barnes told the Los Angeles Times. "It's about how N.W.A. rages violence against women in general. Millions of little boys listen to this crap—and they're going to grow up thinking it's all right to abuse women."

"It ain't no big thing," Young told Rolling Stone. "I just threw her through a door."

Eric Schnurer, a Philadelphia attorney specializing in First Amendment law, says this kind of garbage is protected, just as the Ku Klux Klan has a right to hold a rally and spout its hatred and ignorance.

"Yes, personally I think it's trash and shouldn't be in our society, but the questions go deeper than that," Schnurer says. They go to the issue of limits in a free society, and who sets them. Once you say it's OK to squelch a certain kind of speech because most people don't share the same views, Schnurer says, you cross a dangerous line.

Intellectually, I can understand his point. Emotionally, to borrow an idea, I would still like to see these guys thrown through a door.

But the problem isn't supply; it's, demand. Even if you burned all the albums and tapes today, there'd still be more than one million morons out there who like tapping their toes to the idea of slapping women around and shooting anything that moves.

"The answer is not to throw people in jail for speech that we judge to be bad," Schnurer says. Everybody wants simple legal solutions to complex social problems. Rather, without becoming puritanical freaks, the answer is "to do a better job of promoting better values in society."

Speaking of values, I'll tell you this. If I were a record distributor, I wouldn't offer this junk. If I owned a record store, I wouldn't sell it.

Talk about a ho.

Reprinted with permission from the Philadelphia Inquirer August 18, 1991.

N.W.A. CENSOR ?

. . . Give Me A Break

Dave Marsh

Steve Lopez makes me sick. Literally. Every time I try to read his drivel, I get so angry my head aches and the urge to reach out and twist his neck becomes more and more irresistible. I think it's a waste of *Gauntlet*'s space to run such rubbish, riddled as it is with the gilded dog-shit of cliche and half truth, but I'm not the editor, so let's see if we can briefly address the reasons why this patsy for the status quo is more a protector of garbage than any free speech advocate could ever be.

Lopez is stupid from the git. "If there was any doubt left in America that popular music isn't what it used to be,

along comes a hit album to erase any confusion," he writes. Lopez intends for us to imagine a past benign and far preferable to the situation that pertains today. But in the real past, black musicians were forbidden access to the airwaves, which freed white performers to steal their songs, their rhythms, their ideas and their energy and profit wildly from them. Black musicians remain subject to the rules of a business system that ensures they are unfairly paid, if they are paid at all, for making the music that enriches the white owners of the corporations that market their music, and supplies most of the creative energy to the white musicians who are paid at a higher royalty. Most of them have grown up in environments despoiled in numerous ways by such owners and corporations. This is enough to give anybody, let alone someone defined as a "nigger," an attitude.

To say that this does not justify sexual battery and rape is to say nothing at all, *because that isn't the question.*

The question is why the fuck, in a world where four or five women a minute are battered, our popular music should not reflect such battery—and whether, absent such a reflection, we can do anything to change the situation. The question is whether Steve Lopez, who would kill the messenger, has done fuck-all to reduce the problem. The question is whether killing the messenger would help or hinder a solution. The question is whether Steve Lopez really wants a solution, or just a neater world in which he and his melanin-deficient bosses and colleagues can ignore such issues as *why* there is so much sexual assault. (It ain't because of rap records, fool—ask Tina Turner.)

This problem didn't originate with N.W.A. and I'm not even convinced that N.W.A. makes it worse, because from the point of view of any given victim, *it can t get any worse.* N.W.A. (besides being a musically interesting group in ways that Lopez is apparently too ignorant or too dumb to grasp) is nothing but a scapegoat.

If Steve Lopez really wanted to end sexual battery in the United States, he would not start at the record store. But an end to such problems is the last thing Lopez or his masters want. What they want is to sidetrack the issue by proposing censorship, and then withdrawing that idea as if their dicks would shrivel up if they told the truth about their political aspirations. This leaves us with *no solution.* Having thus frustrated all prospects for change, they can start all over again, returning us to that Reaganite never—land in which *things used to be better.* And they can continue to blame the most destitute, uneducated, helpless parts of the population for the fact that things have gotten worse and continue to deteriorate.

As to cop-killing, if Steve Lopez is so

> But an end to such problems is the last thing Lopez or his masters want. What they want is to sidetrack the issue by proposing censorship . . .

fond of statistics he will be glad to know that eight times as many Americans are killed each year *by* cops as cops are killed by civilians. Hundreds of citizens are shot or otherwise killed by the police; fewer than 100 cops have ever been killed in one year, which is pretty amazing when you think of all the time that cops spend in supposedly vicious neighborhoods. (If those neighborhoods are truly vicious, it would be fair to argue on recent highly public evidence that the cops are generally the most vicious element within them.) The police are a lethal force in all communities, particularly poor and minority ones. For Lopez to pretend that N.W.A.'s songs threatening retaliation are not valid and important examples of political speech is the most deeply dishonest part of his act.

N.W.A. began issuing its inflammatory criticisms of the L.A.P.D. two years before Rodney King had his beating videotaped. For singing such songs, N.W.A. was attacked by the F.B.I. and prevented from singing in concert by the police forces of many American communities in that period. N.W.A. was illegally detained by cops in Detroit in 1990 for singing *one verse* of "F—- Tha Police." Has Steve Lopez ever told his readers about that?

He sure hasn't told the readers of *Gauntlet* any of it. And I wonder: Because he doesn't have the guts, or because he doesn't have the sense?

I hope that Dee Barnes wins every penny in her lawsuit against Dr. Dre. But I know that if she does, it won't diminish N.W.A.'s popularity. Only education can do that, and as long as Steve Lopez is distracting us from getting up and demanding things from our government—I'd say, starting with free speech and some serious bucks for schools—ignorant motherfuckers who value a beat more than ideas are gonna make N.W.A. or somebody like them superstars.

Just the same, if every record store in America stops carrying N.W.A. records, sexual battery will not be reduced. At all.

But censorship—of everything, not just of records that talk about battering women—will increase.

Steve Lopez probably won't have any trouble with that. He's already singing the song the censors want him to. But I don't want to live that way. So fuck him. If I have to choose between two ugly cultural realities, better N.W.A., who possess no hidden agenda, than Lopez, who can't even sing his own song straight.

Or, to paraphrase the ostensible subjects of this "debate": F—- Tha Lopezes of the press.

Dave Marsh is author of **50 Ways to Fight Censorship**, *an invaluable reference book and editor of* **Rock and Roll Confidential**

A female student's group wants men at Brigham Young University barred from being outside on campus Thursday nights. "I want to be able to walk wherever I want, whenever I want without being attacked," said Jill Thompson of VOICE: BYS's Committee to Protect the Status of Women.

The Tupelo

Ayatollah

Skipp Porteous

Under normal circumstances Route 78 from Memphis, Tennessee to Tupelo, Mississippi is a good highway. In the Fall of 1986, on the day I made the 90 mile trip to Elvis Presley's hometown, I encountered torrential rains. At one point visibility was so poor that several vehicles just stopped right in the middle of the road and waited.

To psyche up for my mission I tuned into a local gospel station—pretty easy to find on the dial in that part of the country. There were plenty of programs from which to choose. As I approached Tupelo, "The Don Wildmon Report" began. Good golly Miss Molly!

My purpose in going to Tupelo was to learn more about the operation of the National Federation for Decency (NFD— now called the American Family Association, AFA). The Rev. Donald Wildmon founded the organization 1977. I'd been reading some of Rev. Wildmon's litera-ture and sensed that he would become a major player in the battle for church/state separation, but at that time his name was not widely known. The man's determination, however, told me that he posed a threat to First Amendment freedoms. Wildmon bills his group as "a Christian organization promoting the Biblical ethic of decency in American society with primary emphasis on TV and other media." I had two problems with this statement. First, the "biblical ethic of decency" applies only to the church, not to the state. If he wanted to promote that ideal in his own church, the United Methodist Church, or in Christianity in general, fine, but America is officially a secular nation, not a Christian nation. Secondly, Wildmon says his primary emphasis is on "TV and other media." That is so broad that it could include everything that we hear, read, and see. It covers radio, television, movies, recordings, and newspapers. The only way Wildmon could achieve his goal to affect the media through his so-called "Biblical ethic of decency" is through censorship. Six months earlier I called NFD headquarters to have my name placed on their mailing list. The woman who answered the phone turned my call over to Allen Wildmon, Donald Wildmon's older brother. Allen serves as the NFD/AFA's director of public relations.

Before adding my name to the mailing list, Allen interrogated me. Initially, I had decided to use an assumed name, Rev. Charles Porter. The "Reverend" apparently encouraged Allen to delve into my background and current position. Finding myself on the spot, I improvised.

Before we concluded our conversation, Allen asked me to consider organizing an NFD chapter in Great Barrington, Massachusetts. Choosing the correct buzz words, I said, we'd "pray about it." "We" referred to the "Great Barrington Christian Fellowship" I'd created moments earlier.

A few days later I received a package from the NFD. Included were Donald Wildmon's book, *The Case Against Pornography*, a videotape by a Dr. Holland about child porn, and a packet of materials with which to start an NFD chapter.

I filled out the forms, enclosed a check for $25, and within a month had a bona fide NFD chapter. The following month the NFD asked us to picket our local Cumberland Farms convenience store. Cumberland Farms stores were selected because they sell *Playboy* and *Penthouse* magazines. In order to appear cooperative, we fabricated a newspaper story about the Great Barrington NFD's picketing activities and sent it to, as "Brother Don" likes to put it, the "home office," in Tupelo. To my amazement, the bogus story was published in the November *NFD Chapter Newsletter*.

During the six months The Freedom Writer organization operated our NFD chapter we received reams of materials from Tupelo. On one occasion I wrote to Don Wildmon, and enclosed a stamped, self-addressed envelope in order to encourage a personal response. In the letter

> If he wanted to promote that ideal ("biblical ethic of decency") in his own church, the United Methodist Church, or in Christianity in general, fine, but America is officially a secular nation, not a Christian nation.

I asked Don if he thought pornography could lead to demon possession. He replied, "Concerning pornography leading to demon possession, this could might (sic) well be true since porn is the work of the devil."

About the only remaining opportunity to gather information about the workings of the NFD was an in-person visit. Don was expecting me. When I made the appointment, I neglected to ask for directions, and the only address I had was a post office box. From our files I had a newspaper photo which showed Don at NFD headquarters in a storefront on Main Street in Tupelo. After driving up and down Main Street, I couldn't locate any storefront NFD headquarters. So, I parked the rental car and telephoned. Don's secretary informed me that the NFD moved about two miles outside the center of town. Within minutes I drove into their parking lot.

Located on a side street, the new NFD headquarters was a big step up from the storefront operation. Built especially for the NFD, the new building is a contemporary one-story office building. The NFD logo and name was emblazoned on the front of the building. After entering the building I was struck by the bevy of young beauties in Wildmon's employ. At least four of the young women seated at desks were a prime sampling of the South's delectable belles. I realize the danger of sounding sexist here, but what I'm saying is that I carried a preconceived notion of women with their hair tied up in buns. One young lady arose from her desk and brought me to the desk of Forrest Ann Daniels, Wildmon's executive secretary, and an NFD board member. Forrest Ann, a plain woman, is very charming. She introduced me to Allen Wildmon, who, later, introduced me to Don.

Allen was quite cordial, and he proceeded to give me a tour of the NFD facility. I was impressed. Whether at a desk, or working with specialized equipment, everyone was busy at some project. About a dozen people performed various tasks.

"There are a lot of people out there. Are they volunteers?" I asked Allen.

"No," he replied, "all of 'em are on salary."

Allen proudly showed me their IBM mainframe computer, which keeps their mailing list. He told me they mail out 320,000 NFD Journals a month at a cost of $56,000. [This was 1986.]

The Journal and other typesetting is performed on their own computerized Varityper typesetting equipment. Small printing jobs are done in-house on an AB Dick offset printing press. The envelope stuffing machine I saw was out of order at the time. Allen told me that Richard Viguerie does the direct mail fund-raising for them, although Don writes most of the fund raising letters. With laughter, Allen remarked that Viguerie was good at bringing in the dough. He also commented that Don likes to pay cash for everything.

One room contained four television sets with corresponding VCR's. This equipment is used to monitor prime-time television. Shows are rated according to their sexual content, profanity, violence, and "anti-Christian bias."

After retiring from the insurance business in 1979, Allen began working with his brother at the NFD. His first responsibility was to total the column

inches of advertising each month in *Playboy* and *Penthouse*. Armed with that information, he formed a hit list of national advertisers.

As we toured the building, I mentioned their victory in getting the Southland Corporation, the 7-Eleven franchiser, to stop carrying *Playboy* and *Penthouse*. Allen's response intrigued me.

"Yeah, we were real pleased with that. We got word of it about three days before it happened," he said.

"You mean that they were going to stop the sale of the magazines?" I said.

"Yeah," he said, lowering his voice. "The reason on that occasion is you got Christians on the inside. They will call you. For instance, at the FCC [Federal Communications Commission] we had a lady that would call. She was way up, right close to the head, the head one, Mark Fowler. And she would call us at home, at night, and say, 'Look, you're doin' good, you've got his attention . . . ' The same way at the Justice Department. We even got the magazines out of the Federal prison system, forty-two of them. We had a person on the inside up there that volunteered to call, and says, 'If you keep goin' they gonna pull them! Just need to hold

> With laughter, Allen (Wildmon) remarked that (Richard) Viguerie was good at bringing in the dough. He also commented that Don (Reverend Wildmon) likes to pay cash for everything.

on!'"

"Every time," Allen Wildmon continued, "it just seems like there's somebody—like with the Holiday Inn [For years, Wildmon has led boycotts against Holiday Inn because they show pay-per-view R-rated adult movies]—we've got somebody at the Holiday Inn who calls Don, 'Look, this is what's happening in the front office. Just want you to know what they're thinking up here and . . . ,' you know."

After the tour of NFD headquarters, we took seats in a small reception room and waited for Don. Memorabilia from the NFD's war against porn covered one wall. In the center was a photo of Don shaking hands with President Reagan. I later learned that the picture was taken while Don was at the White House with a group of other ministers. Each of the ministers were allowed to have his photo taken individually with the president. The wall collection included framed magazine covers featuring Don Wildmon. Don's face on the cover of *The Conservative Digest* still stands out in my mind. There were also plaques from Morality In Media—for "victory in the Southland battle"—and from Jerry Falwell's Liberty Broadcasting System; and a plaque from Oklahomans Against Pornography.

Soon, Don arrived, and during the half-hour which followed he did most of the talking. In his rambling discourse, Don said, "There'd be no X-rated book stores open if *Playboy* hadn't been on the stands." He continued, "We're fighting *Playboy* and *Penthouse* on an economic basis."

In reference to then-Attorney General Ed Meese, Don said, "I don't think he's going to try to prosecute *Playboy* or *Penthouse*, of course. What they're [the magazines] afraid of, and what we can do, is in the wave of prosecuting the obscenity and pornography, you can pile in *Playboy* and *Penthouse* with the same. I mean, what you're doing is changing public acception. This is what you're doing when you're out picketing the stores—raising community standards, and also in the same process the community is saying, 'We don't want that garbage, but we don't

Standing United Against Censors

Skipp Porteous

Challenges to Rev. Donald Wildmon and his pro-censorship organization, the American Family Association (AFA), have been successful in several battles. In particular, organization, and legal action, have proven effective.

In one instance, Wildmon went to Orlando, Florida to set up another of his chapters. Local talk show hosts Clive Thomas, Jim Phillips, and Carole Nelson, of WWNZ-AM, asked their listeners to show up at the new group's first public meeting. When 2,000 advocates for free speech showed up, versus about 200 of Wildmon's followers, the fundamentalist preacher stayed in the back of the church and sent word that the meeting was cancelled. Wildmon countered by sending letters to WWNZ's sponsors claiming that the talk show hosts tried to incite a "pro-pornography" demonstration, and called the action an "assault that WWNZ has made on the Christians of central Florida." As a result, the Campbell Soup Company, Allstate Insurance, and a large supermarket chain, pulled their ads. Nevertheless, even with an advertising rate increase, the radio station's ad time continues to be sold out.

"If we don't want our cultural climate set by whoever is the most effective at terrorizing merchants," Clive Thomas said, "we've got to stand up to anybody who wants to deprive us of our country's life blood—the freedom of speech. When even a few people stand up and raise their voices, guys like the Reverend Donald Wildmon literally don't have a prayer."

want *Playboy* or *Penthouse* either.' You may not be able to get *Playboy* or *Penthouse* legally, but you get 'em economically. You can go picket a store."

Wildmon continued, "They're hurtin', *Playboy* and *Penthouse*, hurtin'. I think the tide's going our way, and what we need to do is just keep picketing pretty regular. You won't think it's doin' any good, but it's hurtin' 'em. It's having an affect on 'em, 'cause it's bringing 'em to their knees. We're letting the community know, 'this store's selling porn,' and they got a lot of business at stake, and they [the customers] won't go. They [the stores] won't ever tell you, it embarrasses them. That's the reason Southland pulled it. Because of economics, not because of the Porn Commission report or anything else, pure economics." After awhile, Don excused himself, saying he had work to do. I continued talking with Allen for another hour. While we talked about a number of related topics, I'll just mention a few of his comments.

I commented to Allen about the fact that his brother seemed to be a Fundamentalist, yet he's an ordained Methodist minister. I said that most of the Methodists I knew didn't really preach the gospel.

"They don't down here either, in Tupelo, Mississippi, or anywhere else." Allen said it was his personal belief that Don would have given up the Methodists a long time ago, except that he's trying to turn that church around. Don attends the Methodist church, Allen said, so "he can appeal to the so-called moderates or liberals, maybe have some influence in turning their thinking around."

"You know you're doing some good when the opposition starts screaming," Allen said. "*Playboy*, the recent issue, called Don the Tupelo Ayatollah. But that ain't bad."

He summarized the NFD opposition to erotica in these words: "It doesn't take a person with a doctoral degree to figure out if a dog gets stimulated sexually he's going to look for a female dog. I think humans, they've got sexuality the same as other animals, you know. And if you stimulate them enough, they're going to seek a sexual object."

In another case, members of a local chapter of the AFA visited The Bookman book store in Grand Haven, Michigan, demanding that the owners remove several magazines. Refusal to submit to this pressure provoked boycott threats from the AFA, and a long debate in the local newspaper.

Jim Dana, owner of the bookstore, then founded the 450-member Great Lakes Booksellers Association to counter censorship efforts. The association played a key role in defeating a package of 12 pro-censorship bills introduced in the Michigan state legislature.

A spin-off of the group's activities was the production of an anti-censorship video starring Garrison Keillor. Since its debut, the video has produced more than 40,000 signatures opposing censorship.

Legal efforts against Wildmon continue to beset the AFA. Last year, David Wojnarowicz, a New York artist, obtained an injunction against Wildmon which prohibited him from further distribution of a pamphlet which depicted fragments of the artist's copyrighted work. A federal judge convicted Wildmon of copyright infringement and ordered him to pay a paltry $1 fine. Nonetheless, it cost Wildmon time and money.

When properly initiated, lawsuits against groups such as the AFA are effective. Plaintiffs need the assistance of good pro bono (free) attorneys who specialize in the First Amendment. The American Civil Liberties Union can often be helpful.

In another suit, *Penthouse* magazine continues as the sole plaintiff against the AFA of Florida, and its director, David Caton. The suit charges that Caton and the AFA violated federal racketeering

This comment surprised me for two reasons. First, most Christian Fundamentalists never equate humans with animals, because that indicates some acceptance of the theory of evolution. Secondly, humans can exercise the normal, safe option of masturbation as a way to release sexual urges.

The next morning Allen made a comment which confirmed an attitude I thought I also observed in Don. "This is a business, just like any other business," he said. [Our most recent figures indicate that their "business" takes in $5 million a year.]

I'm glad he said that, for it was not only a revealing statement, but it was the last thing of any use I got from the Wildmons that day. While we sat in the room, the door opened and six other men entered. The party included reporters from the *Jackson Clarion Ledger*, the *Northeast Mississippi Daily Journal*, a detective from the Tupelo Police Department, Don and his son, Tim, and another NFD employee.

Apparently, all my questioning tipped them off that I was not who I said I was. I learned that the night before they did some checking-up on me. They found out that the Cumberland Farms store in Great Barrington hadn't been picketed. And, an Assemblies of God minister in Great Barrington told them that I was "on some sort of crusade against what 'he calls the extreme right.'" He was correct.

Having noticed that I took some pictures inside their building, they insisted on having the film. After exposing the film to the light, I handed it over. Allen gave me ten dollars for it. They wanted to know who I was and who sent me. I refused to answer any questions and said, "I guess our meeting is through," and got up and walked out.

Outside, two patrolman stood by a cruiser. So, I got in the rental car and drove away, nice and slowly.

A blurb about the encounter appeared in the local Mississippi papers. The article noted that I'd done nothing illegal, so no charges were pressed. Wildmon also wrote about the incident in his *NFD Journal*. My sources tell me that Wildmon loves to tell this story to his

laws by creating a scheme to prevent the distribution and sale of *Penthouse*.

The Racketeer Influenced and Corrupt Organizations Act (RICO) makes it a crime for anyone to commit a "pattern" of two or more "racketeering acts" in conducting their affairs. Convictions for violating the RICO act result in stiff penalties, including triple damages, long prison sentences, and the forfeiture of all profits realized by the illegal activities.

This is an important case to watch. If *Penthouse* is successful, RICO statutes can be applied in dozens of other situations around the country.

friends in Tupelo.

What motivates Donald Wildmon? "If you took off all the sex and violence on television, it would still bother me," Wildmon told a reporter in 1986. He said that for a long time he couldn't put his finger on what bothered him about network television. Then, like a light out of heaven, it came to him!

"Clearly, the networks are intentionally pushing a particular value system," Wildmon said. "That value system is secular humanism. That was what had been disturbing me."

In his book, *The Home Invaders*, Wildmon wrote, "We're not engaged in a war against dirty words and dirty pictures." In effect, he said that *Playboy* or *Penthouse* photo features aren't dangerous. "The danger lies not in the vulgar and obscene pictures which grace the pornographic magazines and films or explicit television programs," Wildmon continued. "The danger is the philosophy behind those pictures. That philosophy, the one which the leaders of the media are pushing on the American public, is humanism."

In Wildmon's writings and speeches

he constantly attacks secular humanism. He contends that America was founded upon "the Christian view of man" and that there is some sort of diabolical plot to replace "the Christian view of man" with "the religion of secular humanism."

According to *Christianity and Humanism*, a study guide published by Wildmon, "Humanists believe that man is basically good, and if given the right environment and social context, by reason and intelligence can formulate laws which are in his own best interest." In Wildmon's eyes, this philosophy is evil — from the devil.

Wildmon's "Christian view of man" is in sharp contrast with the "evils" of humanism: "[B]asic to Christian beliefs: is the fallen nature of man.

He is not inherently good . . . his nature is flawed by sin. Not only does he
            need the atonement of Christ, but also he needs the absolutes of the Bible to give order and direction to his life. Man is a sinful creature, and therefore cannot be his own lawgiver and judge. Law must come from God. . . . Scripture ["God's law"] teaches that sex outside of marriage is wrong, sinful and destructive."

In this battle of ideologies, Wildmon perceives, "The struggle will determine whether the Christian view of man will continue to serve as the foundation of our society." Or, will we be a secular nation that will employ reason and logic to serve the needs of our society?

Donald E. Wildmon may well be sincere, but he is undeniably misguided. Secular (which means "not religious") humanism is not a religion, but a term used by the radical religious right to define anything with which they disagree.

As leaders of the radical religious right cleverly focus national and local attention on such topics as "pornography" and the "evils of secular humanism," their real line of attack is on something else—our distinctly democratic values of diversity, dissent, and debate.

Excerpt from **Jesus Doesn't Live Here Anymore—From Fundamentalist to Freedom Writer,** *by Skipp Porteous (Prometheus Books)*

SAN FRANCISCO
VS.
BASIC INSTINCT

Rebecka Wright

In April and May of 1991, San Francisco played hostess to Hollywood. Hollywood demonstrated that it clearly has a lot to learn about sensitivity, among other things. San Francisco just . . . demonstrated.

The occasion was the filming of *Basic Instinct*, a big-budget sex thriller of the gruesome variety that is so common these days: one or more homicidal maniacs are pursued by a brutal cop, who is supposed to be the good guy. Along the way, the landscape is strewn with pretty corpses. In this case, the cop is played by Michael Douglas, who you may remember as the victimized adulterer of *Fatal Attraction*. He is directed by Paul Verhoeven, the Dutch intellectual who is known here in the U.S. for such subtle pieces of artistry as *Robocop* and *Total Recall*. The story is from a $3 million screenplay by Joe Eszterhas, late of *Rolling Stone* magazine, and writer of *Betrayed* and *Jagged Edge*. The corpses are played by various, as always.

The local film making community was happy to have some work in town, less happy that the work itself was such typical trash. It seems that the SF Film Commission is badly understaffed, and the film selection process is not terribly receptive to outside input. Productions that get the green light are normally productions with large budgets, so that the city can rake in some healthy revenues, and are not often of the socially relevant type that would delight the people who live and work here in liberal 'Frisco. *Basic Instinct*, as the title itself suggests, is about as far from elevated consciousness as it gets. One local industry worker mused, "It's peculiar that they choose such sensational and violent films for this beautiful city."

At first, it appeared to be just dreary business as usual. Things heated up real fast though, when the Gay and Lesbian Alliance Against Defamation (GLAAD), a national media watchdog organization, obtained a copy of the script. It seems that

> In part, the demonstrators felt that the movie was inflammatory and would exacerbate the problem of anti-gay violence. To film the movie in an actual gay community establishment, Rawhide II, really added insult to injury.

gay community establishment, the Rawhide II, really added insult to injury.

The Rawhide II is owned by Ray Chalker, the publisher of a local gay weekly newspaper, the *San Francisco Sentinel*. There is little love lost between the more politically active members of the gay community and Mr. Chalker, who has a habit of supporting conservative causes, most recently the election of Republican Pete Wilson to the Governorship of California. (Governor Wilson recently vetoed AB101, a bill that would have outlawed job discrimination based on sexual orientation.) Mr. Chalker says that the film makers assured him that the film was not homophobic (or lesbophobic, as it came to be called), and he believed them, though he had not read the script himself. His cooperation with the makers of *Basic Instinct* lead some in the community to accuse him of profiteering and even treason.

Things started to get ugly. The Rawhide II, neighboring businesses, the *Sentinel* offices, and the Castro district were vandalized, most notably with "Kill Ray" graffiti. Mr. Chalker reported that he was getting death threats on his answering machine. Queer Nation denied any involvement with any of these activities, and concentrated on organizing an advertising boycott of the *Sentinel*. There were rumors bandied about that Mr. Chalker was making up the death threat stories in an attempt to regain the sympathies of the community. This possibility seems only slightly more plausible than 3 rampaging lesbian psycho-killers. Answering machines aside, it's hard to argue with spray paint. The filming moved from the Rawhide II to various other locations around the city, some of which were vandalized, all of which were subject to protests.

this particular film features three women, all of them clearly depicted as either lesbian or bisexual. This wouldn't have been a problem, really, except that all three are also depicted as murderers and at least one as a psychopath. While distasteful and statistically unlikely, to put it mildly, even this could have been tolerated, if it weren't for the fact that gay men and particularly lesbians are portrayed, almost without exception, in just such mentally unbalanced and/or criminal ways every time they appear on the U.S. silver screen. The transvestite psycho-killer (who actually may or may not be gay) in *Silence of the Lambs* was cited as a recent example of this trend. Deciding that enough was enough, GLAAD and Queer Nation protested when filming began at a local gay bar, the Rawhide II.

In part, the demonstrators felt that the movie was inflammatory and would exacerbate the problem of anti-gay violence. While this point is arguable, it was clear that to film it here in San Francisco would be ridiculously insensitive. San Francisco is supposed to be a sanctuary of sorts for gay and lesbian people, though gay-bashing happens here, too. To film the movie in an actual

The demonstrations were modeled after the successful ACT-UP protests of a 1989 episode of NBC's *Midnight Caller*, which was inspired by Randy Shilts' book *And the Band Played On*. ACT-UP was able to shut down production by making so much noise at an outdoor set that it was impossible to film. Filming resumed the next day, but the producers realized that they couldn't afford to shoot in the city if the demonstrators couldn't be mollified. Since the program was very definitely based in San Francisco, moving out of town was considered the course of last resort. They invited the input of the community for a follow-up episode which ran the next season. GLAAD and Queer Nation weren't able to generate the decibel level that would have been needed to shut down *Basic Instinct*, but they were a constant irritant. The resulting publicity generated closer scrutiny by city officials, who were so outraged that they made public statements outlining how outraged they were.

Finally, the *Basic Instinct* film makers agreed to sit down and listen to the protesters' concerns. Screenwriter Eszterhas ended up being sympathetic to the protesters' objections, to the surprise of everyone, including director Verhoeven.

Mr. Eszterhas had previously described his script as "organically constructed", implying that to change anything would compromise the whole. He had also argued that "if we've reached the point where any minority refuses to accept the possibility of a psychotic or murderer among them, then we've reached the state where the only villains can be white male WASPs." (In all fairness, the villain in Mr. Eszterhas' *Betrayed* was a male white supremacist and a previous film by Mr. Verhoeven, *The Fourth Man*, had received kudos from the gay community for its sensitive portrayal of a gay man.) Mr. Eszterhas suggested some changes to the script, which the protesters said were an improvement, although they didn't really change the homophobic character of the film. In any case, the changes were rejected by Mr. Verhoeven. The production company, Carolco Pictures, issued a statement accusing the demonstrators of "censorship by street action."

Carolco got a court order to keep the protesters 100 feet from the filming locations, and banning loud noises, the offensive use of flashlights and glitter. Yes, *glitter*. (It's those little touches that make me love San Francisco.) The protesters kept showing up. Some were arrested. One or two were roughed up by a rogue crew member. Filming wrapped up here and moved on to the next location, as scheduled.

The protesters felt that a victory had been achieved, although no real substantive changes occurred, because the issue of Hollywood homophobia was pushed out of the closet for the first time in years. Many hoped that the issue would continue to be raised. According to a Queer Nation press release: "We will not let up until the censorship of our lives ends, and we finally see our richness and complexity as a community reflected back to us on the silver screen."

ARE PROTESTS CENSORSHIP?

Civil disobedience in this country goes all the way back to the Boston Tea Party. Respect for private property has not figured prominently in its history. Naturally, this troubles business interests, and movie companies are definitely businesses. They are also the creators of a popular art form. While I believe that business is a valid target of protest, the nature of the media business limits the forms of protest which can properly be used against it. The protest must be able to generate heat to be effective, but hope-

> The distillation of this argument is that really bad people do not have the right to be heard. The problem is that this can go both ways.

fully this can be accomplished without extinguishing free speech. It is likewise important for both the protesters and the target of a protest to realize that violence against property or ideas does not justify violence against human beings.

Some people characterized the demonstrations as attempts to shut down the movie entirely. The protesters denied that this was their intention. In combing the records, I have to agree that the goal of the protesters seemed to be dialogue, not censorship. However, some of the tactics that were used teetered dangerously close to interference with the free speech of the film makers. Attempting to shut down production literally means attempting to shut up the producers. Though the possibility of success seems remote, it does happen. ACT-UP successfully, if temporarily, shut down filming on *Midnight Caller*. ACT-UP also succeeded in shouting down U.S. Secretary of Health and Human Services Louis Sullivan at a San Francisco-based international AIDS conference in 1990. Governor Wilson was recently drowned out at a Stanford University function, after he vetoed AB101. Of course, government officials will always have another chance to speak, if not to the same audience, but the people who wouldn't let them talk have lost the moral high ground. Ultimately, it's better to let them have their say. It's possible to learn something, if only where the weakness in their argument lies.

Perhaps some people should not be heard, because they are racist, sexist, homophobic, fascist, or part of a corrupt and even murderous government. These people are dangerous influences. They are bad people. Really bad people. The distillation of this argument is that really bad people do not have the right to be heard. The problem is that this can go both ways. There are plenty of people who would love to deny the right of free speech to pervert homosexuals, godless atheists, morally bankrupt pornographers, disgusting miscegenationists, murdering abortionists, *and* fellow travelers, because, in their view, these are really bad people. Dangerous influences, if you will.

So if we all agree that bad people

should not be allowed to speak, how do we decide who defines what makes a "bad person"?

I'm not willing to give *anyone* the power to decide such a question. I'm too afraid the perverts might come out on the losing end. This is not paranoia on my part. There are many examples in recent history of "dangerous" people being denied their rights by the U.S Government. Japanese-Americans were herded into detention centers during World War II, ostensibly because they were a threat to the war effort. Communists were subjected to social and professional ostracism during the Cold War, because of their "dangerous" ideas. Most recently, the War On Drugs, has enabled the government to severely restrict civil rights, under the cover of protecting the citizenry from a powerful and dangerous enemy. None of these incidents have inspired an enormous outcry from the people of the U.S., demanding that *all* citizens retain their constitutional rights.

For every ACT-UP leader, there is someone like the Reverend Donald E. Wildmon. In the case of the *Midnight Caller* protest, ACT-UP did not approve of the way a bisexual person with AIDS was portrayed. Wildmon and his American Family Association did not approve of the way a homosexual couple was depicted on *thirtysomething*, and so instituted one of their famous write-in campaigns. These groups are on opposite ends of the political spectrum, but they used very similar tools to achieve their goals. Both attempted to bring the network around to their way of thinking by attacking its financial base. The main difference is that ACT-UP attempted to *prevent* the filming of the episode, by making production too expensive, while Wildmon threatened sponsors with boycotts *after* the episode had already aired.

ACT-UP believes that its actions are justified because the very lives of People With AIDS (PWAs) are at stake. There is indeed a state of emergency surrounding the AIDS crisis. (A similar argument could be used by anti-abortion activists, but that's another article.) However, emergencies have often been misused as an excuse to suspend the rights of others:

just ask an elderly Japanese-American or a former '30s-style communist. Hindsight has shown that these people were probably not real threats, and neither was *Midnight Caller*. TV shows don't kill PWAs, AIDS kills PWAs.

The protests of *Basic Instinct* were well conceived, and succeeded in opening the lines of communication between the film makers and the protestors, without overly interfering with free speech on either side. Apparently, at least one mind was changed, though it remains to be seen whether Mr. Eszterhas will ever write a screenplay populated with happy, healthy lesbians. However, the scapegoating of Mr. Chalker was irritating. The vilifying charges of profiteering and treason were thrown around in an irresponsible manner. It is not necessarily treason to disagree with the tactics of your fellows. Mr. Chalker is an active member of the gay community, even though his politics may be objectionable to many. When the protesters began characterizing him as a traitor, the lunatic fringe came out and threatened death to the infidel. Even though they deny responsibility for these threats, the protestors *must* take credit for starting the finger pointing. By casting about for someone nearby to pin the blame on, they set up Mr. Chalker for the nastiness to come. I certainly hope none of the protestors ever has a lapse of judgement like Mr. Chalker's, or they too may feel the wrath of anonymous terrorists.

There are director/auteurs, especially in Europe, who will put non-stereotypical homosexual characters into their films—people like Woody Allen (*Manhattan*), Blake Edwards (*Victor/Victoria*), Paul Bartel (*Scenes of a Class Struggle in Beverly Hills*), and Pedro Almodovar (*Labyrinth of Passion, Law of Desire*). Few of these are considered

"Hollywood" directors. While the protesters are right and their complaints valid, they are sadly mistaken if they think that Hollywood acceptance is worth gaining.

Hollywood movies do not reflect complexity or reality. They never have. That's not what they are for. They are propaganda for the status quo. They can

> Hollywood movies do not reflect complexity or reality. They never have. That's not what they are for. They are propaganda for the status quo. They . . . supply dreams for people who haven'y got enough imagination to dream their own dreams

inspire mindless patriotism, and supply dreams for people who haven't got enough imagination to dream their own dreams. They can make people think that everything is under control and will turn out OK in the end, even as society crumbles outside the theater. I don't think that they have the power to change a bigot's mind, but there isn't any harm in trying, as long as we don't confuse success in the media with success in any other realm of existence. To paraphrase Urvashi Vaid, who wrote about outing in the previous *Gauntlet*, bad characterizations in the movies are not the cause of homophobia—they are merely its exhibits.

People thought that improved media images would improve the lot of African Americans. This is not the case for the majority of American blacks today. Sure, there are a few more acting jobs available. But more and more young blacks die by violence. Poverty is heavily concentrated in the black community. Perhaps all those positive images in the past 3 decades were used as a smoke screen to make people think that some substantive advancements were being made, when the reality was very different. Perhaps these images even acted as a tranquilizer that kept those whose lives were not improving from demanding to know why.

This is not the end I would like to see for the Gay Power movement. I'd like to see some changes happen that really mean something—the repeal of sodomy laws, for instance. A Hollywood confection like *Three Dykes and a Baby* somehow doesn't impress me as a real social gain. Mainstream movies are for the mainstream. It's silly to depend on them for validation. There's no reason why the gay community should need to beg for crumbs of acceptance from a boring, corporate, Hollywood. It certainly hasn't worked for Chicanos, Asian-Americans, or even, after all this time, women. All of these groups are still better served by independent productions than grandiose blockbusters.

That's why it's so great that there are Gay and Lesbian Film Festivals springing up all over the country. Every yearscores of new films from within the community are exhibited.

These are proof positive that homosexuals the world over can speak for themselves, can make their own entertainment, and *can* see themselves reflected off of the silver screen, in all their richness and complexity. Sometimes a few gems leak out into big, bad world out there. There are many artists within the community who deserve our support. People like Jennie Livingston, director of *Paris Is Burning*; Rob Epstein, director of *The Life and Times of Harvey Milk*; Marlon Riggs, director of *Tongues Untied*; Harvey Fierstein, writer/star of *Torchsong Trilogy*; Donna Deitch, director of *Desert Hearts*; Micki Dickoff, director of *Our Sons*, a recent ABC movie; and many, many others. The power lies in seizing the means of production, you see. Then you can always say what you wish, and not beg someone else to say it for you.

Houston Post columnist, Juan Palomo, was fired in late-August for granting interviews disclosing his own homosexuality, a topic his editors had told him not to *write* about. Charles Cooper, Senior Vice President of the *Post* said "The best interests of the *Post* come before the personal agenda of an individual."

IT MUST BE THE CAMERA

Stan Higgins

If a tree falls in the forest and there's no one there to hear it, does it make a noise? If police beat a man and there's no camera to record it, did it really happen?

The evidence is in. We saw it on TV. It's conclusive. Our outmanned, outgunned, underpaid, overworked, and unappreciated public servants do not exercise brutal force . . . unless there's a camera running. Complaints of police brutality are routinely waved away. They are seldom made public. If they are, they're denied. They're investigated by police. Inevitably, such allegations are found to be unwarranted. So it must be true. It never happened. Cops don't lie. Therefore, those sworn to serve and protect, will not, do not, physically abuse suspects, detainees, bystanders, and traffic offenders, unless, it is being filmed. It must be the camera?, right?

Is it the camera? Police chiefs in Boston, New York, Houston, Denver, Los Angeles, and other cities call filmed incidents of brutality an aberration, a regrettable action by a few. I didn't see any divisiveness among the mob of officers beating Rodney King that early Sunday morning in Los Angeles. I saw no officers among the 25 (from two different agencies) break ranks to halt the beating. I saw unanimity. Aberration? It must have been the camera.

Had this not been on film, would it have been another unwarranted "poor me" complaint of a callous, despicable, lying criminal traffic offender? Would we have even heard of it? Is it any wonder that recipients of "aberrations" return to the streets displeased? I think it's clear that without the camera filming it, this would never have happened. And we would believe what we were told.

But there was a camera. A rude, intrusive camera, pulling at the warm, protective blanket of ignorance that protects us all from the difficult, sometimes painful responsibility of making up our own minds. The camera revealed another truth. An uncomfortable truth. A truth at variance with what we are told by those we entrust to tell us the truth.

And a tree falls. Caught on film, we are forced to decide: "Did we hear it?" We are told we didn't.

Blame it on the camera.

THE YEAR IN CENSORSHIP:
THE TOP 10 STORIES OF 1991

John Rosenman

Last year, I selected the emergence of the Politically Correct Phenomenon as my no. 2 story. This year, in a *Gauntlet* issue that focuses on that same subject, it should be no surprise that I list it as no. 1. I do so for three reasons: (1) the "PC Way" is an important story, (2) it permeates many of the top stories in my list below, and (3) it has inspired a national backlash that is reflected in everything from cartoons and newspapers to books and magazines.

1.) THE POLITICALLY CORRECT PHENOMENON

America may be the land of the free, but 137 of its finest universities have recently passed laws restricting free speech. Students must not insult women, gays, blacks, or other sacred cows. At the University of Michigan, a student accused of bad-mouthing homosexuals had to write an apology titled "I.earned My Lesson" to be published in the school newspaper and also attend sensitivity classes. Elsewhere, a *Philadelphia Inquirer* editorial suggesting that poor black women should be provided with free Norplant contraceptive implants created a furor which rivaled the suspension of Pulitzer-Prize winning Jimmy Breslin at *Newsday* for yelling racist and sexist slurs at a female Korean-American reporter who called one of his columns sexist. In short, if you were smart in 1991, you'd opt for wimpdom and shut your trap, or the PC Person (not "Man") would get you.

Fortunately, there's been growing protest against PC orthodoxy. William Lutz, in the Nov. *Family Circle*, rails at being required to call someone "categorically disadvantaged" instead of fat, an "Indigenous Person" instead of an Indian, and—here's my favorite—his pet an

> (Clarence Thomas) . . . cowed senators by describing his confirmation hearings as a "hight tech lynching" of an "uppity black." After *that* charge, to question him at all was tantamount to being a racist.

"animal companion" instead of a cat. Such weasel words distort the truth, and more and more people resent them.

2.) RIGHT-WING POWER GROUPS

ACT-UP for Gays, Animal Rights groups, Ecological/Environmental terrorists: these are just a few organizations that can tell you what to do. As the Jan. *Playboy* warns, "Organized groups of conservatives actively fight sex education, birth control, abortion and erotic expression." *And they are getting stronger.*

(A) Take *NOW*, for example. Tammy Bruce, president of the Los Angeles Chapter of the National Organization for Women, managed to launch a boycott not only against *American Psycho* but all *non*feminist books published by Knopf. Doubtless she would applaud a Berkeley waitress who chastised a customer for reading *Playboy*—"a scolding heard round the world"—as columnist Clarence Page calls it. And let's not forget Holly Dunn's recent pulling of her song "Maybe I mean Yes" because feminists and others felt it encouraged rape. Tammy Bruce (see above) praised the act as showing "an extraordinary realization

of responsibility on the part of the artist."

(B) Next, consider abortion. Such groups as the Alan Guttmacher Institute, Wichita Operation Rescue, and yes, our very own Supreme Court (see no. 3 below) are gradually succeeding in making motherhood mandatory. In fact, thanks to a close, 5/4 vote in *Rust vs. Sullivan*, if you're a doctor or worker at a Government-sponsored clinic, you can't provide any abortion information at all. Of course, if you're rich, it's easy to fix the matter, but if you're poor . . . Well, as Chief Justice Rehnquist said, it's not *his* fault some people are poor. Moving on, Randall Terry, the God-inspired "visionary" behind Operation Rescue, has "logged more than 50,000 arrests . . . for blocking abortion clinics." (Oct. 21 *USA TODAY*) In October, 130 were arrested in Wichita, their most aggressive protest yet.

(C) And last, there's Clarence Thomas and the Political Correctness of being black. Remember when Jesse Jackson said Thomas should "show contrition" for blaspheming Affirmative Action or be considered "a traitor to his heritage"? Ironically, just a few months later, Thomas played a similar card when he cowed senators by describing his confirmation hearings as a "high-tech lynching" of "an uppity black.." After *that* charge, to question him at all was tantamount to being a racist.

3.) THE 'BUSH' SUPREME COURT

Last year, William J. Brennan, one of the greatest Constitutional defenders ever, retired from the Supreme Court. This year, Thoroughgood Marshall followed him and was replaced by Clarence Thomas. Such deterioration caps a decade of destruction by Reagan/Bush nominees whose puritanical bias has shredded the first and fourth amendments. In June, by a narrow, 5/4 majority in *Barnes vs. Glen Theater*, the Court upheld an Indiana law requiring nude dancers to wear pasties and G strings. As Robert Scheer observes in the Oct. *Playboy*, the fact that the Court admitted "the expressive nature of the dancing . . . renders this one of the most serious assaults on the First Amendment in its two centuries of existence." And when it comes to our Fourth Amendment protection, the Court in March ruled in *Arizona vs. Fulminante* that police could board buses and search/interrogate passengers even if they had no reason to believe anyone had committed a crime. Later, in June, *Florida vs. Bostick* excused coerced confessions as harmless errors. Who knows, maybe next the PC Gestapo will be coming through our bedroom windows to see if we're making love in the approved manner or have kiddie-porn photos of children kids in our family albums.

Speaking of PC, note that at Stanford, student law associations for Asians, Blacks, Indians (Whoops!)...I mean "Native Americans," Asian Americans, and Jews now advocate speech codes to combat racism and sexism. Is it possible that these codes will soon be blessed by the Supreme Court?

4.) THE G-RATED WAR

I'm tempted to call this instead "THE WAR THAT WASN'T" or "THE SQUEAKY CLEAN WAR" because it was so sanitized in the media that at times we forgot people were dying across the sea. At home, the numbers of fatalities and pictures of bloodshed were routinely withheld. How many of our soldiers were killed by friendly fire? How many babies and mothers were butchered in February by a Stealth bomber in a Baghdad air shelter? You can be sure the pentagon didn't want us to know, just as CNN didn't want ratings to slip because of an unedited videotape of tortured Kuwaitis. In general, we (or is it our protectors?) prefer a clean, abstract, sugar-coated war unmarred by the truth of what modern technology can do.

Granted, the military should withhold information that would imperil our soldiers, but as syndicated columnist Richard Cohen, comments, censors "interfered in routine news gathering," changing words at will and replacing soldiers' problems and "ordinary gripes" with "football metaphors" and "good news." Not only that, politically correct euphemisms were used to subvert the language. "War" became an "armed situation," "warplanes" were "force packages," and "killing the enemy" was camouflaged with "servicing the target." The worst thing of all, perhaps, is that surveys show the American people actually approve of putting patriotism before journalism. After all, as Robert Scheer points out in the June *Playboy*, it isn't attractive to know that "Japan and Germany, the two countries most dependent on Persian Gulf oil, made only a "checkbook contribution to the coalition victory," or that they "will return to reap the benefits in peacetime." The fact that 15,000 civilian Iraqis may have died in attacks that sometimes violated international law, or that America abandoned the Kurdish revolt after encouraging it, are also items we may choose to ignore. In this battle between a PC war and the First Amendment, the latter was decidedly outgunned.

5.) CENSORSHIP IN THE SCHOOLS

Control the young and what they can read and see and you control the future. An American Booksellers Foundation reports that "Since 1983, challenges to library books have increased by 168%."

> "War" became "armed situation," "warplanes" were "force packages," and "killing the enemy" was camouflaged with "servicing the target."

Little Red Riding Hood, Tarzan, The American Heritage Dictionary are just a few that have been banned. William Noble states that much of the "explosive growth in censorship . . . has occurred in the schools as parents demand control over the books their children read." In "the last three years" alone, "more than 500 books have been challenged in schools throughout the country." Much of the opposition is from groups such as Wildmon's AFA, Concerned Women for America, and the Catholic Church. In New York, the latter "has proved the most formidable obstacle to AIDS education in the public schools and to gay-rights legislation." (Stephen Rae, June *Playboy*) Next door, in N.J., a high school librarian removed a book portraying a woman wearing an apron because of her stereotyped, non-PC role.

School newspapers are also under siege, thanks party to a Supreme Court decision three years ago that gave public school principals the authority to censor student newspapers. In my area alone, student-written stories and editorials on religion, smoking, and school board policies were killed or altered. Moreover, last year even educational TV got switched off, as it was at Madison Middle School, in Eugene Oregon, when Channel One beamed pictures of Michelangelo's David. The media specialist explained that they didn't want to offend parents.

6.) GOVERNMENT EMPLOYEES LOSE FREE SPEECH

This one I had trouble even believing. Starting Jan. 1, 1991, Title VI of the Ethics Reform Act of 1989 becomes effective, which means no officers and employees in the Executive Branch can accept honoraria, however small, for writing or speaking. So, if you're a Civil Service worker and give a speech or write an article on beekeeping and get paid $1, conceivably you can be fined as much as $10,000. The bill, intended to target big-salaried employees and members of Congress, now muzzles thousands of workers who can't even receive token payment concerning interests *totally unrelated* to their jobs. Incidentally, while congres-

sional members stripped workers of their First Amendment privileges, they also had the chutzpah to vote themselves a 23% pay hike.

A friend of mine, a single parent in the Civil Service who really needs extra money, said the following to our state senators in letters she prudently never sent: "How ironic that the Cold War is over, the former Iron Curtain countries have just removed restrictions on writers, and my own country has just imposed them."

7.) SEXUAL HARASSMENT POLICE

Long before Clarence Thomas, people started to monitor and report office chitchat. According to John Leo in the Feb. *Playboy*, "Driven by feminist ideology, we have constantly extended the definition of what constitutes illicit male behavior. Very ambiguous incidents are now routinely flattened out into male predation." Suddenly, sexual jokes, teasing, remarks, and letters are being scrutinized and can backfire by getting one fired or sued. Moreover, there's the danger that employers may become more reluctant to hire and promote women because they might cry "Wolf!"

Am I making too much of this? Two women who I admire contend that men *never* sexually harass by accident, that they *always* know exactly what they're doing. Personally, I think they often know and lie about it, but that mistakes and different perceptions do occur, and with the Anita Hill/Clarence Thomas face-off, they now may occur more often than ever.

Significantly, it's not just suggestive speech, winks, touches, or gestures we're concerned about. In June, Lois Robinson, a female welder, and lawyers from *NOW* convinced a Florida judge that men's pinups of sexy women created a hostile environment. Well, why shouldn't such disgusting, demeaning exploitation of women be removed? One of the problems is that there are *women* who harass men, as well as women who display raunchy pinups of them in the workplace. For instance, because of Lois Robinson's victory, Lauri A. Loftus, who

> ... the question of
> what and how much
> goes onto the Tube is
> obviously part of a
> larger issue. Let's hope
> those like Helms and
> Wildmon don't decide
> it for us.

calls herself a "spayed" ship fitter, had to remove beefcake icons from her locker and toolbox.

If 1991 becomes 1984, perhaps Big Brother will succeed in making us forget that we are a sexual species that desire and seek out erotica and titillation wherever we go. Then, women and Wildmon can get the Supreme Court to airbrush offending billboards along the highways, and outlaw even the mildest of men's magazines.

8.) MEDIA MURDER/ CHARACTER ASSASSINATION

What's happened to Charles Robb and William Kennedy Smith this year raises grave questions about how "free" the media should be. Is it good when yellow journalism results in tabloid lynchings? Even though Ted Kennedy's nephew was found innocent of date rape, the sensationalized publicity he received on NBC's *Hard Copy* and in *The New York Times* prior to the trial alone has forever damned him in many people's eyes. And Robb, though he *may* not be charged with a crime, probably has had his political aspirations guillotined by charges that he had an extramarital affair with a former Miss Virginia/USA *and* attended parties

where cocaine was used. Indeed, we may very well wonder how a man can ever recover from an Oct. *Playboy* cover which blares: *TAI COLLINS: THE WOMAN CHARLES ROBB COULDN'T RESIST.* After peeking at the heart-stopping photos inside, we can only agree that of course, he is guilty, and there's no need for a trial at all.

When does the public's right to know go too far and become trial by media, conviction by accusation? This question applies also to Milquetoast types like Pee Wee Herman who visit porn theaters, to Clarence Thomas who may have rented *Long Dong Silver,* and to the sexist double standard involved in publishing the names of alleged rapists but not their victims. Concerning the women, it is true that disclosing their identities may humiliate and stigmatize them, but what about the men? Who will give them back *their* good names if they are proven innocent after the public instantly judged them guilty?

9.) TV/RADIO INDECENCY BAN OVERTURNED

In May, a federal court struck down a government rule that would have completely banned indecent radio and TV material for 24 hours during the day. The rule, which the FCC adopted in 1988 at Congress's order, was intended to prohibit all programing judged obscene in order to protect children, and it was supported, among others, by Jesse Helms and Donald Wildmon's AFA. Despite our relief that the first Amendment's been upheld and we can continue to watch *Saturday Night Live,* the Government's efforts to control our airways are far from over. In its ruling, the court affirmed the Government's right to protect children and directed the FCC to find a safe time period for "adult" material. As Paul Farhi notes, one of the FCC's options is to "appeal the entire decision to the Supreme Court." If they do that, who knows what will happen. Bullwinkle could be banned next.

Considering what we've already discussed regarding TV laundering of the Gulf War and the smearing of public figures, the question of what and how much goes onto the Tube is obviously part of a larger issue. Let's hope those like Helms and Wildmon don't decide it for us.

10.) THE DEMI MOORE *VANITY FAIR* COVER

This we might call "Vanity-Not-So-Fair" as the whole incident is steeped in hypocrisy. Apparently, it's all right for Tai Collins to accuse a U.S. Senator of extramarital infidelity on the cover of *Playboy*, but not for Anne Leibovitz, a celebrated photographer, to tastefully capture Bruce Willis's nude, seven-month pregnant wife on the August cover of *Vanity Fair*. Outrage immediately ensued, a "firestorm of reaction," according to Roberta Smith of the New York Times News Service, which resulted in feminist bickering and commentary. *Seven* national supermarket chains, including Safeway and Giant, dumped the issue because—here we go again—children needed protectors. Smith also comments that "The outcry suggests that there may be more public tolerance for images of naked women who appear to be available for sex, like those in *Playboy* and *Penthouse*, than a depiction of someone who has clearly had it."

How phony can you get? *Vanity Fair* was snatched from the same racks which trumpet *The National Enquirer* and smutty stories about Martina Navratilova, Ted Kennedy *ad nauseam*. Moreover, Demi Moore, who's shown as enthusiastically awaiting the birth of her second child, was covered up to the nose by an opaque wrapper, so kids couldn't even see her.

Ironically, all this opposition only served to help the issue quickly sell out.

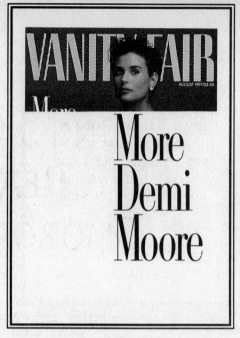

Finally, what is the *funniest* censorship story? This year, by a . . . uh, foreskin, the award goes to the Univ. of New Mexico's Maxwell Museum of Anthropology, whose exhibit "Ancestors" features early human figures without their sex organs. As the June *Playboy* reports, a little girl "chirped, 'Daddy, Neanderthal man doesn't have a penis!'" To which her father replied, "Yes, dear, that's why they went extinct!"

Who knows . . . if certain public protectors get their way, *we* could be the next Endangered Species.

John Rosenman, a freelance writer, is a regular **Gauntlet** *columnist who researches each year's top ten censorship stories. Suggestions, sent to* **Gauntlet,** *will be forwarded to him for future consideration.*

KING'S CRITICS:
A READER'S
SMORGASBORD

Michael R. Collings

George Beahm has noted recently that the number of books about Stephen King now exceeds the number of books by him. Given King's well-earned reputation as a prolific writer, the prospect of such a volume of secondary works is highly intimidating. Furthermore, given that King is contemporary, popular, and (most important perhaps) *still alive*, the fact of that volume verges on the astounding. Fan presses may follow the vicissitudes of a particular writer's career, occasionally making comments and suggestions; but academic and scholarly studies more commonly arise in substantial numbers after a writer is safely dead, after no more books will probably appear to upset a carefully constructed thesis . . . or worse, flatly contradict it. The possibility of a bibliography of roughly 5,000 entries of works by and about King, with over half fall into the *about* category, is therefore startling.

One consequence of such a wealth of material is positive. Students can justify working on King as a high school project; until half a dozen years ago, teachers could legitimately restrict his works as a topic on the grounds that there was no relevant scholarship and hence he would not provide adequate experience in research techniques. Now, if teachers choose to disallow his works, it has to be on more subjective grounds that are often revealed for what they actually are—implicit censorship.

Another consequence, however, is negative. A neophyte interested in discovering what has been said about King confronts a bewildering array of possibilities, from single-author studies, to casebooks on individual novels, to anthologies of articles (themselves ranging from fannishly amateur to stultifyingly academic), to bibliographies and biographies. And the prices range as well—from $4.95 paperbacks to signed and limited collectors' editions priced at

several hundred dollars.

Even so, however, there are some logical starting places.

For general introductions to "things-King," one might best start near the beginning. Douglas Winters' *The Art of Darkness* (1982, 1984, 1986) has the advantage of being both inexpensive and expert. Winter writes effective appreciation-criticism; he avoids academic jargon while including substantive information, much of it through interviews with King. The major disadvantage, of course, is that the text is dated; still, for the early King—and for an overview of the whole phenomenon—Winter remains strong.

George Beahm's *The Stephen King* Companion (1989) offers another route to meeting King. Unabashedly directed toward a popular readership, the *Companion* offers up-to-date information on every facet of King's public life . . . and some insights into his private. A mixture of reprints, interviews, plot summaries, bibliographies, appreciations, short reviews, and critical approaches, the book is accessible, readable, current, and affordable. Beahm's literary biography, *The Stephen King Story* (1991), completes his survey of King's world. Focusing on biographical data as it reflects on King's

published prose, the *SK Story* avoids sensationalism to concentrate on what readers might wish to know about King's life in order to understand his writings.

Two additional surveys, rather more scholarly, are Joseph Reino's *Stephen King: The First Decade* (1988) and Anthony Magistrale's forthcoming continuation, *Stephen King: The Second* Decade—Danse Macabre to The Dark Half (1992). The Twayne studies address general to academic audiences; they avoid the 'gosh-wow' of fan-oriented publications, incorporating instead recent relevant scholarship, bibliographies, and an index. Organized chronologically, they extend material covered in part in my own early study, *The Many Facets of Stephen* King(1985).

For readers wishing even more scholarly approaches to King, the most intriguing (if rather more expensive than some) is Carroll F. Terrell's *Stephen King Man and Artist* (1990). At times idiosyncratic, Terrell's work has the advantage of intimacy; one of King's professors at UMO, Terrell draws on his knowledge of King as student, as person, and as writer to support his thesis that King is a major writer for our time. Favorably comparing King with the likes

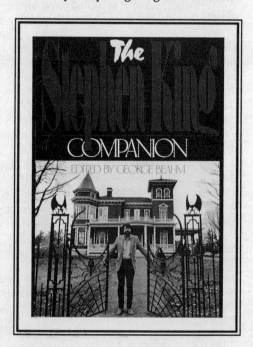

of Shakespeare, Dante, and Dickens, Terrell argues that King is not only an enormously popular writer (that his sales figures adequately demonstrate) but that he is a *great* writer as well. Terrell's approach is sometimes elliptical, at times avuncular, but always stimulating and challenging.

More conventional are a number of edited collections of essays. The first, Tim Underwood and Chuck Miller's *Fear Itself: The Horror Fiction of Stephen King* (1982,1984) sets the style for most—assorted essays on various novels and stories, often by writers whose names are almost as recognizable as King. Gary Hoppenstand and Ray B. Browne's *The Gothic World of Stephen King* (1987) demonstrates the form at its best; the various recent Underwood-Miller limited editions of collected essays and interviews are often far more expensive than their content merits. Anthony Magistrale's 1991 casebook, *The Shining Reader*, is the first in a series of volumes focusing on scholarly and academic responses to individual novels.

Given the amount of information and material available, it was inevitable that research oriented volumes appear to augment these books. Stephen Spignesi's monumental *The Shape Under the Sheet: The Complete Stephen King Encyclopedia* (1991) captures the urge to understand King in almost 800 large-format pages and thousands of entries—concordances to every person, place, and thing in King's writings; indices to first lines, to modes of mayhem and murder; articles and interviews and pictorials about King by friends, colleagues, fellow-writers, and critics. It is hampered by a lack of full cross-referencing and indexing, which makes individual bits of data difficult to locate, and by a $110.00 price tag. But it *is* complete.

At the moment (October *1991*), no comprehensive bibliography is yet available. Winter has been promising one for several years, but the most recent information I've seen suggests that it is not yet prepared . . . and that when it is it will probably not be a full reference bibliography. My *Annotated Guide to Stephen King* (1986), while still in print, is outdated; it will be superseded by *The Work of Stephen King: An Annotated Bibliography Guide*. This 5,000+ item cross referenced and indexed bibliography is current to June, 1991. At roughly 400 pages and tentatively priced at $35-$40 for the paperback edition, the book is scheduled for January 1992. Its format will allow for frequent updates to keep up with King's prolific output . . . and the increasingly more prolific output of his admires, detractors, fans, reviewers, critics and assorted other wordmongers (myself—and this article—included).

Michael Collings is one of the most respected scholars dealing with the work of Stephen King, having written seven books on the man and his work.

CHERI GAULKE:
PERFORMANCE ARTIST UNDER ATTACK

Photo copyright © 1982 by Shiela Ruth

William Relling Jr.

A list of the accomplishments and commendations of Los Angeles-based artist Cheri Gaulke would fill more than a dozen pages. Since earning her B.F.A. from the Minneapolis College of Art and Design in 1975, she has been at the forefront of the avant garde feminist art movement. She is also an environmental activist of renown—a founding member of the anti-nuclear performance art group Sisters of Survival [S.O.S.] that, from 1981 through 1985, toured throughout the United States and Europe. However, it is as a solo artist that she came to the attention of Senator Jesse Helms and others who have expressed opposition to her work. [A performance in Santa Monica, CA, in 1990 titled "Hey Jesse! You Ain't Seen Nothin' Yet!" was her response.]

Recently Gaulke spoke with her high school classmate, writer William Relling Jr., on the subjects of Senator Helms, feminism, history, religion, politics, and censorship

R: Getting right into the political content of your work, I understand you were recently accosted by Jesse Helms. [Gaulke laughs.] If not personally, then certainly through the media. Tell me about that.

G: Basically, my name appeared in the paper one day, in the *Village Voice*, that I was an artist who was doing this kind of "blasphemous" artwork.

R: Was it in connection with a specific piece of work?

G: It was partly "This is My Body," partly "Virgin." They were kind of confused about exactly what they were pinpointing, because their information was a little garbled. They objected to my portraying the Serpent, Eve, Jesus Christ, a witch in performances, in "This is My Body," where I did all that. I'd described, in a press release, the performance being part Christian worship service, part pagan ritual. They objected to that. I'd done another piece about artificial insemination, where I played the Virgin Mary reading a book, *How to Have A Baby Without A Man*, and the angel Gabriel appearing to her and saying, "Try artificial insemination." That was also depicted [in the article].

I wrote about [Helms] in a statement for a performance I did in England [in the Fall of 1991], and I was thinking that in some ways I was flattered to be noticed. Somehow it meant that my message had gotten through. That here I'd been critiquing Christianity's attitudes about sexuality, particularly *female* sexuality for years, and people in politics [finally] noticed.

R: What's the symbolism behind Eve eating the apple in "This is My Body?"

G: Eve eating the apple, in Christian history, has been held up to women as the first woman who was responsible for the demise of humankind. My use of the image is to be critical of Christianity saying that. Eating the apple is a metaphor—a woman exploring her sexuality which gets to be taboo [in Christianity].

R: You were also criticized for your depiction of a woman on a cross in "Passion." What caused the flap there?

G: I was portraying a priest or a monk and I took off my robes and climbed up the cross. The projection of Jesus merges with my body and I began to feel the pain of the choice of putting myself on the cross. This was the first performance where I put myself on the cross—which became a controversial statement; being sort of a female Christ. News articles objected to the fact that I portrayed myself

> . . . he [Jesse Helms] asked the General Accounting Office of Congress to do an investigation of my work [because] I received a NEA grant in 1983. Later I was audited [by the IRS] . . .

as Christ.

R: How did it come to Helms' attention specifically?

G: I think some conservative reporter did research and decided to pinpoint particular artists, then brought it to Helms to bolster his efforts to cut funding for the NEA, funding for the arts. I began to realize that it wasn't really about me, it wasn't really about my work. I was just grist for the mill. I was just being used to further his campaign.

R: What sort of pressure did he put on you?

G: I read in the paper that he asked the General Accounting Office of Congress to do an investigation of my work [because] I received a NEA grant in 1983. But no one ever contacted me personally. Later I was audited [by the IRS], which I thought may or may not have been a coincidence.

That's what's so weird, being aware of all these people talking *about* you, but they never talk *to* you. So you never get to really . . . "defend" myself isn't the right word. You never get to set the record straight. Talk about blaspheming. They're taking *my* name in vain, presenting my work out of context. They're manipulating the emotions of readers, of the public. It's really a cheap shot. Anybody can do that. And it's full of lies.

R: What are your feelings about the relationship between religion and politics? My take on what you do is that it's quite religious, in the sense that there's a spirituality to it, there's a connection to some higher power by whatever name you want to call it— Nature or God. Am I wrong about that?

G: No, you're very right. "Higher power" maybe isn't a [phrase] I would use, because I think I'm more into re-claiming the sacredness within myself and within you and within all beings and all matter. What I think happens in Christianity is that it's very separated from *us*. It's on the outside of us, and we try to attain [salvation]. And of course [Christianity] teaches that we'll never attain it as long as we're in our bodies, because our bodies are flesh and they're evil, and they have sexual desires. So therefore we must repress them and put them down. That for me is very dangerous. What seems spiritual and profound, this belief in God as some higher thing to attain, to me is ultimately extremely dangerous, because it justifies violence. Ultimately it justifies violence against women, against nature, this whole idea of "dominion" over. Rather than seeing that, in fact, we are within nature, we are part of it, we're not separate from it.

[For example] with the whole nuclear issue, I began to realize how ludicrous the idea of destroying the planet was. It's so human-ego invested, because *we* could never destroy the planet. We're just like ants. We're these little, puny, vulnerable creatures. We'll destroy ourselves. We'll destroy the planet's ability to feed us or sustain our lives, because *we're* so fragile. But the planet will continue. The planet, whether you want to call it a goddess or some kind of life form or Nature in the larger, cosmic sense, there's no way we could destroy it.

This has gone off the tangent here a little. But the connection between religion and politics . . . lately I've been doing some research. The so-called "Founding

Photo by Shiela Ruth

Fathers" of our country were not Christians, contrary to what people like Jerry Falwell and Jesse Helms would like you to believe. They were Deists. Which is really humanistic and more where I'm coming from.

R: I suppose if you read Franklin's *Autobiography* or stuff that Thomas Jefferson wrote, you could arrive at that conclusion?

G: There's documented stuff about it. "So help me God," the pledge you take in court? Any kind of swearing of allegiance? That is not actually required. I didn't know that until just recently. Our so-called "Founding Fathers" were into keeping church and state separate. Essentially the Supreme Court is there to be the arbiter between that. What really concerns me is the ways in which people like Falwell and Helms are trying to reconnect those two and equate patriotism with belief in God.

When I read Margaret Atwood's *The Handmaid's Tale*, that to me was the most powerful book. To me it was the feminist *1984*, because it's really my worst fear about where we're heading, in terms of complete enslavement of women. Our only value to this patriarchal culture is that we reproduce. [Atwood's book] may be a paranoid extreme, but I feel like I've seen that happen in history. In the Middle Ages something like nine million people—mostly women—were killed [as witches]. This went on for hundreds of years, this incredible . . . ludicrous . . . it's just laughable, the things they were accused of. [Things like] "removing a male member." Women were completely scapegoated. There were some villages where ever single woman was put to death. What's scary to me is not only did that happen, but that no one talks about it anymore. It's not something that we learn about in history class—it's just like neo-Nazis who say the Holocaust didn't happen. To me that's very scary when the culture loses the history of oppression. We lose the lessons that are learned through those things.

R: So the danger in mixing religion and politics is what?

G: Politics is the enforcer. Religion doesn't have the power to put someone to death or in prison. They need the State to do that. That was the perfect marriage they had going in the Middle Ages. It was a very profit-making industry. A lot of people had the job of locking women up and recording the trials and being the jury. Apparently there were all these different jobs: the job of getting her, taking her from her house. The job of feeding her in jail. The job of bringing her to the courtroom. And guess who paid for it? *She* did. Because they seized her property, and they divided the spoils, and it paid the expenses. God, what a brilliant, capitalist concept! [Laughs.] It was an incredible racket.

R: Are there parallels to things going on today?

G: There are some rackets coming down nowadays. I think what's happening with abortion being threatened is really, really frightening. That's a case where women have [in the past] and will

[in the future] lose their lives. To have the freedom to make that choice . . . such blatant disregard for a woman's sense of her own body, her integrity, her own desires and needs is really what I feel is behind it.

R: Do you find it curious that a lot of these leaders of anti-abortion groups are male?

G: Along with an occasional Phyllis Schlafly. It's not to say that women are superior to men, or that all men are fucked. I don't believe that at all. But it is clear to me who has power in this society, and it's not women.

R: Any number of social critics have referred to where we are now—"we" meaning society—as "post-feminist." What's your take on that?

G: At first I hated that term, because it felt like a put-down to the feminist movement. That somehow we were talking beyond it all, which I really don't think we are. Now I understand it more as a historical term, in terms of meaning that "feminism" as an organized movement doesn't really exist in the way that it did in the '60s and '70s. But I know that feminism is alive and well in the hearts of many women *and* men. I just don't think there's a national strategy.

One of the reasons for that, one of the problems of any kind of movement—[not just] feminism— is that desire to distill a diverse group of people into having a small set of needs and demands. When, in fact, who women are is an extremely diverse cross-section of our society. Women are different races, different classes. Our needs and our issues are very different. That's where feminism broke down.

R: Do you think the current relationship between religion and politics is a reaction to feminism as a movement in the '60s and '70s?

G: When women get strong is there a backlash? Is that the question?

R: Yes.

G: I think that could have something to do with it. When women start to

Photo by Shiela Ruth

get organized, yeah, then I think there is a backlash. In the Middle Ages there was apparently, in the period preceding the witch burnings, there were more women than men. Men were getting killed of by wars, and—this is what I heard one historian say—to some of the plagues, some of the diseases, men were more susceptible than women. So there were more women than men. It meant that women were surviving their husbands, and women were owning more property, that sort of thing. That's interesting to me. [So the men say:] "Okay, we got to *do* something about this! They're outta control!" [Laughs.]

I guess I see history as being two parts. I see this kind of pre-Christian part of history, which women in the past few years have been trying to reclaim. This whole "goddess" movement, which is not a new thing. It's documented that there were thousands and thousands of years during which people existed in cooperation with nature. There was a pantheon of gods and goddesses that were symbolic or metaphoric of cycles of nature. Some people [have suggested] that is was a matriarchal society, [but] I feel uncomfortable with the term "matriarchal," because I think it implies that women ruled over men. I prefer "matristic," a sort of 'woman-centered" culture. But it's clear that [at that time] the female body was respected and worshipped as reflecting the cycles of nature. The difficulty about reclaiming that part of our history is that it's largely oral tradition. It's before the written word, for the most part. But there are objects and there are ruins which have been found.

Then what you have is a shift in power, to patriarchy. At that point, the people with power re-wrote the story. So when you look at something like the Garden of Eden, and you have this case of characters—the evil snake, the tree with fruit on it, the sexual woman who's listening to the snake and eating the fruit—you realize, in fact, it's pre-Christian symbolism. In ancient Egypt, they worshipped Hathor, the goddess of the tree. They believed that the tree was her body, and that she handed out fruit to the dead, which was her gift of eternal life. Serpents were kept in temples, and they whispered to the priestesses, and so on. With the shift to patriarchy, the stories had to be re-written. The good characters had to become bad characters. *All* the stories get re-written—the fairy tales, the definitions of what is "erotic," the laws.

That's why for me there are two phases of history. The earlier phase is when the flesh and the spirit were not thought of a divided. In other words, the —matter was sacred. The earth was sacred. To have a physical presence did not imply carnality and weakness. But after this changed, the flesh and the spirit became divided. The spirit became valued over the flesh, and somehow men, since they were writing the rules, got to be more spiritual than women. Men were the only ones who could officiate and be ministers.

What I saw [for example] when I read [the Book of] Revelations is this story of Jesus coming down as a great warrior to fight the Great Whore of Babylon—who gets to portray the matter, the flesh, the world is this big slut! [Laughs.] Again, it's that desire to destroy the flesh, to destroy nature, to destroy women.

R: I know that censorship is an issue you've had some ambivalence about in the past, in terms of how it relates to pornography. You were involved with an anti-pornography movement for awhile, weren't you?

G: Within the feminist movement, in the '70s, there was a targeting of pornography and violence against women. There was a group called "Women Against Violence and Pornography in Media." They held a conference in San Francisco [in which] I was involved as an artist. Bringing a group of women up there for performances and stuff.

I think what was going on then was really important, [because] it was raising the issue of does pornography lead to violence. There are all sorts of questions about that. [As a consequence] things have changed a lot. I think more women are involved in pornography, in terms of being the creators of it and not just the .. . I don't know if "victims" is the right word. Not just the ones whose bodies are being used.

One of the dangers of what was happening at that time is this discussion of whether to legislate pornography. Should pornography be outlawed, or is pornography freedom of expression? I see how it doesn't really work to legislate it. They

> I don't know if I have a "limit" as far as obscenity goes. Certainly I have limits in terms of what is offensive to me. But it's like the discussion about is there such a thing as "evil." I really don't think there is.

could legislate me just as easily. It's very easy for people like Helms and Falwell to say that *I'm* pornographic and my work is obscene. I think there needs to be an awareness of the issues in terms of is a person being used or abused. I'm not crazy about violence but I certainly feel people have a right to [explore] violence artistically. I'm not particularly aesthetically attracted to violence, although I can be pretty graphic in my performances about violence that's been committed, because I want people to know about that

R: Is there such a thing as obscenity for you? Is there such a thing as pornography?

G: I don't know if I have a "limit" as far as obscenity goes. Certainly I have limits in terms of what is personally offensive to me. But it's like the discussion about is there such a thing as "evil." I really don't think there is. I really don't believe in evil. I think "evil" [like obscenity] is something that's defined by one group to use against another group. Since I happen to be in the group that it usually gets used against, whether that be women or even artists or homosexuals, I see the danger in that.

It's so hard to define it. I feel like there

is a responsibility to protect people who can't protect themselves, like young people. But then you get into people [who] say the unborn are people who can't protect themselves. *That* can get used against you, too. Or the elderly. [Anything] can be used as a way of taking someone else's power.

It's like Bret Easton Ellis's book [*American Psycho*]. There were some feminist groups calling for a boycott of that book. I think that's fine. I boycott Coors. If the workers are striking Corona, I'll boycott Corona. To me that's freedom of expression. But I don't think that [Ellis's book] should be banned or outlawed. He should have every right to write that book and publish it. Bookstores have the right to sell it. I would fight for that right.

R : You're planning a new performance for May. Have you self-censored yourself or don't you care how you are perceived? Does the threat of persecution hang over your head?

G : Yes, I'm always thinking about it. I do have nudity in my new performance, but all of it is behind a scrim, which I've never done before. Now is that because I am putting a layer between myself and the audience? Is that a kind of veiled self-censorship? I don't know. Or is it purely an aesthetic thing? I'm trying not to self-censor, but I am certainly aware of that inner debate.

R : Do you have any fear of being targeted because of the sexual or controversial nature of your performance art?

G : Yes, I do. It's a funny double-edged sword. On the one hand, one gets a lot of visibility for being controversial and I find in some ways I've benefitted by having the finger pointed at me. On the other hand, I've seen artists, who have been more involved in this debate than I have, pay dearly on a personal level. Having to spend so much time fighting those battles can be frustrating and exhausting emotionally. I so identify, his-

torically, with the witch burning period that I fear persecution. I anticipate it in some ways. I do feel, though, that I will be true to what I think is the most important and best image to do in my work; what is best, not work that's the safest. I'm a mature artist. I've been doing this stuff for almost 20 years, so the decisions I make are tempered with experience. I sort of trust my judgment, and if I feel unsure of myself I'll consult with other people that have this experience.

R : Is the climate today more repressive than several years ago? Would your performance pieces, for example, have stirred more controversy if done today?

G : Yes. People are sort of looking for it in a way they weren't looking before. There is a concerted effort by special interest groups to push down women, certain minorities and gays.

R : Why do you think these are more repressive times?

G : I see the economy having a lot to do with it. People feel insecure. There's a feeling there's not enough to go around, so the power groups want to make sure they get their part. That's why David Duke has been so successful. He's tapping into middle class white people's fear of not getting what they perceive as their share. There's a perception that women or minorities have more power.

R : How do you combat this?

G : It's important to keep on doing the work we've been doing. We can't shrink back into the closet and be timid. We have to continue to be aggressive and be aggressive in a responsible way—not do things just for shock value.

William Relling Jr. makes his third appearance in **Gauntlet** *with this interview. His short fiction, censored by various publishers, has appeared in issues #1 and #2.*

The Shameful Enforcement of Video Chastity

Joseph P. Cunningham

As I stood at Showtime Video's checkout counter to rent Clive Barker's *Hellraiser* for about the tenth time, I almost missed the petition. It sat in a clutter of movie ads, but once I saw it my eye was held. A trail of signatures descended below its strong declarative statement:

WE BELIEVE that the First Amendment gives us the right to watch what we choose in the privacy of our own home. WE RESENT attempts by public officials and others to limit this freedom and control what adults are allowed to watch.

"What's going on?" I asked, tapping the page. The manager, Marge Reidmann, began to ring up my rental and explained that a few people from some local churches had formed a "decency" group a few years ago and had been pushing their moral weight around ever since. Marge had been politely dealing with it and had regarded it as one of their smaller problems until three little old ladies filed complaints with the Cambridge Police after having their husbands rent some adult movies.

"Which movies?" I asked as I signed the petition. They were called *Blonde Heat, Naughty Lady,* and *So Many Men, So Little Time.* Pretty typical porno titles, really. I rented one in a pointless gesture of defiance, zipped my coat, told Marge to give 'em hell, and headed out into the Minnesota tundra.

SUPPORT THE **ECCD!**

...BECAUSE A MIND IS A TERRIBLE THING

⬥

For those of you who have been, you know how exhilarating it feels to be idealistic and pissed. This feeling gets especially dizzying when the ideals, which only moments before were completely dormant, come crashing down on you in a storm of fierce tears. I was southbound, doing about seventy with a porno fantasy and Clive Barker's vision of Hell sitting on the seat next to me when my feelings blindsided me with the realization of just how much I hated what those bastards were doing.

It's not that I'm in love with porno movies. They are, for the most part, a class of films which are almost *traditionally* trashy, the embodiment of the cheap thrill. Good artwork tends to appeal to your emotions and challenge your intellect. All porn does . . . in fact, all it is *meant* to do is make you go all warm and stiff (or warm and damp) under your buttonfly. But, as someone once said, knowledge is the birthright of he who seeks it in a free society. Content isn't the point and no one was forcing this degenerate brand of bad film-making onto the decency bunch. The only time they rented it was so they could fuck with everyone else's ability to.

When the East Central Coalition for Decency (ECCD) first got rolling back in 1987, their game plan was to write intimidating letters and distribute a list of all businesses in the county which offered pornographic materials for rent or sale. The blacklist would be distributed by Rev. Paul Lundgren, their leader, at showings of an anti-porn propaganda film by Dr. James Dobson called *A Winnable War.*

Prior to showing the film, the ECCD would send a polite letter to the owner of each business on the blacklist which informed them of their presence on such a list, and that they should "permanently remove the material [before the Dobson film was shown] so that [their] name and business will not be included in the release." Can you say BLACKMAIL, boys and girls? . . . I thought you could.

I was surprised to learn that this tactic *alone* had worked on two video stores. The other stores, Cambridge Video and Showtime Video, were run by people, who apparently, somewhere down the line, invested in a pair of balls. They had taken an I-believe-in-freedom-of-speech-and-nobody's-gonna-tell-me-how-to-run-my-shop stance. The ECCD declared war.

They chose Cambridge Video first because a small mom and pop operation is financially vulnerable. In April of 1990, three ECCD supporters, probably feeling like undercover operatives on a mission from God, rented a few XXX movies and promptly filed complaints with police the next day using a prefabricated form supplied by the Clean Up Project of Minnesota, a religious right-wing group that pumps out a lot of pamphlets and tracts on how to rid your town of filth in ten easy steps.

Complaint filing isn't a big deal unless you've got a Gary Lambert for a police chief. Dennis Coleman, the owner of Cambridge Video, was popped with a search warrant in May of 1990. This was done quietly and the local paper never covered it (Lambert, it seems, filled Mr. Coleman in on the wisdom of a shut mouth). This becomes all the more sickening when you realize that the warrant authorized the seizure of records revealing the names of those who had rented X-rated tapes.

One of the things taken in the raid was a movie called *Exposed*. What follows is an excerpt from Chief Lambert's official police report, which describes the content of the videotape:

Scene 33

Cheerleader is in Willies [sic], (coaches) office. She asks him if this is how she will really get to be head cheerleader (she is sucking and kissing his penis)?

Willie bends her over a desk / pulls down her panties [and] then sticks his penis into her vagina . . . . She rides his penis.

Scene 34

He now masturbates into her mouth. She sucks on his penis. She then "Deep Throats" him a couple of times. Then he wipes some cum [sic] off of her face with his finger, and places it in her mouth.

Lambert later wrote a letter to Coleman, wherein he said, "Please do not make [this film] available to the people of Isanti County . . . . If you do not immediately pull this film from your store, further action may be taken." And that was the end of adult entertainment at Cambridge Video. Can you say GESTAPO-COP boys and girls? . . . I thought you could.

I leaped into the fray as this scenario was being replayed at Showtime Video. The search warrant even read the same, and Lambert kept true to his nazi image by seizing the petition. But this time it got him sued. Unlike Coleman, Showtime owner Steve Davis had a bank account big enough to back up his ballsy stance, and he hired the best law firm in the state.

After the local papers ran front page stories (Davis blew off Lambert's gag-rule), Rev. Lundgren published a letter in the *Star* explaining to the public what they were doing and why. A week later, I fired back with my own letter in which I exposed their tactics and went basically ballistic. I even included my phone number so that support could be rallied for the embattled store. While I did have to field a few calls from indignant bluenoses

> . . . the role we played was critical in making censorship in Cambridge a big steamy shit sandwich for the would-be thought police.

("but we're trying to *protect* you from this sinful filth!"), the positive response was massive. Over eighty-five people stood up to be counted with Americans Together Against Censorship (ATAC), and my phone rang itself sore for two weeks with calls of support. The wife of a local cop (she withheld her name) even helped out with a suggestion for a new petition.

We, the undersigned, believe that if the country is going to censor citizen's private entertainment, then it should also investigate the private sexual practices of the County Attorney, the Police Chief, and numerous police officers in order to determine if these people might be violating adultery or fornication statutes.

Although we didn't dare use it, we did see to it that the suggestion fell into enemy hands.

That was just a small part of the big noise ATAC made, and while it's difficult to be sure, I feel that the role we played was critical in making censorship in Cambridge a big steamy shit sandwich for the would-be thought police.

Over the next few months, the prosecutor's office stalled, and stalled, and stalled some more until we won, when the obscenity statute was deemed unconstitutionally vague by the Minnesota State Court of Appeals. They were filing on a case in Winona that was almost identical to Davis'.

Last month I paid an unexpected visit to an ECCD prayer meeting. After I shook a few hands and was seated, they prayed for Lambert and other local officials, the video store owners and their victims and me. There were also prayers for Pat Robertson, James Dobson, Donald Wildmon, Tipper Gore, and Senator Jesse Helms (and *no*, I'm not kidding!).

Then came the great debate, ten ver-

sus one. When it became painfully obvious that I wasn't going to convert (I felt like Luke resisting Darth Vader's join-me-and-together-we-will-rule-the-universe speech), they gave up and promised to pray for my salvation.

The lesson learned from this entire episode is censorship doesn't look so savory when it's done in broad daylight, and like all shameful activities it must be done under the cover of secrecy.

And darkness.

Joseph P. Cunningham's column "Fighting Back" appears in **Penthouse.** *He is currently working on a book about censorship and a graphic novel,* **Dystopia.**

Censor Me, Please!

Adam Alexander

A xel is famous for not being famous. Lots of people have heard of him, seen him in magazine articles, seen him on little clips on TV. But even before his media appearances, an amazing number of people knew of, had met, or had heard of Axel.

To wear an Axel ring or buckle or even to have a little sculpture around the house, would elicit a sign of recognition from a rather wide range of people. But to know of Axel was to be in on an open secret which is still an open secret, for the world-wide recognition which Axel will certainly some day have is yet to happen. Sort of like what happened to H. R. Geiger after the movie *Alien* when his name became a household word.

So what is it that Axel does that promises such world fame?

Axel is primarily a sculptor of small objects and jewelry. He does his sculpture

Well, that's nice. Sounds like a crafts fair. Where's the point of departure? Well, nothing Axel does looks amateurish; everything he produces looks opulent, well-designed and glitch-free. But that still is not enough to explain his sub-cultural popularity. What explains his popularity is the content of his work. For Axel is a Tabooist and can be considered a founder of the "Tabooist" school of modern design.

Axel's work includes fetuses, genitals, skulls, jokes, strange seeds, animal bones, small shells, funny skeletons on toilets, rings with prongs that extend beyond the knuckle called "protectors", doll's faces with vampire teeth, blobby crosses with a tiny head, a tiny rose, or a tiny skull at the intersection, crucified jesuses off the cross with (cast) butterfly wings between legs and arms called "butterchrists" (or "jesusflies"), lobster carapace forearm covers with horseshoe crab spikes extending over the backs of the hands, nail extensions that fit over the fingertips and extend a couple inches past, one set for vanity another for eating, a spider monkey skull ring with the finger extending through the mouth, a woodpecker skull protector ring, not to mention delicate little gold wedding rings with tiny fiery opals. A skull with Mickey Mouse Club ears becomes "Now it's time to say Goodbye" and a shitting dog with

Ogasming Bat Spoon

Now It's Time To Say Goodbye

in wax and "lost wax" casts it into metal: bronze, silver, and gold. Axel sculpts his wax in a number of ways: taking molds from all kinds of objects, both man-made and natural, and then filling the mold with wax; combining a few or more of these molded fragments; forming soft wax with his fingers; heating and bending sheets and wires of wax; or applying drops of hot wax or a heated dental tool to the piece. Most pieces he does are a combination of these techniques.

its head replaced by a skull becomes "Death takes a shit"; both pieces part of a larger sequence, "the Humiliation of Death."

I have seen middle-aged ladies looking at a spoon which is the image of a masturbating, orgasming, ejaculating bat and admiring the opulence without a clue as to the obvious image before them. On the other hand, any heavy metal kid would immediately see this shock-value, taboo image for what it was.

Axel was influenced by no less an artistic personage than Salvador Dali, with whom he had a personal relationship. Axel would come in from the Jersey shore, where he grew up, and hang out with Dali in the famous St. Regis Hotel where Dali had a suite. Dali would refer to Axel as "My Jesus." Axel created some of his first wax-to-metal sculptures for Dali. From Dali, Axel developed his characteristic surrealistic irreverence by which any aspect of human experience may be commented upon . . . with extra emphasis on the taboo.

Axel exemplifies the basic principle of the Tabooist: a balance between repugnance or shock and attraction or beauty. The Art cop-out of merely presenting the repellent and claiming that the negative emotional reaction is sufficient rationale because it makes people "feel" is not sufficient for a Tabooist. A Tabooist wants neither to be in the interior of repugnance country nor in the interior of beauty country, but to be the border, the interface, between the two. The Tabooist school can be said to include the likes of cartoonist/painter Robert Williams and cartoonist R. Crumb.

In a sense, the essence of Tabooism is the defensibility of taboo or disturbing themes by the sheer beauty of its presentation. "I don't care how beautiful it is, no one is going to show a (penis, vagina, modified jesus, whatever) in our Museum!" At least the Tabooists have a rebuttal.

What Axel is waiting for is the un-

Prickly Subject

deniable exposure to the public after which he himself becomes a household word. Not to take over the industry, but to have a sector all his own, both commercial and one-of-a-kind, pop art and fine art. And presumably, with public attention spiked with an establismentarian frown at the content of his work. Inutherwerds . . . censorship! For no act would give him the pedestal he needs more than an attempt at prohibition on the part of some uptight fool looking to protect the public order from the onslaughts of salacious imagery.

So, if I were Axel, I would say "Censor me, please! Condemn my art in public places and in the news. Say it will hurt the eyes of children and Good Christian Folk. Say only a pervert could like this stuff. Because once I am condemned, the eyes of the nation and the world will be on me! Censor me! Please!!!"

Adam Alexander is an inventor and mathematician who lives in New York City.

A Challenge
To The Media
That
Takes
Itself
Too
Seriously

W. Wilson Goode

Watergate. It seems that since the 1970s, the media has found its own niche in government. No one disputes that Watergate should have been exposed for the sake of our government and society. In this one amazing controversy, though, the media evolved before our eyes from "journalistic" to "policing" reporting. Unfortunately, the Watergate reports were not only good journalism, but great stories; ones that opened new doors of political opportunity for the media. In one major twist of events, the media has found its niche as government's "policing agent" in a way that would sell newspapers and increase television ratings.

The question is, doesn't the media have a larger journalistic role in promoting government through proactive contributions? The answer, of course, is yes: we live in a democracy that works best when all of its citizens are involved, informed, and working together.

How could the media make its greatest contribution to society? It has an important role as journalist and advocate. In a democracy, it is important that *all* sides be heard—more important than to *take* sides. In a society infested with poverty and crime, drug addiction, teenage pregnancy, AIDS, etc., the media must begin to serve as a voice of the people who are rarely heard, rather than the voice of coffeehouse intellectuals or barroom bigots.

If the media does not begin to serve as this protective voice, but acts purely as a reactive voice to government, how are the people empowered over special interests in the media? There is much to be recorded and reported, and even more for which to advocate.

Foremost, citizens of a democracy should better understand government and the democratic process. Therefore, if public education does not properly educate the citizenry about government, the media does a great disservice by so narrowly focusing on political personalities. The citizenry must understand the election process, the balancing branches of government, the budget process, and both the lobbying and legislative process in order to make informed decisions. If, in fact, the government is so "corrupt" that it needs "policing", there must be an understanding of how to alter or change government.

My perception is that our democracy is threatened by the "anti-government", anti-political phenomena that began with Watergate and has been, ironically, fueled by the media politics of the Reagan/Bush Republicans.

For instance, Ronald Reagan was never considered a great government administrator, but he was promoted as the "great communicator." He knew that the average American is no more involved in the democratic process than reading the newspaper or watching the news. Yet, the media never attempted to educate the public on alternative economic policies and social concerns. It must be clear now, to even the media, that the Reagan Revolution was a failure. The current recession and trade deficit is proof of that. The media could have made this easier to understand.

The media can be a powerful communicator for voices that need to be heard. The drug addict's voice needs to be heard as it cries out for rehabilitation. The teenage mother's voice needs to be heard as it pleads for adequate prenatal care. The AIDS victim's voice has stories to tell that could save lives. The media must also tell our society that racism *is* alive and well. To date it hasn't.

The media can be a voice of unity rather than one of divisiveness. Let's hope that in the coming decade, the media rises to the occasion and becomes the voice of unity and hope of this fragile democracy of ours.

W. Wilson Goode is the former Mayor of Philadelphia. He is currently President and CEO of Goode Cause, Inc.

*This issue is dedicated to my mother,
Lenore Hoffman, who passed away in 1991.
She was a class act and will be sorely missed;
and to Danielle Faith Gaines, a sixteen-year-old
former student of mine, with the voice of an angel
who died in a tragic car accident in 1991.
She, too, will never be forgotten.*

HOUSE OF FICTION

T. Liam McDonald

Sibs
F. Paul Wilson
Dark Harvest, $20.95

F. Paul Wilson switches styles and genres with such ease that it's always hard to pin him down. This, of course, is all for the better, and his work displays a breadth and scope and accomplishment that easily puts him at the forefront of modern writers of suspense and horror. A new F. Paul Wilson book is always a special occasion, and *Sibs* is no exception. It is his most compelling book yet, and right from page one you are sucked into a plot that will pull you around countless twists and turns until its shattering climax. This is hot stuff, weaving elements of mystery, suspense, and horror into one powerful tale.

The "sibs" (short for siblings) of the title are Kelly and Kara Wade: identical twins. When Kelly dies in a suspicious fall from the window of a sleazy motel, Kara comes to New York to identify her body and tie up her affairs. With the help of an old boyfriend, Kara learns of the insanity and sexual excess which had be-come part of her sister's life in New York. In the course of searching for answers, Kara is drawn into the same nightmarish world that destroyed her twin.

Sibs is never what it seems to be: every time you think you have a fix on what's happening, Wilson takes you in another direction. It is really one of the few books in a long time that actually has a healthy supply of potent surprises up its sleeve, and jaded dark suspense readers will find it one of the most satisfying reads in a long time. To miss *Sibs* is to miss one of the most exciting books of the year.

Before I Wake
Steven Spruill
St. Martin's $19.95

You heard it here first: *Steven Spruill is going to be big.* We're talking sales and fame in the Mary Higgens Clark, Dean R. Koontz, and Robin Cook range. We're talking feature films and movies of the week. You can take that to the bank. Spruill, who only recently turned his hand to medical thrillers with last year's knock-out *Painkiller*, is back with another medical thriller called *Before I Wake*. The title, by the way, was his publisher's idea, which shows that they have their eyes on the Mary Higgens Clark audience.

Spruill writes drop-dead exciting, well-crafted suspense with a medical backdrop. He knows the *milieu*, too, having labored in the medical profession himself before turning to fiction. In *Before I Wake* he grabs you right from the start with a strangely effective dream-sequence that draws the reader into the recurrent nightmare of the main character: Dr. Amy St. Claire, a physician in charge of a New York City emergency room. When an elderly but otherwise healthy man suffers a fatal heart attack in her ER, she thinks it's strange. But when she learns that other men fitting the same description have also died mysteriously in the same ER, she becomes frightened, especially when she sees that her own father fits the profile of the other dead men.

There's much more to it, of course; but to give any more of the plot away would be, as it was with *Sibs*, unfair. *Before I Wake* is compulsively good reading. It's the kind of book women buy and read and pass around the office: the characterization, especially that of the female characters, is taut; the plotting is compelling; the medical elements ring true. It is everything one could want from a thriller, and more.

When readers think medical thriller, they think *Robin Cook*, which is a shame since Robin Cook is an awful writer. Ten years from now, when people think medical thriller, they will think *Steven Spruill*.

Mortal Remains in Maggody
Joan Hess
Mysterious Press, $18.95

It seems that there are as many Joan Hess books as there are flies on a roadside opossum. Until *Mortal Remains in Maggody* showed up on my doorstep, however, I hadn't read any of them, but I'm going to start. Joan Hess is a funny, entertaining writer who writes a rollicking good mystery. *Mortal Remains . . .* is the fifth *Maggody* book dealing with a police chief, Arly Hanks, in the backwater Arkansas hamlet of Maggody: population 755. Hanks is back in Maggody after living in New York for a stretch, and she's still getting use to the pace of things in her old home town. Not much usually happens in Maggody, but lately an arsonist has been torching abandoned houses. And then things get really strange: a sleazy movie production company comes to Maggody to make a cheapie soft-porn flick called *Wild Cherry Wine*, and soon people are dying or disappearing faster than Chief Hanks can count.

Hess has a masterful way with the offbeat, Twain-esque denizens of Maggody, and this oddball mystery makes for a fine stretch of fiction. It's not easy to write humorous mysteries and actually have them be *good mysteries*. Hess accomplishes both: her characters are strange and funny, yet they manage to

live and breath on the page. Her plots are tight and exciting, and the interesting characters make for enjoyable reading to boot. What more can you ask for from fiction? Do yourself a favor: pick up *Mortal Remains in Maggody*. You won't regret it.

Something Stirs
Charles L. Grant
Tor, $18.95

Year after year you can count on Charles Grant to turn out the most carefully crafted, stylish, evocative horror novels and stories in the genre. Grant has more ability to deliver unease and shivering fear than most modern writers, but his horrors are subtle and cumulative. Like a storm building on the horizon, threatening to explode into violence, a Charles Grant novel weaves deft characterization and a sure sense of place together with strands of horror, creating a tapestry that is as fulfilling as it is disturbing.

Something Stirs is Grant's latest novel, and it follows his recent trend of exploring the turmoils of adolescence. Like a true master, he evokes all the pathos, powerlessness, pain, dislocation, and uncertainty of being a teenager. These novels aren't written specifically *for* teenagers: they are adult novels, but their central concerns touch on a place in time where we all have been. What reader hasn't been a frustrated teenager and known the pain of confusion and uncertainty that comes with maturation? What reader can't relate to the mixture of horror and desire that is part and parcel of gaining one's independence: the desire for freedom mixed with the horror that often accompanies responsibility, the reluctance to shirk youthful freedom in favor of mature obligations? This is Grant's territory, and it is the battle ground of *Something Stirs*, in which fear is a real, tangible thing.

The novel centers around The Pack: a group of real teenagers (as opposed to the teenagers, prevalent in much fiction, who are merely caricatures of what an adult writer thinks a modern teenager should be) who are beset by their own worst fears. The Pack is an anomaly. Vaguely led Eddie Roman, they have styled themselves after members of the youth culture of the fifties: poodle skirts, leather jackets, slicked-back hair, and hanging out at the malt shop. They are James Dean's bastard step-children, plopped down in a culture where "mall-crawling" and girls with fright-wig hairdos are the norm.

Something Stirs begins with the violent murder of Eddie Roman and his father. Eddie is suspected of murdering his father and then killing himself, but how does that explain the post-mortem mutilation of Eddie's own body? Something isn't right with the town of Foxriver New Jersey and the members of The Pack. The teenagers are all seeing things, being followed, living in waking nightmares, aware of some evil pressing down upon them. The tension and the horrors are ever-present, but it is nearly impossible to grasp them and understand them. Are they even real? This way madness lies for the teens. How can you fight what you can't even define or understand?

The thing with Grant's novels, the thing that raises them head-and-shoulders above most modern horror fiction, is their truth: these characters live and breath. These are people we've met, people we've been. Make no mistake about this: Grant's novels are for the careful reader, the reader who wants more than pop-up monsters and cliched, recycled horror. *Something Stirs* is filled with fear that is powerful not in its shock-tactics or graphic detail, but in its skill, elegance, and honesty. This is *real* horror, horror that touches you and stays with you after the last page is turned. From the beginning you know you are in the hands of a master, for no one matches the stylish terrors of Charles L. Grant.

Outrage in the Black Hills:
Censorship and the
New Indian Wars

On June 26, 1975, two FBI agents drove onto the property of a Lakota Indian family named Jumping Bull, in the Pine Ridge Reservation of South Dakota, looking for an Indian youth who they suspected of theft. The rest of the story is hazy, but shots were fired, and the FBI agents and an Indian were killed. A massive manhunt ensued, and in the end a single man, Leonard Peltier, was convicted and sentenced to life imprisonment for the murders. He is still in prison today, fifteen years later. Two small problems: 1) Leonard Peltier is innocent; 2) some very powerful people didn't want you to know his story.

In the Spirit of Crazy Horse, by Peter Matthiessen, is the story of Peltier's case, set against the backdrop of violence towards and oppression of Indians in the disputed Black Hills of South Dakota. The book is a scathing indictment of U.S. policies towards this land's native peoples, and details the long, bloody road that led from the massacre at Wounded Knee to the murder of the FBI agents. It is a story of militaristic oppression by the United Sates, random (government endorsed) attacks on Indians, corruption, lies, and broken treaties. It is a story that the FBI and William Janklow (former governor of South Dakota) did not want you to know. They almost succeeded. You see, *Crazy Horse* was published by Viking in 1983, whereupon it was slapped with $50 million in civil litigation suits for libel. Booksellers were threatened with lawsuits if they sold the book, paperback and foreign publication was blocked, and in the end the book was pulled. The eight years of legal battles that ensued cost the defendants (Matthiessen and his publisher, Viking) $2 million. They finally won, and now the book is available again, with an important afterward by attorney Martin Garbus on the legal battles that kept it off the shelves.

The story of the Black Hills is so long and complex that it can't really be described here. Indeed, it takes two books, Matthiessen's *Crazy Horse* and Edward Lazarus' *Black Hills, White Justice* (Harper Collins) to fully understand it. Much of the violence surrounds a complex web of land disputes between the government and the "Sioux"* Indians which basically boils down to the same old story: the U.S. government will stop at nothing to get Indian lands. This background is essential to understanding

Peltier's case, and Matthiessen spends the first third of his book reciting the litany of horrors brought upon the Indians from 1835 until the Jumping Bull shoot-out. All Americans have a certain vague shame about the disgraceful treatment of the Indians, but too many think it is a thing of the past . . . a wrong that was righted when "Custer died for our sins." Not by a long shot.

Crazy Horse is essential reading for any American, and what it has to say is so disturbing that it should come as no surprise that people would try to suppress the book. You see, the Indian wars are not over. Violence still racked the Pine ridge Reservation in the 1970s, and the ensuing years have only brought a moderate improvement. The U.S. government's standard policy of abusing Indians who disagreed with them was enforced with a vengeance by the FBI, the BIA (Bureau of Indian Affairs), and even COINTELPRO (the FBI's counter-intelligence program). Government sanctioned "goon squads" would beat, rape, and kill Indians at random. Government sponsored clinics would force Indian women to deliver their babies in hospitals under anesthesia, and when the women awoke, they found they had been sterilized without their consent.

You know the operation. It's what we do to cats and dogs.

It's genocide, pure and simple, and *it's not over.*

Why?

Simple: the Indians are in the way, again. The land of the Pine Ridge reservation is valuable, and white rangers and U.S. corporations want it. Plus the Sioux are determined enforce their claims on Blacks Hills, which were given to them in perpetuity in a treaty with the United States. Like so many others, the treaty was broken. The Sioux want the Black Hills back.

These new Indian wars are not being fought on the plains, but in the courtrooms, as *Black Hills, White Justice* so thoroughly details. *Crazy Horse* is even more horrifying in its allegations, which is why it was suppressed for so long. The libel suits filed never had any legal weight behind them, but the plaintiffs used scare tactics to get booksellers to pull the book, and then managed to have the publisher dragged through the morass of the U.S. justice system for eight years, successfully "censoring" the book for a time, at least. As Martin Garbus explains in his afterward, this is one of the most insidious forms of censorship, and if Janklow and the FBI had won, it would have crippled the rights of journalists to present politically unpleasant, and potentially libelous, viewpoints. Freedom of the press would have taken a nose-dive from which it might never have recovered. In allowing the American people to read *In the Spirit of Crazy Horse*, the U.S. judicial system took a stand for the inalienable right of Americans to criticize the actions of our governments and its politicians.

If Matthiessen and Viking had lost, the consequences would have been dire.

Don't shut your eyes to what *In the Spirit of Crazy Horse* and *Black Hills, White Justice* have to say. It's important that we as Americans come to terms with the ghosts of our past and the sins of our present government. It's important that you read what Matthiessen and Lazarus have to say, because the future of an entire race of people is in the balance. Their story is the most tragic of our nation, and it needs to be known.

In the Spirit of Crazy Horse
Peter Matthiessen
Viking $25.00

Black Hills, White Justice
Edward Lazarus
Harper Collins $27.50

*"Sioux"is an English convention used to describe a group of Indians also known as the Lakotas and Dakotas. They do not call themselves "Sioux," but the word has become commonplace in English usage.

T. Liam McDonald is a writer and filmmaker from Northern New Jersey.

TABOO TEXTS

Linda Marotta

The Drug User: Documents 1840-1960
edited by John Strausbaugh and Donald Blaise
Blast Books/Dolphin-Moon Press, $10.95

"Is it not strange that such consciousness and such intoxication can exist in the same brain simultaneously?" —Victor Robinson, from *An Essay on Hasheesh*, 1910

The editors of this superlative collection of drug-related writings specifically chose pre-1960 literature in order to shift our focus away from the news, politics and slogans of the current drug hysteria. John Strausbaugh's introduction and William Burroughs' forward put the War On Drugs in the historical perspective of yet another government sanctioned attempt to suppress free thinking and expression. *The Drug User* reminds us that we've been actively expanding our inner-space frontiers in every culture, in every age. Hell, even animals do it. As Strausbaugh puts it, "It seems that any organism with enough consciousness to be aware of the opportunity to alter it, does." From among the various methods available (prayer, dance, asceticism, alcohol) some folks choose drugs.

The writings flow from the decadently bohemian to the theoretically clinical. The emphasis is on curious, thoughtful investigations into the senses and nature of reality as opposed to reckless abuse. Through drugs, these transcendental explorers escape the physical bonds of the body and the mental constraints of ordinary consciousness sailing into the mysterious Beyond and returning with words that give shape and meaning to the ineffable.

One recurring cosmic puzzle is whether drugs merely amplify our natural perceptions or truly give us access to the Unknown. In Baudelaire's 1858 essay on hashish he states that the intoxication is "nothing but an excess of the natural." Dr. Albert Hoffman, the accidental inventor of LSD, likens the ego to a receiver that picks up different wavelengths of reality when chemically altered. Anais Nin attributes every element of her sensual gold-dusted LSD trip to previous experiences or books, concluding that drugs are an inferior method to the "active, dynamic dreaming" she achieves through art in a sober state. Similarly, after years of peyote use Lakotan Holy Man, Lame Deer decides that "The real vision has to come out of your own juices." Yet, Aldous Huxley predicts a religious revolution due to the imminent wide-spread use of the mystical "new mind changers" in a sadly optimistic 1958 magazine article.

The astounding variety of opinions and styles make this oneof-a-kind anthology both relaxing and exhilarating. The reader drifts through swirling baroque visions then lands at Boxcar Bertha's campsite for a look at drug use among female hoboes. The *salonneuse* Mabel Dodge Luhan relates a hilariously melodramatic account of an almost disastrous peyote party while jazz saxophonist Mezz Mezzrow relives his first reefer high in the middle of a jam. ("Poppa, younever smoked your chops on anything sweeter in all your days of viping.)

There is no need to follow precautions or designate a driver when reading this book since these drug scouts have already taken the risks on behalf of their fellow armchair travelers. Dipping into it as one might a shaman's medicine bag, we discover so many surprises, joys, revelations and terrors that we are reminded of the altered state that can be achieved through the act of reading.

"The Body in Question"
Aperture #121, Fall 1990
Melissa Harris, guest editor
$18.50

Of all the socio-politically relevant books you might have responsibly lining your shelves, this is the one you'll probably read all the way through and leave lying around for your friends to enjoy. This trade edition of the quarterly photography journal *Aperture* focuses on issues of censorship, AIDS, reproductive rights and sexuality. In the spirit of Barbara Kruger's body-as-battleground testament it demonstrates that art and politics become a volatile mix when the human body serves as the vessel. Through photographs, essays, reviews and fiction we witness "the body abused, objectified, discovered, aroused, desired, censored, mythologized, manipulated and celebrated."

The focus of the selection is not anything-goes shock art, but rather varieties of form and feeling. The artists play with diverse methods of representation, flexible gender roles and various expressions of sexuality. The immediacy of photography bridges the borders of identity and desire in the intimate, naked expressions on the faces of Christer Stroholm's prostitutes and transvestites, Donna Ferrato's battered women and in the self-referential portraits of Dorit Cypis. Weilding his "camera in hand" as a weapon, David Wojnarowicz demonstrates the power of the photograph in the battle against our repressive society's "FEAR OF DIVERSITY."

Throughout the book, shots of naked kids and innocent family scenes that have been interpreted as challenging and subversive make us wonder What Are We Afraid Of? and Who Gets To Decide? When *The Wall Street Journal* censored Sally Mann's beautiful cover depicting *Virginia at 4*, Virginia wrote them asking why they covered her body with those awful black bars and received a condescending reply. In "The Right to Depict Children in the Nude" Allen Ginsberg and Joseph Richey argue that our legis-

Sally Mann, *Virginia at 4*, 1989, black and white photograph, as reproduced on the cover of *Aperture* 121, Fall 1990.

Raymond Sokolov, "Critique: Censoring Virginia," *The Wall Street Journal*, 6 February 1991, p. A10.

lators need a remedial course in art history. Although this volume came out in late 1990, it is unfortunately not dated, due to the barely perceptible progress in the fight for individual rights. First to publish Diane Arbus, *Aperture* was dropped by their mailing house as a result of this issue. The editor says she's been called a "pornographer, satanist, and a postmodern Marxist." They lost some old subscribers but gained some new ones.

Among the diverse offerings are fiction by Patrick McGrath and poetry by Karen Finley. Anthropologist Carole S. Vance explains why photography in particular is under recent attack, Herbert Muschamp appraises gay stroke books, Peter Greenaway discusses structure and sensuality in his films, Jenny Livingston (*Paris Is Burning*) deconstructs Harlem drag balls and David Frankel closes with a lively endorsement of the B52's cheerful, hip-to-hip celebration of "the variety of desire." Altogether, it makes for a beautiful chronicle of the current issues in the struggle for freedom of the flesh.

Twisted Sisters: A Collection of Bad Girl Art edited by Diane Noomin Penguin, $14.95

Some bad girls get drunk, do drugs, fuck in public, get abortions, strip or take home men they meet in the street. Lucky for us, some of them draw funny pictures about it. The original *Twisted Sisters* was a "politically incorrect" collaboration between underground cartoonists Diane Noomin and Aline Kominsky put out in 1976. This newer version is a selection of mostly 1980's art and comic strips of fourteen female cartoonists reprinted from magazines such as *National Lampoon*, *Wimmen's Comix*, *Weirdo*, *Young Lust* and

Panel 1: SHE SAW THE DOCTOR BEING DRAGGED AWAY, THE RIGHT-LIFERS KICKING AND BEATING HER WITH OBVIOUS RELISH.

Panel 2: "YOU HAVE THE RIGHT TO REMAIN SILENT," BEGAN ONE OF THE ENFORCEMENT MEN.

SHE DIDN'T REALLY HEAR THE REST...

Panel 3: THE DRUG WORE OFF QUICKLY AS SHE WAS HUSTLED INTO A VAN OCCUPIED BY TWO OTHER PREGNANT WOMEN.

Panel 4: WEEKS LATER AT THE TRIAL, SHE WAS FOUND GUILTY.

Panel 5: SHE WAS SENTENCED TO SERVE THE REMAINDER OF HER PREGNANCY AT THE SYBIL BRAND INSTITUTE UNTIL SHE BORE THE CHILD ... WHICH SHE DID.

Panel 6: THEN SHE WAS TAKEN OUTSIDE AND SHOT.

Tits 'n Clits. They exhibit less sex, drugs and violence than their brother cartoonists, but just enough of that *je ne sais quoi* to get the book rejected by its first printer.

The major bad girl quality the women in this volume share is an autobiographical honesty in their voices and visions and a determination to just not go the fuck quietly. They may complain about crummy boyfriends and roommates but they also admit to their own awkwardness and expose ridiculous pratfalls and personal tragedies. The styles vary from Carol Lay's realistic romantic comic parody to M. K. Brown's funky white girl existentialism to Carel Moiseiwitsch's dark, psychotic portraits and "Priapic Alphabet" (W is for War Widow, Q for Quadriplegic).

They expose their lives and adventures to us through their inkbleeding fingertips. Diane Noomin writes of hickies, dildoes and lox in the Long Island Bagel Belt while Mary Fleener shows us corpse pranks, "torpedo tits" and squishy slugs. Leslie Sternbergh, that goddess of the Lower East Side, takes us on a privileged walking tour of her world (with an emphasis on the *shooze*). Punky Julie Doucet's "Heavy Flow" is a hilariously crazed rendition of how it feels when that blood between your legs becomes the center of the universe.

The book is dedicated to the deceased artist, Dori Seda, whose own intimate tales of eating brains, and her dog's eczema-oozing butt are among the highlights. The breadth and depth of this entertaining collection can be summed up in Krystine Kryttre's screechingly maniacal, yet bittersweet tribute to Seda which rejoices in the wild abandon they shared as friends, then says goodbye to her in a panel that's hard to see through tear-filled eyes.

Twisted Sisters is more fun than riding in cars with boys and hipper than a beehive hairdo. Don't miss it if you're into art beautiful and ugly, stories pleasurable and painful and the truth about naughty games played by little good girls who grow up to be big bad girls.

Whips and Kisses:
Parting the Leather Curtain
Mistress Jacqueline as told to Catherine Tavel and Robert H. Rimmer
Prometheus Books, $21.95

Gollyl! How ever did a nice Jewish girl from the Bronx end up a nasty studded leather whip-cracking dominatrix? This tedious, poorly edited tell-all was put together from tapes by the co-authors of *Raw Talent*, Jerry Butler's disgusting porn star-slamming "autobiography." The result is a relentless exercise in egotistical self-absorption unmarred by the intrusion of depth or perception. A dominatrix friend of mine felt *Whips and Bimbos* would be a more appropriate title. Mistress Jacqueline has a degree in psychology which she waves in our faces to assure us that we will all gain a deeper understanding of the weird and wacky world of S/M by examining her personal discovery of the dominant within. In her boring early years, she goes from being a good girl who keeps her deviant spanking fantasies to herself to a good wife who holds down menial secretarial jobs to support her selfish husband. When the marriage breaks up, she starts drinking, drugging and picking up male strippers. ("No one imagined that there was a hurt little girl hiding behind the mask of a carefree slut.")

If you're skimming for the good parts, about halfway through she answers an ad in a sex tabloid and hooks up with Sir William. Finally she's found a man who'll tell her what to do and arouse her at the same time. He tells her she's a "true submissive." She finds it really weird that he wants her to call him "Sir" and herself "slave." She gapes in Pollyanna astonishment at all the cock-rings, nipple clamps, paddle and videos he shows her at the Pleasure Chest.

Finding she has a real talent for this slave stuff she starts working at the Chalet in Los Angeles. She gets to wear sexy underwear and act slutty while being commanded to lick the toilet bowl, fetch shoes in her mouth and drink her own urine. Of course the drugs helped. "When your brain is obliterated, you'd be surprised at what you'll do." Working at the Chalet gives her life purpose, structure, and acceptance. After all, she's not play-acting like the other women, she's striving to take the most pain, to be the "perfect slave" in her overachieving, co-dependent own little way.

Despite the delivery, a few interesting 'scenes' manage to slip through; for example her introduction to slave training which includes cupping a submissive's just-pierced penis until his blood covers her fist or the man who uses a machine to pump his stomach full of air so that a mistress can punch it flat. But for a psychotherapist, she has surprisingly few theories on the attraction of bondage and discipline. It infuriates her that some people use it to cover up truly abusive relationships when it *should* be all just fun and games. At the same time, she maintains that her services are therapy for the transvestites, human ashtrays, foot fetishists and carpet slaves that make up her clientele. She may very well help them grow through acting-out, but the book contains no proof or examples from her clients lives beyond their gratitude to her. Jacqueline boldly defends prostitution while insisting that it is very different from what *she* does since S/M has nothing to do with sex!

What the hell kind of a free-thinking defender of alternative life styles believes that sex = intercourse?

For a serious look into the politics of pain and the carnal/spiritual connection, pick up instead *Leatherfolk: Radical Sex, People, Politics, and Practice* (Alyson, $19.95). This new collection of writings, edited by Mark Thompson from *The Advocate*, contains personal, historical, political and spiritual accounts of the S/M movement. But only true masochists will want to submit to *Whips and Kisses*.

BEHIND THE MASK:
NON-FICTION
REVIEWS

Matthew J. Costello

Klanwatch, Bill Stanton (Grove Weidenfeld, 1991)

Blood in the Face, James Ridgeway (Thunder's Mouth Press, 1991)

Jesus Doesn't Live Here Anymore, Skipp Porteous, (Prometheus Books, 1991)

Witnesses From the Grave, Christopher Joyce and Eric Stover (Little, Brown, 1991)

Wouldn't It Be Nice?, Brian Wilson (HarperCollins, 1991)

I grew up in Flatbush, Brooklyn. The house that I grew up in was one in a row of red-stone houses with two main floors—each holding a family—and small basement apartment. And next door to our house, in a basement apartment, lived an old woman.

She was different. I grew up knowing that. She didn't look like my family or any of the hordes of Irish-Catholic relatives. She didn't go to our church. My parents—as far as I remember—never spoke to her, though you could have thrown a stone and zipped past her dark basement door.

Eventually, I learned who, or what she was. She was a kike, a hymie, a jew—with the last two letters stretched to almost absurd lengths. My father would often put that word, *jew*, with another word, to form jew-bastard—which was probably someone to be doubly damned. My brothers sat around the kitchen table, working men eating homecooked dinners before they'd flee to wives and their own unhappy homes, and they joined in the name calling.

With more names, like niggers, and jungle-bunnies, and guineas, and wops, and krauts (though there was a little less venom with this one) and squareheads—a who-knows-where it came from appellation for Norwegians.

There were spics, dagos, frogs, and other names that I forget, all dancing around our kitchen, a nice name at hand for anyone who wasn't Irish-Catholic, one of the chosen people.

I never spoke to the old lady next door. But—one day, it was summer day, real hot—she was outside, sitting outside her dark, stuffy apartment, wearing a sleeveless dress. Her arms jiggled, an old woman's arms. I might have been playing stoop ball, throwing the ball against the stoop, back and forth, a game you could play with other kids.

And I looked at the woman. And I saw a tattoo, a small tattoo, a line of numbers inside her arm.

Something jews must have, I thought, throwing the ball again., That's what they have. Secret numbers.

Years later, I learned about the holocaust—not in Catholic Elementary

School, and not even in my Jesuit Prep School. And even later, when I watched the streets fill with hate in the summer of 1991, I knew that hate in Brooklyn was nothing new. Hate anywhere is nothing new.

We have to know that, and watch it. And some new books will be vital to that task . . .

Bill Stanton's *Klanwatch* (Grove Weidenfeld, 1991) documents the heroic work of the Southern Poverty Law Center's Klanwatch Project. The center was launched by Morris Dees, Jr. and Joseph J. Levin, young liberal lawyers. Dees is the guiding force behind the center.

Active in the Democratic Party, Dees was a self-made millionaire many times over. But his life changed when Autherine Lucy, a black woman, attempted to enroll in the University of Alabama. Dees witnessed Klan-led riots on the Tuscaloosa campus. The violence and hate shaped his politics, and gave him the inspiration to use his resources to fight the Klan. Stanton's book documents the important work of Klanwatch and some of its biggest cases, including the defense of Curtis Robinson, accused of shooting Klan leader David Kelso. Klanwatch took the Klan to court for inspiring the violence and initiating the confrontation.

In another case, in the early 1980s, the Texas Knights—one of many Klan splinter groups—attempted to drive away Vietnamese shrimpers out of Galveston Bay. Klanwatch went to their defense, exposing the terrorist tactics of the Klan.

The SPLC wasn't immune form violence itself. IN 1983 arson caused $140,000 worth of damages, which led to an new center being built in downtown Montgomery. In the courts, Klanwatch has been able to hold the Klan culpable for inciting acts of violence, like the 1981 lynching of Michael Donald. Klan members have even agreed, after the Curtis Robinson decision, to take a class on civil rights.

By attacking the organizational structure of the Klan—through the courts—Klanwatch has become an important watchdog on the frontlines of hate.

But the true dimensions of hate in America can't be grasped in Bill Stanton's book. It would still be possible to read that book and think of hate, and white supremacy, and vigilante actions as something restricted to the South and a few backward counties.

But James Ridgeway's brilliant and chilling *Blood in the Face* (Thunder's Mouth Press, 1991) reveals the true dimensions of the beast. Subtitled "The Ku KLux Klan, Aryan Nations, Nazi Skinheads, and The Rise of the New White Culture", Ridgeway's book shows that racism is alive and well in the country, and may be poised for dramatic growth.

Ridgeway documents the different eras of the Klan, from its first inception when it attempted to preserve the withered flowers of the old post Civil War South, through the revival spurred by D.W. Griffith's film, *The Birth of a Nation*, to the recent years when the Klan has learned to control its image and became active—with some success—in mainstream local politics.

There are passages in *Blood in the Face* that are downright scary. The White Aryan resistance is not only open in its position of white supremacy, but it has been willing to use guns to support that position. There are Dial-A-Racist phone lines and WAR computer bulletin boards, as well as well-armed redoubts in the white "homeland" of the Pacific Northwest. In 1983 the Aryan Nations splinter group, the order, murdered the Denver DJ Alan Berg.

The message and symbols of hate, such as the badges of the American Front and the bald-heads of the skinheads, have raised the specter of Naziism, and the proselytizing takes pace in the popular culture of some Rock n' Roll is effective propaganda for intolerance.

Most of these groups are repellent to the average Americans. But others are modeling themselves on the success of Louisiana's David Duke, former Klan leader, who won a seat in the state's House of Representatives—and may even have a shot at a higher office. With a depressed economy, many Midwest farmers have found themselves foreclosed. And the white supremacy group, Posse Comitatus, has been there to tell them that the Jewish bankers have been behind their troubles.

Ridgeway's book includes photographs, such a little skinhead boy giving the Nazi salute, letters, chilling speeches, and copies of newsletters and propaganda posters. As in Weimar Germany, hate can feed on hunger, and Ridgeway's book is an essential volume in fighting back.

Skipp Porteous's *Jesus Doesn't Live Here Anymore* (Prometheus Books, 1991) is his personal story of how he went from being a Fundamentalist Preacher to a nationally-known advocate of the First Amendment.

Porteous tells how he was 'saved' at the age of eleven and then became an effective soldier for the Religious right. Porteous was part of the salvation game, with ministries both on the West Coast and in the East, and radio program reaching out to more distant sinners.

Porteous's own story—how he eventually broke away from the Fundamentalist sub-culture—is fascinating. He then started appearing on radio programs to challenge the rigid, close-minded tenets of Fundamentalist Christianity, warning that there were even greater dangers than mere religious intolerance.

The right wing Christian groups have learned from their attempt to elect Fundamentalist TV Preacher Pat Robertson president during the 1980s. They began concentrating the efforts on local politics, where they could get elected while keeping their larger agenda in the background. An army of the Fundamentalist right is infiltrating all sorts of political infrastructures, under the heading of "Christian Reconstructionism."

The main tenet of Christian Reconstructionism is that the Bible should permeate every facet of life, from how the legal system treats homosexuals to what's permitted on the nation's airwaves.

Fundamentalist Groups, such as Donald Wildmon's American Family Association, attempt to create boycotts against sponsors whose TV shows they find offensive. With a slick newsletter, Wildmon gives marching orders to his Fundamentalist followers who have no compunction about restricting free speech.

Porteous' story is well-told. More importantly, he knows how Fundamentalism works from the inside. He established the Institute for First Amendment Studies and now publishes the Freedom Writer, a national newsletter that defends the separation of church and state. (Editor's note: An excerpt from *Jesus Doesn't Live Here Anymore* appears on page 285 of this issue.)

Clyde Snow solves murders through examination of bones with tape and calipers. An expert in forensic anthropology, Snow is called in when victims of war, violent crime and revolution cannot be identified.

In *Witnesses From the Grave*, (Little, Brown, 1991) Christopher Joyce and Eric Stover recreate encounters with Show, a Sherlock Holmes who has applied his skills to investigate the victims of human rights abuses.

Snow has been connected with some glamorous cases, such his examination of the possible remains of Dr. Josef Mengele in Brazil and his investigation of some of the victims of serial killer John Wayne Gacy. But he has dedicated himself to searching, in South American jungles and cities, for 'the disappeared', the men, women and children who vanished from Argentina during the "dirty war" of the 1970s.

The story is fascinating. But beyond the thrilling nature of Snow's work, there is his grim resolution—Snow objects to anyone suffering the indignity of dying *unknown*. The body tossed into a ravine, or the corpse hacked into pieces are the attempt of someone to hide that crime by destroying the identity of the murder victim.

Snow brings them to light.

I admit to an at-times unfashionable love of the music of Brian Wilson. Where the music of McCartney and Lennon seemed rooted to a time and place, Brian Wilson's paeans to youth, confusion, and love seem timeless and—in some cases—wonderful in their bittersweet beauty.

That such a talent sprung from abuse is hammered home in his autobiography, *Wouldn't It Be Nice* (HarperCollins). Written with Todd Gold, a writer for *People Magazine*, the book describes—with compelling detail—how Wilson was brutalized by his father. Murry Wilson hit Brian with a two-by-four on the side of his head. He made his son defecate on a newspaper.

Murry Wilson, songwriter himself, obviously provided a good Gene pool for the freres Wilson. But he also was an incredible abuser, and his three sons' headlong fall into substance abuse and, in the case of Dennis Wilson, death, can be laid at his doorstep.

By the mid-70s, Brian was a bloated, obsessive and neurotic wreck, not even leaving his bed, when Dr. Eugene Landry entered the scene. Landry's unorthodox procedures got Brian up and about. But Brian's wife and the other Beach Boys, especially Mike Love—who comes off as a near abusive bully boy—forced Landry away. Brian relapsed, growing even larger, consuming even more coke, until Landry once again was summoned to rescue Brian.

Brian Wilson, as he makes clear in his book, wouldn't be here today, making solo cds, if it weren't for Landry. Brian still has to fight the Beach Boys, who support a suit by cousin Steve Love to obtain conservatorship over Brian.

This book should go a long way to helping Brian fight to keep his life-saving relation ship with Dr. Eugene Landry. It's a fast-paced glimpse into that particular heart of darkness of Brian Wilson, the well spring for the California sound of beaches, babes, and teenage angst.

Matthew Costello is a Contributing Editor at **Games Magazine** *and columnist for* **Mystery Scene***. A novelist, with numerous books to his credit,* **Home***, his most recent book will see publication in 1992.*

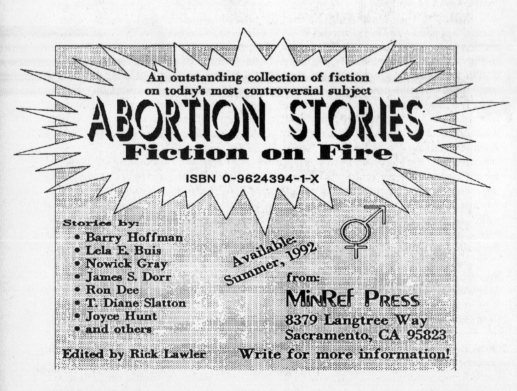

STOP LOOKING AT ME...
AND TAKE A GOOD   LOOK AT YOURSELF!

STOP MAGAZINE.